Dana Andrews

Dana Andrews

The Face of Noir

JAMES MCKAY

McFarland & Company, Inc., Publishers

Jefferson, North Carolina, and London

All photographs provided by Photofest.

Frontispiece: "Man about town." Andrews in a 1949 publicity shot.

LIBRARY OF CONGRESS CATALOGUING-IN-PUBLICATION DATA

McKay, James, 1959–
Dana Andrews : the face of noir / James McKay.
p.   cm.
Includes filmography:
Includes bibliographical references and index.

ISBN 978-0-7864-4614-8
softcover : 50# alkaline paper ∞

1. Andrews, Dana, 1909–1992.
2. Actors— United States— Biography.
I. Title.
PN2287.A615M33   2010   791.43'028'0924 — dc22 [B]   2010006554

British Library cataloguing data are available

Cover image: Dana Andrews as detective Mark McPherson and
Gene Tierney in portrait as Laura Hunt in *Laura*, 1944
(20th Century Fox/Photofest)

Manufactured in the United States of America

*McFarland & Company, Inc., Publishers
Box 611, Jefferson, North Carolina 28640
www.mcfarlandpub.com*

To my wife Christine,
daughter Morgan, son William
and in loving memory
of my mother Francisca.

Acknowledgments

I would like to thank my wife, Christine, and sister-in-law, Joan, for proofing the manuscript; fellow film enthusiast and friend Pete Farley for his useful thoughts on some of the early draft extracts; the helpful staff at the British Film Institute and Columbia University Oral History Research Office; the guys at Photofest for their excellent service in supplying the terrific photo images; my late father for introducing me to the wonders and delights of the "silver screen"; and last but not least Dana Andrews for the many hours of perfect bliss I have enjoyed watching his films. I hope I have done justice to his memory and film legacy.

Table of Contents

Acknowledgments
vi

Preface
1

Biography
3

The Films
23

*Appendix: Major Television,
Theatre and Radio Credits*
215

Notes
223

Bibliography
229

Index
233

Preface

In the 1960s, the classic Hollywood movies entered my world through a small black-and-white television screen — but even in this reduced format, for me, they were still a potent cocktail of romance, mystery and adventure. Comfortably seated alongside my film-buff father, I dodged arrows and bullets with John Wayne, swashbuckled across the seven seas with Errol Flynn, romanced the damsel in distress with Tyrone Power, slapped around the bad guys with James Cagney, and smart-talked my way around town with Clark Gable. And then one day, when the dust had settled on the soundstages and these heroes had wandered off into another sunset to await a new dawn, a fresh experience abruptly invaded my ordered existence: *The Best Years of Our Lives.* For nearly three hours I sat glued to the set, my mind racing: Who was this skillfully restrained actor playing the traumatized airman, this well-meaning "Average Joe" with a distinctive, warm, resonant voice, who possessed a vulnerability which reached out and touched you as if he were in the room. Five-foot-ten and square-jawed, he was tough, but not as tough as Wayne and Cagney; ruggedly good-looking, but not as handsome as Power or Flynn. And yet, he was more real and natural than any other actor that had graced my screen before. As if reading my thoughts, my father whispered, "That's Dana Andrews — one of the tough guys."

That he was indeed a tough guy who could slug it out with the best of them, there can be no doubt, but Andrews was more than simply that. Having starred in a number of groundbreaking films, he proved that he was also a unique performer, who through his understated acting style subtly projected a decent all-American guy, whose outlook was usually tested and tempered by a susceptibility to disappointment, inner bitterness or moral dilemma. As a consequence, his characters were sometimes noted for their ambiguity and air of restrained heroism — qualities that became a hallmark throughout much of his career.

And what a busy career he enjoyed, spanning 45 years, and uniquely covering all the major film genres — westerns, war, film noir, domestic drama, musical, realist thriller, com-

Dana Andrews in 1948.

1

edy, melodrama, romance, spy, horror and science fiction. Indeed, three years ago, when I started this tribute in my spare time, I was simply overwhelmed by the diversity of his film output.

Tracking down the films has been a long and painstaking experience, but certainly a rewarding one. And although I have derived great pleasure from each and every one of them, there are five in particular that I would list as my personal favorites. Indeed, I can confidently recommend that to fully appreciate cinematic art and for pure entertainment value alone, these five are an essential "must see" before you shuffle off your mortal coil: *The Ox-Bow Incident, Laura, A Walk in the Sun, The Best Years of Our Lives* and *Curse of the Demon* (aka *Night of the Demon*). Each film is unique, pioneering and very different, but all of them reveal what Andrews was capable of, given the right material. View each of these films and you are left with no doubt that here was an actor with real screen presence, who fully understood his craft, and honed it to perfection in some of the classics of the "Golden Age" of cinema. These

qualities made him the favorite actor of many of the great directors (Otto Preminger, Lewis Milestone, Fritz Lang and Jacques Tourneur), who instinctively knew how to shape and mold to best advantage the nuances of his persona. In addition to working with these master craftsmen, he also starred opposite some of Hollywood's finest actresses including Gene Tierney, Susan Hayward, Merle Oberon, Joan Crawford and Greer Garson.

Outside of work, Andrews was a private man given to few interviews, and most of the references made to his life have tended to dwell on his drinking problem and not his important contribution to cinema. Researching this tribute has therefore not been an easy one and I apologize in advance for any factual inaccuracies. However, I am a firm believer in my own loose take on the old *The Man Who Shot Liberty Valance* epigram, that if the facts become difficult or impossible to verify, print the legend. So, ladies and gentlemen, without further ado, I give you one of the most undervalued actors in film history — the screen legend, Dana Andrews.

Biography

Carver Dana Andrews was born on January 1, 1909, in Don't (a small town outside Collins), Covington County, Mississippi. He was the third of nine children (eight were boys) of Baptist minister Charles Forrest Andrews and his wife, Anice. His father named him after two professors under whom he had studied in a theological seminary. One of the men was Dr. Carver, the other Dr. Dana. Thus, Carver Dana Andrews took his name from three eminent clergymen. Dana's mother was deeply religious herself, but she wasn't given to preaching. To the rearing of her young family, it is said, she brought a rare combination of patience, humor and tenderness.[1] One of Dana's younger brothers, William, would go on to become a successful film and television actor under the name of Steve Forrest. Despite the trappings of stardom that eventually came his way, Andrews always remained a preacher's son at heart, maintaining a simple lifestyle; his wants were few. His home-loving simplicity was acknowledged by residents of half a dozen southern towns, who would always remember him affectionately as "that nice-looking Andrews boy who sang."

With such a large family to provide for, money was always in short supply in the Andrews household, but their frugal existence never dampened the family's spirit, with the children making the most of the great outdoors— swimming, fishing, riding and camping for three or four days at a time. On summer nights they'd gather around Mother on the front porch, listening to tales of her father's cotton plantation, which they left when Dana was four. Andrews recalled that Don't was the Mississippi town where his father had fallen in love with one of his pupils, Anice Speed. After their marriage, they lived with Grandfather Speed while his father studied theology at the Seminary. Andrews would always remember these early childhood days in Mississippi with much affection.

He further reminisced that in the winter evenings, the family would gather around the piano and, led by their father, sing songs for many an hour. Passed on from their grandfather, the songs had an eerie quality which fascinated the children.

Just as Andrews's eldest brothers, Witon and Harlan, were special friends, so were Dana and his younger brother (by one year), Charles. With such a large brood, self-reliance came quickly to all the children, and there was certainly no place for whining or feeling sorry for oneself. Two days before one particular Christmas, the older boys decided it was time to teach Dana and Charles the truth about Santa Claus, explaining that it was simply a game that adults played for their children. When Charles broke down in tears at the news, it was Dana's reassuring hand and presence that calmed him.

As is the way with large families, the older children educated the younger ones, but there was one lesson, which Andrews recalled, that was strictly the preserve of his father: the art of learning how to swim. Before tossing him into deep water, his father would say, "By the time you come up, I'll be there." As Andrews mused, "If Dad said he'd be there, he'd be there ... and he always was. And you'd grab his shoulder and start kicking your feet and yelling for him to throw you in again."[2]

Throughout his life, Andrews never forgot

his humble beginnings. His affection for his disciplinarian father, who ruled with a firm but fair hand, was further revealed in one of his early recollections of a treasured fishing trip they took together: "Dad pulled beauties out of the river all day long and I never had a nibble. I was feeling pretty low. Just as we were leaving to go home I said, 'I'll show you!' and threw my line over a rocky ledge. I was incredulous when, the moment the hook hit the water, and there was a tug — a big one. I fought that fish for half an hour. Dad would not give me a helping hand — he knew it would make me much happier to land him alone. I did. It was a twenty-pound catfish — the biggest of the day. Dad put his arm around me and said, 'Son, you're the champion fisherman of the family.' Dad is gone now, but I always think of him every time I go fishing."[3]

Andrews was clearly the family show-off, having the confidence to get up in front of a crowd and recite. At age four he appeared on the program of a church entertainment, and at seven he was taking his school reader home and practicing the stories with expression — so much so that when his teacher called on him to read to the class, he would make quite a stir.

At the age of 12, spurred on by fierce determination and great belief in himself, Andrews ran errands for his music teacher to repay her for teaching him to play the piano, from scratch, for a forthcoming recital. Within a short period of time he learned how to play strictly by ear, a fairly complicated march which he carried off with panache, much to the joy of the audience on the day of the recital.

His most notable performance came the following year, when, in the dead of night, he ran away from home, hopping a freight train to San Antonio. For three days, he stuck it out, but eventually his homesickness got the better of him and he returned home, much to the relief of his parents. When his father calmly asked him why he had run away, Andrews in heartfelt tones responded, "I just wanted to make a lot of money, and put you and mother up in a big house."[4]

Poverty also affected Andrews's love life: When he was a young man, his romance to a well-to-do girl was broken off by her father, who disapproved of his poor background and limited prospects.[5] Such personal disappointments would, however, simply add fuel to Andrews's determination to make a success of himself — no matter what.

His father's work involved a lot of relocations; the family moved from Collins to Louisville, Kentucky, and from there to several Texas cities, including Huntsville, where Andrews graduated from high school in 1926. He then enrolled at Sam Houston Teacher College in Huntsville to study business administration. It was here that he further developed his interest in dramatics, after having appeared in several productions during his high school days. Before leaving Huntsville, Andrews worked as a fruit picker, ditch digger, truck driver, plumber's helper and in a number of other manual labor jobs — experience which would stand him in good stead as he later recalled, "I don't regret a minute of it. All this activity kept me in good shape and, although I didn't realize it at the time, it gave me a lot of insight into various characterizations which came in handy when I finally got into acting."

He left college in 1929 and, to earn a living, took another series of jobs which included a short period as an accountant for the Texas Oil Corporation and then as an assistant in a movie theatre, where Andrews claimed he got to know the films by heart and "got bitten by the acting bug." In a 1945 interview with Hedda Hopper, Andrews described how he passed the time in the movie theatre: "Just to entertain myself, I'd reconstruct how they played the parts and imagine how I'd do it. That's when I felt I had acting talent."[6]

Andrews decided to pack his bags and head for Hollywood in 1931. Although he had exactly three dollars in his pocket, Andrews wasn't worried. "I gave up a $175-a-month job as an accountant in order to come to Los Angeles," he related. "It was a long time before I was able to earn that much again.... I just plugged on, driving a school bus, working as a department store stock clerk, selling advertising for a San Fernando newspaper, and finally winding up as a filling station attendant. But always at the back of my mind was an ambition to be a singer."

Having great confidence in Andrews's talent

and aspirations, the owner of the Van Nuys filling station, Mr. Wardlow, and his business partner Stanley Toomey advanced him 50 dollars a week for singing lessons and living expenses until he secured a Hollywood contract (a gesture that Andrews would generously reward when stardom came). Toomey died a few weeks after the last payment, which prompted Andrews to comment, "I felt the world had lost a wonderful man and I a very real friend.... He was always backing someone or doing some fine humanitarian deed."[7]

Away from the gas pump, Andrews would make the rounds of the studios looking for his big break, only to meet with rejection. To improve his acting skills he attended the Van Nuys Amateur Theatre, where he met the woman who became his first wife, Janet Murray. Janet didn't want to be an actress, she'd just joined the class for fun. She had a master's degree in journalism and her job was in the newspaper field. Dana described Janet as an inspiration: "She liked my baritone voice and urged me to become a singing actor, like Lawrence Tibbett."[8]

Inseparable, they rented the upper floor of a duplex, where they invested in a record player and recording machine. Here, they read plays together, made records and played them back. Andrews would sing into the machine and they'd compare them with the previous recording to see if he'd improved.

They married on December 31, 1932, and in the following year their son David was born. Then in 1935, Janet died suddenly after contracting pneumonia. Amidst her own grief, Janet's mother Aggie brought Dana and his two-year-old son into her home, and they became her children. She encouraged and gently prodded Andrews to go back into singing and dramatics.

Heeding the advice of a talent agent that singers were in plentiful supply and that acting was the way forward, Andrews secured a place at the famed Pasadena Community Playhouse, which he would later describe in an interview as a major showcase for talent, with the likes of William Holden, Victor Mature and Robert Preston in attendance. Andrews added, "There were very few girls at the time, because the girls

A youthful Andrews (circa 1920s).

generally got the chance at the studios, but men, no."[9]

Andrews's debut at the Playhouse was as Menelaus in *Antony and Cleopatra*, and it was during this period in his career that he became professionally known as Dana Andrews. A succession of roles followed, including one of the principal leads (Langlois, the sensitive, ironic young Frenchman) in Sidney Howard's dramatization of *Paths of Glory*. One critic wrote, "As for Dana Andrews, playing the soldier whose survival would have meant most to civilization, I find it difficult to restrain my praise...."

For two and a half years he worked his heart out at the Playhouse, learning his trade and developing his technique, playing young and old men in big and small parts. But for all his efforts, his career appeared to be going nowhere, and for the first time he began to feel that he had missed the boat, particularly when some of his Playhouse colleagues (Robert Preston, Laird Cregar and Victor Mature) had moved on to greater things with generous Hollywood contracts under their belts. Andrews recalled that the studios were principally looking for Robert Taylor types, and that Oliver Hinsdale, the man who trained Taylor, enthusiastically introduced him to MGM's casting director, who unfortunately did not share the same enthusiasm. The MGM man told Andrews, "This is not a business for men who don't have what are immediately seen as leading-man qualities. You'll work now and then, but you really won't make a good living."[10]

Undeterred, Andrews continued to pursue his dream. In 1938, while appearing with Florence Bates in *Oh Evening Star*, he was spotted by one of Samuel Goldwyn's talent scouts. This resulted in a successful screen test at the Goldwyn studio in December of that year, and he was signed up to a $150-a-week contract. "Once I had decided that acting was my forte, I stayed put," Andrews recalled. "And did I hold on to my movie salary that first year! I had to. The first thing I had to get off my chest was to pay back that loan for the music lessons."

Goldwyn saw Andrews's potential, but sent him back to the Playhouse to get more experience. Over the next 12 months, Andrews appeared in over 20 productions at the theatre, and it was during this period that he proposed to fellow actress Mary Todd. They were rehearsing *First Lady*, in which Mary played the ingénue opposite Dana. As an actress, film historian and novelist DeWitt Bodeen likened Mary to Marion Davies. Aggie, Dana's mother-in-law, who had been a rock to him during those bleak times three years ago, met Mary for the first time when Dana took them both to a show. Aggie, who was keen to see Dana remarried, later told him, "That's the one. Oh Dana, I'm glad. She's wonderful." To which Dana proudly responded, "Isn't she though!"[11]

Thinking of his career, Andrews sought Goldwyn's approval of the marriage and was surprised when the mogul simply replied that he would think about it. The actor described how anxious weeks went by with no further word from Goldwyn. One day when Andrews was invited to his office, he casually remarked before leaving, "Oh, by the way, you remember my asking about my getting married." To which Goldwyn laughed and replied, "Oh, I forgot all about it. Go ahead, that's fine."[12]

Dana married Mary on November 17, 1939,

and their union was blessed with three children, Katharine in 1942, Stephen in 1944, and Susan in 1948. In 2007, Dana's youngest child, Susan, candidly talked about growing up with her famous father in a podcast interview (an affectionate tribute and a must-listen for all Dana Andrews fans).

Mary was a wonderful mother, which Dana fondly revealed in an interview: "Mary and I have three children and I have a son by my first wife, who died. I shall never forget the happiness I felt over the way Mary took my five-year-old son to her heart when we married. She became his 'mother.' The word 'stepmother' was never used or thought of." In the same interview, Dana also praised Mary's good business sense: "She is a wonderful wife. Thanks to her family bookkeeping and determined budgeting we managed to pay off in full my debt to the man who had taken a chance and put cash straight down the dotted line."[13]

Andrews's life was certainly on the upswing now, with a lovely wife and family, and a blossoming career ahead of him. But he would always look back at his apprenticeship at the Pasadena Playhouse with pride, fully recognizing that he had learned his profession the hard traditional way, without influence or short cuts.[14] Andrews greatly benefited from an amazing photographic memory that enabled him to be word perfect with very little effort, although he was not always able to exercise this skill to its fullest as he once recollected during his early days: "I have memorized five complete operas by heart, but so far I have not yet had the opportunity to use this special gift."[15]

The year 1939 was an important one professionally for Andrews because he was offered his first film role in William Wyler's *The Westerner* starring Gary Cooper and Walter Brennan. Even though the part of Bart Cobble was minor, it was a start in an impressive big-budget movie which would go on to become a classic of its kind. During the making of the film, Goldwyn, forever watchful with his money, sold half of Andrews's contract to 20th Century–Fox, who put him to work straight away as a second lead in two B movies (*Lucky Cisco Kid* and *Sailor's Lady*) and loaning him out to United Artists for a third —(*Kit Carson*).

There was a seven-month gap between *Sailor's Lady* and *Kit Carson* where Andrews didn't work in films at all. To occupy the time, he developed an interest in gardening, which acted as a kind of safety valve for his frustration. He'd never raised so much as a sunflower before, but now suddenly he was absorbed in seed catalogues and books on perennials. "He won't even use plain, ordinary earth," Mary mused to their friends. "It all has to be mixed in the proper proportions, like a martini!"[16]

Both Andrews's mother and father were a little disappointed that none of their boys showed any interest in the ministerial calling, and after some early misgivings about Andrews giving up gainful employment in business, they eventually came to respect his decision to pursue an acting career. His father died while Andrews was away making *Lucky Cisco Kid*, so he never got to see his son on the screen, but he did live long enough to see the hometown boy well publicized in the local press.

In 1941, Andrews appeared in John Ford's version of Erskine Caldwell's novel *Tobacco Road*, which was to be the first of five films he made with his perfect leading lady, Gene Tierney. When Henry Fonda turned down the lead male part in *Belle Starr*, Fox executive Darryl Zanuck provided Andrews with another second lead, supporting Randolph Scott and Gene Tierney as the fiery Belle. This was swiftly followed by one of Andrews's favorites, *Swamp Water*, director Jean Renoir's first Hollywood film.

Later in 1941, Andrews played a slick gangster in another Gary Cooper film, the classic Goldwyn screwball comedy *Ball of Fire,* with Barbara Stanwyck lighting up the stage as "good time girl" Sugarpuss O'Shea. Fox gave Andrews his first leading man starring role in the wartime B movie action thriller *Berlin Correspondent* (1942). This was followed in 1943 with a tribute to the submarine service, *Crash Dive,* where Andrews reverted to playing second fiddle, this time to Tyrone Power.

At age 34, Andrews finally got to prove his acting credentials in his next film *The Ox-Bow Incident* (1943), in which he played the leader of three men condemned to death by a lynch mob for a crime they didn't commit. Although Henry Fonda was the lead in the film, it is Andrews's "heart wringing performance" (as noted by the *New York Times*) that lifts it to classic status. The film was highly praised by most critics, but unfortunately, due perhaps to its grim subject matter, the box-office takings were disappointing. Nonetheless, Andrews would always regard his role as Martin as one of his best acting performances. "Some of the finest roles on stage or screen are minor ones about whom the other characters talk. I learned this early in my career when I was singled out for my part in *The Ox-Bow Incident*. Actually, I was the man hanged, but everyone else in the cast discussed and emoted about me until the final fadeout."

Although his star was steadily on the rise following *The Ox-Bow Incident*, Andrews amusingly recalled how he had yet to become a household name, describing a War Bond Rally he attended where the local emcee paid him scant notice as he introduced him to the audience, making it blatantly clear that he had never heard of Andrews. At the next rally, Andrews took the yokel aside and, informing him of some of the films he had made, asked him to make the introduction with a bit of a buildup this time. The emcee agreed, and gave him this send-off: "Now folks, I want you to meet Dana Andrews, the Hollywood star. He played in *The Ox-Bow Incident* that ran here in town the other night. Personally, I didn't like the picture, but that doesn't mean Dana Andrews isn't any good. I can't remember which part he played anyway."[17]

Notwithstanding this lack of recognition of Andrews in certain backwaters, both Goldwyn and Fox were suitably impressed with his *Ox-Bow* performance to trust him with more lead roles. His career prospects looked even brighter when several of Hollywood leading men (including Fox's Henry Fonda and Tyrone Power) enlisted in the armed services, leaving the field clear for aspiring young actors such as Andrews to make their mark. (Andrews was ineligible for enlistment due to his age and because he was the father of two children.)

Andrews firmly established his leading man credentials with a trio of war films; *The North Star* (1943), *The Purple Heart* (1944), and *Wing and a Prayer* (1944). As the leader of a downed bomber crew in *The Purple Heart,* facing a certain death sentence by a Japanese military court due to trumped-up charges, Andrews was reprising the role of the doomed victim he had played, to magnificent effect, the previous year in *The Ox-Bow Incident.* Wartime audiences sympathized with Andrews's character and connected with his air of heroic vulnerability, which boosted his career to another level. This decent "Average Joe" persona made him the perfect candidate to play the ghost of a dead sailor in the John Ford docudrama December 7th, 1943 about the bombing of Pearl Harbor and America's attempts to hit back at the enemy.

In between these serious war films, Andrews appeared as the romantic lead in the wartime comedy *Up in Arms,* which marked the auspicious debut of Danny Kaye (Goldwyn's replacement for Eddie Cantor). With a busy film schedule, Andrews still made time for his young family, taking them down to the beach whenever possible. Andrews amusingly recalled that one Sunday while riding the merry-go-round at the beach with David and Kathy, he was noticed by a bobby-soxer: "'Look,' she said to her girlfriend, 'there's Dana Andrews.'" The girlfriend fixed Andrews with a haughty stare, then said, "You're crazy. That isn't Dana Andrews. What movie star would spend Sunday at the beach with a couple of kids?"[18]

In another family recollection, Andrews described the birth of his second son, Stephen. He arrived a week early, when Andrews was out with director Lewis Milestone watching some Russian films. When Andrews dropped Milestone off at his home, a frantic head was stuck out at the window: "Mr. Andrews is to call home immediately!" After making the call, Andrews rushed to his car and raced through the rain to his house, narrowly missing a collision by the skin of his fender. Andrews got Mary to the hospital just 14 minutes before Stephen entered the world. With three young mouths to feed now, the time was right for his big break.

Andrews's role as the streetwise cop in the classic film noir *Laura* (1944) finally put him at the top, with audiences and critics unanimous in their high praise of a performance which *Variety* described as "intelligent and reticent." It was also Andrews's initial collaboration with Otto Preminger, who was the first director to recognize the actor's natural ability to play troubled, disillusioned, and morally ambiguous characters—traits he would fully exploit in their next three films together, *Fallen Angel* (1945), *Daisy Kenyon* (1947) and *Where the Sidewalk Ends* (1950).

After the success of *Laura,* Andrews signed a new contract with Goldwyn and Fox that would earn him $1.5 million over five years. With this financial cushion, he was able to indulge in his passion for boats which he preferred to think of as "a wise investment to ensure health and pleasure for myself and the family between pictures." However, with his popularity at its height, Andrews found himself extremely busy with film assignments which, as he explained at the time, left him little time to fully indulge his passion for sailing. "The first good holiday I have, I am going for a South Sea island cruise, but the way parts are lining up, it will be very much in the future. In the meantime, a fishing trip to Mexican waters is about all I get time for—and, of course, each Sunday we go down to Wilmington where we keep the *Katharine* (named after our daughter) tied up."[19]

Andrews was also an avid photographer taking his camera whenever he was working. This culminated in a huge collection of photographs in which just about every major star is represented.

Andrews rarely let success go to his head, as was clearly evidenced when he once walked into a restaurant without a reservation. A long line of people were waiting for tables, but the waiter bowed and winked at Andrews before showing him and his party through to a table. Upset by the preferential treatment, Andrews turned around and walked out with his guests following briskly behind.

With two new budding stars under contract to Samuel Goldwyn, the young Farley Granger and Broadway comic Danny Kaye, Andrews would discover that he was no longer the main focus of attention there. However, his split contract with Fox provided him with a wider choice of roles, which would eventually bring

Publicity poster from *Laura* (20th Century–Fox, 1944). Widely acknowledged as the first film noir, the film boosted Andrews's career to great heights, making him one of the most popular stars at Fox.

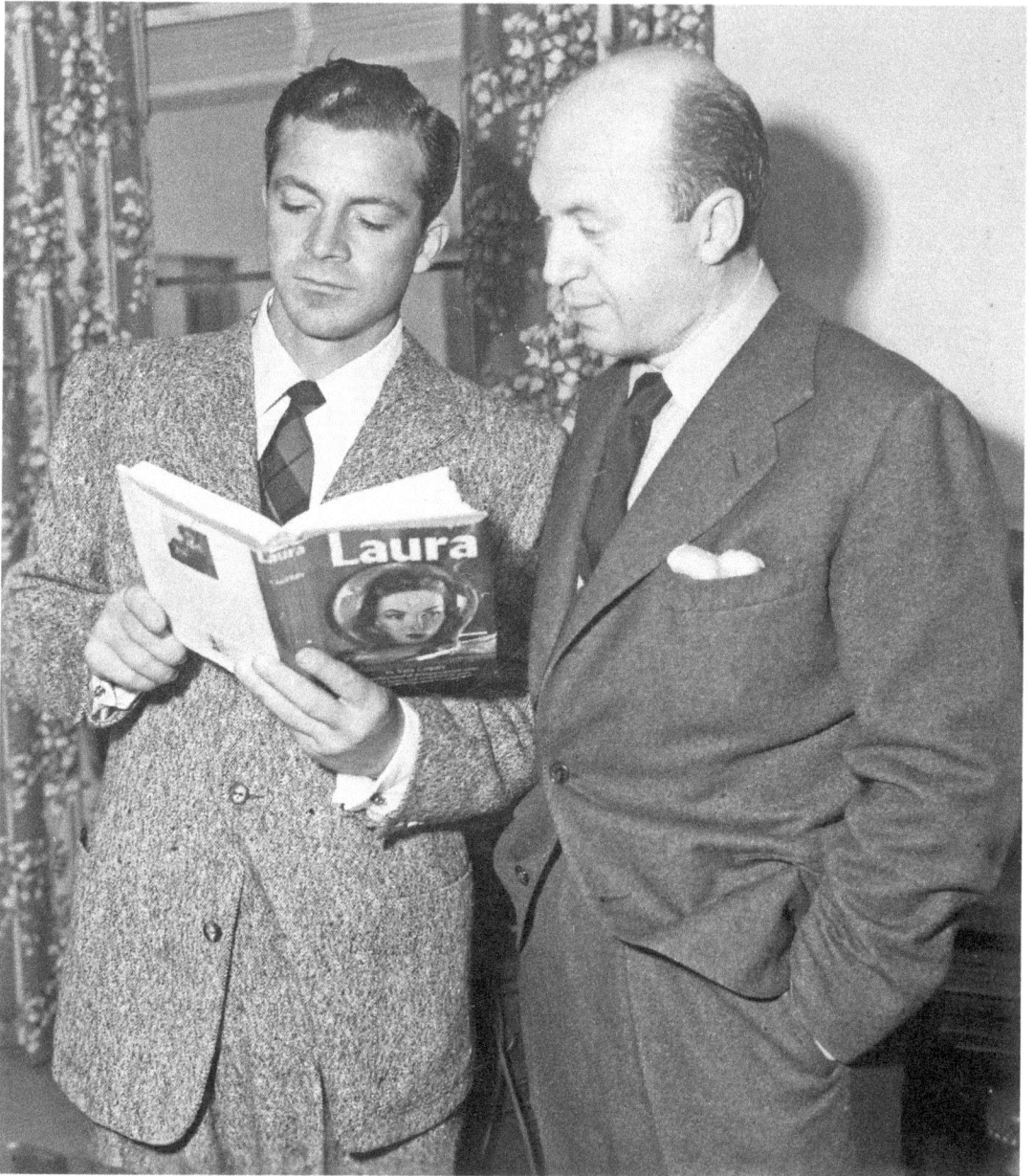

Andrews with director Otto Preminger during the making of *Laura* (20th Century–Fox, 1944).

him the success he had been anxiously awaiting since his early days treading the boards at the Pasadena Playhouse.

Capitalizing on his popularity as a romantic leading man, Fox put Andrews into a musical, Rodgers and Hammerstein's *State Fair* (1945). This time his leading lady was the quintessential "girl next door" Jeanne Crain, who, like Gene Tierney, perfectly complemented An-

drews's understated acting style (they would go on to make another three films together). Even though Andrews possessed a fine baritone singing voice, he kept this to himself, and his singing in the film was dubbed. He later confessed: "I kept my mouth shut.... because I don't like what happens to singers in Hollywood."

Andrews's next assignment, another Mile-

Dana enjoying a relaxing moment with his mother, Mrs. Charles F. Andrews, in 1946.

stone classic, *A Walk in the Sun* (1945) fully explored his manly all–American characteristics. Like *The Ox-Bow Incident* before it, the film fared badly at the box-office, but it would go on to be recognized as one of the classics of the silver screen. Another Preminger entry, the low-key noir *Fallen Angel* (1945), was followed in 1946 by the big outdoor adventure *Canyon Passage* — Andrews's first association with celebrated horror director Jacques Tourneur.

The pinnacle of Andrews's career arrived with Goldwyn's Academy Award winner *The Best Years of Our Lives* (1946), which Andrews described as "the best film I ever made." He was perfect as the traumatized flyer returning home from the war, but his underplaying of the role was taken for granted and he missed out on the Oscar nominations that year (the Academy rarely recognized the skill of minimalist acting). This classic was swiftly followed by another,

Elia Kazan's brilliant drama *Boomerang!*, which one critic described as being "notable for Dana Andrews's best performance to date."

Buoyed by the success of his film career, Andrews began to indulge in the high life of being a star, which left his bank balance dwindling and led to an addiction to alcohol, which would last for most of the rest of his professional career. In rare interviews, Andrews would candidly talk about how his drinking problem, brought on by the pressures of work and the emotional strain of being a star, led to near-disaster in his private and public life. Things hit rock bottom in 1968 when Mary, tired of his heavy drinking, filed for divorce. (They were reconciled six months later.) Andrews blamed drink for the deaths of Natalie Wood and close friend William Holden and fought back tears when Richard Burton once declared, "I'm not an alcoholic, I'm a drunk."[20]

Throughout the rest of the '40s and early 1950s, Andrews's film output remained prodigious. He appeared in a number of highly entertaining and well-received features, but none of them matched the quality of his earlier work. With the end of the war, all the big stars had returned to their studios and the competition for roles in top films became intense. During this period he cropped up in several romantic dramas opposite the likes of Joan Crawford (*Daisy Kenyon*) and Merle Oberon (*Night Song*), but although well-acted and entertaining, these 1947 features were mere trifles. The only memorable entry of the genre in which he appeared was the tearjerker *My Foolish Heart* (1949), which was very much a Susan Hayward vehicle.

Although Andrews worked with some of the most beautiful and glamorous actresses in the business, he was not at all overwhelmed by these encounters, as he was of the firm opinion that beauty was bad for the character, in that, if you were born with something that made life easy, you were not impelled to develop qualities of character.[21]

As the Russian defector in *The Iron Curtain* (1948), Andrews again convincingly played the role of the heroic victim, in a production notable as the first postwar anti–Red film and also for coining the phrase "Iron Curtain." Equally

impressive was *Sword in the Desert* (1949), one of the first films to tackle the Israeli conflict in postwar Palestine, but unfortunately, it was quickly withdrawn due to its Israeli bias. In the late 1940s, Andrews looked to independently produce some small-scale projects in which he could star, but this venture was short-lived when his romantic comedy *No Minor Vices* (1948), which he made with his friend director Lewis Milestone, failed to spark much interest.

Later in 1948, he played a fisherman in the gentle sea tale *Deep Waters*. Amongst the 1949 crop, he starred in his most unusual film, *The Forbidden Street*, a Victorian melodrama made in the United Kingdom, in which he romanced Maureen O'Hara in two different roles, one of which was dubbed.

With Andrews's career in the doldrums, Otto Preminger reappeared on the scene and put the star back on familiar noir ground with the hard-hitting *Where the Sidewalk Ends* (1950), which reunited Andrews with Gene Tierney.

Goldwyn attempted to reprise the glory days of *Best Years of Our Lives* with the family drama *I Want You*, which was set during the Korean War. However, the film was simply seen as a sentimental recruiting poster for the Korean War and it was to be the last film Andrews would make for the mogul. (It was rumored that Andrews paid Goldwyn $100,000 to get out of his contract.) In the same year, Andrews said his goodbyes to the Fox studio with the underwater wartime actioner *The Frogmen* (1951), where he was relegated to second lead, with Richard Widmark topping the bill. The excellent little RKO actioner *Sealed Cargo* gave Andrews the opportunity to work alongside one of the best character actors in the business, Claude Rains.

With his split contract at an end, Andrews was now a free agent, but with all the major studios having their full quota of stars, it was never going to be an easy journey. Before taking a two-year break from filming, Andrews was featured in the espionage thriller *Assignment Paris* (1952), shot on location in Europe. With more time on his hands, Andrews set up his own production company, Lawrence Productions, and returned to the theatre in *The Glass*

The Andrews household (1948). Shown from left: Mary Todd (Mrs. Dana Andrews), Susan, Stephen, Dana and Katherine. In the background is (unconfirmed) a portrait of David, Dana's oldest child from his first marriage to Janet Murray.

Menagerie, co-starring with his wife Mary. He would return to the theatre throughout the rest of his career in productions such as *Two for the Seesaw, The Captains and the Kings* and *Any Wednesday*, the latter also co-starring his wife). To make ends meet, he also got involved in radio drama, signing a ten-year contract to do the weekly drama *I Was a Communist for the F.B.I.* Andrews's radio career also took in several *Lux Radio Theatre* presentations including *Laura* and *Where the Sidewalk Ends.*

In 1954, Andrews got back in front of the camera for two exotic dramas shot on location, *Elephant Walk* with Elizabeth Taylor, set in

F 552- S -202

A proud father with youngest daughter Susan (1948).

Ceylon, and the African adventure *Duel in the Jungle* (his second film with Jeanne Crain).

The 1950s saw a continuance in the western's popularity, and like many of the '40s noir icons (Alan Ladd, Ray Milland and Fred MacMur-ray), Andrews proved he was just as comfortable with a six-shooter as he was with a Smith & Wesson revolver. Striking while the iron was hot, he chalked up four respectable western features in quick succession: *Three Hours to Kill*

Smile, you're on camera! With Katherine and Stephen (1948).

(1954), *Smoke Signal* (1955), *Strange Lady in Town* (1955) and *Comanche* (1956).

Before Andrews could get too comfortable in the saddle, the acclaimed director Fritz Lang set him to work in two film noirs, *While the City Sleeps* and *Beyond a Reasonable Doubt*, both made in 1956. Like Preminger before him, Lang knew how to work the troubled and flawed traits into Andrews's characters.

In 1957, Andrews romanced Betty Hutton in *Spring Reunion* before heading off to England to work for his friend Jacques Tourneur in the brilliant supernatural thriller *Night of the Demon* (U.S. title: *Curse of the Demon*). In this riveting tale, without doubt the finest of its kind, Andrews's performance as the skeptical Dr. Holden is the perfect foil to Niall MacGinnis's black magician, the sinister Julian Karswell.

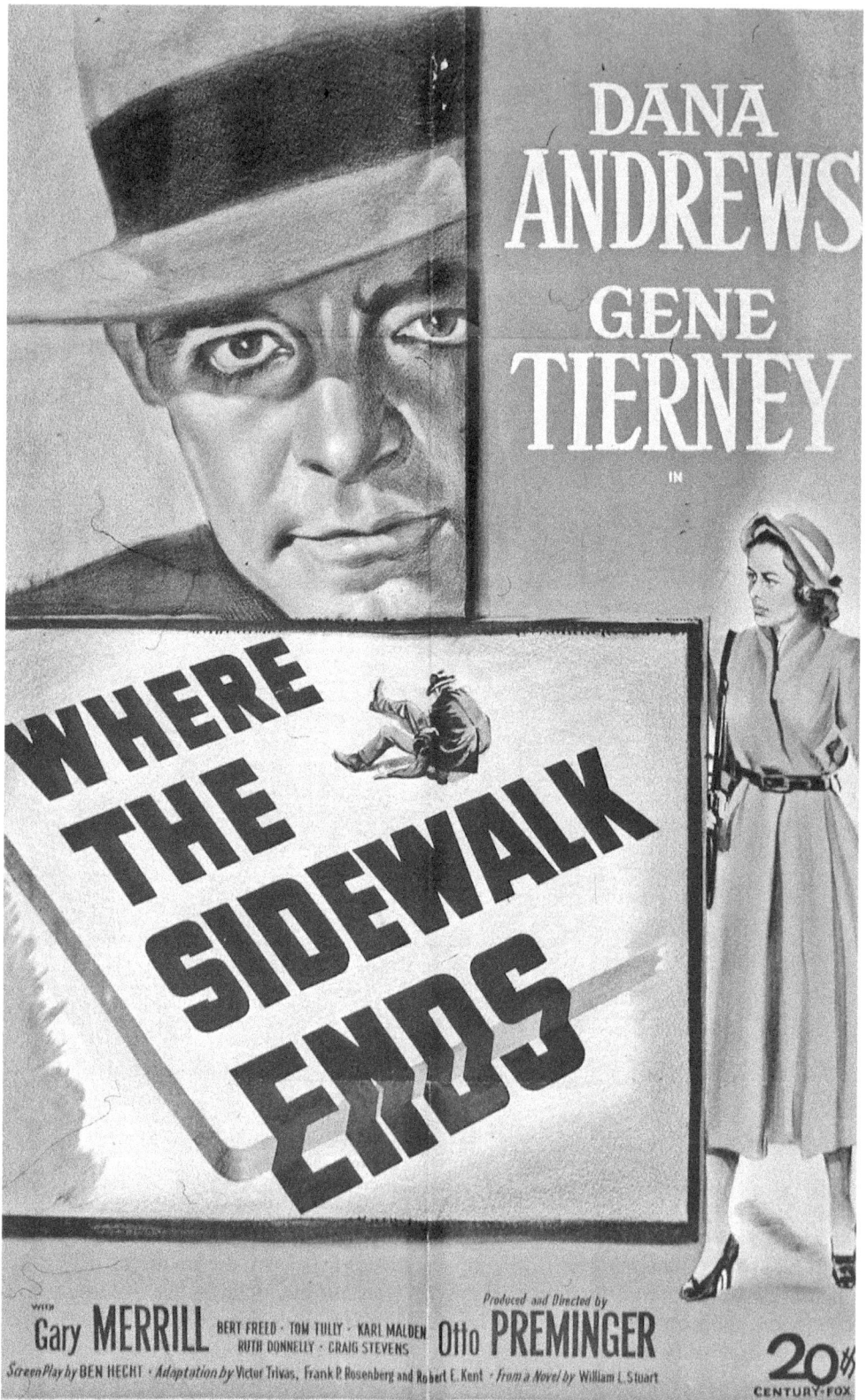

Poster from *Where the Sidewalk Ends* (20th Century–Fox, 1950). Andrews's chiseled features and enigmatic expression prove beyond doubt that he, more than anyone, represented the Face of Noir.

Andrews with Ruth Roman rehearsing for the Lux Radio Theatre broadcast of *The Blue Gardenia* (November 30, 1954).

Returning to the States, Andrews co-starred with Linda Darnell and Sterling Hayden in the suspense-laden *Zero Hour!*, an airborne disaster story by Arthur Hailey which was hilariously spoofed in 1980 by the makers of *Airplane!* This was the first of Andrews's trilogy of airplane disaster films.

Andrews rounded off the 1950s with a dis-

appointing version of Herman Melville's *Typee*, *Enchanted Island* (1958), where he was completely miscast, and another Tourneur thriller, *The Fearmakers*, a tale of subversives in Washington D.C.; Andrews again played the part of a troubled war veteran (*The Best Years of Our Lives* and *Zero Hour!*).

With the dawn of a new decade, Andrews's

life took a new direction when he turned his attention to property development following several months of studying real estate at night school. In 1960, he bought and renovated a North Hollywood apartment building, which he then sold for a profit of $150,000. Other property investments followed, making Andrews financially independent and less reliant on his film career. On the financial rewards of real estate, Andrews commented: "I've made more money during the past three years than I ever did in twenty years of acting."[22] Acting, however, would always remain his first love as he declared, "I make a lot of money, but I'm an actor who is also in business rather than a businessman playing at acting."

Once an actor, always an actor — but with the decline of the big Hollywood studios and the introduction of a new breed of actor such as Brando, Newman and Redford, good film roles became harder to find, which reduced his output in the early 1960s.

After a stint on Broadway with *Two for the Seesaw* (taking over from Henry Fonda) he returned to films, but only made two features in the next four years: *The Crowded Sky* (1960), a star-studded disaster-in-the-air suspenser, and *Madison Avenue* (1962), an advertising jungle melodrama, which reunited him with Jeanne Crain and also included the elegant Eleanor Parker. Andrews was now in his early fifties; his "man about town" character in *Madison Avenue* would be his last significant role as romantic leading man.

His drinking problem still plagued him; it affected his personal life and caused the odd film production headache, but never significantly marred any of his performances, which remained strong throughout his career, regardless of the film's quality.

In 1963 Andrews became president of the Screen Actors Guild, where he aired his concerns over the decline of good quality roles and productions for actors due to influences such as television. "Television has a built-in mediocrity because it is not drama. It is just an adjunct of the advertising business." To restore the actor's standing, he supported the use of Pay-TV. In an interview, Andrews commented on the precarious nature of his profession fol-

lowing the threat from television: "You might be fired tomorrow. So everything depends on what you do today, and what you've done yesterday.[23]

In 1965 tragedy struck when Andrews's eldest son, David (a musician and radio announcer), died after suffering a brain hemorrhage. With this sad loss and his continued drinking, Andrews's personal life hit rock bottom, but in the same year he bounced back with a vengeance, appearing in seven memorable films. Due to his age, leading romantic roles were now behind him, but he now found a new lease on life in smaller character parts and cameos, usually as high-ranking military men, officials, or scientists. Of the 1965 batch, his most notable performances were as the dying scientist in *Crack in the World*, the "stuffed shirt" colonel in *Battle of the Bulge*, and the evil tycoon in *Brainstorm*.

To show he could still whip the bad guys single-handedly, Andrews turned in two impressive performances for veteran western producer A.C. Lyles. *Town Tamer* (1965) and *Johnny Reno* (1966) both made excellent use of Lyles's stable of veteran actors including Lon Chaney, Jr., Lyle Bettger, and Richard Arlen.

With the completion of the made-in-Spain *Battle of the Bulge* (1965), Andrews remained in Europe and made the first of several foreign crime-spy exploitation films which were gaining popularity at the time. The most notable of these excursions were *Berlino, Appuntamento per Le Spie* (*Spy in Your Eye*, 1966), where Andrews played a scientist with a camera implanted in his eye for espionage purposes, and *Il Cobra* (*Cobra*, 1968), where he flexed his muscles as a U.S. Secret Service man fighting opium smugglers in the Middle East.

Many other Hollywood stars made similar European forays, including Stewart Granger, Edward G. Robinson and Van Heflin. Clint Eastwood would of course be the main U.S. export when the spaghetti western hit the screens.

Stopping off in England, Andrews played the most bizarre role in his career as the mad German scientist in a thick slice of low-budget horror hokum, *The Frozen Dead* (1967). In the same year he once again starred with Jeanne Crain in the teenage road rage thriller *Hot Rods*

Poster from the supernatural classic *Night of the Demon* (Columbia, 1957).

to Hell. Both these features clearly fall into the category of being so bad they're actually good.

Having proved his worth as an actor on film and in the theatre, Andrews now turned to television to showcase his talents. He had dabbled with the medium in the '60s, but it was in NBC-TV's daytime serial *Bright Promise* (1969–72) that he really made his mark portraying a college president. Andrews recalled that he was "impressed after reading the first five scripts and felt I had to accept the part."

Many television appearances followed, plus small parts in several films made for television: *The Failing of Raymond* (1971) starring fellow veteran Jane Wyman, *Shadow in the Streets* (1975) and *The First 36 Hours of Dr. Durant* (1975).

However, his most impressive television appearance came in 1971 when he made a public service announcement condemning the evils of alcohol: "I'm Dana Andrews and I'm an alcoholic. I don't drink any more, but I used to—

all the time. I attended [Alcoholics Anonymous] meetings for a time, but in the long run I had to work out my problem for myself." In this candid discussion, Andrews also admitted that his drinking had negatively affected his career.

Having finally beaten the bottle, Andrews turned a corner in his life: "I've got fifteen, maybe twenty years left, and I'm going to live out the twilight my own way." Luckily for his fans, he continued to feature in a number of small and varied roles throughout the '70s and early '80s, despite the fact that with his many investments, he could have easily enjoyed a comfortable retirement.

In 1974, he starred as the hapless pilot who crashes his small plane into a 747 passenger airliner in *Airport 1975*, which completed his trilogy in the airplane disaster genre. And in 1976 he returned to the lavish type of production he had enjoyed under Goldwyn: In *The Last Tycoon,* he played a film director working for a

Andrews (front) with Conrad Nagel in the 1961 theatre production of *The Captains and the Kings.*

character loosely based on MGM "Boy Won-der" Irving Thalberg. This final period in An-drews's film career also included a number of actioners, biopics and political dramas, includ-ing the Vietnam thriller *Good Guys Wear Black*

(1978), *Born Again* (1978) and his final feature *Prince Jack* (1985).

When not filming or attending to his various business interests, Andrews continued to maintain a simple lifestyle at home, with the

Andrews as college president Thomas Boswell, in the NBC-TV daytime serial *Bright Promise,* which ran 1969–72.

film fan magazines of the day listing his interests as Dickens, Shakespeare, Rachmaninoff's Piano Concerto No. 2 in C Minor, Van Gogh, A.J. Cronin, Maxwell Anderson, Grant Wood, Abraham Lincoln, the Philadelphia Symphony and amateur photography.[24] With Ralph Edwards presiding, Andrews's personal and professional life was celebrated in a 1973 episode of *This Is Your Life.*

In February 1983, Andrews was further honored with a retrospective film festival at Mississippi State University in Starkville, Mississippi. In addition to the screening of eleven of Andrews's films, the nine-day event (February

16–24) included a series of discussions and a musical performance, with Dana, accompanied by his wife Mary, arriving on campus for a series of lectures, receptions and banquets. Andrews was selected to be honored because he was born in Mississippi, of which he was proud, and had achieved a status in his profession unequalled by any other Mississippian. Clyde Williams, English professor at MSU and coordinator of the festival, said that Andrews received this tribute because "his life and his films are the embodiment of the American dream." Andrews acknowledged that he epitomized the concept of "the poor boy who makes good." One of the highlights of the event for Andrews, and audience alike, was a presentation to the actor of an album of movie stills autographed by other cast members. Entitled "You Have Friends—Dana Andrews," the album included luminaries such as Clayton Moore, Richard Webb, John Agar, Evelyn Finley, Marc Lawrence, George Montgomery, Henry Brandon, Gene Tierney, Virginia Mayo, Kirk Douglas, Myrna Loy and many more.[25]

Even though money was not an issue, the Andrews family resided in a relatively modest Studio City, California, home where Andrews spent much of the latter part of his life. In 1990, he suffered a series of small strokes and was diagnosed with multi-infarct dementia, a condition similar to Alzheimer's disease.

Seriously ill, he soldiered on for another two years, living at the John Douglas French Center for Alzheimer's in Los Alamitos, Orange County, California. At age 83, he died of congestive heart failure and pneumonia on December 17, 1992, at the Los Alamitos Medical Center. *The Guardian Obituary* succinctly summed up his unique contribution to the world of cinema: "There were more showy, charming, and exciting male stars in Hollywood in the 1940s, but there were few as subtle, enigmatic and moody as Dana Andrews...."[26]

And so ended the story of a fine actor. I hope you enjoy this tribute to his film work. But if you don't, in the words of the great man himself, "Go ahead and spit if that'll make you feel better."*

---

*Andrews's Mark McPherson says it in Laura, in response to Bessie Clary's swipe, "I ain't afraid of cops. I was brought up to spit whenever I saw one."

The Films

Lucky Cisco Kid
20th Century–Fox, 1940

Cast: Cesar Romero (Cisco Kid); Mary Beth Hughes (Lola); Dana Andrews (Sergeant Dunn); Evelyn Venable (Emily Lawrence); Chris-Pin Martin (Cordito); Willard Robertson (Judge McQuade); Joe Sawyer (Bill Stevens); Johnny Sheffield (Tommy Lawrence); William Royle (Sheriff); Francis Ford (Court Clerk); Otto Hoffman (Storekeeper); Dick Rich (Stagecoach Driver); Spencer Charters (Hotel Guest); Jimmie Dundee, Adrian Morris, William Pagan (Stagecoach Passengers); Frank Ellis, Ethan Laidlaw (Henchmen); Bob Hoffman, Boyd "Red" Morgan (Soldiers); Lew Kelly (Station Agent); Frank Lackteen (Bandit); Henry Roquemore (Diamond); Gloria Roy (Dance Hall Girl) ; Blackie Whiteford (Spike); Syd Saylor (Hotel Clerk); Harry Strang (Corporal).

Credits: Sol M. Wurtzel (Producer); H. Bruce Humberstone (Director); John Stone (Associate Producer); Based on the character created by O. Henry; Julian Johnson (Story); Robert Ellis, Helen Logan (Screenplay); Cyril J. Mockridge (Music); Lucien N. Andriot (Cinematography); Fred Allen (Editor); Richard Day (Art Direction); William H. Anderson, Bernard Freericks (Sound); Thomas Little (Set Decorations); Helen A. Myron (Costume Design). Running time: 67 minutes

Through a reign of terror, corrupt Judge McQuade, assisted by a gang of crooks led by Bill Stevens, hopes to drive settlers off their land and buy it for himself, all the while placing the blame on the Cisco Kid. Pursued by Sergeant Dunn (Dana Andrews) and his cavalry unit, the Kid, assisted by his loyal companion Cordito, seeks to round up the crooks and prove his innocence. Throughout the chase, the Kid finds time to romance Dunn's dancehall sweetheart Lola and the attractive widow Emily Lawrence.

The character of the Cisco Kid was created by author O. Henry in his short story "The Ca-ballero's Way," published in 1907. Although portrayed by Hollywood as a Mexican hero, in the original story he was a non–Hispanic character and a cruel outlaw who was probably modeled on Billy the Kid. The caballero featured in numerous films between 1929 and 1950, portrayed by Warner Baxter, Cesar Romero, Gilbert Roland, and Duncan Renaldo; this was followed by a television series that ran from 1950 to 1956. Unlike the traditional stereotype of the Mexican bandit — greasy, vicious, insidious, lazy and licentious (I think that covers them all) — the Cisco Kid was a more refined, dashing Californio, a kind of Robin Hood type. And, like that other Hispanic hero Zorro, the Kid played out his south of the border adventures in a mythical land bursting at the seams with guitar strummers, groveling peasants and feisty spitfires.

It is fair to say that the Mexican got a rawer deal than the Native American Indian when it came to stereotyping in Hollywood. Whereas characterization of the Indian was fully explored over time, the Mexican male basically fell into one of two camps— the poor, vulnerable "dirt farmer" peasant or the snarling, bloodthirsty bandit, the Alfonso Bedoya type: "Badges? We ain't got no badges. We don't need no badges. I don't have to show you any stinking badges." I must stop watching repeats of *The Treasure of the Sierra Madre*, but I think you'll agree that the Cisco Kid and Zorro were like a breath of fresh air.

Director H. Bruce Humberstone was no stranger to series characters, having made his name with some of the Charlie Chan films. He was adept with all genres, but with no distinct directing style; his most notable films included *Sun Valley Serenade* (1941), *I Wake Up Screaming*

(1941), and *Pin Up Girl* (1944). In at the beginning of Andrews's career with *Lucky Cisco Kid*, Humberstone also produced and directed the actor's last feature as a romantic leading man 20 years later, *Madison Avenue*.

Lucky Cisco Kid was Cesar Romero's third outing as the Kid, out a series of six he made between 1939 and 1941. Prior to being typed as a Latin lover in Hollywood, Romero had made his reputation as a dancer. Critics and fans generally agree that his best performance was as the Spanish explorer Cortez in *Captain from Castile* (1947). In the 1960s he gained a cult following for his role as the Joker in the hugely successful *Batman* television series.

In addition to being Andrews's debut film appearance (he made *The Westerner* first, but this was released later), *Lucky Cisco Kid* was the first of his many westerns. Although he would be more readily associated with film noir, realist thrillers and war films, he actually notched up 13 entries in the western genre.

As the young Sergeant Dunn in this deliciously ripe "saddle saga," Andrews cuts a dashing figure in two different cavalry uniforms (no doubt he had a third for formal evening wear in his saddle bags), vying with the charmingly roguish Romero for the attention of Mary Beth Hughes. Andrews shouldn't have been unduly concerned as the Kid rarely got too serious where females were concerned, much preferring to ride off into the sunset with his paunchy pal Cordito, played in this instance by Chris-Pin Martin. In return for Andrews's solid support throughout the proceedings, Romero returned the favor eight years later when their starring roles were reversed in the salty tale *Deep Waters*. Mary Beth Hughes and Chris-Pin Martin also worked again with Andrews in the western tragedy *The Ox-Bow Incident*.

Romero's lively performance as the gay caballero is equally matched by Andrews's spirited turn as the no-nonsense Sergeant Dunn. In hot pursuit of the Kid, he has little time for romance with his "babe" Lola (Hughes), who is being wooed by Dunn *and* the Kid, *and* is also the object of desire for bad guy Bill Stevens. No small wonder Dunn gets increasingly snappy as the story unfolds. Andrews would go on to play a similar role in *Belle Starr*— again in charge of a cavalry unit, but this time chasing outlaw Sam Starr around the country, with both men falling

for the lovely Belle, played exquisitely by Gene Tierney.

With Andrews's first screen lines, we get an idea of Dunn's dogged determination to catch that daring outlaw rascal, the Cisco Kid.

> SGT. DUNN: Look at it, 10,000 square miles of nothing.... May as well be looking for a rabbit. Maybe that's why he calls himself conejito.
> CORPORAL: What does that mean?
> SGT. DUNN: Conejito— that's Spanish for little rabbit. If ever I get my hands on him, he'll be a hung goose.

The film also dishes up a fair slice of humor, particularly in the scene where Dunn describes the Kid to Lola while the Kid, immersed in a bubble bath next door, amusingly listens on. With a spot-on description from the stage driver, Dunn spits out, "He's a big, ugly-looking galoot with a face like poison. He's got great big eyes and when he's gonna slit your throat, he smiles like he's enjoying it."

No creaky old western would be complete without the "I'm so bored and easily led; let's lynch somebody" mentality rearing its ugly head during the proceedings. In this case, the Kid lives to woo the womenfolk another day when Dunn pulls him away from an excited mob that wants to string him up from the nearest post. Lynching would become a recurring feature in several of Andrews's westerns, with our hero playing the role of victim or rescuer with equal indignation.

Andrews was one of the first Hollywood actors to work under a split contract, dividing eleven years of his early career between the Samuel Goldwyn studio and 20th Century–Fox. In this period he played the second lead in a number of B pictures including *Lucky Cisco Kid*. Unlike some of his Hollywood contemporaries such as John Wayne and Robert Mitchum, Andrews's B-movie apprenticeship was comparatively short — in total, three features produced and released in rapid succession in 1940.

Sailor's Lady

20th Century–Fox, 1940

Cast: Nancy Kelly (Sally Gilroy); Jon Hall (Danny Malone); Joan Davis (Myrtle); Dana Andrews (Scrappy Wilson); Mary Nash (Miss Purvis); Larry "Buster" Crabbe (Rodney); Kay Aldridge (Georgine); Harry Shannon (Father McGann); Wally Vernon

(Goofer); Bruce Hampton (Skipper); Charles D. Brown (Capt. Roscoe); Selmer Jackson (Executive Officer); Edgar Dearing (Chief Master-at-Arms); Edmund MacDonald (Barnacle); William B. Davidson (Judge Hinsdale); Lester Dorr (Assistant Paymaster); George O'Hanlon, Steve Pendleton, Murray Alper, Bud Carpenter, William H. Conselman, Jr. Don Forbes, Eugene Gericke, Eddie Hall, John Kellogg, Tom Seidel, Charles Tannen (Sailors); Matt McHugh (Cabby); Peggy Ryan (Ellen); Ward Bond (Shore Patrolman); Barbara Pepper (Maude); Eddie Acuff (Guide); Edward Earle (Navigator); Pierre Watkin, Paul Harvey (Captains); Emmett Vogan (Medical Officer); Don "Red" Barry (Second Paymaster); Robert Shaw (Ensign); Frances Morris, Gladys Blake, Marie Blake (Beauty Operators); Claire Du Brey (Old Maid); Kane Richmond (Lt. Wood).

Credits: Sol M. Wurtzel (Producer); Allan Dwan (Director); Lieutenant Commander Frank "Spig" Wead (Story); Frederick Hazlitt Brennan (Screenplay); Ernest Palmer (Cinematography); Fred Allen (Editor), Samuel Kaylin (Music Direction); Lewis H. Creber, Richard Day (Art Direction); Thomas Little (Set Decorations); Herschel McCoy (Costume Design); William H. Anderson, Eugene Grossman (Sound). Running time: 66 minutes

Sailor Danny Malone plans to marry his girl Sally Gilroy when he returns from sea, but things become complicated when the bride-to-be is put in charge of an orphaned one-year-old boy called Skipper. The baby is accidentally left on board a battleship following a visit and is later discovered during a battle maneuver. Amidst the resulting chaos, the sweethearts try to reunite to sort out the mess, but are thwarted by Danny's buddy, Scrappy Wilson (Dana Andrews), and Sally's previous partner Rodney.

Tagline: "50,000 SAILORS— Can't Go Wrong."

One television promotion hailed *Sailor's Lady* as one of the most hilarious nautical comedies ever filmed. A slight exaggeration, yes, but this Fox second feature was certainly a lively affair with enough fun, laughter and romance to keep you in your seat for a little over an hour.

Former Navy aviator Lt. Commander Frank "Spig" Wead turned to writing as a second career following a tragic accident which left him paralyzed. His writings led him to Hollywood and an eventual friendship with director John Ford. Wead received two Academy Award nominations in 1938, one for Best Original Story for *Test Pilot* and a second for Best Screenplay for *The Citadel*. His other notable successes based on naval and aviation themes include *Dive Bomber*

(story, 1941) and *They Were Expendable* (screenplay, 1945). In 1957, Ford made *The Wings of Eagles* which was based on Wead's life, with John Wayne ("I'm gonna move that toe, I'm gonna move that toe!") taking the central role and Ward Bond playing John Ford in the character of John Dodge.

Director Allan Dwan, who was also a notable producer and screenwriter, directed over 400 films in his long and successful career, including several with Mary Pickford and Douglas Fairbanks, and other acclaimed classics such as *Heidi* (1937) and *Sands of Iwo Jima* (1949). Eighteen years after *Sailor's Lady*, he again directed Andrews in the South Seas drama *Enchanted Island* (1958).

Following the making of *The Westerner*, Sam Goldwyn sold half of Andrews's contract to 20th Century–Fox, where he was immediately cast in two B movies *Lucky Cisco Kid* and *Sailor's Lady*. This arrangement lasted for eleven years with each studio, according to Andrews, splitting his paycheck if he was in between assignments.

Scrappy Wilson is a die-hard bachelor hellbent on keeping his buddy Danny single and in the navy by thwarting his plans to marry Sally. This is by far Andrews's most mischievous character. It's a role that calls for a boisterous performance, especially in the scene where he and cohort Goofer (Wally Vernon) incite a riot at a party arranged by Danny and Sally, who are trying to convince Skipper's stuffy guardian Miss Purvis that they would be perfect parents.

In contrast to the serious one-woman characters in his other two B features that year, Scrappy marks Andrews's debut as a love 'em and leave 'em type, which would resurface in various guises throughout his career —*State Fair, Fallen Angel, My Foolish Heart* and *Madison Avenue.*

We first detect this cavalier attitude toward the opposite sex in a bar scene when Scrappy shares a drink with Danny. Danny is upset about his break-up with Sally — a break-up orchestrated by Scrappy, who thinks marriage is for suckers.

OLD FLAME: Danny, darling, don't tell me you're back in circulation.

SCRAPPY: Sure he is— sit down and feel his pulse.

When one recalls Andrews's rugged, square-jawed persona, tough guy names such as Mark

All at sea in *Sailor's Lady* (20th Century–Fox, 1940). From the left: Andrews as mischievous sailor Scrappy Wilson followed by Kay Aldridge, Jon Hall, Nancy Kelly, Wally Vernon and Joan Davis.

McPherson (*Laura*), Mike Dillon (*Sword in the Desert*) and Brett Halliday (*Smoke Signal*) immediately come to mind. Scrappy Wilson, however, even stretches *my* overworked imagination. But with comedy high on the agenda in the early war years, anything was possible, and there was no doubt that *Sailor's Lady* more than did its bit to address the wartime slogan, "Keep 'em laughing."

Titled *Sweetheart of Turret One* during production, *Sailor's Lady*'s story, in keeping with most of the escapist fare during this period, is episodic and merely serves as a loose framework for a series of comedy and musical numbers. Amidst the bedlam is ten-month-old Bruce Hampton as the stowaway baby, who during filming had five attendants, as well as a double and a stand-in.[1] Four years later, in Andrews's second nautical romp *Up in Arms*, Danny Kaye took over where Bruce Hampton left off, as the source of chaos afloat.

Although it is a B movie, this entertaining nautical comedy boasts an impressive cast which is a veritable delight for film buffs:

- Son of a Tahitian princess, husky leading man Jon Hall was usually cast as a South Sea islander or Arabian adventurer, and made his mark with a series of escapist exotic adventures with Maria Montez in the early 1940s.
- Former child star of the 1920s, Nancy Kelly played the lead in both A and B movies in the 1930s before returning to the stage. She received a Tony Award for her part in the play *The Bad Seed*, and was honored again when her performance in the 1956 film version earned her a Best Actress Oscar nomination.
- Champion swimmer Larry "Buster" Crabbe won the bronze medal for the 1500-meter freestyle in the 1928 Olympic Games and the gold medal for the 400-meter freestyle in the 1932 Games. In 1933, he starred in a Tarzan serial that launched a successful movie career, which was topped with the classic *Flash Gordon* serial in 1936.
- Best known for her dancing feet, Peggy Ryan found fame dancing alongside Donald

O'Connor; they were Universal's answer to Judy Garland and Mickey Rooney. In later years she played a small recurring part as the secretary in *Hawaii Five-O* (1968–1976).

- Don Red Barry acquired the nicknamed "Red" from the *Red Ryder* western character he successfully portrayed in the famous 1940 Republic Pictures serial. Due to his feisty nature and short stature, Republic tried to present him as their version of James Cagney. He worked with Andrews again in the classic World War II drama *The Purple Heart* (1944).
- Wally Vernon made a name for himself as the ubiquitous comic relief in many a Republic western in the 1940s and 50s.
- Comic actress Joan Davis enjoyed a successful career in vaudeville, film, radio, and television, but is most fondly remembered as the manic wife of mild-mannered community judge Jim Backus in *I Married Joan*—a television show very much in the *I Love Lucy* vein.
- With her beauty, sparkling wit and vivacious personality, former model Kay Aldridge enthralled audiences in the 1940s as the heroine in Republic's cliffhanger serial *Perils of Nyoka*, which saw her regularly tied to posts and suspended over flaming pits.

For several members of this fine ensemble, tragedy was lurking in the wings:

- In 1935, Andrews's first wife Janet, whom he had married in 1932, contracted pneumonia and died. Their only child David was born in 1933, but died in 1964 of a cerebral hemorrhage. Adding to this pain, Andrews's constant battle with alcoholism would further damage much of his personal and professional life.
- At the age of 66, Jon Hall shot himself in 1979 after being bedridden for nine months following surgery for bladder cancer.
- Wally Vernon was killed by a hit-and-run driver near his home in 1970.
- With his film career very much at an end, Don "Red" Barry committed suicide by shooting himself in 1980.
- In 1961, Joan Davis died of a heart attack at the age of 53. Two years later, Davis's mother, daughter and grandchildren all perished in a house fire.

Kit Carson
United Artists, 1940

Cast: Jon Hall (Kit Carson); Lynn Bari (Dolores Murphy); Dana Andrews (Captain John. C. Fremont); Harold Huber (Lopez); Ward Bond (Ape Eaton); Renie Riano (Miss Pilchard); Clayton Moore (Paul Terry); Rowena Cook (Alice Terry); Raymond Hatton (Jim Bridger); Harry Strang (Sergeant Clanahan); C. Henry Gordon (General Castro); Lew Merrill (General Vallejo); Stanley Andrews (Larkin); Edwin Maxwell (John Sutter); George Lynn (James King); Charles Stevens (Lieutenant Ruiz); William Farnum (Don Miguel Murphy); Iron Eyes Cody, Charles Soldani (Indians); Bill Hazlet, Al Kikume (Indian Chiefs); Tex Cooper, Julian Rivero, Al Haskell (Californians); Harry Semels (Aide).

Credits: Edward Small (Producer); George B. Seitz (Director); Evelyn Wells (Short Story); George Bruce (Screenplay); Edward Ward (Music); John J. Mescall, Robert Pittack (Cinematography); William F. Claxton (Editor); John DuCasse Schulze (Art Direction); Edward G. Boyle (Set Decorations); Howard A. Anderson, Jack Cosgrove (Special Effects); Edward P. Lambert (Costume Design); Richard V. Heermance (Sound); Don L. Cash (Makeup). Running time: 97 minutes

En route to California, Kit Carson and his buddies Lopez and the boomerang wielding Ape Eaton are endangered by Indian attacks orchestrated by the Mexican government in an attempt to prevent Americans from colonizing what they see as part of Mexico. They escape unscathed and get to Fort Bridger, where Captain John Fremont (Dana Andrews) hires them to lead a wagon train to California. On the way, both Carson and Fremont fall for pioneer girl Dolores Murphy, but their rivalry is soon forgotten when they join forces to fight off another Indian attack. Upon arriving in California, the two heroes initiate a campaign to free the state from Mexican control.

Taglines: "The Thundering Spectacle of America's Most Fabulous Days"; "Thrill to DANA ANDREWS' Greatest Role ... Fighter ... Lover ... Adventurer."

Director George B. Seitz started his career in the theatre and by writing screenplays for action serials such as *The Perils of Pauline* (1914) and *The Iron Claw* (1916), and he is best remembered for directing most of the entries in MGM's immensely successful Andy Hardy series. The adventurous biopic *Kit Carson* gave him the opportunity to stamp his mark on the life of the legendary frontiersman.

Western explorer Captain John C. Freemont (Andrews, right) discusses the orders of the day with legendary scout Kit Carson (Jon Hall) in the thrilling western *Kit Carson* (United Artists, 1940).

B movie icon Jon Hall enjoyed a temporary break from his usual trademark South Sea garb when he played the Western legend, whose services as a scout were celebrated in John C. Fremont's widely read reports of their expeditions (from Oregon to California, and through much of the Central Rocky Mountains and the Great Basin).

One of the most celebrated western explorers, Fremont served as U.S. Senator from California and, in 1856, became the first Republican candidate for president of the United States. He served in the Union Army during the Civil War, and afterwards was territorial governor of Arizona.

Captain Fremont was Andrews's first substantial part and a role he clearly relished, judging by the vigor of his performance. It was an inspired piece of casting made possible through a Fox loanout to independent filmmaker Edward Small, whose company, Reliance Pictures (formed

in 1932), distributed the film through their releasing deal with United Artists.

Fremont and Sergeant Dunn (*Lucky Cisco Kid*) were the first of many dependable, "ordinary guy" roles that Andrews cut his teeth on, before hints of vulnerability and moral ambiguity were teased out of such characters in later features. These roles also kicked off Andrews's long association with military and "authority" types. And when it comes to authoritative soldiering, there's no upper lip or collar stiffer than that of Andrews's Captain John C. Fremont as we regularly see in his exchanges with the legendary scout Kit Carson. ("The difference between you and me, Carson, is that you do as you please. I'm governed by orders and regulation.")

Fremont's initial disdain for Carson and his two rough-and-ready sidekicks is laid out when he explains to Dolores Murphy, "These scouts, they see an Indian behind every bush. You mustn't forget that they've lived amongst savages so long, they're practically savages themselves." Andrews sported a mustache, which was always guaranteed to add that final touch of authority to any historical military part. However, Andrews lacked the requisite "knowing smile," perfected by the likes of Gable and Flynn, to make this facial accessory a permanent feature. The actor recalled that in the late 1930s, his agent built him up as the next Clark Cable around the studios, but no one took the bait.

Lynn Bari also enjoyed a brief reprieve from her usual "B" movie roles when loaned out to independent producer Edward Small to play the Spanish-American heroine in *Kit Carson*, which was considered a big-budget western at the time. In the 1930s and '40s, Bari made over 100 films for 20th Century–Fox (usually B-movies), specializing in sultry, exotic bad girls.

Kit Carson also featured Clayton Moore, who was an aerialist in the circus and a male model before entering the world of B movies. His most famous role was as the masked hero on the TV series *The Lone Ranger*.

In another supporting role, the ubiquitous Ward Bond proved yet again that he was a force to be reckoned with. This was the second of four features he made with Andrews (the others being *Sailor's Lady*, *Swamp Water* and *Canyon Passage*).

The film's big budget is evident in a particularly exciting sequence where the settlers circle their covered wagons to fend off the hostile Indians. Serial king Seitz borrowed Cecil B. DeMille's famous bathtub sequence to spice up the proceedings, with the curvaceous Lynn Bari sharing bath time with Jon Hall, Ward Bond and Harold Huber. Don't get too hot under the collar, we are talking titillation, 1940s style — and if you want to know what happens to Hall's soap, get your own copy of the video.

If marauding Injuns and saloon gals weren't enough, this rousing adventure climaxes with General Castro's attack on the small garrison at the hacienda, which plays like a rematch of the Alamo. Drifting into parallel worlds, I figure Andrews as Travis without the attitude, Hall as Crockett without the coonskin cap and Ward Bond as Bowie without the knife, but just as lethal with a boomerang (which incidentally shares the same nickname as Crockett's frontier rifle — Old Betsy).

With the many traditional western songs incorporated into the storyline, you could be forgiven for thinking you had drifted into a John Ford feature. They are "Prairie Schooner," "Buffalo Gals Won't You Come Out Tonight," "Jeanie with the Light Brown Hair" and "Taps."

One critic wrote: "The photography is good; there are adequate action sequences and a more realistic portrayal of Navajo Indians than most, but it has little to do with the life of Kit Carson." (This is not altogether surprising, as the exploits of Kit Carson, like many other Western heroes, were heavily fictionalized during his own lifetime.)

According to the *New York Times*, "It was a straight old-fashioned action picture with more violent mayhem per linear foot of celluloid than we've seen in recent weeks."

It was rather fortunate for Andrews that he had a split contract, as Goldwyn's film output was low, and at this stage in his career Andrews needed exposure and experience, which he got with films such as *Sailor's Lady* and *Kit Carson*. With *Kit Carson* in the can, Andrews's agent rubbed his hands gleefully, exclaiming, "They'll be fighting over you for romantic leads now, kid."[1]

The Westerner

Produced by Samuel Goldwyn and distributed by United Artists, 1940

Cast: Gary Cooper (Cole Hardin); Walter Brennan (Judge Roy Bean); Doris Davenport (Jane Ellen Matthews); Fred Stone (Caliphet Mathews); Forrest Tucker (Wade Harper); Paul Hurst (Chickenfoot); Chill Wills (Southeast); Lilian Bond (Lily Langtry); Charles Halton (Mort Borrow); Tom Tyler (King Evans); Lucien Littlefield (A Stranger); Arthur Aylesworth (Mr. Dixon); Lupita Tovar (Teresita); Julian Rivero (Juan Gomez); Dana Andrews (Bart Cobble); Roger Gray (Eph Stringer); Jack Pennick (Henry Williams); Trevor Bardette (Shad Wilkins); Bill Steele (Tex Cole); Blackjack Ward (Buck Harrigan); James "Jim" Corey (Lee Webb); Buck Moulton (Charles Evans); Ted Wells (Joe Lawrence); Joe De La Cruz (Mex); Frank Cordell (Man); Philip Connor (John Yancy); C. E. Anderson (Hezekiah Willever); Arthur "Art" Mix (Seth Tucker); William Gillis (Leon Beauregard); Buck Connors (Abraham Wilson); Dan Borzage (Joe Yates); Aleth Hansen (Walt McGary); Gertrude Bennett (Abigail); Miriam Sherwin (Martha); Annabelle Rousseau (Elizabeth); Helen Foster (Janice); Connie Leon (Langtry's Maid); Charles Coleman (Langtry's Manager); Lew Kelly (Ticket Man); Heinie Conklin (Man at Ticket Window); Corbet Morris (Orchestra Leader); Stanley

Andrews (Sheriff); Phil Tead (Prisoner); Henry Roquemore (Stage Manager); Bill Bauman (Man Getting Haircut); Hank Bell (Deputy).

Credits: Samuel Goldwyn (Producer); William Wyler (Director); Stuart N. Lake (Story); Niven Busch, Jo Swerling (Screenplay); Gregg Toland (Cinematography); Dimitri Tiomkin (Music); James Basevi (Art Director); Daniell Mandell (Editor); Walter Mayo (Assistant Director); Julia Heron (Set Decorations); Fred Lau (Sound); Irene Saltern (Costumes). Running time: 100 minutes

Drifter Cole Hardin, falsely accused of stealing a horse, is brought before Judge Roy Bean, the sole law west of the Pecos. Discovering the judge's great admiration of Lily Langtry, Cole cleverly cons the judge into believing that he knows her. Envious, the judge has Cole reprieved so that he (Cole) can get him a lock of Lily's hair. On his way to California, Cole happens to stop at the farm of Caliphet Mathews, whose daughter Jane-Ellen convinces him that the homesteaders are right in their fight with the cattlemen, who with the assistance of the judge are trying to drive them out of the territory. Cole goes back into town and declares himself on the side of the homesteaders. After a series of stampedes and fires which culminates in the killing of Jane's father, Cole sets out after the judge, who has gone to nearby Fort Davis to see Lily Langtry on stage. Inevitably, the two shoot it out after the show ends and the judge is mortally wounded. In a gesture of respect, Cole picks him up and escorts him to Lily, whose hand he kisses before he dies.

Tagline: "Outlawed! But fighting for an empire! Era of flaming feuds and new frontiers!"

Having observed his competitors enjoying box-office success with Westerns such as *Stagecoach* (United Artists), *Jesse James* (Fox) and *Destry Rides Again* (Universal), Samuel Goldwyn decided to put his own brand on the genre with *The Westerner*. Goldwyn wanted the film to be made quickly, but still budgeted it at more than a million dollars. The film was shot in four weeks with Tucson, Arizona, filling in for the Texas frontier.

Although the title of the film refers to the character of Cole Hardin, nonchalantly played by Gary Cooper, the movie primarily focuses on the life of the legendary "Hanging Judge" Roy Bean, who held court sessions in his saloon along the Rio Grande in West Texas from the 1880s until his death by natural causes in 1902.

In real life, Bean never got to meet Lily Langtry, but the actress did travel by train to Langtry, Texas, in 1904 to pay posthumous respects to one of her biggest fans.

Notwithstanding Cooper's top billing, the real star of *The Westerner* is Walter Brennan, who played the ornery Judge Bean to perfection and earned a Best Supporting Oscar for his performance. Both stars enjoyed Oscar success in their careers; Cooper for *Sergeant York* (1941) and *High Noon* (1952), and Brennan as Best Supporting Actor for *Come and Get It* (1936) *Kentucky* (1938) and *The Westerner* (1940).

Perfectionist William Wyler became known as "Ninety-Nine Take Wyler" for his insistence on shooting scenes over and over until he was satisfied with the results. Nominated 12 times for Academy Awards, he won the Best Director Oscar three times, for *Mrs. Miniver* (1942), *The Best Years of Our Lives* (1946), and *Ben-Hur* (1959). His varied 45-year directorial career also includes such classics as *Dead End, Jezebel, Wuthering Heights, Roman Holiday,* and *The Big Country.*

Interviewed years later, Andrews discussed working with Wyler on *The Westerner* and describe a scene where he was nearly killed by some fence posts that rolled off a speeding wagon turning a corner. According to the actor, Wyler's first reaction to the incident was to inquire about the condition of the fence posts, leaving Andrews in no doubt that at this early stage of his career, his value to the director was less than that of set materials.[1]

Andrews recalled the release of *The Westerner*: "Probably my biggest 'sheer chance' thing happened right down there on 44th Street in New York. I had just made my first movie, *The Westerner*, starring Gary Cooper. Down there, they put up a huge sign ... *The Westerner*, it said, starring Gary Cooper and Dana Andrews. I had exactly four lines in the picture. Nobody had ever heard of me. But the publicity department had done that for all the billboards. They thought Andrews was a girl's name, and was the girl in the picture, and that it looked more exciting to have Cooper and a girl.... If I'd used my first name, Carver, maybe I'd never have made it."[2]

Like Wyler, Goldwyn was forever the perfectionist and insisted that Andrews practice his acting skills on stage before appearing in a movie. As a consequence, the actor prepared for his four lines in *The Westerner* by appearing in two dozen Pasadena Playhouse productions.

Andrews as Bart Cobble: We hired out for farm work, miss— not a civil war. This ain't no fit place to homestead in.

> FARMHAND: Land's no good if there's always lead flying over it.
> JANE: If you'd shoot back, maybe they'd stop bothering you.
> FARMHAND: We did shoot back.
> BART COBBLE: And so did Chad Wilkins. But he ain't trying it no more!

During filming, Andrews obeyed Goldwyn's instruction to wear a dental brace and had to seek the mogul's permission before getting married to actress Mary Todd. Although he was grateful for his big break, the timing of the decision to cast him in the film left a lot to be desired, as Andrews amusingly recollected: "[W]e had arranged the wedding, and about a week before the wedding was planned, I got a call from the casting director: 'Let your hair and your beard grow; you're going to be in a Western.' So I had a week's growth of beard at my wedding, and in the society column of the Santa Monica paper (where my wife lived) there was a big picture of the two of us, me with this beard, and it said, "Mr. Andrews is an actor. Note the beard."[3]

Cooper's love interest in the film, Doris Davenport, tested for the part of Scarlett O'Hara in *Gone with the Wind*, but *The Westerner* was her only major feature before drifting into B productions and then out of the business altogether. The film also provided a 21-year-old Forrest Tucker with his debut role. Giving the movie a unique touch of authenticity, the role of the bartender is played by 82-year old Cal Cohen, the original bartender from Judge Bean's saloon.

Although the film bravely tried to detach itself from the traditional western plot and character formula, it opened to mixed critical reviews; according to the *New York Morning Telegraph*, "All of these recognized artists of the cinema, Cooper, Wyler, et al., apparently believed that they could put some very artistic stuff into what is nothing more or less than a good old-fashioned hoss opera, and it's a debatable question as to whether artistic stuff really belongs in such a work." It was perhaps for this reason that Wyler steered clear of the genre until

his triumphant return in 1958 with the sweeping epic *The Big Country*.

Paul Newman played the role of Bean in *The Life and Times of Roy Bean* (1972), a solid version which nonetheless lacked the wry humor and atmosphere of its predecessor.

Having impressed in this, his first rustic outing, Andrews was given another opportunity to play a hot-headed hick the following year in Jean Renoir's *Swamp Water*, with Walter Brennan once again in the star line-up.

The theme of a man's obsessive love for a remote unattainable beauty fuelled by her ethereal image in a painting would crop up again in one of noir's finest entries (and although it's also a worthy film, you're way off beam if *The Woman in the Window* first comes to mind).

Tobacco Road
20th Century–Fox, 1941

Cast: Charley Grapewin (Jeeter Lester); Marjorie Rambeau (Sister Bessie Rice); Gene Tierney (Ellie May Lester); William Tracy (Dude Lester); Elizabeth Patterson (Ada Lester); Dana Andrews (Capt. Tim Harmon); Slim Summerville (Henry Peabody); Ward Bond (Lov Bensey); Grant Mitchell (George Payne); Zeffie Tilbury (Grandma Lester); Russell Simpson (Chief of Police); Spencer Charters (County Clerk); Irving Bacon (Bank Teller); Harry Tyler (Auto Dealer); Charles Halton (Mayor); George Chandler (Hotel Clerk); Robert Shaw (Hillbilly); Charles Trowbridge (Rector); Charles Waldron (Mr. Lester); Dorothy Adams (Payne's Secretary); Erville Alderson (Driver of Car Hit by Dude Lester); Francis Ford (Vagabond); David Hughes (Coroner); Mae Marsh (County Court Assistant); John "Skins" Miller (Auto Dealer's Mechanic); Jack Pennick (Deputy Sheriff).

Credits: Darryl F. Zanuck (Producer); Jack Kirkland, Harry Oshrin (Associate Producers); John Ford (Director); Based on the play by Jack Kirkland and the novel by Erskine Caldwell; Nunnally Johnson (Screenplay); Gene Bryant, Edward O'Fearna (Assistant Directors); Arthur C. Miller (Cinematography); David Buttolph (Music); Barbara McLean (Editor); Richard Day, James Basevi (Art Directors); Thomas Little (Set Decorations). Running time: 84 minutes

This movie was adapted from Erskine Caldwell's novel and Jack Kirkland's Broadway play concerning life among poor inbred whites in the Georgia backwoods during the Great Depression. Jeeter Lester, a lazy but lovable old reprobate, is the patriarch of a large backwoods clan who are about to be thrown off their land for non-payment of rent. Their ancestors had prospered on the rich farmland, but the land became fallow, leaving the family to scrape for food. Threatened by a bank's attempts to take over the land for more profitable farming, Jeeter, supported by his long-suffering wife Ada, faces the uncertain future with a spirited sense of humor. His unwillingness to work runs in his family of 17, including Dude, who is more interested in cars, and daughter Ellie May, who is in love with her brother-in-law Lov Bensey. Sympathetic to the family's plight, Capt. Tim (Dana Andrews) lends a financial hand with the rent and money for seed.

"All that they were, and all that they had, is gone with the wind and dust."

No— not a line to mark the entrance of "Fiddle-dee-dee" Scarlett O'Hara, but a suitably plaintive statement to introduce the "poor white trash" that scratched out a living in Georgia at a time when Southern belles, balls and beaus had become consigned to distant memory. With Jeeter and wife Ada hard-pushed to even remember the names of members of their huge brood, who have mostly moved away and don't write, it is quite apparent that family values have also gone with the wind.

In the opening shot we are informed that the Jack Kirkland stage play, was originally presented in New York City on December 4, 1933, and has played continuously since then, breaking all records for length of run in the history of American theatre.

When 20th Century–Fox decided upon making a movie version, they wisely retained Charley Grapewin who had played a significant part in the show's Broadway success. Grapewin made his mark in Hollywood at the age of 60 playing wise, wheezy, humorous characters, usually against a rustic setting. He is best remembered for playing Jeeter Lester, Grandpa Joad in *The Grapes of Wrath* (1940), and Inspector Queen in the *Ellery Queen* series in the early 40s. Versatile Marjorie Rambeau was twice nominated for Academy Awards, as the prostitute mother of Ginger Rogers in *Primrose Path* (1940) and the mother at odds with daughter-star Joan Crawford in *Torch Song* (1953).

In keeping with all of John Ford's films, the imagery and photography in *Tobacco Road* is first class. It was made during a period in his career which was characterized by an almost expressionist style.[1] And when you get past the cu-

riosity value behind this production, it is quite clear that Ford plays much of the film for laughs, and they hit you in every shape and form —from zany slapstick to rib-tickling lines, with everyone getting in on the act. One remark in particular had me off my stool wildly slapping the ground: When a hungry Dude asks about the whereabouts of the harness, Ada Lester casually replies, "I think Grandma ate it."

And when it comes to their views on womenfolk, the men are certainly in top form (or perhaps on another planet), with Jeeter declaring that the first ten years of marriage as being the happiest, because in that period Ada never spoke a word. And if you think he's long overdue for the men in white suits, check out Lov Bensey, who thinks that people will laugh at him if he takes Ellie May as his wife, because at the ripe old age of 23, she's well and truly past her sell-by date.

Continuing the lunacy, the courting ritual between Ellie May Lester and Lov Bensey has to be seen to be believed, as they slither towards one another in the dirt. But this is surpassed by Dude's outrageous "Keystone Cop" approach to driving a new car, which leaves the vehicle a wreck and his new bride penniless after she uses $800, left to her by her deceased spouse, to pay for it — which is totally bizarre when you consider that these folks are so hungry they fight over a turnip.

Although he plays a small supporting role, Andrews's performance showed real potential and he was mighty grateful for the opportunity, particularly as it was his first significant A picture role. In a 1977 interview, Andrews explained that back in the 1940s, Fox had two units, the Wurtzel unit which churned out low-budget fillers and another, managed by Zanuck, which produced the A pictures. "This was a chance to break into the better class and after that I never played in any B pictures for a long, long time," the actor told the interviewer."[2]

With all the characters clearly as mad as a box of frogs (must be something in the moonshine in them thar parts), Andrews's two short scenes as the level-headed Captain Tim Harmon are like a breath of fresh air and certainly give you an opportunity to pick yourself up off the floor and resume your composure before the tomfoolery starts again. As the paternalistic Captain Tim, intervening in a landscape completely devoid of family values and work ethic, we get an early indication of Andrews's natural air of authority, tinged with compassion for his fellow man.

In his scenes with Jeeter and Ada, we see in Captain Tim a man who deeply cares for his poor neighbors and who is saddened by the degeneration of a way of life. Although financially strapped himself, he remains unperturbed and constantly chipper. When he lays eyes on Jeeter after a spell away, his love for the old man shines through: "Look at him, the old scoundrel — still full of beans."

And when the chips are down, and Jeeter and Ada have no option but to head off to the poor farm, Captain Tim rides to their rescue, staking them with his last $60 ($50 for six months rent, plus $10 for seed) to work their own land. In her gratitude Ada pipes up, "Do you mind if he gets me some snuff out of that ten dollars?" to which

Andrews as the paternalistic Captain Tim Harmon in John Ford's humorous take on Southern rural life, *Tobacco Road* (20th Century–Fox, 1941).

Captain Tim joyously replies, "If snuffs gonna help you to get Jeeter to work Ada, get all you want."

Even though Andrews's role was relatively minor compared to the leads, it was enough to impress the mighty John Ford, who during filming encouragingly informed Andrews, "You look very good."[3]

Tobacco Road was the first of five films in which Andrews appeared with Gene Tierney, but they would have to wait until their next film *Belle Starr* before sharing a scene together. A strikingly beautiful actress, Tierney played a variety of roles in a number of 1940s classics including *Leave Her to Heaven* (for which she received an Oscar nomination), *Laura*, *The Razor's Edge* and *The Ghost and Mrs. Muir*. In 1955 she suffered a mental breakdown, which virtually marked the end of her movie career except for a short-lived comeback in the early '60s.

Ford's humorous take on rural life in *Tobacco Road* was perhaps overly rich and too much of a contrast with his earlier serious masterpiece *The Grapes of Wrath*, and as a consequence the film opened to mixed reviews.

The Hollywood Reporter described the film as "the most daring movie of all time." This comment was no doubt influenced by the seduction scene between Gene and Ward Bond, which required them to grope and paw each other in the dirt, which so embarrassed Gene that she asked John Ford to clear the set first. Ellie May was certainly a far cry from her usual glamorous roles, for each morning, to get into character, Gene's hair was caked with mud and her arms, legs and face were covered with oil before being smeared with dirt.[4] (What's the betting the makeup guys were fighting over that assignment?)

Charmingly sincere and wholly believable in a rustic setting, Andrews was rewarded with a leading role in another slice of Americana produced that same year — Jean Renoir's *Swamp Water*.

Belle Starr

20th Century–Fox, 1941

Cast: Randolph Scott (Sam Starr); Gene Tierney (Belle Shirley, later Belle Starr); Dana Andrews (Major Thomas Grail); Shepperd Strudwick (Ed Shirley), Elizabeth Patterson (Sarah); Chill Wills (Blue Duck); Louise Beavers (Mammy Lou); Olin Howland (Jasper Tench); Paul E. Burns (Confederate Sergeant); Joe Sawyer (John Cole); Joe Downing (Jim Cole); Howard C. Hickman (Colonel Thornton); Charles Trowbridge (Colonel Bright); James Flavin (Sergeant); Charles Middleton, Hooper Atchley, Norman Willis, Davison Clark (Carpetbaggers); Matthew "Stymie" Beard (Young Jake); Franklyn Farnum (Barfly); Mae Marsh (Preacher's Wife); Kermit Maynard (Union Officer); Clarence Muse, Clinton Rosemond (Black Men); Elena Verdugo (Young Girl); Cecil Weston (Mother).

Credits: Darryl F. Zanuck (Producer); Kenneth Macgowan (Associate Producer); Irving Cummings (Director); Niven Busch, Cameron Rogers (Story); Lamar Trotti (Screenplay); Ernest Palmer, Ray Rennahan (Cinematography); Alfred Newman (Music); Richard Day, Nathan Juran (Art Direction); Thomas Little (Set Decorations); Robert L. Simpson (Editor). Running time: 87 minutes

At the end of the Civil War, Confederate guerrilla leader Sam Starr hates carpetbaggers and Yankee soldiers with equal measure and, with a group of renegades, takes to riding throughout the land raiding banks and the railroads. During his escapades he meets up with Belle, a member of the landed gentry, who joins forces with the rebels when the Yankees burn down her home as punishment for harboring the guerrilla leader. Together they become outlaws, hoping to avenge the fallen South. Along the way the pair get married and become a Missouri legend, raiding and chasing out the carpetbaggers, much to the anger of the Yankee forces trying to capture them. Their pursuers include Major Thomas Grail (Dana Andrews), a childhood friend of Belle's, who is compelled by duty to bring her to justice in spite of his love for her. When Belle is killed by a fatal shot from town low-life drunk Jasper Tench, who is out for the reward money, Sam Starr turns himself in to Major Grail, and both men grieve over the woman they loved.

Tagline: "A GREAT NEW SCREEN PERSONALITY!... Miss GENE TIERNEY FLAMES TO STARDOM AS 'THE BANDIT QUEEN!' No woman was ever a more tender sweetheart ... or a more relentless champion of right!"

Broadway actor turned director Irving Cummings took a break from his staple fare of big, splashy Fox musicals (which in 1945 included Andrews's *State Fair*), to direct this dramatized account of the legendary female outlaw, Belle Starr.

Belle Starr was Andrews's third film in a row based on a legendary western character, follow-

Andrews's first screen embrace with his perfect leading lady, Gene Tierney, in the post–Civil War adventure *Belle Starr* (20th Century–Fox, 1941).

ing *Kit Carson* and *The Westerner* (Judge Roy Bean) the previous year. Andrews got his role because Henry Fonda refused to play the male lead, which forced Darryl F. Zanuck to reconsider casting. Randolph Scott was switched from the role of the Army major to Sam Starr, and Andrews took the part of the major. Again he

was playing an Army officer vying for the attention of the leading lady, but losing out to the leading male.

Craggy-faced Randolph Scott, who always looked middle-aged, started his Hollywood career in light comedies and dramas before attaining stardom in westerns. In the 1950s his successful partnership with producer Harry Joe Brown and director Budd Boetticher injected new life into the genre with the likes of *Seven Men from Now* (1956) and *The Tall T* (1957). Possessing a shrewd head for investments, he accumulated a personal fortune of $100 million during his lifetime.

Even though Andrews's was a supporting role as the honorable by-the-book major who is in love with Belle but puts duty first, we get an early glimpse of the troubled type of character fighting inner turmoil, which he would fully explore and perfect in later years. Andrews's few scenes with Gene Tierney are particularly moving, laying the seeds for their electric reunion three years later in *Laura*. He is also nicely balanced alongside Randolph Scott and their final scene together, when they both struggle to maintain their composure as they mourn the death of Belle, is particularly touching.

Scott shines in the role of Sam Starr, but as *The New York Herald Tribune* reported, "Dana Andrews in the unpleasant role of the Yankee major is equally good." Andrews's Major Grail is a man who will stand no nonsense in the pursuit of his duty. Determined to bring his man to justice, he informs Belle of his intentions to hang Starr and his outlaw gang from the highest tree. When Belle quips that this would require a good deal of rope, he counters, "Fortunately, we have an ample supply."

Andrews cuts a dashing figure in uniform with the obligatory Errol Flynn mustache, and his beautifully photographed romance in-the-moonlight scene with the gorgeous Gene Tierney is as pretty as a postcard. Resolute in his duty, he nonetheless shares Belle's respect for the Confederacy, and in an effort to overcome her disdain for his Yankee uniform he graciously concedes, "Oh, but look, Belle, in the moonlight it's almost gray."

Suitably impressed with Andrews's performance and clearly aware of his star potential, director Irving Cummings informed him on set one day, "You're a good actor. They should give you a lead."[1] Andrews didn't have to wait long for this opportunity, taking one of the principal roles in his next film, *Swamp Water*.

The part of Belle was originally earmarked for Barbara Stanwyck, who pulled out at the last minute. Stanwyck would probably have given the character the extra edge that it really required, but there is no doubt that Gene was a more appropriate leading lady to play opposite Andrews and Randolph Scott. The chemistry between the three leads was spot on, but the production was by no means a smooth affair. Gene developed a severe eye condition, which stopped filming while she recovered. With the studio losing money with every lost day, she ran the risk of being replaced in the role, but her fledgling career was saved when Randolph Scott kindly intervened, waiving his right to any additional payment for every day over schedule.[2] Thereafter, to play safe, Gene refused to wear eye makeup in future productions, and was one of the few actresses who was naturally beautiful enough to get away with it.

With its Civil War theme, fiery Southern heroine complete with obligatory loyal mammy, *Belle Starr* was clearly Fox's attempt to cash in on the popularity of *Gone with the Wind* (1939). However, there was no equivalent return to Tara for our headstrong Belle, but instead, a lasting legacy, which imbued her spirit with the characteristics of a red fox according to her old former slaves.

Belle's story was embellished by Richard K. Fox's dime novel *Belle Starr, the Bandit Queen*, published in 1889. There are no records that she ever got involved with robbing trains and stagecoaches, but she was charged with horse theft. She grew up with the likes of the Younger brothers and the James boys, and in her lifetime had several husbands including Cherokee Sam Starr, who was killed by an Indian policeman on the reservation. Belle herself was ambushed and killed by an unknown assassin. The character would go on to appear in several other films, including *Belle Starr's Daughter* (1948) with Ruth Roman and *Montana Belle* (1952) with Jane Russell. *Bewitched* star Elizabeth Montgomery breathed new life into the myth with the 1980 TV movie *Belle Starr*.

Swamp Water

20th Century–Fox, 1941

Cast: Walter Brennan (Tom Keefer); Walter Huston (Thursday Ragan); Anne Baxter (Julie); Dana Andrews (Ben); Virginia Gilmore (Mabel MacKenzie); John Carradine (Jesse Wick); Mary Howard (Hannah); Eugene Pallette (Sheriff Jeb McKane);

Ward Bond (Tim Dorson); Guinn "Big Boy" Williams (Bud Dorson); Russell Simpson (Marty McCord); Joe Sawyer (Hardy Ragan); Paul E. Burns (Tulle McKenzie); Dave Morris (Barber); Frank Austin (Fred Ulm); Matt Willis (Miles Tonkin); Red Larkin (Clem Hooper); Mae Marsh (Mrs. McCord); Charles F. Miller (Fiskus); Sherman Sanders (Caller).

Credits: Irving Pichel (Producer); Jean Renoir (Director); Len Hammond (Associate Producer); Vereen Bell (Story); Dudley Nichols (Screenplay); Peverell Marley (Cinematography); David Buttolph (Music); Richard Day, Joseph C. Wright (Art Direction); Guy Pearce (Makeup); Sam Benson (Costume); Alfred Bruzlin, Roger Heman, Sr. (Sound); Walter Thompson (Editor). Running time: 86 minutes

Wrongly accused of murder and sentenced to hang, Tom Keefer escapes from prison and hides out in the Okefenokee swamps of Georgia. A trapper, Ben Ragan (Dana Andrews), is out looking for his dog when he encounters Keefer and the two become friends. They go trapping together and Ben sells the pelts, passing on Keefer's share of the proceeds to his daughter Julie, who has been living in the nearby town. Ben's trapping expeditions go against the wishes of his strict father Thursday Regan, who fears for his son's safety in the dangerous uncharted swamplands. As they get to know each other better, Ben eventually falls in love with Julie, which incurs the anger of Ben's girlfriend, Mabel. Feeling jilted, she reveals to the authorities her suspicions that Ben is aware of Keefer's hiding place. Ben refuses to cooperate with officials seeking to hunt down the fugitive, and he and Julie set out to prove her father's innocence. When questioned by Ben, Jesse Wick, who was the chief witness at Keefer's trial, reveals that the real murderers were the Dorson brothers. Realizing that the game is up, the brothers set out to conceal their guilt by getting rid of Ben and Keefer. Their attempts in the swamp fail, with Bud meeting his fate in quicksand and Tim forced to hide out in the wilderness in the same way Keefer had to survive. Finally cleared of the murder, Keefer returns to town to start a new life with Julie and prospective son-in-law Ben.

Tagline: "The Swamp!—sinister—mysterious—it shaped the lives, and loves and hates of the people who lived around its edges."

Fritz Lang was originally chosen to direct *Swamp Water*, but production chief Zanuck reassigned it to Jean Renoir when the distinguished French director expressed an interest in the script. This was Renoir's first Hollywood film following a successful career in Europe in the 1930s. Perhaps the greatest of French directors, his many classics include *La Grande illusion* (1937), *La Regle du jeu* (1939), *The Southerner* (1945) and *The River* (1951). Renoir declined the offer of using the studio's top stars for *Swamp Water*, preferring lesser-known faces. He commented: "I would rather have people who are still hesitant so that I can work with them, so that I can direct them."[1] Initially, Zanuck cast Fox's new glamorous star Linda Darnell and the virtually unknown Andrews as young lovers Julie and Ben. Renoir thought Darnell unsuited to the part, preferring instead 18-year-old ingénue Anne Baxter. Zanuck conceded but had a change of heart over Andrews, suggesting newly signed Shepperd Strudwick. Fortunately for Andrews, Renoir persuaded Zanuck to keep to his original choice.[2]

Starting her career as a child star on Broadway, Anne Baxter went on to receive an Oscar for *The Razor's Edge* (1946) and an Oscar nomination for *All About Eve* (1950). However, her talent was stifled by the excesses of studio policy and as a consequence, in common with Andrews, she never quite reached the upper ranks of Hollywood stardom.

Adapted from a *Saturday Evening Post* story by Vereen Bell, *Swamp Water* has the distinctive feel of a John Ford movie with its Southern, rural setting and its use of Ford stock players—Walter Brennan, Ward Bond and John Carradine. And just as Ford coached the best out of Henry Fonda in the mother of all hillbilly films *The Grapes of Wrath*, Renoir achieves the same success with Andrews in *Swamp Water*. As the homespun rustic, Andrews is thoroughly convincing, handling the hillbilly accent and mannerisms with natural ease. Although he took fourth billing in the film, he is in no way overshadowed by the other stars, who all have the effect of drawing different emotions from his character Ben. He is tender and decisive with Anne Baxter, naive and awestruck in the company of Walter Brennan and magnificently indignant and independent in his confrontations with his curmudgeon father, played to the hilt by Walter Huston. Indeed, Andrews's scenes with Huston were so convincing that Andrews's eldest son and biggest fan David (age eight at the

Fur trapper Ben Ragan (Andrews) contemplates his future with wholesome gal Julie (Anne Baxter) in eminent French director Jean Renoir's first Hollywood film, *Swamp Water* (20th Century–Fox, 1941).

time), who was watching filming one day, walked off the set, mightily upset, when Huston beat the blazes out of Andrews in one of their heated exchanges.[3]

As a pleasant diversion from some of the more serious moments on set, Renoir's accent was occasionally a source of amusement during filming. One day, while giving instructions to Anne Baxter's stand-in, who was on the other side of the river and had to get into a boat, he told her to "wait a little," but it came out like "wet a little." She looked at Andrews and said, "Does he really want me to...?" to which he wickedly replied, "These foreign directors sometimes have strange ideas."[4]

To instill a sense of realism, Renoir wanted to shoot the film on location in the Okefenokee Swamp of Georgia. To reduce costs, Zanuck would only allow Andrews and his dog Trouble to accompany Renoir for two weeks of filming in Georgia. As a result, only five minutes out of the 86-minute running time were actually filmed in

the swamp (plus some background plates for rear-projection). The rest of the exteriors were shot at a ranch near Los Angeles. While on location, Andrews roamed around every night with a local taxi driver to pick up the Georgia cracker drawl he had to use in the film, but the cabbie never did catch on who his famous fare was. He thought Andrews was a carpenter in the crew.

With his naturally warm Southern voice and subtle movements, Andrews was faultless in the role of the young trapper. As a press release stated, "He was fortunate in having a part that showed his versatility. He was gentle and kind and courted the girl he loved with a want of confidence that was sober reality." Noting his fine voice and delivery, the studio release concluded, "Dana Andrews will be a star one of these fine days." Throughout his career, Andrews would regard *Swamp Water* as one of his favorite films.

Perhaps in recognition of the uniqueness of

the story and the rarity of strong hillbilly roles, Andrews gave a spirited performance, imbuing Ben with grit, confidence and good old-fashioned rustic charm, which we amusingly observe when he buys his gal a dress for a dollar and a half, and later when he steals a kiss from her: "I've never in my life asked for no kiss— always did took 'em. But I'd be dogged if I ain't just askin' you Julie. Do you mind?"

His enthusiastic characterization makes for riveting viewing, particularly in his excited interrogation of Jessie, wonderfully played by John Carradine. "No, I'm not wrong, Jessie. You killed him or the Dorsons did it, and you seen 'em! That's it, just as plain as the look on your face. You're just as guilty as they, Jessie — and if they hang for it, you're going to hang, too!" The two stars would go on to work together again, to equal effect, in *Fallen Angel* (1945).

Despite the many qualities of the film (great performances from all concerned, an absorbing tale that worked on many levels, great photography and music, and the magnificently eerie swamp setting), it opened to bad reviews in November 1941, with *Variety* reporting: "That it's something less than an auspicious beginning for Renoir over here is not entirely his fault. Giving him a story dealing with a segment of the U.S. population with whom not even many Americans are familiar appears open to debate." On a slightly more positive note, another critic commented that "the film was so bad it's terrific."

I guess I must be a dumb old hick myself, and perhaps one alligator short of a swamp, for I say, forget the critics of the day and enjoy — because it's brilliant!

Twentieth Century–Fox remade *Swamp Water* in 1952 as *Lure of the Wilderness* with another French director, Jean Negulesco. Water Brennan reprised the role of Tom Keefer, and Jeffrey Hunter and Jean Peters played Ben and Julie.

Ball of Fire

RKO, 1941

Cast: Gary Cooper (Professor Bertram Potts); Barbara Stanwyck (Katherine "Sugarpuss" O'Shea); Oscar Homolka (Professor Gurkakoff); Henry Travers (Prof. Jerome); S.Z. Sakall (Prof. Magenbruch); Tully Marshall (Prof. Robinson); Leonid Kinskey (Prof. Quintana); Richard Haydn (Prof. Oddly); Aubrey Mather (Prof. Peagram); Allen Jenkins (Garbage Man); Dana Andrews (Joe Lilac); Dan Duryea (Duke Pastrami); Ralph Peters (Asthma Anderson); Kathleen Howard (Miss Bragg); Mary Field (Miss Totten); Charles Lane (Larsen); Elisha Cook, Jr. (Nightclub Waiter); Charles Arnt (McNeary); Alan Rhein (Horseface); Eddie Foster (Pinstripe); Aldrich Bowker (Justice of the Peace); Pat West (Bum); Addison Richards (District Attorney); Kenneth Howell (College Boy); Tim Ryan (Motor Cop); William A. Lee (Benny the Creep); Gene Krupa (Orchestra Leader); Eddy Chandler, Ken Christy, Dick Rush, Lee Phelps, Oscar Chalkee Williams (Cops); George Barton, Walter Shumway (Garbage Men); Doria Caron, Merrillee Lannon (Girls in Subway); Edward Clark (Motor Court Proprietor); Chet De Vito (Tollkeeper); Geraldine Fissette (Hula Dancer); Pat Flaherty, George Sherwood (Deputies); Catherine Henderson, Helen Seamon (College Girls); Otto Hoffman (Stage Doorman); June Horne, Ethelreda Leopold (Nursemaids); Mildred Morris (Chorus Girl); Edward Mundy (Spieler); Gerald Pierce (Delivery Boy); Francis Sayles (Taxi Driver).

Credits: Samuel Goldwyn (Producer); Howard Hawks (Director); Based on the Story "From A to Z" by Thomas Monroe and Billy Wilder; Charles Brackett, Billy Wilder (Screenplay); Gregg Toland (Cinematography); Alfred Newman (Music); Perry Ferguson (Art Direction); Howard Bristol, Julia Heron (Set Decorations); Thomas T. Moulton (Sound); Edith Head (Costumes); Daniel Mandell (Editor). Running time: 111 minutes

Bertram Potts, a linguistics professor, and his seven older, scholarly associates are preparing a treatise on slang for an encyclopedia. As part of their research they enlist the help of a burlesque stripper, "Sugarpuss" O'Shea. When she comes to stay with Potts and his fellow professors to explain slang expression, they are unaware that she is trying to escape her gangster boyfriend Joe Lilac (Dana Andrews). Lilac is suspected of murder and Sugarpuss's testimony could put him away. Her presence upsets the regulated, stodgy lifestyle of the professors and their housekeeper, but in time they all grow fond of her. Potts is particularly taken with their house guest, but he conceals his true feelings until Lilac and his henchman, Duke Pastrami, show up to claim her. Lilac has plans to marry her so she can't testify against him, but the professors come to the rescue and Potts wins the girl.

Tagline: "I LOVE HIM because he don't know how to kiss—THE JERK!"

Rather surprisingly, Barbara Stanwyck was not Goldwyn's initial choice for the role of "Sugarpuss" O'Shea. Ginger Rogers was considered first, but after winning an Oscar for *Kitty Foyle*

Andrews played Joe Lilac (his first and only gangster role) alongside Barbara Stanwyck as "Sugarpuss" O'Shea in Howard Hawks' sparkling comedy *Ball of Fire* (A Goldwyn Production released through RKO, 1941). At right is Eddie Foster.

she thought the role too frivolous now that she had established herself as a serious actress. The script was then sent to Jean Arthur and Carole Lombard, but Columbia would not agree to loan Jean out and Carole was not interested in the part.[1] Had Carole accepted the role, it is very likely that she would have attended the opening of the film at Radio City on January 16, 1942, instead of taking off on a bond-selling tour, which ended in disaster when the plane crashed into Table Rock Mountain near Las Vegas, killing all on board.

Stanwyck received a Best Actress Oscar nomination for her role, missing out on the night to Joan Fontaine for her performance in *Suspicion*. Nominations were also received for the sound recording, Alfred Newman's score and Billy Wilder's original story.

Initially, Goldwyn was opposed to Andrews playing the part of a hood, protesting to direc-

tor Howard Hawks, "He can't play gangsters." However, very much his own man, Hawks ignored the advice and Andrews got the part.

During production, the Goldwyn publicity machine tried to promote Andrews as a new face on the tough guy scene, noting for the press that he had a freshly evil look about him, which was quite distinct from the familiar image conveyed by the likes of Cagney and Bogart. As the villain of the piece, snappy dresser Joe Lilac, Andrews was ably supported by fellow tough-guy actors Dan Duryea and Allen Jenkins. Whether in film noir or in westerns, Duryea was one of the silver screen's finest purveyors of nastiness, which was in complete contrast to the family man who was married to his wife, Helen, for 35 years. If Andrews needed any further influences to help him put a harsher edge to his screen image, he was given the perfect opportunity at the premiere of the film where he was able to mix with real-life

gangster Benjamin "Bugsy" Siegel. In a life-im-
itates-art reversal, Virginia "Sugar" Hill, the
mistress of Siegel, was cast as a showgirl in the
film.

At such an early stage in his screen career, and
acting opposite two Hollywood giants, Andrews
handles his role as a gangster with confident
panache, clearly relishing the opportunity to play
a bad guy with a pinch of humor. When the district attorney threatens him with a specially
heated 20,000-volt chair, he casually responds
"AC or DC?" And to counter the DA's boast that
finding "Sugarpuss" should present no problem
to his boys who can find a needle in a haystack,
Joe, in true wise-guy style, idly quips "Why,
that's a cinch. All you have to do is set a horse to
eat the hay, then x-ray the horse."

With production starting on August 6, 1941,
the film wrapped one day ahead of schedule on
October 16 at a total cost of $1,152,538. Opening
at Radio City Music Hall on January 16, 1942,
the film generated $2,200,000 in rentals, making
it the 25th biggest box-office attraction for that
year.[2]

The movie was clearly an update on the story
of *Snow White and the Seven Dwarfs*; one reviewer described the elderly professors as playing close parallels to the well-varied dwarfs;
Cooper as a very shy Prince Charming; Stanwyck as a decidedly worldly-wise Snow White;
and Dana Andrews, combining both charm and
vicious sadism, as a neat male counterpart to the
Wicked Witch. The *New York Times* noted,
"Dana Andrews, Dan Duryea and Allen Jenkins
do handsomely in minor tough-boy roles."

With the success of the film, director Billy
Wider rang Goldwyn requesting the $2,500
bonus he had been promised by the mogul.
The ever money-conscious Goldwyn conveniently had no recollection of this "gentlemen's
agreement," which so infuriated Wilder that he
slammed down the receiver after telling Goldwyn that he wanted nothing more to do with
him. Ten minutes later Goldwyn rang back:
"Look, Billy," he said, "I don't want people going
around Hollywood saying I'm not honest. Come
on over, right now ... and pick up the $1500."[3]

Keen to capitalize on good material, Goldwyn
and Hawks remade the film in 1948 as a vehicle
for Danny Kaye under the title *A Song Is Born*.
The new film earned Goldwyn the worst critical reviews of his career.

Joe Lilac was Andrews's first stint as a villain,
and was the type of character he would later be
wiping the smile off in *Where the Sidewalk Ends*
(1950). He would never again play a gangster,
but clearly had the ability to play cold and calculating characters, which he proved to chilling
effect in the later features *Beyond a Reasonable
Doubt* (1956), *Brainstorm* (1965), *The Frozen
Dead* (1967) and *Innocent Bystanders* (1972).

Berlin Correspondent
20th Century–Fox, 1942

Cast: Virginia Gilmore (Karen Hauen); Dana An-
drews (Bill Roberts); Mona Maris (Carla); Martin
Kosleck (Captain von Rau); Sig Ruman (Dr. Diet-
rich); Kurt Katch (Weiner); Erwin Kalser (Mr.
Hauen); Torben Meyer (Manager); William Ed-
munds (Hans Gruber); Hans Schumm (Gunther);
Leonard Mudie (George, English Prisoner); Hans
von Morhart (Actor); Curt Furburg (Doctor); Henry
Rowland (Pilot); Christian Rub, Egon Brecher, John
Bleifer (Prisoners); Rudolph Anders (Guard at Air-
port); Louis V. Arco, Arno Frey (Censors); John
Epper (Searchlight Operator); Frederick Giermann,
Rudolf Myzet (Waiters); Henry Guttman (General's
Aide); Otto Reichow, Harold Schlickenmayer, Bob
Stevenson, William Yetter Sr. (Guards); Lionel Royce
(High Official); Walter Sande (Red, Reporter);
Richard Ryen (Official); Paul Seidel (Radio Man);
Nicholas Vehr (Orderly); Emmett Vogan (Radio An-
nouncer); Paul Weigel (Patron); Wolfgang Zilzer
(Patient).

Credits: Bryan Foy (Producer); Eugene Forde (Di-
rector); Steve Fisher, Jack Andrews (Screenplay);
William Goetz (Executive Producer); Virgil Miller
(Cinematography); David Buttolph (Original
Music); Emil Newman (Music Director); Richard
Day, Lewis Creber (Art Direction); Hal Herman (As-
sistant Director); Thomas Little (Set Decorations);
Herschel McCoy (Costume Design); Joseph E.
Aiken, Harry M. Leonard (Sound); Fred Allen (Ed-
itor). Running time: 70 minutes

An American correspondent Bill Roberts
(Dana Andrews), stationed in Berlin in the
months before Pearl Harbor, hopes to alert
America and the world to the truth about Nazi
Germany by sending out coded messages in his
seemingly innocent daily program. Beginning
to suspect, the Gestapo sends Captain Carl von
Rau to investigate. He, in turn, assigns Karen
Hauen to spy on Roberts. She turns her back on
the Nazis when she discovers that her father is
the source of the reporter's information. When
her father is sent to a concentration camp, she

appeals to Roberts for help. Having fallen in love with the girl, and out of loyalty to his old friend, he agrees to help them both escape. After several tight spots, Roberts manages to spring the father. The three keep one step ahead of their Gestapo pursuers and finally find their freedom in Switzerland.

Tagline: "He Lived Thru a Nazi Nightmare You'll Never Forget!"

Andrews as Bill Roberts in the opening scene: "Hello this is Bill Roberts, Berlin, on this bleak Thanksgiving Day. It seems good to be broadcasting to an America that is still at peace with the world — but while you over there are enjoying your turkey dinner, the news for the democracies is still ominous."

With such an opening line you know you're in for a rough-and-ready propaganda ride, 20th Century–Fox style — but who cares? Even with its implausible twists and turns, this is still top drawer entertainment with an excellent cast that delivers on tap. Andrews excels as our all–American hero, who appears to be having great fun giving the Nazis the runaround. His warm Southern voice never sounded better and his vi-

American news reporter Bill Shepperd (Andrews) finds it difficult to broadcast the truth to the world with the Nazis looking over his shoulder in *Berlin Correspondent* (20th Century–Fox, 1942).

vacious performance neatly falls in with the brisk pace of the story, which gives him several opportunities to reveal his ability to play light comedy — gloriously conveyed in the scene where he is one step ahead of his Nazi tail: "For a moment I thought I'd lost you. Come on — let's go." The wicked humor kicks in again when Andrews (disguised as a German officer) orchestrates the escape of Karen's father, then with tongue firmly in cheek, chastises the prison guards for their incompetence (it's a hoot!).

Indeed, throughout the proceedings, Andrews memorably demonstrates that he's no lightweight in the snappy dialogue department, particularly in the restaurant scene where Karen tries to ensnare Bill with her damsel-in-distress act — in this case being caught short with the bill. When the waiter curtly remarks that this type of behavior might cost Germany the war, Bill with a broad grin on his face, enthusiastically chips in, "Oh! Do you really think so?"

Bill may well be a gentleman, but he's certainly no pushover when it comes to feminine wiles, as we clearly observe in the scene where Karen pleads with him to help her free her father. Her plea elicits Bill's indignant response, "Listen sister — I'm just an American newspaper guy. If I were one of your German supermen it might be different."

As an action thriller this is real "Boy's Own" stuff which never takes itself too seriously, even though several dark themes are touched upon, particularly the interrogation scene where Col. von Rau and two bare-chested Gestapo brutes give their prisoner a real taste of what the future would hold under the rule of a murderous dictator. The final scene wickedly reinforces the film's propaganda credentials when the German pilot in the plane commandeered by Bill and Karen has a pang of conscience about the perils of Nazism and decides to join in their escape plan.

The film's subtle vein of humor came courtesy of producer Bryan Foy, son of the famous vaudevillian Eddie Foy, who began his career in vaudeville as a member of the Seven Little Foys before going on to direct comedy shorts for Fox in 1918. He freelanced as a joke writer for Buster Keaton before making his mark as the head of Warners' B-unit in the '40s. His most notable production was the landmark 3-D film *House of Wax* (1953).

The tense, exciting pace was set by director Eugene Forde, part of 20th Century–Fox's busy B units in the 1930s and '40s churning out entries in many series (including the Charlie Chans and Michael Shaynes). Virgil Miller's crisp photography added to the film's production values which greatly belie its modest budget.

As Andrews's love interest, Virginia Gilmore never looked lovelier or more appealing. (Six years later, Andrews would again be subjected to such female cunning by the equally alluring June Havoc in *The Iron Curtain.*) This was Gilmore's second film with Andrews, having played his spurned girlfriend, Mabel McKenzie, the previous year in *Swamp Water.* She was married to Yul Brynner from 1944 to 1960; her career suffered in the 1950s as a consequence of a drinking problem. (Was there anyone in Hollywood who didn't succumb to the bottle?)

Dubbed "the definitive Nazi swine" by one critic, Martin Kosleck specialized in portraying Nazis and sinister villains, which was quite ironic considering he was Jewish. In reality, he was an outspoken anti–Nazi in the German film industry, and was forced to flee to America one step ahead of a Gestapo death squad when Hitler came to power in 1933. In his film career, he played Goebbels, Hitler's propaganda minister, five times.

As Captain von Rau's female assistant Carla, Mona Maris once again showed her deft hand at playing bad girls. Born to a wealthy Argentine family and educated in France, Maris's film roles were usually confined to Hispanic stereotypes.

Although *Berlin Correspondent* had the right credentials for A movie status, it was regarded by the trade as a program filler, oddly playing the lower half of a double-bill with *Bambi* when it did the rounds in the New York area in 1942.

The film is notable as Andrews's first starring role. As a typical piece of wartime propaganda, it was a taut, well-acted drama, but the reviews upon release didn't reflect its excellent entertainment value. The *New York Times* felt that the film was "too pretentious for its own good." The *New York Herald Tribune* commented, "More than a few of the best sequences of *Berlin Correspondent* lose weight soon after the synthetic suspense has worn off, when one has time to appreciate how implausible they actually are."

Nonetheless, Andrews's confident handling of the title role was enough to impress Fox, who next starred him alongside Tyrone Power in *Crash Dive* (1943).

Crash Dive
20th Century–Fox, 1943

Cast: Tyrone Power (Lieutenant Ward Stewart); Anne Baxter (Jean Hewlitt); Dana Andrews (Lieutenant Commander Dewey Connors); James Gleason (Chief McDonnell); Dame May Whitty (Grandmother); Henry "Harry" Morgan (Brownie); Ben Carter (Oliver Cromwell Jones); Frederic Brunn (Q-boat Lieutenant); Frank Conroy (Captain Bryson); Minor Watson (Admiral Bob Stewart); Kathleen Howard (Miss Bromley); Florence Lake (Doris); John Archer (Curly); Frank Dawson (Henry, the Butler); George Holmes (Crew Member); Paul Stanton (Officer); Betty McKinney, Ruth Jordan, Dorothy Brent, Sally Harper, Ruth Thomas, Sue Jolley (Schoolgirls); Fred Aldrich (German Seaman); Stanley Andrews (Shipwrecked Captain); Paul Burns (Simmons, Desk Clerk); Gene Collins (Boy in Lifeboat); James Conaty (Hotel Desk Clerk); Steve Forrest, Harry Carter (Sailors); Charley Grapewin (Pop); Thurston Hall (Senator from Texas); Trudy Marshall (Telephone Operator); Lelia McIntyre (Senator's Wife); Edward McWade (Crony); Hans Moebus (German Officer); Otto Reichow (German Signalman); Gene Rizzi (Seaman Rizzi); Charles Tannen (Seaman Hammond); Hans von Morhart (Y Gun Operator); Chester Gan (Lee Wong, the Waiter); Bruce Wong (Waiter); Edward Earle, James Metcalf (Men); Lionel Royce (Captain of Q-boat); Cecil Weston (Woman); Peter Leeds (Shore Police).

Credits: Milton Sperling (Producer); Archie Mayo (Director); W.R. Burnett (Story); Jo Swerling (Screenplay); M.K. Kirkpatrick, Commander, U.S.N. (Technical Advisor); Leon Shamroy (Cinematography); Fred Sersen (Special Effects); David Buttolph (Music); Emil Newman (Music Director); Richard Day, Wiard B. Ihnen (Art Direction); Thomas Little, Paul Fox (Set Decorations); Roger Heman Sr. (Sound); Ray Curtiss, Walter Thompson (Editors). Running time: 105 minutes

Set during World War II, this morale-booster is a tribute to the submarine service. Lt. Ward Stewart after having served with distinction as the commander aboard a PT boat, is reassigned against his wishes by his uncle Admiral Bob Stewart to a new job as the executive officer on a submarine. While en route to Washington for a spot of leave, he meets and falls in love with pretty schoolteacher, Jean Hewlitt, but soon discovers that she is already engaged to his commanding officer, Lt. Comdr. Dewey Connors

(Dana Andrews). Matters are further complicated because the two men have become friends following a successful first mission in which they destroyed an enemy ship. Ashore on leave, Dewey becomes aware of Ward's feelings for his girl before the two set off on their next mission, to locate a secret German naval base. Putting their differences aside, the two work together to destroy the base, which culminates in a daring commando raid led by Ward and an equally fearless escape through a sea of flaming fuel oil, with Dewey steering from a damaged submarine bridge. On the return to base, Dewey graciously gives up Jean when he realizes that the love between her and Ward is the real thing.

Tagline: "Tyrone Power — Leading a reckless crew on the war's most daring mission! Battling death in a depth-bombed submarine! Blasting Nazis on a bold Commando raid! Finding love in precious, stolen moments! Crashing his way to unforgettable glory in...."

Crash Dive was purposely designed as a farewell film for Tyrone Power before he entered active service in the United States Marines. (At 34 years of age and the father of two children, Andrews was ineligible for enlistment.) The film nicely contrasts the different acting styles of the two actors — Power's dashing exuberance clearly in keeping with the Errol Flynn school of theatrics, while Andrews's more restrained, understated style was very much in the Henry Fonda mold. In common with Flynn, Power tended to get typecast in one-dimensional action-adventure swashbuckler roles that made him a top star — *The Mark of Zorro* (1940), *The Black Swan* (1942) and *Captain from Castile* (1947). After demobilization, he tried to break free of this tag and would have relished the opportunity to portray the multi-faceted and morally ambiguous type of characters that came Andrews's way. Perhaps the closest he got to this was as the unscrupulous mentalist in *Nightmare Alley* (1947), where he, arguably, gave the best performance of his career.

This was Andrews's second of three films with Anne Baxter, and once again in true second lead fashion he loses the girl to the principal male. In between romancing Baxter and the lively action scenes, Andrews and Tyrone share one of the film's lighter moments when they give us an insight into the deprivations of the submariner. Ashore after a long underwater patrol, the first

things they have a hankering for (before gals and the nearest bar) are sun ray lamps, milk, fruit and more milk. As the waiter cheerfully remarks, "Can't get milk like that from a sea cow."

Not to be outshone by Power after he leads a successful commando raid, Andrews takes a turn at the heroics when atop a submerged and shell-damaged bridge he bravely guides the submarine out of perilous waters (what a guy!). Joining the action and adding further quality to the film, we see the ever-dependable Henry "Harry" Morgan and James Gleason in excellent supporting parts. Morgan would go on to play a number of significant supporting roles in notable films such as *The Glenn Miller Story* (1953) and will be fondly remembered as Officer Bill Gannon, Joe Friday's partner in the revised version of *Dragnet* (1967–70) and as the crazed Major General Bartford Hamilton Steele on *M*A*S*H*. James Gleason, who as a young man fought in the Spanish-American War, carved a niche in films as likable wisecracking characters, earning an Academy Award nomination for *Here Comes Mr. Jordan* (1941). He would work alongside Andrews again in *Spring Reunion* (1957).

The cast also included Ben Carter, whose character was clearly modeled on Doris Miller, the first African-American hero of World War II. Miller, a navy mess man with no gunnery experience, manned an anti-aircraft gun during the Japanese attack on Pearl Harbor. (For his extraordinary courage under fire, Miller was awarded the Navy Cross by Fleet Admiral Nimitz in 1942. In 1944, Miller died in action in the Pacific when his ship was hit by a torpedo from a Japanese submarine.) Blink and you will probably miss Andrews's brother Steve Forrest, who appears uncredited as a sailor.

Notwithstanding the film's high production and entertainment values, career-wise for Andrews his Lt. Comdr. Connors is just another variation on his Captain Fremont from *Kit Carson* and his Major Grail from *Belle Starr* — all courageous, steadfast and rational men with a tendency to conceal their inner thoughts and emotions. In complete contrast, Power's impetuous Lt. Stewart is a man who wears his heart on his sleeve and believes himself capable of winning the war single-handedly. But in time, he eventually heeds the cautious Dewey who, following a deadly depth charge attack, calmly advises, "When you can't get away, Mr. Stewart,

Andrews's sub commander is at odds with his executive officer Tyrone Power (left) in the wartime tribute to the submarine service, *Crash Dive* (20th Century–Fox, 1943).

you play possum." With both characters facing adversity together, a mutual respect evolves which we observe in their good-natured raillery over torpedo boats and subs:

> LT. COMDR. DEWEY CONNORS: I'm thinking one day they'll make a torpedo boat that will submerge.
> LT. WARD STEWART: It's funny that you should mention that, captain, because I've been thinking of how to make a submarine go about 50 knots.

When the enemy takes a licking in the final mission, we see a more animated Dewey, who proves he can be just as exuberant as the next guy when he exclaims, "Holy mackerel! Look at those shore installations and that harbor jammed with shipping. Boy, that looks like a grand slam!"

Fred Sersen's photography and Roger Heman's sound didn't go unnoticed, both receiving Academy Award nominations. When making *Crash Dive* in Connecticut, Andrews befriended some Naval radar men who, when later passing through Los Angeles, came to the house for dinner. Forewarned of the visit, Andrews's eldest son, David, astounded everyone throughout the evening with his knowledge of condensers, circuits and amperes. Suitably impressed, one of the radar men exclaimed, "Looks to me like you've got a fine junior radar man there."

"Or a fine actor," said Andrews. "I'll let you know later."[1]

Although serving well as an exciting recruiting picture for the all-volunteer submarine service, *Crash Dive* (like many flag-waving service films of this period) had its fair share of historic inaccuracies. The U.S. Navy didn't use American submarines in the North Atlantic as there were no German surface ships to attack; instead they were mainly deployed in the Pacific theatre from the earliest days of the war. In addition, American submariners rarely conducted commando operations themselves.[2]

Time magazine called *Crash Dive* "a technical submarine story, which should appeal to the boy in every man who wants to be an officer and a gentleman. The best parts of the film are its scenes of serious submarine business." The *Morning Telegraph* succinctly wrote, "It's a humdinger of a show..." and the *New York Times* reported, "Mainly the picture is romance and thriller of the most fictitious sort. It leaves one wondering blankly whether Hollywood knows we're at war."

A trifle harsh you might think, for don't we, at the very least, learn from Lt. Stewart's ravings that PT boats are better than subs, frigates, sliced bread, bottled beer, ma's cooking, Betty Grable's legs, Alice Faye's smile, Veronica Lake's Peek-a-Boo Bang, and Uncle Tom Cobbley and all? The *Times* further noted, "Dana Andrews plays the submarine commander with commendable second lead charm." With the film's box office success, Fox were impressed enough to offer him the most important role of his screen career to date, that of the helpless victim in the classic *The Ox-Bow Incident*.

In a moment of amusing self-deprecation, Andrews recalled the night he took his son David to a movie house to see *Crash Dive*. Coming out after the picture, he casually asked his son how he liked it. David seemed torn by some kind of violent emotion, but finally spoke right out. "Well, Dad," he said, "you were pretty good and all. But that Tyrone Power — wow! What a man!"[3]

The Ox-Bow Incident

20th Century–Fox, 1943

Cast: Henry Fonda (Gil Carter); Dana Andrews (Donald Martin); Mary Beth Hughes (Rose Mapen); Anthony Quinn (Juan Martinez/Francisco Morez); William Eythe (Gerald Tetley); Harry Morgan (Art Croft); Jane Darwell (Jenny Grier); Matt Briggs (Judge Daniel Tyler); Harry Davenport (Arthur Davies); Frank Conroy (Maj. Tetley); Marc Lawrence (Jeff Farnley); Victor Kilian (Darby), Paul Hurst (Monty Smith); Chris-Pin Martin (Poncho); Willard Robertson (Sheriff); Ted North (Joyce); George Meeker (Mr. Swanson); Almira Sessions (Mrs. Swanson); Margaret Hamilton (Mrs. Larch); Dick Rich (Deputy Butch Mapes); Francis Ford (Old Man Halva Harvey); George Lloyd (Moore); Tom London (Deputy); Stanley Andrews (Bartlett); Hank Bell (Red); William Benedict (Green); Paul Burns (Winder); George Chandler (Jimmy Cairnes); Forrest Dillon (Mark); Rondo Hatton (Gabe Hart);

Frank Orth (Larry Kinkaid); George Plues (Alec Small); Leigh Whipper (Sparks); C.E. Anderson, Tex Cooper, Dan Dix, Larry Dods, Tex Driscoll, Don House, Frank McGrath, Ed Richard, Walt Robbins, Clint Sharp, Ben Watson (Posse).

Credits: Lamar Trotti (Producer); William Wellman (Director); Based on the novel by Walter Van Tilburg Clark; Lamar Trotti (Screenplay); Arthur C. Miller (Cinematography); Cyril J. Mockridge (Music); Richard Day, James Basevi (Art Direction); Thomas Little, Frank Hughes (Set Decorations); Alfred Bruzlin, Roger Heman (Sound); Sam Benson (Wardrobe); Guy Pearce (Makeup); Allen McNeil (Editor). Running time: 75 minutes

This dark psychological western depicts an incident which is said to have happened in Nevada in 1885. Two saddle-sore cowboys, Gil Carter and Art Croft, passing through the town of Bridger's Wells after a long winter on the range, incite the anger of the locals when they get embroiled in a barroom fight. However, the attention of the townsfolk is soon diverted when news arrives that a local rancher, Kincaid, has been killed and his cattle stolen. With the sheriff out of town, the deputy and a former Confederate officer, Major Tetley, organize a lynch mob. Riding through the night, the posse comes across three outsiders sitting around their campfire — young family man Donald Martin (Dana Andrews), a Mexican and a senile old man. In possession of Kincaid's cattle and with no bill of sale, the men are put on trial then and there. Despite their protestations that they purchased the cattle, small pieces of circumstantial evidence point to their possible guilt, and all three are sentenced to hang on the spot. Gil and Art are joined by an old storekeeper Davies, Sparks the preacher and Tetley's pacifist son Gerald, in their efforts to restrain the vigilantes, but their pleas are lost on a mob hungry for revenge. Martin is allowed to write a letter to his wife, which Gil promises to deliver. After the crack-of-dawn lynching, the mob rides back to town only to discover from the sheriff that Kincaid is not dead and that he did sell the cattle to Martin. Derided by his son for causing the death of three innocent men, Tetley returns home and shoots himself.

In the sullen quiet of the saloon, Gil shames the members of the mob by reading aloud Martin's poignant letter to his wife. Gil and Carter then ride out of town to deliver the letter.

The somber tale of *The Ox-Bow Incident* was

considered a poor box office attraction and the film came into existence only because Henry Fonda and director William Wellman were so enthusiastic about Walter Van Tilburg Clark's novel and Lamar Trotti's script that they managed to persuade Darryl F. Zanuck to make it. In return they both agreed to work on some more commercially viable films that Zanuck had in the pipeline. For his part, Fonda, who rose to fame with such classics as *Young Mr. Lincoln*, and *Jesse James* (both 1939), and *The Grapes of Wrath* (1940), agreed to star in a minor comedy called *The Magnificent Dope* (1942). Wellman, who directed the classic *Wings* (1927), *The Public Enemy* (1931) and *A Star Is Born* (1937), fulfilled his part of the bargain by directing *Thunderbirds* (1942) and *Buffalo Bill* (1944).

Securing the role of Martin was a significant breakthrough in Andrews's career; it allowed him to escape the small parts and supporting roles he had played since arriving in Hollywood. Although he initially found it difficult to convince people to give him the part, Andrews's persistence paid off because the role of the heroic helpless victim, Donald Martin, fully showcased his acting abilities. With his big sad eyes and sincere face, he skillfully underplayed the role, which made for a haunting and memorable performance. The scene where Major Tetley gives the doomed men two minutes to pray before sentence is carried out is particularly moving, with the desperation and despair in Andrews's eyes conveying more than words can ever say. The image is so strong, it will stay with you long after the credits have rolled.

Shortly after this, with his hands tied behind his back, Martin pleads with Tetley to consider his (Martin's) wife and two children; it's one of the most poignant scenes in the film:

> Justice! What do you care about justice? You don't even care whether you've got the right men or not. All you know is you've lost something and somebody's got to be punished. I told you there's nobody to look out for them, they're in a strange place, can't you understand...! You butcher!

Andrews would always regard his role in *The Ox-Bow Incident* as a personal favorite and as one of his most enduring performances, in that it allowed him to stretch his range by playing a sensitive character who was not in any way weak.

Essentially non-violent, compassionate men, the characters played by Andrews and Henry Fonda are so similar that the two actors could have easily switched roles without upsetting the fine balance of this tragic tale. Fonda also considered this one of his favorite roles and his performance, in keeping with the rest of the cast, was faultless. Anthony Quinn was excellent as the fatalistic Mexican drifter, as was Francis Ford (brother of director John Ford) as the old man and Frank Conroy as the tyrannical martinet Major Tetley. Jane Darwell proved she could play against type as the goading Ma Grier, who discovers a willing ally in her gallows humor with the equally obnoxious Monty Smith (Paul Hurst). As the pretty Rose Mapen (Gil's lost love), Mary Beth Hughes is the only decorative image in an otherwise bleak, claustrophobic landscape. Harry Davenport also makes his mark as Arthur Davies, the man who tries to stop the hanging, as does Leigh Whipper in the role of Sparks, the town's unofficial preacher (one of the first serious film roles given to an African-American).

Notwithstanding the gloomy subject matter, spirits were high on set, with everyone pulling their weight and getting on with one another during production like one big happy family. Andrews, Henry Fonda, and Francis Ford were particularly well liked and respected by their co-workers.

During filming, Andrews lightened up the atmosphere one day by recounting his early days as a movie projectionist in Huntsville, Texas. The 19-year-old student was showing Wellman's *Wings* and, since the theatre wasn't yet equipped to handle the production's musical soundtrack, Andrews created his own system with a phonograph and several well-placed speakers. However, in his enthusiasm he inadvertently synchronized lilting violin music to the battle scenes and heavy drum rolls to the romantic moments.[1]

Andrews's daughter Kathy was born during filming. When Andrews came to work after a sleepless night awaiting the delivery, Wellman kindly rearranged the shooting schedule to allow him to do a sleeping scene out of sequence. The resultant scene is particularly realistic for when Andrews was asked to go to sleep he did so quite naturally.[2] Of the director, Andrews had this to say: "Mr. Wellman is, not without cause, called 'Wild Bill Wellman.' He's a very dominant, two-

Young family man Donald Martin (Andrews) restrained by Paul E. Burns, destined to hang for a crime he didn't commit, pleads his innocence as sympathetic cowpoke Gil Carter (Henry Fonda, left), helplessly looks on in the somber western classic *The Ox-Bow Incident*. (20th Century–Fox, 1943).

fisted sort of a man. I have been told ... and I think I've observed it very frequently ... that this covers up a very sensitive interior, but nevertheless, it's pretty successfully covered up. For the actor, sometimes it's very hard to probe down and find out what he's actually trying to say." Of the teary scene before the men are hanged, Andrews recalled that it was difficult to get into character, because Wellman cracked a funny joke after the cameras rolled. When he asked his good friend for an explanation, Wellman replied, "I was afraid you'd ham it up if I didn't."[3]

To cut down on production costs, the film was mostly shot in the studio, which created a claustrophobic feel that was superbly complemented by the shadowy photography to give a noirish edge to the doom-laden tale. As a stylish photographic touch, in the two main exterior shots which neatly bookend the film, we see a dog crossing the deserted street in the opening sequence when Art and Gil ride into town, and making its return journey at the end when the two ride out to deliver Martin's letter.

The film was nominated for the Academy Award for Best Picture (it lost out to *Casablanca* — so we can forgive that one) and has been deemed "culturally significant" by the Library of Congress and selected for preservation in the United States National Film Registry.

Because of its bleak qualities, a running time of 75 minutes and an uncompromising ending, Fox released the film as the lower half of a double-bill. Wellman recollected, "The film came and went in the States ... but when they sent it overseas it was an instant success." However, it was denied a release in Germany until 1964 because fascist undertones associated with the crazed brutality of the vigilantes flew in the face of the country's de–Nazification.

There are a handful of films which have a lasting impact on you and this is certainly one of them, particularly the scene where Gil reads out Martin's letter in the hushed silence of the saloon. It will reduce you to tears as his tragic character laments in prose that there can't be any civilization unless people have a conscience, ending the note with, "Kiss the babies for me and God bless you. Your husband, Donald."

Bosley Crowther of the *New York Times* called Andrews's sincere portrayal of Martin a significant contribution to the success of the film: "A heart-rending performance by Dana Andrews as the stunned and helpless leader of the doomed trio does much to make the picture a profoundly distressing tragedy."

In 1955, Fox made a 45-minute television version of *The Ox-Bow Incident*, with Cameron Mitchell (Buck in TV's *The High Chaparral*) taking Andrews's role as the doomed Donald Martin.

The North Star

RKO, 1943

Cast: Anne Baxter (Marina Pavlova); Dana Andrews (Kolya Simonov); Walter Huston (Dr. Pavel Grigorich Kurin); Farley Granger (Damian Simonov); Jane Withers (Clavdia Kurina); Eric Roberts (Grisha Kurin); Walter Brennan (Karp); Dean Jagger (Rodion Pavlov); Ann Harding (Sophia Pavlova); Carl Benton Reid (Boris Stephanich Simonov); Ann Carter (Olga Pavlova); Esther Dale (Anna); Ruth Nelson (Nadya Simonova); Paul Guilfoyle (Iakin); Erich von Stroheim (Dr. Otto von Harden); Tonio Selwart (German Captain); Peter Pohlenz (First Lieutenant); Gene O'Donnell (Russian Co-Pilot); Frank Wilcox (Petrov); Lynn Winthrop (Guerrilla Girl); Charles Bates (Petya); Robert Lowery (Russian Pilot); George Lynn (German Pilot); Minna Phillips (Old Lady in Wagon); Bill Walker, Clarence Straight (Young Men in Wagons); John Bagni (Guard at Desk); Patricia Parks (Sonya); Ferdinand Schumann-Heink (Doctor's Assistant); Harry Strang (Guerilla); Inna Gest, Marie Vlaskin, Tamara Laub, Clair Freeman, William Sabbot, Jack Valskin, George Kole, Tommy Hall, Eric Braunsteiner (Specialty Dancers).

Credits: Sam Goldwyn (Producer); William Cameron Menzies (Associate Producer); Lewis Milestone (Director); Lillian Hellman (Screenplay); Aaron Copland, Ira Gershwin (Songs); Aaron Copland (Music); James Wong Howe (Cinematography); David Lichine (Choreography); Perry Ferguson, McClure Capps (Art Direction); Howard Bristol (Set Decorations); Sam Nelson (Assistant Director); Fred Lau (Sound); R.O. Binger, Clarence Slifer (Special Effects); Daniel Mandell (Editor). Running time: 106 minutes

Set in a peaceful Ukrainian farming collective known as the North Star, this slice of World War II propaganda opens in June 1941 with a delightful depiction of rural life: farmers expecting bountiful harvests and young people occupying their minds with thoughts of love and marriage. However, this idyllic way of life is abruptly shattered when Nazi Germany, in defiance of previous peace treaties, launches a surprise Stuka attack which is swiftly followed by a brutal occupation. Each member of the community does their bit in the struggle against the Nazi oppressors—bombardier Kolya (Dana Andrews) returns to his bomber squadron to take the fight to the air and Rodion takes to the hills with most of the men to form a guerrilla movement, while those who remain behind, including Kurin, Marina and Damian, bravely defy the occupying forces led by Dr. Otto von Harden. The barbarity of the Nazis is clearly demonstrated when the children are rounded up to be used as a constant source of blood transfusions for wounded German soldiers. Justice is finally delivered when the guerrillas, now armed after a brave group of children and one old man run some guns through to them, defeat the Nazi garrison and retake the village.

Tagline: "A rolling wall of hell that couldn't be stopped.... A handful of men who had to stop it!"

America's relationship with the Soviet Union was a mite confusing during World War II. In the '30s, with hopes of the Soviet Union becoming an ally in the coming war, there was a cooling of anti-communist sentiment, which quickly returned to animosity when the Nazi-Soviet Pact was created in 1939. With the German invasion of the Soviet Union in the summer of 1941, age-old differences were conveniently discarded and the Americans once again looked upon the Soviets as their allies.

The North Star was intended to drum up American support for its Russian ally and followed a popular movie theme in the 1940s of villagers defending their homeland against the Nazi aggressor — with Norwegians in *Edge of Darkness*, the French Resistance in *Assignment in Brittany* and Czechs in *Hitler's Madman* (all 1943).

This film was the first of four Andrews made with distinguished director Lewis Milestone (followed by *The Purple Heart*, *A Walk in the Sun*, and *No Minor Vices*). With a dearth of directors and actors as a consequence of war service, Goldwyn was quite fortunate to engage Milestone, who had made his name with the monumental *All Quiet on the Western Front* in 1930. Looking back over his early career, An-

drews recalled that he enjoyed working under Milestone's direction and that they became very good friends. With many of the big stars, such as Tyrone Power and Henry Fonda, now in uniform, Andrews had a perfect opportunity to

Andrews takes time out in the company of Walter Brennan (Karp) during the making of *The North Star* (RKO, 1943).

stamp his presence on screen and Milestone was the ideal director to fully explore his quiet resilience, which was revealed to great effect in their three war pictures together.

For this, his pet project, Goldwyn was also fortunate to enlist the services of one of America's important dramatists, Lillian Hellman; but with the many rewrites prompted by both producer and director, her experience of writing the film was not a happy one. Milestone suggested to Hellman that he wanted to show the Nazi atrocities that she only hinted at. As a result, a German doctor was created; played to the hilt by Erich von Stroheim, he was responsible for taking blood from the village children. His battle of words with the village doctor (Waler Huston) on the rights and wrongs of oppression formed the script's centerpiece from which the individual feats of heroism radiated. Hellman raged to her dying day that Goldwyn "phonied" up her film, incensed at what she believed was a dumbing-down of her screenplay. (On a similar note, in the previous year Hellman walked out of a screening of her friend William Wyler's *Mrs. Miniver* claiming that the great director had reduced the story to "a lot of sentimental crap.")

In portraying the Stalin-enslaved Soviets as proto–Americans holding democratic values, *North Star* was very much keeping in with several other pro–Soviet melodramas, which were used as propaganda to allay xenophobia — notably *Mission to Moscow* (1943) and *Song of Russia* (1944).

Goldwyn reportedly spent about $3,000,000 in 18 months of production on the film and certainly didn't scrimp when it came to casting. Headed by Walter Huston and Ann Harding, fresh from starring in Warners' *Mission to Moscow*, the stellar line-up, in addition to Andrews, also included handsome 17-year-old newcomer Farley Granger, Zanuck's latest discovery Anne Baxter, Eric von Stroheim and the ever-dependable Walter Brennan and Dean Jagger. Granger later recalled that on set Andrews was always word-perfect, and was constantly there for him, but away from the cameras he tended to be taciturn. Walter Brennan reassured Farley that it was nothing personal, explaining that Andrews was just hung over and trying to get it together each morning.[1]

Teresa Wright was initially chosen to play the romantic interest opposite Granger, but had to drop out of the picture when she discovered that she was pregnant. Goldwyn always suspected that her husband, novelist and screenwriter Niven Busch, whom he had recently sacked, got her pregnant on purpose so she could be excused from playing such a minor part in the film.

Although Andrews also played a relatively minor part, as the forthright bombardier Kolya, he had the opportunity to bow out in a blaze of glory when he guides his crippled bomber into the path of a convoy of German tanks. As he lines up the target for the final run, we hear his last avenging words: "I'm coming down and it's going to hurt you. And I'm coming down just where I want to, because I was a good bombardier and a good pilot, too."

Before this magnificent departure in true "Hollywood World War II" fashion, we learn a good deal about Kolya during his walk to Kiev in the company of Damian, Marina and Clavdia. (The latter is infatuated with him, but is too young and immature to be taken seriously.) In their good-natured exchanges as they sing and joke, we observe that the jovial Kolya is a born leader, dedicated to duty, wise beyond his years and concerned about his young comrades. The character also gave Andrews a rare opportunity to show off his fine singing voice when he takes a turn with a lively Russian folk song as they stroll along. Andrews went on to play another ace wartime bombardier in *The Best Years of Our Lives*.

The idyllic mood of the journey is shattered in one of the film's memorable scenes: Kolya stops the group's singing to listen to the drone of approaching aircraft. Alert to the imminent dangers, he desperately tries to clear the road before the bombs rain down seconds later. Despite his efforts there are many casualties including a young boy who loses a limb. Moved to tears by the carnage and the plight of the boy, Clavdia is consoled by the compassionate Kolya, who informs her that there is no shame in airing one's true feelings: "You are what you are, Clavdia. It is my opinion that the trouble in the world comes from people who don't know who they are — they pretend to be something they're not."

As a small part of such an impressive cast, it would have been difficult for Andrews to make a significant impact. While *The North Star* did little for his career, the film was nominated for six Academy Awards (including one for

Hellman's screenplay). Incidentally, the film re-united Andrews with the three principal players from *Swamp Water*— Walter Brennan, Walter Huston and Anne Baxter.

Bosley Crowther of the *New York Times* wrote: "It is a heroic picture, the force of which is weakened by the fact that Mr. Goldwyn and Mr. Milestone have too freely mixed theatrical forms. The first part of the film, in which the village and its inhabitants are idyllically introduced, is distinctly in the style of operetta.... The contrast is therefore too prodigious when the bombs suddenly come raining down and the style of the film abruptly changes to one of vehement reality. The switch is too obvious a reminder of the theatrical nature of the film."

However, most of the New York press found the film moving enough to compensate for its so-called "departures from reality." Time called it a "cinemilestone."

Proud of his work, Goldwyn said when the film was released: "I don't care if this picture doesn't make a dime, just as long as every man, woman, and child in America sees it."

With the advent of the Cold War, *The North Star* was criticized by the House Un–American Activities Committees and re-edited into *Armored Attack* with much of the pro–Soviet propaganda deleted. In addition, a clumsy voice over was added that made the film a narrative about the 1956 Soviet invasion of Hungary. All very interesting, but *I* say, ditch the politics, because when all is said and done, this is a stirring and exciting war film that pulls out all the stops in true Hollywood style.

Up in Arms

RKO, 1944

Cast: Danny Kaye (Danny Weems); Dinah Shore (Virginia Merrill); Dana Andrews (Joe Nelson); Constance Dowling (Mary Morgan); Louis Calhern (Colonel Ashley); George Mathews (Blackie); Benny Baker (Butterball); Elisha Cook, Jr. (Info Jones); Lyle Talbot (Sergeant Gelsey); Walter Catlett (Major Brock); George Meeker, Richard Powers (Ashley's Aides); Charles Arnt (Mr. Higginbotham); Margaret Dumont (Mrs. Willoughby); Tom Dugan (Pitchman); Sig Arno (Waiter); Donald Dickson (Singer at Dock); Charles Halton (Dr. Roger B. Freyheisen); Harry Hayden (Dr. Weavermacher); Charles D. Brown (Dr. Campbell); Maurice Cass (Dr. Jones); Fred Essler (Head Waiter); Virginia Mayo (Nurse Joanna) Knox Manning (Narrator).

Credits: Samuel Goldwyn (Producer); Don Hartman (Associate Producer); Elliott Nugent (Director); Based on the play *The Nervous Wreck* by Owen Davis; Don Hartman; Allen Boretz (Screenplay); Ray Rennahan (Cinematography); Perry Ferguson, Stewart Chaney, McClure Capps (Art Direction); Howard Bristol (Set Decorations); Ray Heindorf (Music Arranger); Louis Forbes (Music Director); Harold Arlen, Ted Koehler, Sylvia Fine, Max Liebman (Songs); Louis Germonprez (Assistant Director); Fred Lau (Sound); Clarence Slifer, R.O. Binger (Special Effects); Daniel Mandell (Editor). Running time: 106 minutes

To his surprise, Danny Weems, a hypochondriac elevator operator, is drafted into the army during World War II. After training, he and pal Joe Nelson (Dana Andrews) board an overseas transport ship bound for a South Seas island. En route, Danny is kept busy keeping his colonel from discovering that his girlfriend, Mary Morgan, is a stowaway. To further complicate matters, unbeknownst to Danny, his girl is really in love with Joe, and her best friend Virginia Merrill, a navy nurse, has similar feelings for Danny. Many romantic moments ensue on ship and land before Danny emerges as the hero of the hour after rounding up a troop of invading Japanese soldiers.

Tagline: "Oh Kaye!"

Up in Arms, Andrews's first musical, marked the film debut of comedian Danny Kaye. Traditionally, the role played by Kaye would have been secondary to the male lead, usually seen as the hero's clownish best buddy, but in *Up in Arms* the character was elevated to the lead role to capitalize on Kaye's inimitable comic skills. After his sterling performances in *Crash Dive* and most notably *The Ox-Bow Incident*, Andrews could have been excused for feeling that his role in the film was perhaps a backward step in his career. Andrews played a likable character, but the film was clearly built around Kaye, and there was little for Andrews to do except smile on cue.

The screenplay was based on the Broadway comedy *The Nervous Wreck*, which had been the basis for an Eddie Cantor stage vehicle called *Whoopee!* With this choice of material, Goldwyn was clearly trying to develop Kaye into another Cantor and it is said that he even called him "Eddie" from time to time.

With his unique skill in delivering tongue-

Andrews as all-around decent guy Joe, playing the straight man to Danny Kaye (right) in the comedy musical *Up in Arms*. Love interest Mary Morgan (Constance Dowling) tries to keep her head down. (A Goldwyn Productions released through RKO, 1944.)

twisting songs and monologues, Kaye went on to become Goldwyn's leading star in a number of hit movies including *Wonder Man* (1945), *The Secret Life of Walter Mitty* (1947) and *Hans Christian Andersen* (1952).

Dinah Shore and Constance Dowling also made their film debuts in this musical comedy. Originally a child star named Fanny Rose, Shore made her first recordings with bandleader Xavier Cugat. She was married to George Montgomery from 1943 to 1960, and a decade after their split she had a long affair with Burt Reynolds. Dowling's film career faded in the 1940s and she went to live in Italy in 1947, appearing in some unmemorable Italian films before returning to America where she retired from acting in 1955. Before going under contract to Goldwyn, she had an affair with director Elia Kazan and later in life was linked with the Italian poet and

novelist Cesare Pavese, who committed suicide after being rejected by her. A newcomer on the Hollywood scene, Virginia Mayo unsuccessfully tested for the part taken by Dowling, but did appear in the film as part of the chorus line.

Although Andrews possessed a fair singing voice, having taken singing lessons early in his career, he didn't sing in this musical, but instead chose to keep this talent a secret. Andrews later revealed the reason for this: "I didn't tell Darryl Zanuck or Sam Goldwyn because you're dead in Hollywood if you're a singer. Nobody will accept you as an actor. About the time I'd hit Hollywood, they'd stopped making musicals. I'm no fool. I just kept my mouth shut."[1] Andrews described his singing voice as deep and dramatic, more suited to opera than ballads.

Constantly at odds with exhibitors, Goldwyn was concerned that his two-million dollar production would not show a profit. Of the big five exhibitors (Paramount, Loew's, Warners, 20th Century–Fox and RKO), only RKO would provide him with favorable terms to run his films in their theatres. (For example, a Goldwyn film in a Warners theatre might earn as little as one-eighth of what it might have earned elsewhere.) With such antitrust practices being investigated by the Society of Independent Motion Picture Producers, Goldwyn went to great lengths to expose the problem. In Reno, rather than conceding to the unreasonable demands of the theatre owners, Goldwyn decided to screen *Up in Arms* in the town's ballroom. To overcome the many obstacles thrown his way, such as safety laws and city building ordinances, the ballroom seats were secured to the floor and a platform was built outside one of the windows, through which they could project the film. With guest speaker Mary Pickford railing against the distribution monopolies, Goldwyn had all the publicity he needed to get his message over and at the same time boost box office takings.[2]

The critics loved the film and it became one of Goldwyn's biggest moneymakers, earning $3.3 million according to *Variety*.[3] Frank Quinn of the *New York Daily Mirror* wrote, "Not since Greta Garbo made her cinematic bow has there been anything so terrific as the inimitable Danny."

Although Andrews had clearly shown in *Berlin Correspondent* that he could naturally convey light comedy touches when required, *Up in Arms* gave him little opportunity to do so with Kaye fielding all the humor. However, Andrews did get the opportunity to exercise his romantic abilities during his flirtations with Constance

Andrews and Constance Dowling in a scene from *Up in Arms* (RKO, 1944). (A Goldwyn Production released through RKO, 1944.)

Dowling in the role of Mary. As the star-struck lovers, they make a cozy couple as wonderfully conveyed in two simple scenes. Huddled together on Mary's doorstep after a night out on the town, amused by Danny's early morning raid on the milkman, Joe quips, "That Danny's doing all right — that must be his third bottle of milk. He's gonna drink himself white. He's quite a guy." To which Mary replies, "Yes he is. He's going to make some woman a wonderful medicine cabinet someday." And in the shadow play sequence at the fair, where Joe ribs Mary that her graceful swan "looks more like a wombat or something."

Andrews's Joe clearly represents the all-American "boy next door" type in this flag-waver, with his keen sense of duty to country equaled by his loyalty to his buddy Danny. This is revealed at the draft board with Joe's attempts to get himself enlisted in place of Danny: "Maybe he's not really sick, but he thinks he is and that amounts to the same thing ... I can't figure it, you take fellas like Danny, and I've been here dozens of times...."

However, much to his delight, Joe is finally enlisted, providing Kaye with a solid straight man for his seaborne tomfoolery. And it is a true mark of Andrews's professionalism that at no stage in the proceedings does he attempt to upstage the fledgling Kaye in this, his debut film.

The film boasts some great musical numbers, including the spectacular fantasy dream sequence with Kaye in a devil's suit, and Tess's Torch Song with Kaye and Dinah Shore. But there is no doubt that the highlight of the film, for audiences of the day, was Kaye's classic comedy tongue-twisting monologue in the lobby of the movie theatre. In the finale, Danny single-handedly captures a platoon of Japanese soldiers who are mercilessly stereotyped as squint-eyed, buck-toothed knuckleheads (but what the heck, we *are* talking wartime propaganda).

Although the film was undoubtedly a big success, for Andrews it was just another entry in a long list of supporting roles (something he desperately wanted to break free from). With all of Goldwyn's attentions now focused on his new discovery Danny Kaye, it was Andrews's split contract with Fox that would provide him next with the right vehicle to fully showcase his leading man credentials.

The Purple Heart
20th Century–Fox, 1944

Cast: Dana Andrews (Capt. Harvey Ross); Richard Conte (Lt. Angelo Canelli); Farley Granger (Sgt. Howard Clinton); Kevin O'Shea (Sgt. Skvoznik); Don "Red" Barry (Lt. Peter Vincent); Trudy Marshall (Mrs. Ross); Sam Levene (Lt. Wayne Greenbaum); Charles Russell (Lt. Kenneth Bayforth); John Craven (Sgt. Martin Stoner); Tala Birell (Johanna Hartwig); Richard Loo (Gen. Mitsubi); Peter Chong (Mitsuru Toyama); Gregory Gaye (Voroshevski); Torben Meyer (Kappel); Kurt Katch (Kruger); Martin Garralaga (Silva); Erwin Kalser (Schleswig); Igor Dolgoruki (Boris Evenik); Alex Papana (News correspondent); H.T. Tsiang (Yuen Chiu Ling); Philip Ahn (Saburo Goto); Keye Chang (Admiral Yamaguchi); Luke Chan (Court Stenographer); Benson Fong (Moy Ling); Lee Tung Foo (Third Judge); Wing Foo (Police Captain); Paul Fung (Court Clerk); Allen Jung (Itsubi Sakai); Joseph Kim (Prosecutor); Clarence Lung (Japanese Lieutenant); Nestor Paiva (Francisco De La Santos); Marshall Thompson (Morrison); Beal Wong (Toma Nogato); Spencer Chan, Johnny Dong, Roque Espiritu, Harold Fong, Leon Lontoc, Bruce Wong (Naval Aides); Angel Cruz, Pete G. Katchenaro, King Kong, Eddie Lee, James B. Leong (Army Aides).

Credits: Darryl F. Zanuck (Producer); Lewis Milestone (Director); Darryl F. Zanuck as Melville Crossman (Story); Jerome Cady (Screenplay); Arthur Miller (Cinematography); Fred Sersen (Special Effects); Alfred Newman (Music); Artie Jacobson (Assistant Director); James Basevi, Lewis Creber (Art Direction); Thomas Little, Walter M. Scott (Set Decorations); Sam Benson (Wardrobe); Alfred Bruzlin (Sound); Douglass Biggs (Editor). Running time: 99 minutes

During the 1942 Doolittle bombing raid on Tokyo, a U.S. bomber is downed and the eight-man crew is captured by the Japanese. The men are put through a military "show trial" on a charge of committing war crimes. Before a court of paid-off witnesses and Axis journalists, the men are falsely accused of bombing schools and hospitals. With the men facing certain death as war criminals, the Japanese judge promises to be merciful if they reveal information about the secret locations from which the bombers took off. Led by Captain Harvey Ross (Dana Andrews), the heroic pilots defy their captors and are individually subjected to torture in an attempt to wring information from them. As a result of his failure to break the resolve of the Americans, the chief prosecutor commits suicide, and Capt. Ross and his men, who prefer death to dishonor, proudly march out of the courtroom to their execution.

Tagline: "NOW it can be told! You'll burn with rage ... and thrill with pride!"

In the early stages of the Pacific War, 1942's daring Doolittle Raid showed that it was possible to launch Army twin engine bombers (B-25 "Mitchell" medium bombers) from an aircraft carrier and attack the Japanese mainland. Jimmy Doolittle led the air group which consisted of six-

Downed pilots Harvey Ross (Andrews), Greenbaun (Sam Levene) and Vincent (Donald Barry) await their fate at the hands of their Japanese captors in the wartime flagwaver *The Purple Heart* (20th Century–Fox, 1944).

teen B-25s, each with a five-man crew. As the aircraft carrier, the *Hornet*, steamed towards the launch point, it encountered enemy picket boats, which took away the element of surprise. Most of the aircraft attacked the Tokyo area, but the damage inflicted was more to Japanese pride than to targets of military value. Unsettled and deeply embarrassed by such an audacious attack, the Japanese vented their anger by beheading three of the eight downed airmen they had captured.

Although the characters in *The Purple Heart* are fictional, Lewis Milestone's direction produced a film which seemed so real that people thought 20th Century–Fox had been provided secret information about the downed flyers. A *Newsweek* reviewer wrote, "If this film isn't the macabre McCoy, it is a reasonable approximation. Darryl Zanuck, hiding behind his favorite pseudonym (Melville Crossman), has written a plausible and shocking story of the American flyers who are charged with murder on the spu-

rious grounds of having strafed non-military objectives.... With Dana Andrews and Sam Levene heading his capable cast, Milestone achieves not only an expert job of moviemaking but a propaganda film that will leave you as disorganized as a haymaker to the midriff."

Andrews later recalled that Fox's head of distribution, Mr. Spyros Skouras, informed him that it was *The Purple Heart* that finally made the actor a star. Andrews attributed this success to the nature of the character he portrayed: "[W]omen all over the country, whose men were away at war, identified their husbands as being that sort of man." This was clearly evidenced at an event in Philadelphia which Andrews attended with many other stars and studio personnel to help promote the film *Wilson* (1944). When introduced on stage, he was met with a standing ovation from the audience, who stamped their feet and screamed like little girls as if Sinatra himself had made an entrance.[1]

An indignant Captain Harvey Ross (Andrews) makes it clear to General Mitsubi (Richard Loo) that he and his men will never give in to his demands in the compelling *The Purple Heart* (20th Century–Fox, 1944).

Zanuck and Skouras also attended this promotion and, having witnessed Andrews's great reception, were convinced he had the makings of a star. Andrews later discovered the reason for this particular outburst of public fervor was that many of the women in the audience were Air Force pilots' wives who had seen him in *The Purple Heart* the previous week and were indeed reminded of their husbands.

Unashamedly a propaganda piece, *The Purple Heart* nonetheless, through its tight script and solid acting, powerfully puts over its depiction of the enemy as a bunch of sadistic "saber-rattling" samurai, who need to be eradicated whatever the cost if mankind is to have any real future. Tapping into the mood of a nation and reflecting America's anger with the treatment of its downed flyers, Andrews's Captain Harvey Ross gives one particularly impassioned speech, ending with the immortal lines "This is your war. You wanted it. You asked for it. You started it. And now you're going to get it. And it won't be finished until your dirty little empire is wiped off the face of the earth."

In another memorable scene, Ross and his men drop their aviator wings into a vase in a secret ballot, with the understanding that if even one is broken they will comply with Mitsubi's demands. Ross is without doubt a courageous man, and in common with all of Andrews's wartime characters (particularly his Sergeant Tyne in *A Walk in the Sun*) he is no stranger to fear, which he openly confesses to nervous young Sergeant Clinton, beautifully played by Farley Granger. Describing his own shaking hands and pounding heart before take-off, he reassuringly reminds the airman that a man is only a coward when he allows his fears to get the better of him.

Fear and anxiety can sometimes erupt into anger, and nobody does moral indignation and manful defiance better than Andrews. Furious at the accusation of hitting civilian targets such as hospitals and schools, he bites back that their mission was to destroy oil storage centers, airports and shipyards and nothing else. His defiance, is matched by his compassion for his fellow man, which we observe when General Mitsubi boasts that their important buildings are constructed to withstand air raids. Contemptuous of the remark, Captain Ross responds, "That makes it tough on the little guys who live in the paper houses, doesn't it, general!"

Andrews's outstanding performance, and those of the other members of the strong cast, produced a truly moving piece of wartime propaganda. Some of the other stars would, like Andrews, go on to carve a niche in the murky world of film noir. Russian-born Sam Levene appeared in many classics including *The Killers* (1946), *Brute Force* (1947) and *Crossfire* (1947), and he worked with Andrews again in the memorable *Boomerang!* (1947). Richard Conte also teamed with Andrews again in another Milestone war epic, *A Walk in the Sun* (1945), before chalking up a number of noir credits including *Call Northside 777* (1948), *Thieves' Highway* (1949), *The Blue Gardenia* (1953), and *The Big Combo* (1955). Ironically, Conte was promoted by Fox as the "New John Garfield," the very man who helped discover him at New York City's Group Theatre. Conte starred as Don Corleone's rival Don Barzini in *The Godfather* (1972) and was considered for the title role before the casting list was reduced to Laurence Olivier and Marlon Brando.

Born in Hawaii of Chinese parentage, Richard Loo turned to acting when his business as an importer was hit by the Wall Street crash of 1929. In a long movie career he was stereotyped as a movie villain, usually as a Japanese tormentor, most notably in this film and *China Sky* (1945). Don "Red"' Barry was loaned out to Fox from Republic and saw this as his big break into A movies, but Republic's top man Herbert Yates had other ideas, keeping his star in B westerns.

In many ways, the bleak claustrophobic feel of the film mirrors the mood conveyed in the equally tragic *The Ox-Bow Incident*, with the victims in both films facing certain death at the hands of their unsympathetic captors. Andrews's Captain Ross is very much an older version of Donald Martin operating in a different era, but with the same sense of courage and morality. It is a testament to Andrews's superb acting that he not only evokes great sympathy for both characters, but also a courageous inner strength which must have touched audiences at the time. Indeed, in the final scene of *The Purple Heart*, as the determined Captain Ross and his men gallantly march off to their execution in step to a rousing rendition of "Into the Wild Blue Yonder," you can almost hear the roar of applause in the auditorium.

The *New York Times* noted, "Dana Andrews is magnificently congruous as the leader of the bomber crew." *Variety* was certainly impressed: "An intensely moving piece, spellbinding, although gory at times, gripping and suspenseful for the most part. Scenes depicting tortures strike home with terrific impact." *Time* labeled it as Milestone's best since *All Quiet on the Western Front*.

Wing and a Prayer
20th Century–Fox, 1944

Cast: Don Ameche (Flight Comdr. Bingo Harper); Dana Andrews (Lt. Comdr. Edward Moulton); William Eythe (Ensign Hallam "Oscar" Scott); Charles Bickford (Capt. Waddell); Cedric Hardwicke (Admiral); Kevin O'Shea (Ensign "Cookie" Cunningham), Harry Morgan (Ens. Malcolm Brainard); Richard Jaeckel (Beezy Bessemer); Richard Crane (Ens. Gus Chisholm); Glenn Langan (Executive Officer); Renny McEvoy (Ens. Cliff Hale); Robert Bailey (Ens. Paducah Holloway); Reed Hadley (Comdr. O'Donnell); George Mathews (Dooley); B.S. Pully (Flat Top); Dave Willock (Ens. Hans Jacobson); Murray Alper (Benny O'Neill); Charles Lang (Ens. Chuck White); Eddie Acuff (Pharmacist's Mate); Stanley Andrews (Marine General); Irving Bacon (Scissors, Sailor Projectionist); John Miles (Ens. "Lovebug" Markham); Harry Carter (Telephone Orderly); George Chandler (Sailor Assisting Projectionist); Robert Condon, Jimmie Dodd, Blake Edwards, Frank Ferry, Mike Killian, William Manning, Mel Shubert (Pilots); Eddie Friedman, Frank Marlowe, Sidney Miller, George Offerman, Jr., Wallace Scott, Ray Walker (Sailors); Billy Gilbert, Alice Faye, Betty Grable (Archive footage from *Tin Pan Alley*); Joe Haworth (Murphy); John Kellogg (Assistant Air Officer); Carl Knowles (Marine Orderly); John Kelly (Lew); Selmer Jackson, Frank McClure, Jack Mower, Albert Van Antwerp, Edward Van Sloan, Charles Waldron, Pierre Watkin, Crane Whitley, Frederick Worlock (Admirals), Billy Lechner, Raymond Roe (Gunners); Chet Brandenburg, Terry Ray, Robin Short, Jay Ward (Mail Orderlies); Jerry Shane (Foley); Charles B. Smith (Alfalfa); Larry

Squadron leader Edward Moulton (Andrews) looking up "into the wild blue yonder" with Flight Commander Bingo Harper (Don Ameche) in Darryl F. Zanuck's rousing homage to the aircraft carrier, *Wing and a Prayer* (20th Century–Fox, 1944).

Thompson (Sam Cooper); Charles Trowbridge (Comdr. L.M. Hale). William Colby, Harry Strang (Bit Roles).

Credits: William A. Bacher, Walter Morosco (Producers); Henry Hathaway (Director); Jerome Cady (Screenplay); Glen MacWilliams (Cinematography); Hugo Friedhofer (Music); Emil Newman (Music Direction); Lyle R. Wheeler, Lewis Creber (Art Direction); Thomas Little, Fred J. Rode (Set Decorations); Henry Weinberger (Assistant Director); Alfred Bruzlin (Sound); Sam Benson (Wardrobe); Ben Nye (Makeup); Fred Sersen (Special Effects); Watson Webb, Jr. (Editor). Running time: 99 minutes

In the lead-up to the Battle of Midway, a U.S. aircraft carrier is dispatched on a decoy mission around the Pacific with orders to enact a non-combat strategy in hopes of misleading the Japanese before the crucial battle. The carrier is commanded by a tough flight officer, Bingo Harper, who loses the respect of his pilots due to his rigid and unyielding manner. Led by Edward Moulton (Dana Andrews), the young pilots become increasingly frustrated and bitter about the avoidance of combat, particularly when the casualties begin to pile up. Their resentment towards their commander turns to respect when they are finally given the opportunity to fight. With the great battle turning in their favor, they realize that his tough methods were right all along.

Tagline: "The Most Dangerous Mission in the War."

Darryl Zanuck recognized that whereas there had been two wartime movies glorifying submarines, *Crash Dive* and *Destination Tokyo* (1943), no such tribute had been paid to aircraft carriers since Pearl Harbor. To avoid the usual conventional melodrama associated with service pictures, he insisted that *Wing and a Prayer* must not depend on plot, but instead should concentrate on casting, dialogue and battle sequences. He assigned the challenge to the studio workhorse, the consummate professional Henry Hathaway.

Hathaway progressed through the ranks from child star to film director in a 40-year career which saw him at his best in westerns and crime films. In his directorial debut *Heritage of the Desert* (1932), he gave Randolph Scott his first starring role, and in the postwar period he pioneered the making of films in a semidocumentary style (*The House on 92nd Street, 13 Rue Madeleine* and *Call Northside 777*). This style also found full expression in *Wing and a Prayer* with its need for realism and naval detail.

Heading the cast with Andrews was Fox's bon vivant young man-about-town Don Ameche in possibly his last great film from his golden era, which included classics such as *The Story of Alexander Graham Bell* (1939) and *Heaven Can Wait* (1943). When his film career faded in the 1950s he turned to radio, returning to films in the 1980s with *Trading Places* (1983) and *Cocoon* (1985), for which he received an Academy Award for Best Supporting Actor. Ameche recollected that during the filming of *Wing and a Prayer*, in between shots the actors used to pass the time discussing the jobs they held down before securing movie contracts; Andrews kept them amused with tales of his exploits as a gas station grease monkey, which paid for his singing and acting lessons.[1]

The supporting cast was also first class, with Charles Bickford giving one of his consistently solid performances as Captain Waddell and William Eythe showing he had great leading man potential as the reckless glam-boy flyer Oscar Scott. Bickford teamed again with Andrews a year later in Preminger's classic noir *Fallen Angel*. Eythe made his film debut alongside Andrews the previous year in *The Ox-Bow Incident*, but after a promising start his film career went into decline in the late 1940s. Like many young Hollywood hopefuls he turned to drink, which culminated in his untimely death in 1957 at age 38.

Andrews recalled in an interview that during production Hathaway asked him to go out one Saturday evening to learn the rudiments of flying a plane, which would help him to play the part of a pilot. Andrews made it known to the assistant director that he felt this was not necessary because they always cut above the shoulders in a plane shot and therefore it didn't matter what the hands were doing. Although he was ordered to attend the lesson, it turned out to be to his advantage, because during the lesson he bumped into Darryl Zanuck's wife who, after their long conversation, told him that she thought he had leading man potential.[2] Such a compliment would been a tremendous boost to his confidence with the likes of Tyrone Power and Henry Fonda still the top boys at the Fox studio.

Wing and a Prayer was the only time that Andrews worked with Henry Hathaway, who in a 1973 interview recalled the actor's remarkable ability to be word-perfect with little effort: "Dana had a quality. I'll tell you one thing he had like nobody I've ever seen in my life. Drunk or sober, he comes in, in the morning and they're making him up and he'd say, 'What do I do today?' And you say, 'Do this.' And he'd look at the script and he goes out ... and he never misses a word."[3]

Andrews plays Lt. Comdr. Moulton in his moderately resolute way. Happy to throw in with the guys, Moulton is nonetheless a stickler for doing things according to the book and shows no hesitation in issuing reprimands when the occasion suits; following one of the many landing scenes using actual crash footage, he tears a strip off glam boy pilot Scott for his recklessness and failure to follow signals. "What do you think the flagman was doing ? Waving byebye?!"

In many ways Moulton is just as rigid and unyielding as Flight Commander Bingo Harper when he knows there's a job to be done, particularly on the attack run: "Moulton to Squadron. Remember, when you think you're in close, go in closer before you drop that fish."

To enhance the action scenes, a construction crew built a mock-up of a section of a carrier flight deck on the Fox backlot to serve as a stage for exterior scenes footage Hathaway had taken the previous year aboard the USS *Hornet*. The film has the distinction of showing the first War Department–approved footage of action on board one of the new post–Pearl Harbor aircraft carriers. Leftover footage from the film was put to good use in the documentary feature *The Fighting Lady*, made that same year.

As well as combining actual combat footage with soundstage action, the film also intertwined image and reality when Andrews rebukes one of his glory-seeking pilots: "As for you, Scott, there are no stars out here — this isn't Hollywood. When the time comes for you to take the bows, we'll turn on the spotlights." For his brisk script, Jerome Cady was nominated for a Best Original Screenplay Oscar.

Although the film did portray life on board a carrier with some authenticity, it did not accurately reflect events during the first day of battle at Midway. Direct hits were made on Japanese carriers by U.S. Naval aircraft, but this damage was inflicted by dive bombers and not by torpedo planes as depicted in the film.[4]

Personal heroics are practically non-existent in *Wing and a Prayer* and that tends to give added realism.... The personal side of the story is rather routine, but it does not intrude too often and the various players ... give effective performances.—*New York Times*

Andrews reprised the role of the junior officer at odds with his disciplinarian commanding officer in another service film, *The Frogmen* (1951), with Richard Widmark assuming "the Don Ameche role."

"Into the Wild Blue Yonder" played out the final scene in *The Purple Heart*; the equally rousing "Anchors Aweigh" brought the curtain down in *Wing and a Prayer*. With this one in the can, there was no doubt that Andrews had starred in two of the finest wartime propaganda films.

Laura
20th Century–Fox, 1944

Cast: Gene Tierney (Laura Hunt); Dana Andrews (Det. Lt. Mark McPherson); Clifton Webb (Waldo Lydecker); Vincent Price (Shelby Carpenter); Judith Anderson (Ann Treadwell); Dorothy Adams (Bessie Clary); James Flavin (McAvity); Clyde Fillmore (Bullitt); Ralph Dunn (Fred Callahan); Grant Mitchell (Corey); Kathleen Howard (Louise); Harold Schlickenmayer, Harry Strang, Lane Chandler (Detectives); Frank La Rue (Hairdresser); Lee Tung Foo (Waldo's Servant); William Forrest (Important Client); Buster Miles (Office Boy); John Dexter (Jacoby); Jane Nigh (Secretary); Alexander Sascha, Dorothy Christy, Aileen Pringle; Terry Adams, Jean Fenwick, Yolanda Lacca, Forbes Murray, Cyril Ring, Nester Eristoff, Kay Linaker, Cara Williams, Gloria Marlen, Beatrice Gray, Kay Connors, Frances Gladwin (Bits).

Credits: Otto Preminger (Producer-Director); Vera Caspary (Story); Jay Dratler, Samuel Hoffenstein, Betty Reinhardt (Screenplay); Joseph LaShelle (Cinematography); David Raksin (Music); Emil Newman (Music Director); Johnny Mercer ("Laura" Lyric); Lyle Wheeler, Leland Fuller (Art Direction); Thomas Little (Set Decorations); Tom Dudley, Robert Saunders (Assistant Directors); Sam Benson (Wardrobe); Bonnie Cashin (Costumes); Guy Pearce (Makeup); Fred Sersen (Special Effects); Harry M. Leonard, E. Clayton Ward (Sound); Louis R. Loeffler (Editor). Running time: 88 minutes

The story opens in New York with the discovery of the facially disfigured body of the beautiful girl of the title, Laura Hunt, murdered by a

Andrews's lovesick flatfoot Mark McPherson gazes starry-eyed at a painting of the object of his desire, the captivating Laura Hunt (Gene Tierney), in chic noir classic *Laura* (20th Century–Fox, 1944).

shotgun blast to the face. Police detective Mark McPherson (Dana Andrews) interviews each of the suspects: Laura's intellectual mentor, the bitchy society columnist Waldo Lydecker; Laura's weak playboy fiancé Shelby Carpenter; and Ann Treadwell, a wealthy older woman in love with Shelby. During the investigation, Mark becomes fascinated with Laura and is bewitched by her painted portrait. Alone in her apartment looking for evidence, he falls into a hypnotic daze staring at the portrait, but is abruptly brought back to his senses with the opening of the door and the surprise appearance of Laura. She informs Mark that she has been away in the country reconsidering her forthcoming marriage to Shelby. Further evidence reveals that the dead girl is a model, Diane Redfern, who was once romantically connected with Shelby. With jealousy high on the agenda, all the suspects have a motive: Lydecker or Anne might have killed Diane in the mistaken belief that the model (in Laura's apart-

ment and wearing one of Laura's furs) *was* Laura; Shelby might have been disposing of his ex-girlfriend; and Laura herself might have resented Diane's attachment to her husband-to-be. With the discovery of the murder weapon, the finger of blame points to Lydecker, who enters Laura's apartment to ensure that if *he* can't have Laura, then no one will. Mark arrives in the nick of time to save the girl, and during the course of the rescue, Lydecker is fatally wounded.

In the opening soliloquy, crisply delivered by Clifton Webb in the role of Waldo Lydecker, Andrews's character, detective Mark McPherson is casually introduced to the audience:

> I shall never forget the weekend Laura died. A silver sun burned through the sky like a huge magnifying glass. It was the hottest Sunday in my recollection. I felt as if I were the only human being left in New York.... And, I had just begun to write Laura's story when another of those detectives came to see me....

Opening lines don't come any better and street-wise cops don't come any finer than Andrews's Mark McPherson. At the top of his profession and looking every bit the tough, world-weary detective, Andrews was tailor-made for the part. In many ways, his McPherson formed the bedrock for subsequent character portrayals. Sure, they became more cynical, jaded, embittered and in some cases traumatized or devious as the years moved on — but essentially at the core, they were McPherson, an honest, hard-working guy trying to make his way, to the best of his ability, in a harsh, unforgiving world.

The production of *Laura*, which is widely regarded as the first full-fledged Hollywood film noir, was by no means a smooth affair. Darryl F. Zanuck originally assigned Rouben Mamoulian to direct the classic Vera Caspary murder mystery, with Otto Preminger producing, but after viewing some early rushes both Preminger and Zanuck were disappointed with the results. In an effort to revive the film, all the early footage was scrapped and Mamoulian was taken off the project and replaced by Preminger. A portrait of Laura painted by Mamoulian's wife was also cast aside and replaced by a photograph of Gene that was enlarged and painted over to give the impression of an oil.

Before Mamoulian was chosen to direct, Andrews recalled that his old buddy Lewis Milestone was offered the job, but turned it down. While driving home with Andrews after a day's location shoot for *The Purple Heart*, Milestone told the actor that, although he had turned down the assignment, he thought that the part of the detective would make his friend a star. Milestone gave Andrews the script and, after reading it, Andrews set out to get the part. He first met Preminger at a party at Milestone's house, where he learned that Zanuck had John Hodiak down for the role. Full of determination, Andrews got columnist Hedda Hopper to put a heavy hint in her column advocating, "Andrews for *Laura*." His chances were also possibly enhanced following a chance meeting with Zanuck's wife during the making of *Wing and a Prayer* when, after their long conversation, she realized his star potential. Despite all the pressure, Zanuck still had Hodiak in mind following the actor's hit performance in *Lifeboat* (1944) and was of the opinion he oozed more sex appeal than Andrews, who was Preminger's first choice. However, Preminger's persistence paid off and Andrews got the part.[1]

The film marked the sound film debut of Clifton Webb and brought him to prominence after a long career on stage as a dancer and actor. Webb, however, was not the first choice to play the bitchy intellectual Waldo Lydecker, as Zanuck originally wanted Monty Woolley or Laird Cregar. Zanuck's reluctance to use Webb was due to the actor's known homosexuality, but Preminger eventually convinced him that Webb was perfect for the part. Reginald Gardiner was considered for the role of Shelby Carpenter before it went to Vincent Price, giving the actor his big break. Having proven herself in notable films such as *Rebecca* (1940), where she played Mrs. Danvers, Judith Anderson was a sure bet for the role of Ann Treadwell.

Jennifer Jones was offered the part of Laura, but turned it down because she felt that the role was minor.[2] It was subsequently offered to Gene Tierney, providing the actress with a film comeback after a year off due to pregnancy. Initially, Gene had her own doubts about the role, complaining, "Who wants to play the part of a painting?" Interestingly, other actresses considered included Hedy Lamarr and Marlene Dietrich. Lamarr certainly had that essential enigmatic beauty to pull if off, but Dietrich — no! You can just picture the scene: Mark, asleep in the chair facing the portrait of the handsome fraulein, the hypnotic background beat of "Lili Marlene" filling the air, when all of a sudden, Laura makes her entrance, shaking him abruptly from his dreamy slumber with the question, "Who are you? And vot are you doing in my apartment?" (Cut! Next screen test, please!)

In an interview, Andrews described Preminger's and Mamoulian's original thoughts on the nature of his character, Mark McPherson: "What conversations they'd had between themselves, I don't know, but they were in agreement in talking to me, that they wanted this character played as though he were a student of criminology from Yale or Harvard or something like that, and not at all the hard-boiled detective that you generally see."[3]

Andrews went on to describe how the character was played this way for the first two weeks before Zanuck intervened on his return to the studio after a stint out of town. Preminger, Mamoulian and all the leads were summoned to

Zanuck's office, where the mogul told Andrews that he wanted the character to be played as a streetwise type, very much in the Pat O'Brien vein.[4]

With his sonorous voice and inimitable deadpan style, enhanced by the obligatory cigarette tightly wedged in the corner of his mouth, Andrews was the ideal candidate to deliver some of the best hard-boiled lines in noir history. With Lydecker as a great feed man, the smart remarks come thick and fast. When asked whether he'd ever been in love, Mark nonchalantly responds, "A doll in Washington Heights once got a fox fur out of me." And amidst all the chaos, he remains defiantly calm, amusing himself with a hand-held pinball puzzle while interrogating the suspects and witnesses. Amongst that ensemble is Laura's domestic maid Bessie Clary, who makes it abundantly clear that she has no time for cops and was taught to spit whenever she saw one. The remark taps into Mark's caring and understanding side for the little people, as he amusingly replies, "Okay, go ahead and spit, if that'll make you feel better."

Indeed, brought up from the streets, Mark is very much a man of the people who clearly has little time for Laura's ne'er-do-well friends: "I must say, for a charming, intelligent girl, you certainly surrounded yourself with a remarkable collection of dopes."

In perhaps the most memorable sequence, Mark gazes upon the portrait, clutching a drink, with Laura's theme music fuelling his haunted obsession with the unattainable beauty. The obsession is not unnoticed by Lydecker when he drops by, having seen the lights on in Laura's apartment. Annoyed by Mark's prying into Laura's letters and his growing interest in the girl, Lydecker glibly warns the detective that he could be the first patient locked up for falling in love with a corpse. But our detective is too far gone to take much notice — until Laura's unexpected return to her apartment a short while later abruptly interrupts his reverie. Shocked by his presence, she threatens to call the police, which tees Mark up for one of the best lines in the movie when the equally startled detective responds, "I *am* the police."

Despite some mixed reviews (how bizarre!), *Laura* nonetheless went on to win an Oscar for Joseph LaShelle's captivating black-and-white cinematography and was also nominated in four other categories: Best Director (Preminger), Best Supporting Actor (Webb), Best Art Direction and Best Screenplay. Astonishingly, one of the film's major assets, the haunting score by David Raksin, was not even nominated. When Johnny Mercer added lyrics, the melody became a classic song popularized by Frank Sinatra. Interestingly, Preminger originally wanted George Gershwin's "Summertime" or Duke Ellington's "Sophisticated Lady" as the theme, but Raksin won the day when he successfully rose to Preminger's challenge to compose the perfect score over a weekend. According to Raksin, on the Sunday night he was no further forward with his assignment until he read a "Dear John Letter" from his wife informing him that their marriage was over; this triggered a burst of creative genius, giving birth to the haunting melody of *Laura*.[5]

Laura was shot between May 1 and June 26, 1944, at a cost of $1,075,000 (approximately $20,000 above the original budget), and earned $2 million in domestic rentals.

One critic perfectly summed up Andrews's unique screen presence in the film: "With his haunted eyes, taut yet sensitive mouth, and softly insinuating voice, Andrews is a highly evocative screen presence, conveying more with a look than many actors do with a soliloquy."

Andrews received one of his best reviews from the *New York World–Telegram*: "Dana Andrews has consistently outdone each of his successive performances.... The smoldering force with which he plays the detective leaves one pretty sure that the chain of topping himself will be broken with this picture — unless he turns out to be just about the finest actor of our time."

The *New York Times* reviewer wrote, "Mr. Andrews is fast proving himself to be a solidly persuasive performer, a sort of younger-edition Spencer Tracy," and the *Daily Telegraph* was all praise for the film: "One of the best thrillers ever made, as good as *Double Indemnity*, better than *Casablanca* or *The Maltese Falcon*. ... [T]he plot is brilliantly contrived, the characters live, the dialogue is witty without being forced, laconic without a lot of hammy biting on the bullet."

Film historians Rudy Behlmer and Jeanine Basinger provided some excellent commentary for the special edition DVD release in 2006, with Basinger noting that Andrews's enigmatic, tense, off-hand presence did much to imbue his character with a sense of mystery.

Andrews's acclaimed performance in *Laura* elevated his career to new heights, making him one of Fox's most popular stars on the fan mail front. He rose from 12th position to the number one slot in this, his first crack at being a romantic leading man.

Vincent Price always cited *Laura* as the best movie he was in.[6] He regarded all the actors as good friends who were delighted with the opportunity to work together. Forty years later, in 1984, the surviving cast members, including Vincent, Gene and Andrews, met up again at a reunion to honor the film.[7]

In the 1955 CBS-TV television version of *Laura*, Mark McPherson was played by Robert Stack, Laura by Dana Wynter, and Waldo Lydecker by George Sanders. Both Stack and Sanders went on to reprise their roles in the 1968 ABC-TV version with Lee Radziwell (younger sister of Jacqueline Kennedy) as Laura and Farley Granger as Shelby Carpenter. In the 1954 *Lux Radio* presentation, Mark McPherson was played by Victor Mature; Andrews played Mark in the 1945 *Lux* presentation. Hugh Marlowe played the detective in the 1947 New York stage play.

Although not in the same league, shades of *Laura* can be observed in *Chicago Deadline* (1949) with Alan Ladd as the hard-boiled type investigating the mysterious death of enigmatic beauty Rosita, played by Donna Reed.

State Fair

20th Century–Fox, 1945

Cast: Jeanne Crain (Margy Frake); Dana Andrews (Pat Gilbert); Dick Haymes (Wayne Frake); Vivian Blaine (Emily Edwards); Charles Winninger (Abel Frake); Fay Bainter (Melissa Frake); Donald Meek (Hippenstahl); Frank McHugh (McGee); Percy Kilbride (Dave Miller); Harry Morgan (Barker); Jane Nigh (Eleanor); William Marshall (Marty); Phil Brown (Harry Ware); Paul Burns (Hank); Paul Harvey (Simpson); Josephine Whittell (Mrs. Metcalf); Tom Fadden (Eph); William Frambes (Pappy); Coleen Gray (Girl with Pappy); Steve Olson (Follies Barker); Neal Hart, Walter Baldwin (Farmers); Margo Woode, Jo-Carroll Dennison (Girls); Francis Ford (Mr. Martin, Whirlwind's Owner); Will Wright (Hog Judge) Harry Depp (Judge's Secretary); Earle S. Dewey, Wheaton Chambers (Assistant Hog Judges); Almira Sessions, Virginia Brissac (Farmer's Wives); Brooks Benedict (Hammer Contest Spectator); Eddie Borden, Harry Semels (Follies Spectators);

Harlan Briggs (Food Judge); John Dehner (Hog Contest Announcer); Cathy Downs (Girl on Carousel); Eddie Dunn (Roller Coaster Attendant); Jim Farley (Ticket Taker); Alice Fleming (Food Judge); Ralph Sanford (Police Chief); Diane Florentine (Police Chief's Daughter); Louanne Hogan (Margy Frake's Singing Voice); Bess Flowers (Woman in Pickle Crowd); Reed Howes (Horse Race Spectator); Frank Mayo (Man Margy Bumps); Emory Parnell (Sen. James A. Goodheart).

Credits: William Perlberg (Producer); Walter Lang (Director); Philip Strong (Novel); Sonya Levien, Paul Green (Adaptation); Oscar Hammerstein II (Screenplay); Richard Rodgers; Oscar Hammerstein (Songs); Alfred Newman, Charles Henderson (Music Directors); Edward Powell (Orchestrator); Leon Shamroy (Cinematography); Lewis H. Creber, Lyle R. Wheeler (Art Direction); Thomas Little, Al Orenbach (Set Decorations); Rene Hubert (Costume Design); Sam Benson (Wardrobe); Gaston Glass (Assistant Director); Bernard Freericks, Roger Heman Sr. (Sound); Fred Sersen (Special Effects); J. Watson Webb, Jr. (Editor). Running time: 100 minutes

In this Rodgers and Hammerstein musical, the setting is the annual summertime Iowa State Fair, and the four members of the Frake family are looking forward to a memorable experience. Abel wants to win first prize for his huge hog and his wife Melissa has similar ambitions for her mincemeat in the "best pickle" contest. Their teenage children Margy and Wayne are more interested in romance, which they find, respectively, in the form of a newspaper reporter, Pat Gilbert (Dana Andrews), and dance band singer Emily. After several musical numbers and romantic complications, Abel's hog wins the blue ribbon, Melissa's brandy-spiked mincemeat gets the winning "thumbs up" from the judges, Wayne takes up with his old high school sweetheart when he discovers that Emily has a husband and, after a brief separation, Margy and Pat decide to get married.

Tagline: "For the young in heart! And romantic oldsters, too!"

With the world still at war, film studios were encouraged to make pictures which would not only serve as a comforting diversion for the good folks at home, but also as a homely reminder to the boys and gals serving in uniform overseas. Hollywood responded with a memorable stream of Americana musicals including Warners' *Yankee Doodle Dandy* and MGM's *For Me and My Gal* and *Meet Me in St Louis*. Keen to do their bit, 20th Century–Fox pitched in with *My Gal Sal* and *State Fair*.

Fox was keen to make a Rodgers and Hammerstein musical and initially focused their sights on making *Oklahoma!* However, with the show's huge success on Broadway, Dick and Oscar weren't quite ready to kill the golden goose just yet, so instead, Fox decided to make a musical version of Phil Strong's charming novel *State Fair*, which the studio had previously made as a non-singing film back in 1933 with Will Rogers, Lew Ayres and Janet Gaynor. This musical remake downplayed the older characters in favor of the younger members of the cast, which included the wholesomely beautiful Jeanne Crain in the role of Margy. Jeanne, a former Miss California, enjoyed most of her success in the 1940s with notable performances in *Apartment for Peggy* (1948) and *Pinky* (1949), her performance in the latter earning her an Oscar nomination (she lost to Olivia de Havilland for *The Heiress*). The natural chemistry between Jeanne and Andrews was clearly evidenced in *State Fair* and the couple went on to star together in another three films—*Duel in the Jungle* (1954), *Madison Avenue* (1962) and *Hot Rods to Hell* (1967). Like Andrews's career, Jeanne's was less memorable in the 1950s but, considering she was a mother of seven, she continued to look stunning in all her roles.

One of the unsung greats of the Hollywood musical, director Walter Lang was responsible for many of the Fox tunefests of the 1940s and '50s, including *Tin Pan Alley* (1940), *Moon Over Miami* (1941), *Coney Island* (1943), *There's No Business Like Show Business* (1954) and *The King and I* (1956) for which he received an Academy Ward nomination. In keeping with these timeless classics, his *State Fair* was big, glossy, wholesome and shot in gloriously garish 20th Century–Fox Technicolor.

As in *Up in Arms*, Andrews had an opportunity to show off his singing skills, but once again chose not to reveal to the studio that he was a trained singer. Instead, he was dubbed by another singer, who was paid $150. Andrews later explained that he remained silent about his operatic voice because the dubbing singer probably needed the money and he didn't want to put anyone out of work. His singing voice in the film was provided by Esther Williams's soon-to-be second husband, radio singer and announcer Ben Gage, who had also dubbed for Victor Mature's singing in *My Gal Sal* (1942).[1]

Although cast in several musicals, Jeanne herself was not a singer. In *State Fair* and all her other musicals she was dubbed by Louanne Hogan. No dubbing was required for the perfect singing voices of Dick Haymes and Vivian Blaine; both made a distinctive contribution to the masterful score, which included "Our State Fair," "That's for Me," "Isn't It Kinda Fun," "It's a Grand Night for Singing" and the Oscar-winning "It Might As Well Be Spring" (sung by Louanne Hogan); this, rather surprisingly, was Rodgers and Hammerstein's only Oscar. The film's lasting appeal and charm is undoubtedly down to the clever use of these songs as part of the plot.

In addition to the catchy songs, colorful sets and some delightful boy-meets-girl interplay, the film's many highlights include a scene-stealing cameo from Donald Meek (who died in 1946 — remember him in the role of the mild-mannered passenger in *Stagecoach*) as one of the mincemeat judges and some lovely images of folksy Americana, particularly the fairground scenes where Andrews's confident newspaperman, Pat Gilbert, exercises his prowess with a chat-up line on Margy: "I've been standing there, watching you walk away. Every step you took, your hair bounced up and down on the back of your neck. Very nice. I dunno if that's what caught me, but here I am. Now it's your turn to say something."

And with an all-knowing look, there's no mistaking, that at face value, our Pat's definitely a "no strings" type, telling Margy that if ever things went cold between them, she would go east and he would go west, with no hard feelings. Savvy as they come, Pat is one of those guys who will happily throw in the towel if things get too serious, further informing a doting Margy when she broaches the subject of marriage, "[I]f I ever found a girl I cared that much about, I'd care too much about it, to wish a guy like me off on her." Grossing over $4 million, *State Fair* ranked second in Fox's top moneymakers that year, and was described by Zanuck as "the most popular musical we have had in years and the business nationwide is just sensational."

The *New York Post* hailed it as "a honey of a picture"; equally impressed, *Time* magazine described the film "as happy as a hayride down the

Wholesome country girl Margy Frake (Jeanne Crain) shares a soda with fresh, streetwise reporter Pat Gilbert (Andrews) in the glorious Rodgers and Hammerstein musical *State Fair* (20th Century–Fox, 1945).

middle aisle of *Oklahoma.*" On a similar note, Tony Thomas in his book *The Films of the Forties* noted, "*State Fair* has a genial atmosphere, and it glows with the wit and compassion of Oscar Hammerstein II."

This was Andrews's second performance as a newspaperman following *Berlin Correspondent* three years earlier, proving yet again that he was the ideal choice to play "street-wise" characters. He would reprise the role of the reporter in three other films—*Assignment Paris* (1952), *While the City Sleeps* (1956) and *Beyond a Reasonable Doubt* (1956).

Alice Faye was originally considered for the role of Emily, ultimately played by Vivian Blaine. However, Faye did appear as the mother in the disappointing 1962 remake with Bobby Darin, Pat Boone, Ann Margret and Pamela Tiffin substituting for Andrews, Dick, Vivian and Jeanne.

In addition to being possibly the most wholesome tale on film, this is, without doubt, one of the best sing-along movies ever made. Oh, it's a grand night for singing, la da dee da dee da!

P.S. If you're in the mood for some great tunes, grab a copy of the brilliantly conceived CD "Music from the Movies of Dana Andrews 1944–1949."

A Walk in the Sun
20th Century–Fox, 1945

Cast: Dana Andrews (Sgt. Bill Tyne); Richard Conte (Pvt. Rivera); George Tyne (Pvt. Friedman); John Ireland (Pvt. Windy Craven); Lloyd Bridges (Sgt. Ward); Sterling Holloway (McWilliams); Norman Lloyd (Pvt. Archimbeau); Herbert Rudley (Sgt. Eddie Porter); Richard Benedict (Pvt. Tranella); Huntz Hall (Pvt. Carraway); James Cardwell (Sgt. Hoskins); George Offerman, Jr. (Pvt. Tinker); Steve Brodie (Pvt. Judson); Matt Willis (Sgt. Pete Halverson); Chris Drake (Rankin); Victor Cutler (Cousins); Alvin Hammer (Johnson); Jay Norris

(James); John Kellogg (Riddle); Harry Cline (Corp. Kramer); Dick Daniels (Long); Anthony Dante (Giorgio); Danny Desmond (Trasker); Robert Lowell (Lt. Rand); Grant Maiben (Smith); Burgess Meredith (Narrator); Malcolm O'Guinn (Phelps); Don Summers (Dugan); George Turner (Reconnaissance).

Credits: Lewis Milestone (Producer-Director); Harry Brown (Novel); Robert Rossen (Screenplay); Russell Harlan (Cinematography); Frederic Efrem Rich (Music); Millard Lampell, Earl Robinson (Songs); Colonel Thomas D. Drake (Technical Advisor); Max Bertisch (Art Direction); Maurice M. Suess (Assistant Director); Sam Benson (Wardrobe); Duncan Mansfield (Editor). Running time: 117 minutes

Set during the 1943 invasion of Italy, this semi-documentary World War II drama concentrates on a platoon of infantrymen as they advance one morning from a beach landing at Salerno to the capture of a German-held farmhouse six miles away. Each of the soldiers reveals his background and character against a canvas of danger, fear and death. Amongst the ranks, Windy finds escape from the horrors of war by composing letters in his mind to his sister, while cheeky machine-gunner Rivera keeps a positive outlook with his infectious humor.

After a series of casualties, intelligent and sensitive Corporal Tyne (Dana Andrews), now elevated to sergeant, assumes command of the platoon in their desperate bid to take the heavily fortified farmhouse. A natural-born leader, Tyne succeeds in harnessing the best from the men as they complete the mission by storming the stronghold and overthrowing its defenders.

In the opening ballad, we hear a stirring tribute to the men of a fine fighting platoon who "came across the sea to sunny Italy. To take a little walk in the sun."

The mixed group of infantrymen that takes this particular "walk in the sun" are individually introduced to us as they march along to the opening narration, with Andrews's Sgt Tyne described as a home-loving man who "never had much urge to travel. Providence, Rhode Island, may not be much as cities go but it was all he wanted — a one-town man." The rest of the impressive cast are for the most part newcomers to the big screen, including Richard Conte, Lloyd Bridges, John Ireland, Norman Lloyd and Steve Brodie.

In the role of the wisecracking "nobody dies" Rivera, Conte is particularly outstanding. His perfectly timed, humorous exchanges with George Tyne in the role of Pvt. Friedman set the pace throughout the film.

Lloyd Bridges made his first films in 1936 and although he kept busy, usually as unreliable types (most notably as the deputy in *High Noon* [1952]), he didn't enjoy major success until he broke into television with the hugely popular *Sea Hunt* (1958–1961); the spoof disaster film *Airplane!* (1980) brought him a new legion of fans. It is a little-known fact that he was offered the part of Captain Kirk before the role went to William Shatner.

John Ireland's first big break came as the letter-writing GI in *Walk in the Sun*, and in 1949, he was Oscar-nominated for Best Supporting Actor for his role as the reporter in *All the King's Men*. Usually cast as the villain in the 1940s, he became the brooding hero in a number of American and British B movies of the 1950s. The second of his three wives was Joanne Dru (from 1949 to 1958).

With his freckle-faced country bumpkin demeanor and trademark near-falsetto voice, Sterling Holloway was almost exclusively cast in comic roles, but in *A Walk in the Sun* he was notably cast against type as the thoughtful Pvt. McWilliams. He later enjoyed worldwide fame as the voice behind many Walt Disney characters, particularly Winnie the Pooh. Dead End Kid-East Side Kid Huntz Hall appeared in several war films after his army discharge, receiving the New York Theatre Critics Circle Blue Ribbon Award for his memorable performance as Pvt. Carraway in *A Walk in the Sun*.

Harry Brown was an Army private during the Second World War and his novel upon which the film was based, memorably portrays the fear, anxieties, boredom, determination and weary triumph of the average soldier. Skillfully combined with Robert Rossen's unsentimental screenplay and Lewis Milestone's expert direction, the film is rightly considered one of the greatest war films. There are no "Errol Flynn–type" heroics; instead the emphasis is very much on characters who are linked together through the perfect use of repetitive GI banter and the thoughts of Ireland's character as he composes letters to his sister in his head.

Andrews's role was perfectly summed up in *The Great War Films* by Lawrence J. Quirk:

Andrews as Sergeant Tyne heeding some helpful advice from his director-friend Lewis Milestone during the making of *A Walk in the Sun* (20th Century–Fox, 1945).

Dana Andrews is particularly fine as the sergeant playing with quiet and eloquent square-jawed intensity, a man who realizes he has responsibility for others as well as himself. [A]s their leader, he is the perfect battle-scarred, yet battle-hardened fighting man — balanced, sensitive to his men, determined to do his duty, yet saddened by the horrifying costs entailed.[1]

Many years later, Andrews said that for this independent production Milestone personally selected him for the Sgt. Tyne role, which Andrews considered meaty and important in terms of his career. Having great respect for the director, he described him as something of a poet with the camera, working by inspiration and from sketch camera layouts provided by an artist who worked alongside him. He further praised the director's ability to capture faces on camera.[2]

The unassuming Sgt. Tyne (Andrews, center) takes a walk in the sun with Pvt. Rivera (Richard Conte, left) and Pvt. Porter (Herbert Rudley) in Lewis Milestone's wartime epic *A Walk in the Sun* (20th Century–Fox, 1945).

This is memorably demonstrated in one scene, which also enabled Andrews to utilize his unique ability to convey raw emotion through his facial expression. As you watch Tyne crawl slowly toward the German farmhouse, pondering on how long it would take to crawl around the world, pure fear and trepidation starkly stare back at you through the intensity in his eyes.

Despite the focus on characterization, the film does have some first-class action sequences, particularly the platoon's encounter with a German half-track and the near-suicidal finale with their frontal assault on the German-held farmhouse. Milestone cleverly made use of heroic ballad-verse to link the action scenes with the character vignettes. The film's sense of purposelessness, with the average soldier resigned to a grand plan he has no real comprehension of, would again be explored by Milestone in *Halls of Montezuma* (1950) and *Pork Chop Hill* (1959).

With his younger brother, Steve Forrest, away on active service during the war, Andrews would learn first-hand the uncertainties and tensions of those on the front line. "My brother was in the Battle of the Bulge and he says that nobody in there had any idea what was happening to them — all they knew was, they were surrounded and they just had to make the best of it."[3]

With their rich blend of inner thoughts, fears, and profound observations, interlaced with GI banter, the lines are sheer poetry. And slipping snugly into the part of the unassuming Sergeant Tyne like a well-worn glove, Andrews delivers his share of them to maximum effect, such as his thoughts on what to expect when they hit France: "I bet it's just a long concrete wall with a gun every yard. Maybe they'll set the water on fire with oil, too. Boy, when that day comes, I wanna be somewhere else." An all-around decent guy, Tyne is a man you can depend on to give reassuring comfort and sympathetic leadership when the men most need it. However, beneath that quiet, dignified authority, he is just as anxious and fearful as the next guy, as we

Crawling to the German-held farmhouse, the stench of death in the air, Sgt. Tyne (Andrews) ponders how long it would take to crawl around the world in *A Walk in the Sun* (20th Century–Fox, 1945).

learn when he confesses to one of the men before the assault on the farmhouse, "My stomach feels like it's tied into a tight knot ... feel a little sick, a little dizzy." But when the chips are down, you intuitively know he'll lead from the front until the job's accomplished, with the minimum of fuss and casualty.

With the mission successfully completed, the bitter irony of war is summed up in Windy's closing thought-composed letter to his sister, "We just blew a bridge and took a farmhouse. It was easy. Terribly easy."

Although the film marked Andrews's first official feature as a lead star, its arrival in 1946 coincided with war-weary audiences and as a consequence, on its initial release, it fared badly at the box office, which prompted Fox to sell it to a small British distributor. Retitled *Salerno Beachhead*, the film was highly praised by the British critics with some hailing it as the greatest war film since Milestone's classic *All Quiet on the Western Front* (1930).

The *New York Herald Tribune* commented,

"Dana Andrews [plays] with the quiet intensity one might expect from a knowing star...." According to *Variety*, "Dana Andrews gives one of his invariably forthright performances as the sergeant, and the rest of the impressive cast know their way around a script." The *New York Times* went even further in their praise of his performance: "Most impressive is Dana Andrews, who makes of Tyne an intelligent, acute, and sensitive leader of the pathetically confused but stubborn group."

Fallen Angel
20th Century–Fox, 1945

Cast: Alice Faye (June Mills); Dana Andrews (Eric Stanton); Linda Darnell (Stella); Charles Bickford (Mark Judd); Anne Revere (Clara Mills); Bruce Cabot (Dave Atkins); John Carradine (Professor Madley); Percy Kilbride (Pop); Olin Howland (Joe Ellis); Wally Wales (Police Officer Gus Johnson); Mira McKinney (Mrs. Judd); Jimmy Conlin (Walton Hotel Clerk); Broderick O'Farrell (Policeman); Lelia

McIntyre (Bank Clerk); Garry Owen (Waiter); Horace Murphy (Sheriff); Martha Wentworth (Hotel Maid); Paul Palmer (Detective); Paul E. Burns (News Vendor); Herbert Ashley, Dave Morris (Reporters); Matthew Beard (Shoeshine Boy); William Haade, Chick Collins (Bus Drivers); Dorothy Adams (Stella's Neighbor); Betty Boyd (Bank Clerk); Gus Glassmire (San Francisco Hotel Clerk); Dick Haymes (Juke Box Vocalist); Adele Jergens (Woman in Audience); J. Farrell MacDonald (Bank Guard); William H. O'Brien (Bus Passenger); Harry Strang (Policeman); Brick Sullivan (Honky Tonk Dance Extra); Max Wagner (Bartender); Franklyn Farnum, Tiny Jones, Frank O'Connor, Hal Taggart (Extras).

Credits: Otto Preminger (Producer-Director); Marty Holland (Story); Harry Kleiner (Screenplay); Joseph LaShelle (Cinematography); David Raksin (Music); Emil Newman (Music Direction); David Raksin, Kermit Goell (Songs); Lyle Wheeler, Leland Fuller (Art Direction); Thomas Little, Helen Hansard (Set Decorations); Tom Dudley (Assistant Director); Fred Sersen (Special Effects); Bernard Freericks, Harry M. Leonard (Sound); Bonnie Cashin (Costume Design); Ben Nye (Makeup); Harry Reynolds (Editor). Running time: 98 minutes

Eric Stanton (Dana Andrews), a down-on-his-luck press agent, drifts into Walton, a small coastal town in Northern California. Shortly after stepping off the bus he meets an assortment of characters in "Pop's Eats," including the diner's beautiful waitress, Stella. In exchange for a room for the night, Stanton agrees to help promote the visiting mentalist Professor Madley and his companion Joe Ellis. Becoming a regular in the diner, Stanton falls in love with Stella, but she refuses to take him seriously due to his poor finances. From information gleaned from Madley, Stanton sets out to romance and marry the wealthy and respectable June Mills, with the intention of acquiring her money following a divorce so that he can marry Stella. Although June's sister Clara is skeptical of his intentions, Stanton and June get married, but things take a turn for the worse when Stella is murdered. Initially the main focus of retired cop-turned-detective Mark Judd's investigation is Stella's ex-boyfriend, the slick Dave Atkins, but soon the cloud of suspicion falls on Stanton. He flees to San Francisco with June, who still loves him even though she is aware of his dishonest plans. While trying to prove his innocence, Stanton eventually reciprocates these feelings of love, and he and June return to town and prove that the murderer is actually Judd, who was secretly obsessed with Stella.

Taglines: "The creator of *Laura* does it again!"; "The Screen's Most Gripping Drama of Murder — and Desire."

With the film's opening credits jumping out in the form of roadside signs as the Greyhound bus rumbles along the highway at night, you immediately know that a journey into noir territory beckons. And as the bus abruptly stops on the outskirts of town, we are introduced to noir's archetypal character, sleeping passenger Eric Stanton, a loner with a past, looking for a future. His make-believe slumber is disturbed by the hostile bus driver "Hey you, come on, I've seen that sleeping act before. Your ticket ran out at the last stop." Unperturbed, Stanton nonchalantly responds, "How much to San Francisco?" Down to his last dollar and short of the fare, he steps off the bus into a strange town, and so our tale begins.

Fallen Angel was a follow-up to director Otto Preminger's hugely successful *Laura* the year before and although the film is not as chic or moody as *Laura*, time has lent it some endearing qualities of its own. However, these qualities were not enough to convince a doubting Andrews, who reluctantly took on the role of the itinerant Stanton. In an interview, he voiced his dislike for the vagrant nature of his character: "Mr. Preminger more or less forced me into this picture which sort of put Alice Faye out of business."[1]

Even though Andrews's relationship with Preminger was as close as any actor could get with a director, he did feel that after the success of *Laura* the director was responsible for putting him into two films which he didn't want to do, *Daisy Kenyon* and *Fallen Angel*. At first he turned down the part of Stanton, which he considered "in bad taste" and "unbelievable," and acceded only following much persuasion from Preminger and the threat of a studio suspension.[2]

Despite Andrews's reluctance to accept the role, Preminger described the actor as "a director's delight. He always knows his lines, arrives on time, and knows what he wants to do with a part."

Following a successful career in musicals including *Weekend in Havana* (1941), and *Hello, Frisco, Hello* (1943), Alice Faye focused her sights on playing more dramatic roles and rejected almost three dozen scripts before accepting the lead in *Fallen Angel*. However, she was less than

Drifter Eric Stanton (Andrews) eavesdrops on Stella (Linda Darnell) and Pop (Percy Kilbride) in director Otto Preminger's *Fallen Angel* (20th Century–Fox, 1945).

satisfied with the outcome of the film, claiming that the strength of her character was weakened by Darryl Zanuck and Preminger, in favor of the part played by Linda Darnell. Incensed with the editing, she retired on the spot. During filming, Andrews recalled an upbeat Faye enthusing, "This is going to be great. It's terrific," but when she saw the completed film, he remembered her stating, "I'll never do another picture."[3] And indeed she didn't for another 16 years, returning to the screen as Pat Boone's mother in the 1962 remake of *State Fair.* In truth, it could be argued that Faye's movie career really ended in 1945 when Betty Grable replaced her as Hollywood's favorite musical-comedy actress.

Andrews very much sympathized with Faye's predicament, particularly when he learned that having seen his performance in *Laura,* she told the studio that she would only accept the role in *Fallen Angel* on condition that he was included in the cast.[4] Interestingly, Zanuck initially considered borrowing Olivia de Havilland from

Warners to play June Mills, a role to which she would have been eminently suited (and perhaps we could have had her regular screen partner Errol Flynn as a swashbuckling noir womanizing drifter, with not so much a chip on his shoulder, but more of a mischievous glint in his eye).

Groomed by Fox as a lightweight sex symbol, Linda Darnell was a piece of inspired casting as the smoldering Stella in *Fallen Angel.* This was acknowledged by Andrews when he claimed, "Linda Darnell was the best thing in the picture. The scene I had with her was at least showy." Darnell played the tramp with such gusto there was even talk of her receiving an Academy Award nomination.[5] To help get into character, Darnell worked as a waitress in the Fox coffee shop for a week.[6] One of Hollywood's most popular stars of the 1940s, her career went into rapid decline in the early '50s when Fox ended her contract, and tragically she died in a house fire in 1965 at the age of 41.

Greatly enriching its hard-boiled noir creden-

Stanton (Andrews) grabs a coffee in Pop's Diner while sultry waitress Stella (Linda Darnell), unexpectedly returning from a night out and feeling ravenous, bites into the hamburger he ordered from café owner Pop (Percy Kilbride, center) in *Fallen Angel* (20th Century–Fox, 1945).

tials, the film enjoys some robust supporting play from Charles Bickford, who skulks under his hat as the menacing police detective Mark Judd, Percy Kilbride as the likable Pop and Bruce Cabot as the traveling salesman who endures a brutal interrogation at the hands of Judd (Judd simply doesn't like his face). Also excellent are Anne Revere as June's knowing sister and John Carradine and Olin Howland as the traveling hypnotists. Like *Laura,* the film benefits from a lingering David Raksin theme song, "Slowly," a low, sultry love ballad which when played on the diner's jukebox for the umpteenth time prompts Andrews to ask Darnell, "Does that song play all day?" Bored to death, she rings up a sale on the cash register and, without even looking at him, snaps back, "I like it!" (Classic noir!) Alice Faye did a rendition of the song, which was dropped from the film. (Burning the midnight oil, Zanuck didn't just tinker with the editing — he wiped out entire scenes.)

David Raksin was full of praise for Andrews, describing him as "a man's man, a great guy really and so easy to work with. At Fox he was one of Otto's favorites."[7]

Such praise was not undeserved, with Andrews delivering another forthright performance, making it look so terribly easy. With his deadpan, quizzical expression, he makes the most of his lines, which were exquisitely penned by Harry Kleiner, one of Preminger's Yale Drama School students.

Living off his wits, Andrews's Eric Stanton is constantly searching for an angle to pay for his next meal or bed for the night. When phony hypnotist Professor Madley hits town, Stanton makes out that he knew him from the good old days to gain the confidence of Madley's front man, Joe Ellis. When Ellis questions, "How old?" Stanton confidently replies, "Old enough to be good."

Stanton may be nobody's fool, but he's still a

sucker for a pretty face, and he is willing to take it on the chin when a ravenous Stella heartily tucks into his main meal of the day. Unperturbed, he glibly comments, "That's the best hamburger I never ate." Wildly infatuated with the beautiful waitress, he nonetheless reserves his best line in flattery for his next hit, the lonely June Mills. Working his way into her affections in order to get his hands on her money, he compliments her organ playing, claiming that Beethoven never sounded so good. When she informs him that it was Brahms, he swiftly changes his pitch: "Why, sure it was Brahms. The old boys do sound alike don't they?"

On the surface, Stanton initially comes over as a shallow opportunist, but we soon come to appreciate that, as with most of Andrews's characters, there are more facets to him. At heart he is a well-meaning guy who has turned bitter and cynical after losing half of his public relations business in a rigged poker game. With his natural ambiguity, Andrews's portrayal of his multilayered character is both stark and suitably morose. One critic wrote, "Andrews remains one of the better young dramatic actors in this film, although his character is not always clearly defined in the writing."

Eric Stanton is perhaps Andrews's first real loner, a man with a grievance who occasionally erupts into self-pity, particularly in the scene with June where he bares his sole, describing himself as a washout at 30: "I got everywhere talking fast in a world that goes for fast talking — and ended up with exactly nothing."

Andrews went on to play a public relations man in two of his later films, *The Fearmakers*, where again he loses his business as the result of foul play, and *Madison Avenue*, where he finally hits the big time with his fast line in talk.

Fallen Angel is notable for Joseph LaShelle's excellent camerawork, which skillfully showcases the characters and the sharp contrasts between the two ends of the coastal town — from the seedy diner and rundown hotels to the respectable suburban houses. Every scene simply drips with atmosphere, and the ending, when the real murderer is revealed, is a real knockout.

Filming started on May 1, 1945, and ended on June 26, on a budget of $1,055,136. As well as taking the lead, Andrews also narrated the film's trailer.

Time magazine commented, "If you go for

Andrews and Linda Darnell in a publicity shot from *Fallen Angel* (20th Century–Fox, 1945).

whodunits, a hard-boiled one with fancy trimmings, you can go for this; and you'll get your money's worth." The *New York Times* noted, "As the frustrated adventurer, Dana Andrews adds another excellent tightlipped portrait to a growing gallery."

As to the film's title — well, I'm still trying to figure that one out. On face value, one would assume we are talking about Stella, but it is clear that at no stage in her life was she ever an angel. The same could also be said of Eric Stanton and Mark Judd, so I guess it's open to your own interpretation. Or am I just too plain dumb to see it?

Canyon Passage
Universal, 1946

Cast: Dana Andrews (Logan Stuart); Brian Donlevy (George Camrose); Susan Hayward (Lucy Overmire); Patricia Roc (Caroline Marsh); Ward Bond (Honey Bragg); Hoagy Carmichael (Hi Linnet); Fay Holden (Mrs. Overmire); Stanley Ridges (Jonas Overmire); Lloyd Bridges (Johnny Steele); Andy Devine (Ben Dance); Victor Cutler (Vane Blazier); Rose Hobart (Marta Lestrade); Halliwell Hobbes (Clenchfield); James Cardwell (Gray Bartlett); Onslow

Stevens (Jack Lestrade); Tad Devine (Asa Dance); Denny Devine (Bushrod Dance); Erville Alderson (Judge); Richard Alexander, Jack Clifford, Karl Hackett, Daral Hudson, Joe Mack, Gene Roth (Miners); Harlan Briggs, Eddie Dunn, Jack Ingram, Peter Whitney (Men); Chester Clute (Portland Storekeeper); Frank Ferguson (Preacher); Sherry Hall (Clerk); Willy Kaufman, Rex Lease (Card Players); Francis McDonald (Cobb); Virginia Patton (Liza Stone); Dorothy Peterson (Mrs. Dance); Ralph Peters (Harry Stutchell); Jack Rockwell (Teamster); Wallace Scott (Mack McIver); Harry Shannon (McLane); Jay Silverheels (Indian); Ray Teal (Neal Howison); Chief Yowlachie (Indian Spokesman); Janet Ann Gallow, Ann Burr, Mary Newton (Girls).

Credits: Walter Wanger (Producer); Alexander Golitzen (Associate Producer); Jacques Tourneur (Director); Ernest Haycox (Story); Ernest Pascal (Screenplay); Edward Cronjager (Cinematography); Frank Skinner (Music Direction); John B. Goodman, Richard H. Riedel (Art Direction); Russell A. Gausman, Leigh Smith (Set Decorations); Travis Banton (Costume Design); Jack P. Pierce (Makeup); Fred Frank (Assistant Director); Bernard B. Brown (Sound); Milton Carruth (Editor). Running time: 92 minutes

In 1856, Logan Stuart, an ambitious general store and freight owner, escorts his friend's fiancée, Lucy Overmore, from Portland to the mining settlement of Jacksonville, Oregon. During the journey Logan falls in love with Lucy and then avoids her out of loyalty to his friend, George Camrose, a local banker with a weakness for gambling. Taking his mind off Lucy, Logan courts Caroline Marsh, a daughter of an Englishman killed by Indians, who lives with homesteaders Mr. and Mrs. Dance. To feed his gambling addiction, Camrose steals from the miners' gold deposits entrusted to him and ends up killing one of them. Johnny Steel, a friend of the dead miner, rouses the locals to hang Camrose on the spot, but Logan convinces them to give him a trial. Proceedings are put on hold when Logan's enemy, the brutish Honey Bragg, incites an Indian uprising by killing a young Indian girl. Logan rallies the community to defend the settlement and in the ensuing battle Camrose is killed and Logan's store is burned to the ground. Realizing that she could never be happy with the restless Logan, Caroline releases him from any commitments, and he and Lucy are at last free to pursue their love for each other.

Producer Walter Wanger arrived in Hollywood after serving as an Army Intelligence Officer during World War I. In a varied career

working for the studios and as an independent, his many notable productions include *The Trail of the Lonesome Pine* (1936), *Stagecoach* (1939), *Scarlet Street* (1945) and the leviathan that bankrupted Fox studios, *Cleopatra* (1963). In 1951, he received some unwanted publicity and a short prison sentence when he shot the agent of actress-wife Joan Bennett in the groin after suspecting them of having an affair.

With a big budget at his disposal, Wanger was determined to top his previous Western classic *Stagecoach*, which was also by the same author, Ernest Haycox. Many of the directors he initially considered for the assignment (George Marshall among them) were unavailable, which provided Jacques Tourneur with a great opportunity to broaden his directorial experience.

Having built his reputation with low-budget horror films (*Cat People* [1942] and *I Married a Zombie* [1943]) Tourneur got to make his first Western (and his first film in color). With its richly assorted cast of characters, the film cleverly portrays almost every aspect of realistic life in the Old West, embracing adventurous pioneers, hostile Indians and a colorful array of villains.

With five westerns under his belt at this stage, Andrews was certainly no stranger to the genre, but *Canyon Passage* was notable for being his first western outing as a leading man. The film was also the first of three he made with Tourneur (*The Fearmakers* and *Night of the Demon* being the other two), and through their shared passion for sailing they became good friends.

Andrews was not the first actor considered for the role of young entrepreneur Logan Stuart, as the part was initially earmarked for Susan Hayward's husband Jess Barker. Feeling confident that the part was his following a test , Barker convinced Tourneur to offer a reluctant Susan the part of the leading lady, Lucy. However, this was not destined to become a family affair for the Barkers because before production got underway Wanger had decided on Andrews for the male lead instead of Jess.[1]

But there was no change of heart where Susan Hayward was concerned, with Wanger clearly recognizing her great star potential which to date had been generally overlooked by Hollywood. Starting out as a photographic model in New York, Hayward came to Hollywood to test for the Scarlet O'Hara role in 1937. When she signed a seven-year contract with Wanger, she had yet to develop the mannerisms that would later become her trademark; they gave her *Canyon Passage* performance an unstudied and natural quality that perfectly complemented Andrews's understated style of acting. By the time the pair starred together again in *My Foolish Heart* (1949) the distinctive Hayward voice, walk and hand gestures were more developed and the contrast between their two styles became more marked. Susan displayed these mannerisms to full effect in two of her most memorable films, where coincidently, in common with *My Foolish Heart*, each of the characters she plays suffer from a drinking problem: *Smash Up: The Story of a Woman* (1947) and *I'll Cry Tomorrow* (1955).

The other love interest in *Canyon Passage* was played by vivacious English actress Patricia Roc. Described by J. Arthur Rank as "the archetypal British beauty" and the "Goddess of Odeons," Roc was the first homegrown British star to go to Hollywood under a lend-lease deal between Rank Pictures and Universal Studios. Her debut performance in *Canyon Passage* prompted co-star Hayward to comment, "That Limey glamour girl is a helluva dame." During filming Roc was romantically linked to aspiring actor Ronald Reagan. However, despite a promising start in *Canyon Passage*, she failed to click with American audiences, which led to her return to England shortly afterwards. Back on home turf, she went on to star in some of her most notable films including *Jassy* and *The Brothers*, both made in 1947.

The pedigree cast also included the rugged-looking, mustachioed Brian Donlevy in the role of Logan's friend George. Donlevy's early life was just as colorful as any of the roles he played in films: He served with the U.S. Expeditionary Force, which was sent out to pursue Pancho Villa, before joining the Lafayette Escadrile as a pilot during World War I. Despite a drinking problem his performances remained top drawer including *The Great McGinty* (1940) and his Oscar-nominated role as the sadistic sergeant in *Beau Geste* (1939). *Stagecoach* supporting star Andy Devine also appeared in the film with his two sons Tad and Dennis.

Canyon Passage was shot on location in and around Diamond Lake and Medford, Oregon, in August 1945 and was one of the few Tourneur films to use a second unit. Although Edward

Cronjager's photography is of the highest order, one of the major concerns Wanger had about the production was Tourneur's tendency to shoot medium and long exterior shots, seemingly paying little regard to close-ups. In an anxious telegram, Wanger sent a clear instruction that the scene between Andrews and the brutish villain, played by Ward Bond, outside Dance's cabin should be shot in close-up. "Andrews should be really angry in this close-up.... Explain to Tourneur that in color you have to use more close-ups than in black and white, as characters fade into background with scenery and story points lost because we cannot see facial expressions and eyes."[2] For a minimalist actor like Andrews, who tended to convey a great deal of expression through his eye movements, this advice would have clearly helped to show off, to best advantage, his excellent performance in the film.

Pipe in hand and at complete ease with the world, this is Andrews in Walter Pidgeon mode. Although he is clearly a restless man, Logan is nonetheless a solid member of the community with the strength of character to rise above the type of "life's challenges" (such as moral dilemma, fear and disillusionment) which usually plagued Andrews's characters. In his personal life, he is quite happy to conceal his true feelings for Lucy and allow his friend George first refusal on the marriage front. This relaxed attitude also permeates into his business life, when he lends George $2000 without batting an eyelid. If his business failed, he would simply "get a new deck and deal again." Need a strong pair of hands to help you raise a cabin? Logan's your man. And if the brutish Honey Bragg steps out of line, Logan's just the man to stand up to him.

> HONEY BRAGG: What do you have against me?
>
> LOGAN STUART: You ought to know.
>
> HONEY BRAGG: You're talking in riddles, Logan. What's in your mind ?
>
> LOGAN STUART: A picture of a tree — with you swingin' from it.

Three Hoagy Carmichael compositions were featured in the film: "Rogue River Valley," "I'm Getting Married in the Morning" and "Ole Buttermilk Sky."

Interestingly, after composing "Ole Buttermilk Sky," Carmichael thought the song too corny and didn't want to include it in the film. However, Wanger insisted on its inclusion

A man you can depend on, freight owner Logan Stuart (Andrews), delivers Lucy Overmire (Susan Hayward) to her fiancé and his best friend, scheming gambler George Camrose (Brian Donlevy), in Andrews's first of three films for sailing buddy-director Jacques Tourneur, *Canyon Passage* (Universal, 1946).

and the song went on to pick up an Academy Award nomination, losing out to "On the Atchison, Topeka, and the Sante Fe" which featured in the Judy Garland musical *The Harvey Girls.*

In addition to the Carmichael compositions and the excellent photography, the film benefited from an atmospheric score by Frank Skinner, which emotively conveyed the expanse and hardships of the Oregon frontier. At a cost of $2.3 million, *Canyon Passage* was Walter Wanger's most successful postwar film both financially and aesthetically.

Time noted, "Unlike bridge, alcohol, the ponies and popular forms of escape, this brilliantly engineered movie is non–habit-forming and has no nagging after effects. *Canyon Passage* has all this and more — plus better-than-average dialogue and competent players...." The *New York Times* particularly enjoyed the bout of

fisticuffs between Andrews and Ward Bond, commenting, "It is customary for the hero in such films to mix it up for the sake of his honor with a bruiser almost twice his size, and the slaughter involving Dana Andrews and Ward Bond is really something to behold. ...[This is] a whopping Western show, with a lot of good old-fashioned thrills."

Modern-day critics have gone even further in their praise of Andrews's performance, with Brian Garfield in *Western Films — A Complete Guide* commenting that Andrews's part in the film as the steady-nerved, pipe-smoking Stuart may be the best of his career.[3] This opinion was shared by Chris Fujiwara in his book on the work of Jacques Tourneur: "Dana Andrews ... gives one of the best performances of his career: Andrews's precise minimalism proves ideal for Tourneur, as it also did for Preminger."[4]

The Best Years of Our Lives

RKO, 1946

Cast: Myrna Loy (Milly Stephenson); Fredric March (Al Stephenson); Dana Andrews (Fred Derry); Teresa Wright (Peggy Stephenson); Virginia Mayo (Marie Derry); Harold Russell (Homer Parrish); Cathy O'Donnell (Wilma Cameron); Hoagy Carmichael (Butch Engle); Gladys George (Hortense Derry); Roman Bohnen (Pat Derry); Ray Collins (Mr. Milton); Minna Gombell (Mrs. Parrish); Walter Baldwin (Mr. Parrish); Steve Cochran (Cliff Scully); Dorothy Adams (Mrs. Cameron); Don Beddoe (Mr. Cameron); Victor Cutler (Woody Merrill); Marlene Aames (Luella Parrish); Charles Halton (Mr. Prew); Ray Teal (Mr. Mollett); Dean White (Mr. Novak); Erskine Sanford (Mr. Bullard); Michael Hall (Rob Stephenson); Howland Chamberlin (Mr. Thorpe); Norman Phillips (Merkle); Teddy Infuhr (Dexter, Brat in Drugstore); Ralph Sanford (George Gibbons); Bert Conway (ATC Sergeant); Blake Edwards (Corporal); Jack Rice (Desk Clerk); Harry Cheshire (Minister); Ben Erway (Latham); Clancy Cooper (Taxi Driver); Mary Arden (Miss Barbour); James Ames (Jackie); Claire Du Brey (Mrs. Talburt); Ruth Sanderson (Mrs. Garrett); Al Bridge (Gus, Salvage Superintendent); Donald Kerr (Steve the Bartender); Joyce Compton (Hat Check Girl); Pat Flaherty (Salvage Foreman); Tennessee Ernie Ford (Night Club Hillbilly Singer); Ray Hyke (Gus the Foreman); Chef Milani (Giuseppe); Caleb Peterson (Black Soldier at Airfield); Jan Wylie (Saleswoman); Tom Dugan (Doorman), Mady Correll (Announcer); Mickey Roth (Boy at Soda Fountain); Ernesto Morelli, Stephen Soldi, Joe Palma (Card Players); Roy Darmour (Parking Lot Attendant).

Credits: Samuel Goldwyn (Producer); William Wyler (Director); MacKinlay Kantor (Novel — "Glory for Me"); Robert E. Sherwood (Screenplay); Gregg Toland (Cinematography); Hugo Friedhofer (Music); Sidney Arodin, Hoagy Carmichael (Song); Emil Newman (Music Direction); Perry Ferguson, George Jenkins (Art Direction); Julia Heron (Set Decorations); Irene Sharaff (Costume Design); Robert Stehanoff (Makeup); Joseph Boyle (Assistant Director); Richard De Weese (Sound); Daniel Mandell (Editor). Running time: 172 minutes

At the end of World War II, three veterans flying home to Boone City get acquainted and share their anxieties about how they will readjust to civilian life. Reunions with loved ones prove awkward as each of them tries to adapt to the lost years. Sergeant Al Stephenson returns to his wife Milly and teenage children, Peggy and Rob, and discovers that although their mutual love has not changed, attitudes have. His frustration increases when he returns to his old job at the bank and tries to persuade his risk-averse bosses to provide non-collateral loans to ex–GIs. Captain Fred Derry (Dana Andrews), a decorated bomber pilot, returns to find that his wartime achievements mean nothing in civilian life and that his glamorous but gaudy wife, Marie, whom he married only weeks before departure, has become a stranger to him. When he takes up his old job as a soda jerk, she becomes bitter at his inability to advance himself; to escape her dreary world, she takes up with other men. Sailor Homer Parrish, lost both hands in a torpedo blaze and has been fitted with hooks; he has learned to live with it but his over-caring family finds it hard adjusting to his disability and he begins to fear that his girl, Cathy, no longer loves him, but feels only pity. During a night on the town with his family, Al gets drunk, and his daughter Peggy finds love for the first time when she meets Fred — a feeling he reciprocates. As the protective father, Al attempts to break them up because he doesn't want his daughter hurt through involvement with a married man. Meanwhile, back in the Parrish household, Homer eventually realizes that Cathy's feelings of love are genuine and the two decide to get married. By the time of Homer's wedding, Al has happily settled back into the comforts of his old lifestyle and is more receptive to Peggy's relationship with Fred when he learns that Fred has arranged to divorce his wife.

Taglines: "THE SCREEN'S GREATEST LOVE STORY IS THE BEST FILM THIS YEAR FROM HOLLYWOOD!"; "Samuel Goldwyn's greatest production"; "Three wonderful loves in the best picture of the year!"; "Filled with all the love and warmth and joy ... the human heart can hold!"

The pinnacle in Samuel Goldwyn's career, *The Best Years of Our Lives*, was inspired by an article his wife Francis read in the August 1944 issue of *Time* magazine, concerning the problems that awaited veterans in their readjustment to the routine and tensions of civilian life. Goldwyn recognized that the story would make a good movie and assigned screenwriter MacKinlay Kantor to write the screenplay, which culminated in *Glory for Me*, a novel of blank verse about three returning soldiers. Goldwyn initially thought the novel too difficult to film and the idea would have been abandoned were it not for reassurances from director William Wyler and screenwriter Robert Sherwood (who reworked

The pinnacle of Andrews's career, the multi–Oscar winning *The Best Years of Our Lives* (RKO, 1946), with Andrews's traumatized airman Fred Derry (center) sharing a homecoming "night out on the town" with Homer (Harold Russell), Peggy Stephenson (Teresa Wright), Milly Stephenson (Myrna Loy), Butch Engle (Hoagy Carmichael, standing) and Al Stephenson (Fredric March).

Kantor's novel) that the story had great potential.

The film's title can be interpreted in two ways: Either servicemen had the best years of their lives in wartime or they lost their best years through being on active service. Of the three returning servicemen, it is perhaps Andrews's character, Fred Derry, who is open to both. The war gave him respect and made him a hero, but it also robbed him of his youth and an opportunity to rise above his previous job as a soda jerk.

One of the major problems Sherwood encountered in writing the screenplay was how to strengthen the storyline associated with Andrews's character. In Kantor's novel, Fred's marriage to wife Marie is over too quickly when he discovers her infidelity. In the reworked screenplay, he is unaware of his wife's affair until later in the film, which presents him with the moral dilemma of whether he should leave her for the

new love in his life, Peggy Stephenson. Sherwood also experienced difficulties with the character of Homer, the disabled veteran. Kantor's Homer was disabled by spastic paralysis, but both Wyler and Sherwood felt that the role would be better suited to an amputee. They visited the Veterans' Hospital in Pasadena where they discovered real amputee Harold Russell, who was perfect for the part. Russell was an Army sergeant who had lost his hands during a training exercise in North Carolina when some dynamite exploded without warning.

The role of Homer had originally been earmarked for a professional actor, with Farley Granger at the top of the list. Goldwyn also had set his sights initially on Fred MacMurray and Olivia de Havilland to play Peggy's parents, Al and Milly, but they felt that the parts were insubstantial (MacMurray remarked that he thought they were "third banana"[1]). Fredric

March was a versatile actor who had won an Oscar for *Dr. Jekyll and Mr. Hyde* (1931), but his days as a leading man were behind him and he readily accepted the part of Al. Fondly remembered for the *Thin Man* series, Myrna Loy had an acting pedigree which equaled that of March, but she required a little more coaxing from Goldwyn to play the part of Milly (apparently she had heard that Wyler could be a bit of a bully). Even though her part was not the largest, she still received top billing. The rest of the roles went to Goldwyn's stable of contract players including Andrews, Virginia Mayo and Teresa Wright. To round things off, the inspired cast included that welcome addition to any movie, the inimitable Hoagy Carmichael, who, as usual, played himself.

In a 1977 interview, Andrews recalled that Wyler originally didn't want him for *The Best Years of Our Lives*. The director had seen none of Andrews's subsequent work since he played a small part in the director's *The Westerner* in 1939. (As the actor explained, during this intervening period, Wyler had been in England serving with the 8th Air Force.) Andrews described their encounter on the first day, when Wyler called him over after shooting a scene and asked him, "What happened to you? You're a very good actor!" In response, Andrews laughed and countered that having made many pictures since they last worked together, he'd be a pretty stupid actor if he hadn't improved.[2]

When the script was finally completed, Goldwyn still had concerns that with the war over, audiences would not take to the grim subject matter and would perhaps prefer something more glamorous such as a musical. However, his fears were overcome when the Audience Research Institute reported that the public were very much interested in the plight of returning war veterans.

Completed in four months (from April 15 to August 9, 1946) at a cost of $2.1 million, the film was shot in black and white to give it a sense of realism. To add to this feel, Wyler also got the actors to wear department store clothes, which they were asked to wear for a few weeks before filming began.[4]

In a later interview, Andrews commented upon Wyler's meticulous attention to detail in the drug store scene, where Fred is trying to sell a bottle of perfume, and as part of the sale a series of decreasing-in-size perfume boxes are displayed: "Mr. Wyler stopped production for three hours to get a new box made. He had to have one made. He had a guy searching and also had the property man making one, and they finally came up with one that was satisfactory to him. There were 200 extras sitting around. This must have cost $5,000. But he didn't want it without that little touch. That is just indicative of the care with which he directs."[5]

Wyler's drive for perfection was also evidenced in a simple scene which called for Andrews to emerge from the back seat of a car. Upon exiting, Andrews accidentally bumped his head, which so enthralled Wyler due to its naturalness, he asked Andrews to repeat it about 20 times to get it perfect. As fellow star Teresa Wright described it, "He just kept hitting his head harder and harder, I just cringed.... What is so strange is that it was such a contradiction of the Willy I knew. He was not the milk of human kindness, but he was always so much fun to be around. And he loved Dana. He had the best rapport with him, Freddie and Myrna that I have ever seen."[6]

To this day, the scene in the film which has the most impact is the airplane graveyard scene, where Andrews sits in the cockpit of a partly dismantled Flying Fortress and mentally relives his days as an Air Force bombardier. Andrews's anguished look, as the trauma of his wartime experience overwhelms him, dramatically captures the moment and leaves you in no doubt that here was a an actor of great depth and range at the peak of his profession. (It was a brutal injustice that his performance wasn't rewarded with an Oscar, or at the very least a nomination.)

Andrews had this to say of the symbolic scene and the film as a whole when he viewed it for the first time on opening night at the Astor in New York on November 22, 1946: "The scene where Fred Derry is looking at all those old planes—I thought that was a waste of film, just Wyler indulging himself in nostalgia for the 8th Air Force. I thought it would wind up on the cutting room floor. It turned out to be one of the most impressive scenes in the picture! Here's this guy, he's leaving town, and here are the remnants of what were the best years of his life—a graveyard of planes. A very strong point in the picture." To show his appreciation, Andrews walked up to Goldwyn after the film and heartily

Fred Derry (Andrews) and Peggy Stephenson (Teresa Wright) discover that true love can happen at first sight in Goldwyn's "crowning glory" *The Best Years of Our Lives* (RKO, 1946).

congratulated him "Sam, that was really wonderful!" To which Goldwyn responded, "I'm glad to do it for you."[7]

Andrews had several other memorable scenes, including a touching reunion with his wrong-side-of-the-tracks folks; a moving nightmare piece where he is haunted by his combat memories; and a brilliant scene in Butch's bar where Al tells Fred that he wants him to stop seeing his daughter. Once again Andrews's facial expressions speak volumes when he reluctantly agrees to this request. The moment is further heightened by the ingenious use of the deep focus lens of cinematographer Gregg Toland, which places Fred in the top-left corner of the frame when he goes to telephone Peggy to tell her it's over, with Al, Homer and Butch sitting at the piano playing "Chopsticks" in the right-hand foreground. Although the camera's eye was on Al, the audience could clearly understand Fred's conversation with Peggy without hearing a single word of it.

In addition to the film's excellent photography, the 24-carat script is particularly memorable, providing Andrews with some of the best lines in his career. We kick off with an early conversation with Peggy when he informs her of his pre-war occupation. After the initial shock of learning he was a soda jerk, she says, "I betcha mixed up a fine ice cream soda," to which Fred responds, "You're darn right. I was an expert behind that fountain. I used to toss a scoop of ice cream in the air, adjust for wind drift, velocity, altitude. Then, *wham*, in the cone every time. I figured that's where I really learned to drop bombs."

After the trauma of his wartime experiences, Fred is clearly at ease with the understanding Peggy, but to his trashy wife, whom he hastily married during training, he is a complete stranger. We observe the fragile nature of their relationship when Fred reminds her of their "for better or worse" marriage vows. When Marie asks when she can expect to see the better times, he replies, "Whenever I get wise to myself, I guess. Whenever I wake up and realize I'm not an officer and a gentleman any more. I'm just another soda jerk out of a job."

Clearly a resourceful man, Fred eventually finds work as a junkman in the aircraft grave-yard, but not before the foreman gives him his earnest views on flyboys:

> FOREMAN: I see. One of the fallen angels of the Air Force. Well, pardon me if I show no sympathy. While you glamour boys were up in the wild blue yonder, I was down in a tank.
>
> FRED: Listen, chum. Some time I'd be glad to hear the story of your war experiences. What I asked you for is a job. You got one?

In one of the film's most touching scenes, we get a clear understanding of Fred's heroism when his father reads to his wife their son's dis-tinguished medal citation: a Distinguished Fly-ing Cross for valor and heroism in the skies over Germany, when wounded and with complete disregard for his own safety he guided his forma-tion on a perfect run over the target.

Possessing a natural, understated acting style similar to Andrews's, Teresa Wright was the ideal candidate to play his love interest Peggy. In the role she is not only understanding, intelligent and vivacious, but also amusing. When Fred mentions that she doesn't seem like Al's daugh-ter, she idly quips, "Actually, I'm not. He's my son by a previous marriage."

Wright has the distinction of being the only actor to be nominated for an Oscar for her first three films—*The Little Foxes* (1941), *The Pride of the Yankees* (1942), and *Mrs. Miniver* (1942). However, weary of the lack of privacy and tired of being traded like cattle by producers, she re-belled against the studio system and as a conse-quence her film career went into decline after *The Best Years of Our Lives.*

In the role of Fred's avaricious, flighty wife Marie, glamorous blonde Virginia Mayo was also a casting success. Once described by the sul-tan of Morocco as "tangible proof for the exis-tence of God," Mayo starred alongside the likes of Danny Kaye and Bob Hope in a number of '40s comedies and musicals, before turning her hand to westerns and adventure films in the 1950s and '60s. She was also capable of taking on straight dramatic roles, which she proved to much acclaim in *The Best Years of Our Lives* and as James Cagney's scheming wife Verna in *White Heat* (1949).

In addition to expert direction, innovative camerawork and top-notch acting, *Best Years* also benefited from an excellent score by Hugo Freidhofer. But Goldwyn was concerned that the three-hour film might be too long for audiences. When it premiered in October 1946, all thoughts of cutting it were dismissed when the audience reaction was fantastic. The film was a success worldwide, grossing ten million dollars in its first year of release, making it the second biggest financial hit to date in talking movie history (*Gone with the Wind* held first place).

Its huge popularity was further evidenced when it picked up nine Academy Awards: Best Picture, March for Best Actor, Russell for Best Supporting Actor, Wyler for Best Director, Sher-wood for Best Screenplay, Friedhofer for Best Scoring, Daniel Mandell for Best Editing, the Irving Thalberg trophy (awarded to Goldwyn "for the producer whose creativity over the years reflects consistently high quality of motion pic-ture production") and a Special Award for Rus-sell "for bringing hope and courage to his fel-low veterans through his appearance in *The Best Years of Our Lives.*" Although Andrews delivered a totally sincere performance in a difficult role, his underplaying was taken for granted and his vital contribution to the success of the film was completely overlooked by the Academy Award fraternity. Justly outraged by this oversight, someone, back in 1946 put an advertisement in *Variety* saying, "I would surely like you to watch *The Best Years of Our Lives* one more time and tell me what Dana Andrews has to do to win an Academy Award."[8]

Fully appreciating Andrews's intrinsic part in the film, the *New York Post* reviewer commented, "Caught in a role at once glamorous and trite, he, does his actor's job, as always, with integrity and intelligence." *Variety* called the film "one of the best pictures of our lives" and *Newsweek* de-scribed it as "epic art."

To help publicize the film, Goldwyn agreed to appear on Bob Hope's radio show, and a few days before going on air, he asked one of his writers what he should say. The writer replied, "You have Hope say to you, 'Well, Mr. Goldwyn, how have things been going since I left your stu-dio?' And you reply, 'I'll tell you, Bob—since you left, we've had the Best Years of Our Lives.'" On the night and as rehearsed, Hope fed him his line, "Well, Mr. Goldwyn, how have things been going since I left your studio?" Forgetting his script, Goldwyn replied, "Since you left, things are better than ever." The audience looked confused and Hope doubled over with laughter.[9] (Goldwyn's mispronunciations and misuse of the English language were legendary.)

Boomerang!
20th Century–Fox, 1947

Cast: Dana Andrews (Henry L. Harvey); Jane Wyatt (Mrs. Harvey); Lee J. Cobb (Chief Harold F. Robinson); Cara Williams (Irene Nelson); Arthur Kennedy (John Waldron); Sam Levene (Dave Woods); Taylor Holmes (T.M. Wade); Robert Keith (Mac McCreery); Ed Begley (Paul Harris); Karl Malden (Det. Lt. White); Barry Kelley (Desk Sgt. Dugan); Lewis Leverett (Whitney); Philip Coolidge (Crossman); Lester Lonergan (Carey); Wyrley Birch (Father George A. Lambert); E.J. Ballantine (McDonald); Royal Beal (Johnson); Helen Carew (Annie); John Carmody (Thomas Callahan); William Challee (Stone); Clay Clement (Judge Tate); Isabel Cooper (Church Choir Member); Jimmy Dobson (Bill); Bert Freed (Herron); Richard Garrick (Graham Rogers); Walter Greaza (Mayor Swayze); Helene Hatch (Catherine Manion); Bern Hoffman (Tom); Joe Kazan (Paul Lukash); Ben Lackland (Commissioner James); Ida McGuire (Miss Roberts); Lawrence Paguin (Sheriff); George Petrie (Harry O'Shea); Leona Roberts (Mrs. Crossman); Anthony Ross (Warren); Dudley Sadler (Dr. Rainsford); Lucia Backus Seger (Mrs. Lulash); John Stearns (the Rev. Gardiner); Edgar Stehli (Ryan the Coroner); Fred Stewart (Graham); Guy Thomajan (Ronolo Cartucci).

Credits: Darryl F. Zanuck (Executive Producer); Louis de Rochemont (Producer); Elia Kazan (Director); Fulton Oursler [using the nom de plume Anthony Abbot] (Magazine Article); Richard Murphy (Screenplay); Norbert Brodine (Cinematography); David Buttolph (Music); Alfred Newman (Music Direction); Richard Day, Chester Gore (Art Direction); Thomas Little, Phil D'Esco (Set Decorations); Kay Nelson (Costume Design); Ben Nye (Makeup); Tom Dudley (Assistant Director); W.D. Flick, Roger Heman, Sr. (Sound); Harmon Jones (Editor). Running time: 88 minutes

Boomerang! is based on a true story about the unsolved murder of a priest in Bridgeport, Connecticut, in 1924. He was killed by a gun fired at close range. It was shot mostly on location in a semi-documentary style; the central character is state's attorney Henry L. Harvey (Dana Andrews), who is called upon to defend vagrant John Waldron, accused of killing a much-respected priest. Waldron vehemently denies the crime, but with the evidence stacked against him and a local community out for a quick conviction, nobody believes him except Harvey, who decides to probe deeper into the case. Putting his career and political ambitions at risk, he runs a gauntlet of pressures, exerted by the police, politicians and media, who are more interested in concluding the case than establishing the truth. After two days of police grilling, Waldron, exhausted and full of despair, gives a forced confession. Fortunately, Harvey remains resolute in his belief that the man is innocent and manages to discover evidence that clears him. The identity of the real culprit was never discovered.

Tagline: "It comes back at you again and again!"

Introductory narration: "Some wag once remarked that after New York it's all Connecticut...."

Wag humor aside, if ever a film put Connecticut firmly on the map, it was this gem from the hands of Elia Kazan, in which Andrews convincingly demonstrated that he was just as comfortable and equally effective delving into chicanery in small-town America as he was in the big city. And in Henry Harvey he found a peach of a role to convey a solid, upright, unflappable character with high ideals. Like his Fox colleague Henry Fonda, Andrews had a reassuring face and presence that inspired confidence, which made him the ideal choice to play the highly respected district attorney. Variations on this type of strong, intelligent, dependable and incorruptible character can be found in Andrews's Logan Stuart (*Canyon Passage*), Hod Stillwell (*Deep Waters*) and Father Roth (*Edge of Doom*).

The film was shot on location in Stamford, Connecticut, and White Plains, New York. (Officials for the actual scene of the crime, Bridgeport, had refused permission to shoot in its streets). Andrews and Kazan attended the film's premiere at the Palace Theatre in Stamford on March 5, 1947. It was Elia Kazan's third film, marking his return to America not as an actor but as a director. Producer Louis de Rochement had pioneered the use of reconstructions in documentary films through his *March of Time* series, and he developed this style to critical acclaim with semi-documentary features such as *The House on 92nd Street* (1945) and *13 Rue Madeleine* (1946). Very much in this vein,

Boomerang! used location shooting, night-for-night shots, an incisive Reed Hadley baritone voice-over, high-contrast cinematography and an extremely mobile camera to enhance realism and the urgency of the story. Kazan claimed in a 1947 newspaper interview that with the complete absence of studio shots, *Boomerang!* was the "Best film fun I've ever had."

If there were any doubts that Andrews was at the forefront of 20th Century–Fox's drive for realist dramas, this taut little drama clearly dismissed them. The film was based on Fulton Oursler's (under the name Anthony Abbot) *Reader's Digest* article "The Perfect Case," about the real unsolved murder in 1924 of Father George A. Lambert in Bridgeport, Connecticut. The story covers an early episode in the career of Homer Cummings, who as state's attorney becomes convinced he is about to prosecute an innocent man for murder. Homer went on to become Franklin Roosevelt's first attorney general.

Proudly representing this staunch defender of justice, Andrews is on top form in the terrific scene where Harvey illustrates his point that Waldron's gun couldn't have been used in the murder. Calm and collected, he bravely gets his assistant to fire the loaded gun into the back of his head while the courtroom audience looks on in stunned disbelief. Apologizing for the use of the theatrics, Harvey points out that there's a defect in the gun's firing pin, making it impossible to fire in this position. Also, the dull army finish of the gun conflicts with eyewitness accounts of a weapon that glistened at the scene of the crime. It is this vital inconsistency which prompts Harvey to unravel the case as he makes clear to the court: "Your honor, I submit that a gun specifically designed not to reflect sunlight could hardly glitter at night. It was the first inconsistency of testimony, your honor, which first struck me. I believe there are others."

To enhance the film's unique grip, Kazan combined non-actors (playing most of the minor roles) with Broadway actors, who at this stage had yet to make their mark on the silver screen: Arthur Kennedy, Lee J. Cobb, Ed Begley and Karl Malden.

Boomerang! was Arthur Kennedy's first film as a freelancer. Kennedy got his break when he was discovered by James Cagney and given his first film role as Cagney's brother in *City for Conquest* (1940). From then on, he carved a successful career playing good and bad guys in many classics including *Champion* (1949), *Bright Victory* (1951), and *Bend of the River* (1952). Kennedy shared the record with Claude Rains for four Best Supporting Actor Oscar nominations without a single win.

Lee J. Cobb gave his greatest performance on stage as Willy Loman in Arthur Miller's 1949 play *Death of a Salesman*. On screen, his tough, growly persona enhanced such films as *On the Waterfront* (1954) and *The Brothers Karamazov* (1958). Chief Robinson, a man who has little time for the shenanigans of politicians, was a role tailor-made for his gruff style and surly way with a line.

A native of Connecticut, Ed Begley was a natural for sweaty, aggressive and nervous types films like *12 Angry Men* (1957) and *Sweet Bird of Youth* (1962), for which he won an Academy Award for Best Supporting Actor. As *Boomerang!*'s corrupt Commissioner of Works Paul Harris, he certainly has enough reason to work up a sweat with his dodgy land deal dependent upon his party being elected, which will only happen if they secure a quick conviction for Waldron. His over-eagerness does not go unnoticed by Henry, who accusingly counters, "You're making a lot of fuss for a Commissioner of Works."

Henry's no-nonsense approach is summed up in another scene with Paul, when he threatens, "I've had a pretty trying day, Paul. I'm gonna give you just one minute to get out of here and then I'm going to throw you out."

Only two of the leading actors in *Boomerang!* were well-known by the movie going public, Andrews and Jane Wyatt. A diminutive beauty, Wyatt will always be remembered as Ronald Colman's love interest in *Lost Horizon* (1937) and as the wife of Robert Young in the television sitcom *Father Knows Best* (1954–1960). Strong performances were also delivered by Karl Malden, Sam Levene and Robert Keith (it seemed like no Andrews film was complete without Robert Keith appearing in support). A marvelous character, Keith, father of actor Brian Keith, is fondly remembered as the policeman in two very different Brando classics, *The Wild One* (1953) and *Guys and Dolls* (1955).

In *Boomerang!*, his character Mac McCreery helps us to identify with Henry's dilemma: McCreery asks the DA if he can prove his hunch that Waldron is innocent. Knowing that the odds are stacked against him, Henry confesses, "I don't know. I thought I had the case going perfectly straight and then all of a sudden it comes back and hits me right between the eyes. I just don't know." (It was at this point that the meaning behind the title hit *me* between the eyes; I have to admit, it had me 20th Century–Foxed for some time.)

The on-screen chemistry between Andrews and Jane Wyatt works a treat. They certainly look the ideal couple with their intimate little exchanges while cuddled in a chair. She even gets him to drink milk, quite a rarity in a Andrews movie. (Well, okay, he and Tyrone Power drank gallons of the white stuff while on shore leave in *Crash Dive*.)

In his autobiography, Karl Malden recalled Elia Kazan's concerns over Andrews's drinking.

Thinking that Andrews could not possibly be up to the job of remembering his lines after a night of boozing, Kazan decided to teach the actor a lesson by ordering a rewrite of a lengthy courtroom summation he was scheduled to deliver on set that day. Asked to memorize it at short notice, Andrews confidently replied, "Give me about twenty minutes." Returning from his dressing room, he was word-perfect. In Malden's experience, Andrews was one of the few actors he had come across who was able to pull off that kind of memorization sober or otherwise.[1]

Once again in a Andrews film we experience a community with a lynch mob mentality, in this instance a vengeful citizenry willing to sacrifice justice for selfish expediency. If the film had been made a few years earlier, there is every possibility that Andrews might well have found himself in the role of the victim, innocent war veteran

A staunch defender of justice, District Attorney Henry L. Harvey (Andrews, standing) takes on the seemingly impossible case of murder suspect John Waldron (Arthur Kennedy) in Elia Kazan's drama *Boomerang!* (20th Century–Fox, 1947).

John Waldron. Waldron is similar to Andrews's character Fred Derry from *The Best Years of Our Lives*: Both characters are disillusioned and bitter when they return to civilian life following war service, with little prospect of a decent job.

Andrews commented that the film "reached the proportion of my fans who are intelligent and appreciate the type of story this is; it was also a good character, but not in the romantic he-man vein."[2]

The critics were unanimous in their high praise of Andrews's performance. *Variety* noted, "[Andrews'] role is realistic and a top performance job as the prosecutor who establishes the innocence of the law's only suspect." The *New York Times* reported: "In the fluid performance of this story, Dana Andrews does another sensitive job as the tortured but steadfast State's attorney." *Variety* said, "An excellent movie of its kind — and its kind is very good and rare indeed."

Another critic noted, "A study of integrity, beautifully developed by Dana Andrews against a background of political chicanery that is doubly shocking because of its documentary understatement."

The Henry Harvey type as portrayed by Andrews, who is very much his own man, unswayed by majority opinion and pressure, would crop up again in the equally powerful movie *12 Angry Men* (1957), with Henry Fonda taking the lead this time as the staunch defender of justice for the "little man." And in common with *Boomerang!*, the success of this movie lay with the excellent character actors who graced the bill, including, incidentally, *Boomerang!*'s Ed Begley and Lee J Cobb.

The subject of proving someone's guilt beyond reasonable doubt would provide the main plot for Andrews's big noir comeback in the 1950s, *Beyond a Reasonable Doubt*.

Daisy Kenyon

20th Century–Fox, 1947

Cast: Joan Crawford (Daisy Kenyon); Dana Andrews (Dan O'Mara); Henry Fonda (Peter Lapham); Ruth Warrick (Lucille O'Mara); Martha Stewart (Mary Angelus); Peggy Ann Garner (Rosamund O'-Mara); Connie Marshall (Marie O'Mara); Nicholas Joy (Coverly); Art Baker (Lucille's Attorney); Robert Karnes (Jack, Assistant Attorney); John Davidson (Mervy, O'Mara's Butler); Victoria Horne (Marsha); Charles Meredith (Judge); Roy Roberts (Dan's Attorney); Griff Barnett (Will Thompson); Tito Vuolo (Dino); Marion Marshall (Telephone Operator); Ann Staunton (Secretary); George E. Stone (Waiter); John Garfield (Himself, Cameo in Stork Club Bar); Norman Leavitt, Jimmy Ames , John Butler, Les Clark (Cab Drivers); Monya Andre (Mrs. Ames); Mauritz Hugo (Mr. Ames); Roger Neury, Don Avalier (Hotel Captains); William H. O'Brien (Bartender); Mae Marsh (Woman Leaving Apartment); Leonard Lyons, Damon Runyon, Walter Winchell (Themselves); Jeffrey Sayre (Stork Club Manager). Running time: 99 minutes

Credits: Otto Preminger (Producer-Director); Elizabeth Janeway (Story); David Hertz (Screenplay); Leon Shamroy (Cinematography); David Raksin (Music); Alfred Newman (Music Direction); Lyle Wheeler, George Davis (Art Direction); Thomas Little, Walter M. Scott (Set Decorations); Charles Le Maire (Costume Design); Fred Sersen (Special Effects); Tom Dudley (Assistant Director); Eugene Grossman, Roger Heman Sr. (Sound); Louis Loeffler (Editor).

Daisy Kenyon, a commercial artist living in Greenwich Village, is in love with high-powered lawyer Dan O'Mara (Dana Andrews), who happens to be married to bitchy Lucille and is the father of their two children. The fact that Dan won't leave his wife puts a strain on Daisy, who resigns herself to the situation until she meets Sergeant Peter Lapham, just home from the war. Peter is keen to resume his career as a boat designer and live the simple life in Massachusetts. He falls in love with Daisy and the two marry, setting up home in his Cape Cod cottage. When Dan's wife overhears a telephone conversation between him and Daisy, she becomes hysterical; this culminates in the two getting a divorce. Free from his wife, Dan calls upon Daisy and tries to win her back. When Peter leaves the decision of which man to choose to Daisy, she realizes that her love for Dan has run its course and that it is Peter she really loves.

Tagline: "These Three Together.... In a Love Only Two Can Share!"

Daisy Kenyon was very much a Joan Crawford film, with Andrews and Henry Fonda, for the most part, acting as mere props in another of the actress's familiar portrayals of a woman successful in business but unlucky in love. Rather surprisingly, Fonda took third billing in this soap opera; this wasn't because Andrews had finally eclipsed the star status of his Fox colleague, but was due to the fact that Fonda had come to the

High-powered lawyer Dan O'Mara (Andrews) resigns himself to the fact that, due to circumstances beyond his control, he is losing the love of his life (Joan Crawford) in *Daisy Kenyon* (20th Century–Fox, 1947).

end of his detested seven-year contract with the studio and cared very little about what they placed him in at this point.

Crawford only agreed to do *Daisy Kenyon* if she could have Henry Fonda and Dana Andrews as her co-stars. Both actors were reluctant to work with her, but they had little to say on the matter due to their contractual commitments. Throughout filming, Crawford flirted with Fonda, surprising him with a present in the form of a jock strap made from rhinestones, gold sequins, and red beads. During a scene in which he carries her up the stairs, she whispered in his ear, "How about modeling it for me later?" In disbelief Fonda nearly dropped the actress and they had to shoot the scene again.[1]

Although clearly falling into the melodrama genre, the film is beautifully shot in a film noir style with its shadowy lighting. It also has sharp dialogue, an excellent David Raksin score and brisk direction by Otto Preminger, who skillfully coaches first-rate performances from the leads. Indeed, the success of the film very much lies in the fact that the love triangle is nicely balanced and (unusually for Crawford) she doesn't overshadow her male co-stars. As Andrews's highly strung wife, Ruth Warrick is also excellent value, as is Peggy Ann Garner as one of his daughters. Warrick made her film debut as another unhappy wife in *Citizen Kane* (1941).

Andrews had his misgivings about the story because he thought it too much of a soap opera in which Fonda had the better part. As he later recalled, "Preminger wanted me to do it, so I did it."[2] Despite these reservations, Andrews did concede that the film was quite a success. Although Fonda was only suited to the wholesome role of Peter, the returning serviceman who wants to design yachts, Andrews could have played either role with equal aplomb.

During production, Crawford's new contract allowed her to control the temperature on set, which she fixed at a chilly 58 degrees (apparently at age 43 she was suffering life-changing hot flashes). This prompted Andrews and Fonda to complain that it was too cold. Not wishing to upset the actress, the studio told the two co-stars to wear heavy sweaters or coats.[3] Andrews may well have achieved star status, but screen legends such as Joan Crawford still reigned supreme on set.

The suffering heroine in movies like *A Woman's Face* (1941) and *Mildred Pierce* (1945), Crawford was clearly a natural in anguished roles, which she proved once again in *Daisy Kenyon*, particularly in the scene where Daisy is imagining she is hearing phones ringing—a scene, very reminiscent of her thriller *Possessed* which was released that same year.

Andrews's initial reluctance to take on the part of the married cad in no way mars his performance, re-emphasizing how capable he was of moving away from highly principled good guys to compassionately playing shallow characters. Preminger coached a similar performance out of Andrews in *Fallen Angel* (1945), and in 1962 Andrews excelled again as the "heel with a heart" in *Madison Avenue*.

Arguably, the role of the smart corporate lawyer Dan O'Mara, living in two separate worlds and failing to find true happiness in either of them, is one of Andrews's most interesting. On face value, he may appear superficial and self-centered, but scratch away at the surface and a multi-faceted character emerges. These characteristics are fully explored through Andrews's inspired performance, which is suitably jagged to give this soap opera the noir edge it requires. Trapped in a loveless marriage, with the pressures of teenage children, a high-profile job, and a mistress who has set her sights on another lover, Dan is certainly on a roller-coaster ride and we see the full gamut of his emotions.

In the opening scenes at Daisy's apartment, he appears as a slick, self-satisfied character, quick with a quip ("Don't girls ever die in bed in your magazines?" he teases with Daisy's visiting editor friend). But beneath that suave demeanor, his insecurity about his relationship with Daisy smolders. He believes that by refusing his offer of a swank apartment uptown, she is simply punishing him for being married.

At the family home, when he is in conversation with his youngest daughter Marie, we observe a father showing tenderness and understanding combined with a pinch of subtle humor, as evidenced in the scene where he defuses an angry clash between her and her mother. Taking his daughter aside, he jokingly tells her that being rude to your parents is a greater crime than murder or stealing. However, when bitchy Lucille loses her temper with him and the children, we witness a tormented husband maintaining a dignified composure.

To compensate for his failed marriage, he excels in his work as a lawyer for his father-in-law's firm. But beneath that corporate exterior, there lurks a man of principle not purely driven by wealth and power. Dan will readily risk his reputation by taking on a hopeless no-fee case involving a Japanese-American war veteran who after serving the U.S. with honor and distinction returns home to find that his farm has been confiscated. Excitedly Dan discusses the case with Daisy, speculating that his father-in-law will flip his lid when he finds out. When confronted by Pops on the matter, Dan is manfully defiant, having suppressed his nobler instincts for far too long, "If it gives me pleasure to fight some lucrative race prejudices, including your own, that's my sport. Do you understand?"

That he is a man of hidden depths, there can be no question; Daisy comes to appreciate this *after* she has married Peter.

With love rival Peter, his exchanges are nothing less than congenial; on the surface, he bears no ill will or malice. But Dan is clearly a man who successfully suppresses his feelings, unless you push him too far and then anything is possible, as we see in the scene when he confronts Lucille after she hysterically interrupts his discreet telephone conversation with Daisy, "For a while I didn't think you were worth killing, but you are," he snarls at her with the utmost contempt. We are certainly shocked by this outburst of rage; it surfaces again when he tries to force himself on the married Daisy, but he is thwarted by her resistance.

Dan does get to reveal, later on in the film, that he is more than just a two-timing heel, when he breaks down in tears after discovering that his mean wife has been taking out her anger by abusing one of the daughters. With the strict morality code at the time, there was little chance that Andrews's character would be able to totally abandon his wife and children and it was therefore inevitable that Crawford would walk off into the sunset with Fonda, who is the more likable of the two male characters.

Apart from the chilly temperature on set, the production was relatively a smooth affair, with all participants going about their business in a very professional manner. The film came in two days ahead of schedule (it was shot from June 16 to August 12, 1947) and at $100 less than the original budget of $1,852,000.[4]

The *New York Herald Tribune* reported, "Preminger accomplishes no mean feat in guiding these people in and out among the interweavings of their own complexes, and he does wonders in varying the action of similar scenes. Working with Miss Crawford's iridescence, Fonda's diffidence, and Andrews' aggressiveness, he stages these synthetic involvements as though he believed every minute of them."

The *New York Times* noted, "Miss Crawford is, of course, an old hand at being an emotionally confused and frustrated woman and she plays the role with easy competence. Henry Fonda, too, is likable but somewhat more sympathetic and passive than a husband in such circumstances has any right to be. As the philandering father, Dana Andrews gives a performance that is full of vitality and technical grace, but it lacks authority. Mr. Andrews, somehow, just doesn't appear the type."

Interestingly, *Daisy Kenyon* was Andrews's second feature as a character trapped in a loveless marriage, having seen off trashy wife number one in *The Best Years of Our Lives.* In 1956, he made the wrong choice of bride again in *Beyond a Reasonable Doubt,* but in this story, divorce plays second fiddle to murder.

According to Preminger's niece, who visited during filming, the sets were dark "to hide Joan Crawford's wrinkles,"[5] which prompts the question, was film noir simply devised as a form of anti-aging cream for wrinkly middle-aged divas? It's a topic worthy of a thesis, perhaps.

Night Song
RKO, 1948

Cast: Dana Andrews (Dan Evans); Merle Oberon (Cathy); Ethel Barrymore (Miss Willey); Hoagy Carmichael (Chick); Artur Rubinstein (Himself); Eugene Ormandy (Himself); Jacqueline White (Connie); Donald Curtis (George); Walter Reed (Jimmy); Jane Jones (Mamie); Whit Bissell (Ward Oates); Lennie Bremen (Chez Mamie Headwaiter); Luis Alberni (Flower Vendor); George Chandler (Bartender); Hector Sarno (Proprietor); Charles Cirillo, Victor Romito (Sailors); George Cooper (Bellboy); Suzi Crandall (Fur-coated Pedestrian); Herbert Evans (Butler); Antonio Filauri (Chef); Jack Gargan, Alex Melesh (Waiters); Harry Harvey (Postman); Hercules Mendez (Headwaiter); Eva Mudge (Woman); Howard Keiser (Newsboy); Ervin Richardson (Artist).

Credits: Jack J. Gross (Executive Producer); Harriet Parsons (Producer); John Cromwell (Director); Dick Irving Hyland (Story); Frank Fenton, Dick Irving Hyland (Screenplay); DeWitt Bodeen (Adaptation); Lucien Ballard (Cinematography); Leith Stevens (Music); C. Bakaleinikoff (Music Direction); Hoagy Carmichael, Fred Spielman, Janice Torre (Song); Albert S. D'Agostino, Jack Okey (Art Direction); Darrell Silvera, Joseph Kish (Set Decorations); Gordon Bau (Makeup); Orry-Kelly (Wardrobe); Maxwell Henry (Assistant Director); Russell A. Cully (Special Effects); John Tribby, Clem Portman (Sound); Harry Marker (Editor). Running time: 101 minutes

Struck blind in an accident, brilliant pianist-composer Dan Evans (Dana Andrews) now scratches out an existence as a pianist in a back alley dance club in San Francisco. His bitterness about his condition causes him to abandon the brilliant concerto he was composing before the accident. Hearing him play one evening, a beautiful heiress, Cathy, recognizes his potential and hatches a plan to get him to regain his confidence. She gains his sympathy by pretending to be poor and blind and thus encourages him to enter a music composition contest which she has secretly organized. Dan enters the contest with his completed concerto and wins first prize. He uses the prize money to have his eyesight restored and takes up with his rich benefactress in New York. On the opening night of his concerto in Carnegie Hall, Dan remembers the poor blind girl who inspired him and realizes that he really loves her. In the rush to be with her, he discovers to his joy that she and the rich girl are the same person.

In the opening scene, the beautiful Cathy, seated at the jazz club after a night at the opera, suddenly becomes conscious of the haunting, introspective beat of the music. In a kind of hypnotic trance she crosses the floor to the piano and notices the player for the first time. In his blue eyes she sees a sad, faraway look which deeply stirs her. Without glancing her way he suddenly speaks: "Light me a torch, chum."

Realizing that the request is meant for her, she hands him a lighted cigarette, and only at this point does she realize that he is blind.

"Light me a torch, chum," blind pianist Dan Evans (Andrews) asks the fixated onlooker, Cathy (Merle Oberon), in the 1940s fairy tale *Night Song* (RKO, 1948).

In keeping with the likes of "Play it again, Sam," such scene-stealing lines undoubtedly give rise to the quaint expression "They don't make them like that any more." That is perhaps very true, but back in the '40s, Hollywood regularly indulged its passion for a good old fairy tale, which in 1947 found full expression in the RKO release *Night Song*. In time-honored fashion, these tales usually entailed our two lovers gazing starry-eyed at opposite ends of the social hierarchy, and *Night Song* was no exception. As the personification of elegance and sophistication, Merle Oberon is of course the rich gal to Andrews's impoverished musician ("I've been so poor, the cockroaches walked out of the place!").

This bittersweet tale was one of Oberon's first features in a six-picture deal with RKO, but unfortunately the film (*and* her next entry *Berlin Express*) slipped to the lower halves of double bills. Born in Bombay in 1911, Merle Oberon had stunning, exotic looks which were the result of mixed parentage: Her mother was Ceylonese and her father a Welsh mining engineer. Discovered by Alexander Korda, whom she subsequently married in 1939, she was catapulted to stardom by her critically acclaimed performance as Cathy in *Wuthering Heights* (1939). After her divorce from Korda in 1945, Merle married *Night Song*'s cameraman Lucien Ballad, who like Merle was of mixed blood (part–Cherokee Indian). When the actress suffered facial scars from a car crash, Ballard developed a camera-mounted compact spotlight which lighted the subject head on, thus reducing the incidence of unflattering lines and shadows.

As well as taking the shine off Oberon's star, *Night Song* also marked a slight downturn in Andrews's career after the success of the previous six years. The role of a blind pianist certainly showcased Andrews's acting versatility, but with audiences he was more readily identified with battle-weary servicemen, tough cops, or determined district attorneys. Although Andrews coped admirably with the part, it was perhaps more suited to the likes of Cornel Wilde (*A Song to Remember*), which incidentally also starred Merle Oberon, or Tyrone Power (*The Eddy Duchin Story*). However, it could equally be argued that Dan was simply another entry in Andrews's impressive repertoire of bitter, disillusioned characters.

Casting debate aside, *Night Song* is still a thoroughly entertaining weepie in the best traditions of Hollywood, which reveled in the plight of musicians who "give it all for their art." It was certainly "bread and butter" fare for director, John Cromwell, who had firmly established himself with *Since You Went Away* (1944), *The Enchanted Cottage* (1945) and *Anna and the King of Siam* (1946). Andrews had this to say of the director: "Mr. Cromwell is of course an actor himself, and is certainly very well able to explain to an actor what he wants."[1]

Producer Harriet Parsons (daughter of Louella Parsons) had appreciated Andrews's acting talents since his appearance in *Swamp Water* and *The Ox-Bow Incident*, and even as far back as his time at the Pasadena Community Theatre, and was, therefore understandably overjoyed when he

Andrews and Merle Oberon in a publicity shot from *Night Song* (RKO, 1948).

accepted the role of the blind pianist. Regarding him as the "hottest actor in Hollywood," she described how they got together to do business: When she asked him whether he played the piano at all, he explained in a dreamily amused tone, "I did once. A long time ago. I was nine and mad for a little girl who was giving her first piano recital. Despite my charms, she wasn't impressed. So I told my music teacher she had to teach me a piece I'd decided on for the recital. She was very cold to the idea. According to her, it was way over my head. Well, I learned it, played it at the recital, and that's the story of my piano career to date."[2]

"Fundamentally, he's well-informed, broadminded and seriously intelligent," said Parsons. "He's quick to grasp and help solve any problem that has to do with making a picture. That's why he'd be a good producer himself." Andrews casually said of her comment, "So far, I haven't found a story I think enough of, to want to produce."[3]

Parsons explained how Andrews had to wear contact lenses to help him play a blind person, and notwithstanding the complexity of the role, he was always remarkably on cue with the music and his lines.

Andrews's deftness at the keyboard was also noted by Charles Higham and Roy Moseley in their 1983 biography of Merle Oberon. They reported that Andrews worked with great intensity on the fingering, made more difficult by the fact that he could not seem to be looking at the keys. The book also revealed that Andrews felt slightly disconcerted by the fact that Merle only made moderate, subtle advances toward him in front of her husband, who was photographing them. He felt embarrassed because the slightest indication of feeling would be clearly observed by Ballard. The Czech leading man Charles Korvin, who starred with Merle in *This Love of Ours*, supported Andrews's opinion that Merle liked to make it appear to her husband that she was attracted to her leading man. Andrews recalled that, much to his dismay, Merle would often whisk him away to lunch, leaving Ballard behind.[4] These mind games did nothing to endear Andrews to his beautiful co-star, whose circle of social set friends were from a different world than Andrews's more down-to-earth cronies (the likes of Henry Morgan, Victor Jory and Robert Preston).

Adding his customary warmth to the film is wandering minstrel Hoagy Carmichael in his third and last film with Andrews (after *The Best Years of Our Lives* and *Canyon Passage*). *Night Song* cast him as Chick, a clarinet-playing bandleader, who abandons music to help Dan. For his own song "Who Killed 'Er (Who Killed the Black Widder)," Hoagy switched from clarinet to piano-vocal. In addition, the film also showcased Artur Rubinstein at the piano and Eugene Ormandy conducting the New York Philharmonic, the orchestra that played the finished concerto (actually written by Leith Stevens) in Carnegie Hall. Contrary to the critics of the day, I think that Stevens' concerto is a wonderfully fitting piece for the finale — both haunting and dramatic.

As well as a great cast, the film also benefits from Ballard's inspired photography, which perfectly complements the mood and atmosphere of this tale. The sumptuous production values are also helped by Ethel Barrymore as Oberon's wise old aunt (did she ever make a bad film — here reprising her wry, knowing character from the 1949 *Portrait of Jenny*).

Having played a character suffering from mental trauma in *The Best Years of Our Lives,* Andrews now got his first opportunity to play a character with a *physical* disability, and in true Hollywood style he takes out his bitterness on anyone who comes near him. This bitterness is heightened by the fact that he was blinded not in the war, but by a freak accident afterwards, when a truck crashed into a drug store he was sitting in — a tragic accident which cruelly curtailed his ambitions to become a music composer. We get a taste of his frustration and despair when he first comes into contact with Cathy at the jazz club. Staring ahead, with Cathy looking on, he utters in an offhand manner, "I'm exhibit 'A' here. I'm the blind piano player. She wants to know how I can find the keys with only my fingers. You tell her it's a Braille piano."

The contrast between her sheltered society background and his struggles in a bleak world is laid bare when she associates the sound of rain on a window pane with music, and he in turn looks upon it, simply, as rotten cold rain that drips into your shoes, when you're out trudging though a downpour looking for a job. However, as the story unfolds, Cathy's kindness finally softens Dan's bitterness, and with the bleak days behind them he whispers, "We were two blind people in a city full of eyes."

This is easily Andrews's corniest film, mawkish with a capital M, but once you've suspended your disbelief with the unlikely plot, it still represents one of Hollywood's finest 1940s love stories, where rich girl and poor boy finally put aside their backgrounds and come together in holy matrimony. Andrews had another opportunity to tickle the ivories seven years later in *Elephant Walk,* where his plantation manager Dick Carver impresses another beautiful brunette, Elizabeth Taylor, with yet another take on Chopin.

Andrews's next opportunity to play a character with a physical ailment (with the exception of his terminal illness in *Crack in the World,* 1965) came 20 years later in *Hot Rods to Hell* (1967) where his character is once again consumed with bitterness following a car accident which left him with a serious back problem.

David Meeker's *Jazz at the Movies* succinctly summed it up: "Intelligent, entertaining melodrama with Dana Andrews as a blind pianist-composer who graduates from a dance band to the Philharmonic."

The Iron Curtain

20th Century–Fox, 1948

Cast: Dana Andrews (Igor Gouzenko); Gene Tierney (Anna Gouzenko); June Havoc (Nina Karanova); Berry Kroeger (John Grubb); Edna Best (Mrs. Albert Foster); Stefan Schnabel (Col. Ilya Ranov); Nicholas Joy (Dr. Norman); Eduard Franz (Maj. Semyon Kulin); Frederic Tozere (Col. Trigorin); Noel Cravat (Bushkin); Christopher Robin Olsen (Andrei); Peter Whitney (Cipher Lt. Vinikov); Leslie Barrie (Editor); Mauritz Hugo (Leonard Leitz); John Shay (Lt. Pyotr Sergeyev); Victor Wood (Capt. Donald P. Class); Reed Hadley (Narrator); Anne Curson (Helen Tweedy); Helena Dare (Capt. Kulina); John Davidson (Secretary to the Minister of Justice); Eula Morgan (Mrs. Trigorin); Michael Dugan (Policeman); Joe Whitehead (William Hollis); Arthur Gould-Porter (Mr. Foster); John Ridgely (Officer Murphy); Charles Tannen (Voice of Radio Commentator).

Credits: Sol. C. Siegel (Producer); William Wellman (Director); Igor Gouzenko (Based on his personal story); Milton Krims (Screenplay); Charles G. Clarke (Cinematography); Dimitri Shoshtakovich, Serge Prokofiev, Aram Khachaturian, Nicholas Myaskovsky (Music); Alfred Newman (Music Direction); Lyle Wheeler, Mark-Lee Kirk (Art Direction); Thomas Little (Set Decorations); Bonnie Cashin, Charles Le Maire (Costume Design); Ben Nye, Dick

Smith (Makeup); Fred Sersen (Special Effects); William Eckhardt (Assistant Director); Bernard Freericks, Harry M. Leonard (Sound); Louis Loeffler (Editor). Running time: 87 minutes

Based on a true story, this semi-documentary style Cold War drama concerns the defection of Soviet embassy code specialist Igor Gouzenko (Dana Andrews) during the atomic spy scandal. Arriving in Canada from Soviet Russia, Gouzenko is exposed to the cold and suspicious nature of his government's regime as he works at the embassy, which is linked to the network of Communist agents and sympathizers who supply the information sent to Moscow. Chief amongst these are NKVD officer Ranev and spy network head Grubb. Hounded by his superiors and feeling the effects of suspicions and tyranny at the embassy, Gouzenko becomes disillusioned with his government and begins to see it as more of a threat than that posed by the good citizens of Canada. The simplest basic rights and pleasures are even denied him when he is refused time off to be with his wife Anna at the birth of their son. Instead, he is ordered to radio reports on the atomic bomb research to Moscow from his hidden office in the embassy. Fearing that he might be recalled to Russia with his wife and child, he decides to take matters into his own hands by stealing secret information with the intention of handing it over to the Canadian Ministry of Justice. At first, his revelations are dismissed, which enables the Soviet agents to close in on him. Confronted by Ranev and his men, he is about to give himself up when the Canadian Mounted Police, summoned by neighbors over the ruckus, arrive on the scene. When the true nature of the stolen information is revealed, the spies are rounded up and Gouzenko and his family are put in the protective custody of the Canadian government.

With the Cold War heating up in 1947, Darryl Zanuck decided to do his bit to counter the accusations that Hollywood was not doing enough to hold back the tide of communism. Inspired by a J. Edgar Hoover speech claiming that Soviet spies were active in the United States, Zanuck set to work on the fact based espionage melodrama *The Iron Curtain*.

Shifting the "Red Threat" to Canada, *The Iron Curtain* was shot in a quasi-documentary style to reinforce the serious message that Soviet spies were operating in North America. Realism was enhanced by using newsreel clips, voiceover narration and the actual Ottawa locations where the spy network operated. The film was possibly the first of many features made after World War II which pursued an anti-communist theme. The title phrase "the Iron Curtain" was first used in 1920, but did not come into general use until 1946, when Winston Churchill used it in his "Sinews of Peace" address. The film was written by Milton Krims, who helped pen the model for all Cold War films, *Confessions of a Nazi Spy* (1939), which dealt with a Nazi spy ring in the U.S.

As Andrews had shown in *Boomerang!* (1947), his minimalist acting lent itself superbly to the quasi-documentary filming style, which didn't go unnoticed by director William Wellman, who coached the actor to another fine, understated performance. Andrews was no stranger to Wellman's directing style, having successfully collaborated with the director five years earlier in the classic *The Ox-Bow Incident,* in which Andrews gave possibly the strongest performance in his career. Andrews was in familiar territory playing a victim with strong values. He had previously played a more youthful Russian of similar character in the Goldwyn epic *The North Star* (1943), although on that occasion the Nazis were the bad guys. The "Red Menace" surfaced again in Andrews's 1958 thriller *The Fearmakers.*

With close-cropped haircut, shabby suit and his customary tight-lipped grimace, Andrews certainly looked the part of the downtrodden Russian. Fresh off the plane, his Gouzenko is still very much a man of the Party prepared to do his duty without question, informing wife Anna that as simple people they must have faith in their leaders.

Even though he is a simple man, he is wise to the wiles of Ranev's secretary, Karanova, and her attempts to test his mettle through seduction. Unimpressed by her efforts, he tells her his only two secrets, that like any good Russian he drinks vodka and that his wife is very beautiful. And to make doubly sure that Karanova gets the message, he casually informs her before he leaves that her beauty is carved out of granite with no body or soul.

Andrews again enjoyed the benefit of having the lovely Gene Tierney as his co-star in this, her first film project after giving birth to her baby daughter Tina. To enhance credibility, both stars expertly underplayed their parts and were fortunately not required to accent the dialogue, which might have undermined the film's sense of realism. Their well-balanced, subtle performances expertly conveyed the effect of suspicion and fear on the Gouzenkos' frugal existence, which is only brightened by their love for one another and Anna's pregnancy. But even with this simple pleasure, the realities of life under the communist yoke cannot be ignored, with Gouzenko pinning his hopes on a boy because boys can expect a better future than girls under the red flag.

The communist operatives are also well cast, with June Havoc (sister of the famous striptease artiste Gypsy Rose Lee) appropriately viperous in the role of the scheming Karanova, who tries to seduce Gouzenko. Barry Kroeger is equally memorable as the sinister Grubb and Eduard Franz is in excellent form as the disenchanted, alcoholic Major Kulin. (You could always recognize the Soviet bad guy in a Hollywood movie:

Apart from having had a personality bypass, his skewed, screen-filling shadow seemed to assume a life of its own when making an entrance or chasing down an alleyway.)

For maximum effect the film was released simultaneously in 500 American theatres with the Fox publicity machine boasting, "The most amazing plot in 3300 years of recorded espionage." However, in some places where it played, pro–Soviet protestors clashed with anticommunists groups, and many of those involved in the film, including Andrews, received abusive letters.[1] When the film went into general release internationally, many governments considered the subject matter too controversial and banned it. To ensure that the public got the message that Andrews in no way had any communist tendencies his brother Steve Forrest claimed in an international magazine article, "He has just the right amount of liberalism — he's a full-fledged American without going overboard for

Disillusioned with his government, the dissident Soviet Igor Gouzenko (Andrews) contemplates the future for him and his forthcoming family under the communist yoke, while concerned wife Anna (Gene Tierney) looks on in the fact-based Cold War drama *The Iron Curtain* (20th Century–Fox, 1948).

any 'isms."[2] The inflammatory nature of the film was underlined by the fact that during production, visitors were barred from the set, and those involved in its production were almost quarantined.

Keen to show their Soviet allegiance, the four Russian composers (Shostakovich, Prokoviev, Khachaturian and Myaskovsky) whose music was played in the film tried to sue Fox Studios for using it without their permission, but their endeavors failed because their work was not protected by copyright in America. Zanuck was totally perplexed as to why anyone would support what he saw as an authoritarian regime, where the government had the last say on script approval. He wrote in a note to producer Sol Siegel, "Can you imagine our not being able to make pictures that were critical of America such as *Grapes of Wrath, The Best Years of Our Lives, Gentleman's Agreement* and hundreds of others?"[3]

In post-production, to make it perfectly clear what prompted Gouzenko's actions, Zanuck inserted a scene in which the disillusioned Kulin tells Gouzenko about how he was forced to shoot five Russian comrades to get a volunteer for a mission. When Kulin is ordered to return to Russia to await his fate for disloyalty to the party, he idly remarks that he would prefer a firing squad, because drinking oneself to death would take too long.

All these messages reinforced the notion that Communist values cared little for the sanctity of a single life, which prompts Gouzenko to turn his back on the party, informing his wife that they will not be returning to Russia. The main reason behind this brave decision is etched clearly over Gouzenko's face when he looks at his baby son and contemplates a better future for him.

Little is known about the real-life Gouzenko and his family after they were given new identities, but it is understood that they lived a middle-class existence somewhere in Canada. During his lifetime, Gouzenko penned two books (one an account of his defection) and made occasional appearances on television, always with a hood covering his head. In 2003, the Canadian Government put up memorial plaques in Dundonald Park commemorating the courage shown by the defector, who had died of a heart attack in 1982.

Director William Wellman maintained that his films, such as *The Iron Curtain* and *Blood Alley,* were more about action than politics, informing an interviewer, "Hell, I don't make political films. After *The Ox-Bow Incident* and *Wild Boys of the Road*, I was accused of being a liberal. After *The Iron Curtain*, I was a leftist. I mean, I'm Republican, but I loathe all politicians."[4] During the making of *Johnny Reno* in 1965, a period when many stars were rushing into politics, Andrews revealed in the film's pressbook that he had no political ambitions himself: "I'll leave the politicking to Sen. Murphy [former actor George Murphy] and to Ronnie Reagan. I believe an actor's place is in front of the footlights or the camera."[5]

With all the scaremongering of the period, which culminated in the "McCarthy Era," *The Iron Curtain* was clearly Fox's attempt to prove its all–American credentials; however critic James Agee saw the film in a less serious light, writing, "If it could be proved that there is any nation on earth which does not employ spies, that would be news. This is just the same old toothless dog biting the same old legless man. However, it is efficient melodrama, and fairly constrained in delivering its world-shaking message."

In contrast, the *New York Herald Tribune* commended the film's "provocative ideological chord," but added that it "does not stack up well as propaganda or entertainment." Looking beyond the politics, one critic noted, "Dana Andrews does one of his best jobs as Gouzenko, making the character as real on the screen as it is in real life."

A sequel, *Operation Manhunt* (1954), purported to show a failed Soviet attempt to draw Gouzenko out of hiding to kill him. In the epilogue, the real hooded Gouzenko stresses vigilance regarding Soviet activities. (Are you still looking under your bed?)

Deep Waters
20th Century–Fox, 1948

Cast: Dana Andrews (Hod Stillwell); Jean Peters (Ann Freeman); Cesar Romero (Joe Sanger); Dean Stockwell (Danny Mitchell); Anne Revere (Mary McKay); Ed Begley (Josh Hovey); Leona Powers (Mrs. Freeman); Mae Marsh (Molly Thatcher); Will Geer (Nick Driver); Bruno Wick (Druggist); Cliff Clark (Harris); Eleanor Moore (Secretary); Harry Malcolm Cooke (Bus Station Operator); Raymond Greenleaf (Judge Tate); Harry Tyler (Hopkins).

Credits: Samuel G. Engel (Producer); Henry King (Director); Ruth Moore (Novel *Spoonhandle*); Richard Murphy (Screenplay); Joseph LaShelle (Cinematography); Cyril J. Mockridge (Music); Lionel Newman (Music Direction); Lyle Wheeler, George W. Davis (Art Direction); Thomas Little (Set Decorations); Charles Le Maire (Wardrobe); Ben Nye, Harry Maret (Makeup); Joseph Behm (Assistant Director); Fred Sersen (Special Effects); Bernard Freericks, Roger Heman Sr. (Sound); Barbara McLean, Gilbert Hackforth-Jones, H.G. Stoker (Editing). Running time: 85 minutes

Set against the backdrop of the Maine fishing community, the story concerns the plight of a troubled orphan boy, Danny Mitchell, who runs away from his foster home after he is caught stealing. Welfare worker Ann Freeman takes charge of the boy and introduces him to her boyfriend, lobster fisherman Hod Stillwell (Dana Andrews), in the hope that he will be a good role model for the boy. While taking care of Danny, Ann and Hod maintain an on-off romantic relationship due to Hod's refusal to give up the sea for a safe and secure job ashore. Ann is further concerned when Danny also develops a hankering to go to sea. Taking Danny under his wing, Hod grows fond of the lad and, with the help of his fisherman friend Joe Sangor, brings out the best in his character. In turn, Danny rekindles the romance between Ann and Hod and brings them together after Ann finally accepts Hod's and Danny's love for the dear old briny.

Taglines: "The Sea is a Woman ... beautiful.... And like you ... Cruel!"; "Dana Andrews— A Man possessed by the sea.... And something more..."; "Jean Peters— A portrayal as exciting, as in *Captain from Castile.*"

Lobster fisherman Hod Stillwell was the first of four seafaring roles Andrews played in his movie career. In 1949, he was a freighter captain in *Sword in the Desert*, in 1951 a fishing boat captain in *Sealed Cargo* and in 1958 a whaler in *Enchanted Island*. In common with the archetypal noir and western loner, the hardy mariner is essentially a drifter with no ties, taking each day as it comes, knowing that one day his roving ways will be over. His restless soul roams the seas like the proverbial Flying Dutchman in search of his true love, which in this case comes in the form of Jean Peters's prissy landlubber Ann Freeman, who finally surrenders to our lobster man when she eventually learns to respect his seafaring way of life. Clearly playing fast and loose with Ruth

Moore's novel *Spoonhandle*, a compelling story of an island community in Maine, *Deep Waters* nonetheless delivers its wholesome tale with much warmth and sentiment.

With his simple outlook on life and his love of the great outdoors (the open sea), Hod is very much an older and wiser version of Ben, Andrews's trapper character from *Swamp Water* (1941). Hardened by the wild, tough environment in which they make their living, both men are nonetheless gentle characters with a great deal of compassion for their fellow men, with Ben's empathy for escaped convict Keefer matched by Hod's concern for wayward orphan Danny. Their strong moral fiber is also underpinned by sheer courage in the face of adversity, particularly when they are pitted against the elements— Ben in the unforgiving swamplands and Hod in the stormy seas off Maine. Hod's grit and determination in risking his own life to save the boy from being dashed on the rocks is an excellent example of Andrews's square-jawed natural ability to play the resolute hero. Courage is etched all over his face as he tries to steer the boat away from the jagged rocks, and when Joe exclaims "Santa Maria, how did we do that?" he nonchalantly replies, "I dunno. We were born to be heard, I guess." This steely-eyed resolve would surface again in *The Crowded Sky* (1960), when as the captain at the controls of the stricken airliner, he doesn't bat an eyelid when one of the failed engines nearly drops off.

This was the only time that Andrews worked with the eminent film director Henry King, who rather surprisingly never won an Academy Award despite having a career which spanned half a century and included such classics as *Stella Dallas* (1925), *Jesse James* (1939), *The Song of Bernadette* (1943) and *Twelve O'Clock High* (1949).

With his nostalgic love of wide open spaces and all things Americana, King would have found the quaint setting of *Deep Waters* much to his liking. Indeed, the impressive Maine locations are one the most striking features of this simple romantic tale. *Deep Waters* was shot on location in Vinalhaven, Maine (an island ten miles off the mainland), and all the studio equipment had to be brought in on a barge because the local ferry was too small to handle the job.

Andrews's love interest Jean Peters came to Hollywood in 1946 after competing in a beauty contest in her home state of Ohio. *Deep Waters* was her second film after her successful debut opposite Tyrone Power in the 1947 hit *Captain from Castile*. At the height of her career ten years later, she secretly married Howard Hughes; the couple divorced in 1971. With the lure of an expensive ring and moonlight, Hughes tried to persuade Peters to consummate their relationship prior to marriage, but she laughed off his proposal before setting off for Maine to film *Deep Waters*.[1]

In the role of welfare worker Ann Freeman, Peters is suitably authoritative, but her hard-and-fast objections to Hod's love for the sea puts a strain on their relationship. Their uncomfortable stand-off is clearly in evidence when Hod returns the boy to her custody after rescuing him from the perilous seas. When Ann gives the boy the once-over and declares he's wet, Hod cuts to the chase, informing her, "Yeah, he fell in the water again. Every time you do that, you get wet."

But in time Hod and Ann come closer when Hod explains to a puzzled Ann that Danny, like his (Danny's) fisherman father, has the sea in his veins, and that the real problem is not Danny's love of the sea, but her own fear of it: "[T]here's one thing you didn't tell me or I was too stupid to see it: You're afraid, Ann, you're afraid of the sea, you're scared to death of it."

Such fears were certainly not shared by Andrews and Cesar Romero, who took to their seafaring roles "like ducks to water." Looking very much at home as hardy men of the sea, both approached their parts with great subtlety, which created a natural partnership on screen. Eight years earlier, Andrews started out his film career playing second fiddle to Romero in *Lucky Cisco Kid*; now the roles were reversed. The film also reunited Andrews with Anne Revere (*Fallen Angel*) and Ed Begley (*Boomerang!*), both actors once again making it look so effortless in their supporting roles.

With his natural interest in fishing, Andrews

Fisherman Hod Stillman (Andrews) and welfare worker Ann Freeman (Jean Peters) are starry-eyed lovers sharing an affectionate moment in the charming sea tale *Deep Waters* (20th Century–Fox, 1948).

jumped at the opportunity of playing the part of a lobsterman, and during production he made three extra-curricular lobster fishing expeditions to familiarize himself with the job.

In between filming, Andrews also spent many an hour searching for arrowheads and other island relics, hitting the jackpot one day when he discovered an extremely rare soapstone pipe used for ritualistic purposes by the Algonquin Indians who inhabited the island 500 years ago.[2]

In addition to the fine acting and superb photography, the film also features a memorably haunting score by veteran composer Cyril Mockridge, which wonderfully captures all the romance and mystery of the sea. Cleverly woven into this memorable theme, we are also treated to a burst or two of "I Can't Begin to Tell You" when our two lovebirds get together.

For its six-minute storm sequence, the film earned an Oscar nomination for special effects, but lost out that year to David O. Selznick's enchanting *Portrait of Jennie*, a classic film that *also* featured a breathtaking storm sequence set against Maine's rugged coastline.

Shot on a tight budget, the film paid for itself and returned a small profit. One critic referred to Andrews's performance as "magnificent." Another commented that the film was "contrived but a pleasant enough romantic tale."

Deep Waters was based on a popular literary theme skillfully explored in another two films, *Captains Courageous* (1937) and *Down to the Sea in Ships* (1949), the latter also starring Dean Stockwell as the boy.

No Minor Vices

Enterprise-MGM 1948

Cast: Dana Andrews (Dr. Perry Aswell); Lilli Palmer (April Ashwell); Louis Jourdan (Octavio Quaglini); Jane Wyatt (Miss Darlington); Norman Lloyd (Dr. Sturdivant); Bernard Gorcey (Mr. Zitzfleisch); Roy Roberts (Mr. Felton); Fay Baker (Mrs. Felton); Sharon McManus (Gloria Felton); Ann Doran (Mrs. Faraday); Beau Bridges (Bertram); Frank Kreig (Cab Driver); Kay Williams (Receptionist); Robert Hyatt (Genius); Jerry Mullins (Boy); Inna Gest (Mrs. Fleishgelt); Joy Rogers, Eileen Coghlan (Nurses); Frank Conlan (Window Cleaner).

Credits: Lewis Milestone (Producer-Director); Arnold Manoff (Story and Screenplay); George Barnes (Cinematography); Franz Waxman (Music); Nicholai Remisoff (Production Designer); Edward G. Boyle (Set Decorations); Marian Herwood Keyes (Costumes); Gus Norin (Makeup); Nate Watt (Assistant Director); Frank McWhorter (Sound); Robert Parrish (Editor). Running time: 96 minutes

In this light comedy of marital jealousy, successful pediatrician Perry Ashwell (Dana Andrews) and his attractive wife April lead sedate, conservative lives, with the self-satisfied Perry taking his wife and friends very much for granted. The status quo of their cozy existence is rudely interrupted when Perry permits rich and eccentric artist Octavio Quaglini to enter his home and office. In his attempt to sketch the concealed "inner self" of the Ashwells, Octavio, a handsome Continental type, soon causes disharmony and discourse within the household when he set his amorous sights on April. However, the artist's presence and non-conventional ways have the opposite effect with Perry's lovelorn colleagues Miss Darlington and Dr. Sturdivant, who eventually find solace in each other's arms. Confessing his love for April, Octavio attempts to steal her away from Perry. Although flattered by his attention, she realizes that her heart belongs to Perry, who after much soul-searching finally realizes the error of his ways.

In the 1940s, several challenges were made to the stranglehold of the major studios. In a bid for both artistic and financial freedom, various producers, directors and stars got together to form independent film companies, only relying on the majors for their distribution networks. Frank Capra, George Stevens and William Wyler got together to form Liberty Films, which collapsed shortly after two expensive box office disappointments, Capra's 1946 classic *It's a Wonderful Life* (I know — totally unbelievable) and 1948's *State of the Union*. Unlike the big studios, who could balance out the hits and flops across a wide production schedule, these fledgling independents relied too heavily on individual film projects, which exposed them to high financial risk. Another company that learned this the hard way was Enterprise Studios, which was essentially an extension of the independent producing activities of David Loew, the twin brother of MGM's foreign sales executive Arthur M. Loew and son of MGM founder Marcus Loew.

In its brief existence, Enterprise churned out a handful of films including the minor classic *Force of Evil* (1948) and the expensive flop that

Self-satisfied pediatrician Perry Ashwell (Andrews, right) keeps a watchful eye on eccentric artist Octavio Quaglini (Louis Jourdan), who has designs on Perry's wife, April (Lilli Palmer) in the romantic comedy *No Minor Vices* (MGM, 1948).

bankrupted it, the Ingrid Bergman vehicle *Arch of Triumph* (1948), which United Artists called "probably the greatest commercial failure in the history of motion pictures."

No Minor Vices was conceived as a means to keep the company going until all the anticipated money rolled in from *Arch of Triumph,* with director Lewis Milestone describing it as "a little comedy ... that we tossed off for Enterprise because they wanted to keep the gates open." It was literally a case of Milestone getting some pals together, including Andrews, to make a film which would cash in on the interest in psychoanalysis which had been created by *Lady in the Dark* (1944) and *Spellbound* (1945). With the lure of profit participation, Andrews invested some of his own money, which he lost when the film bombed. Fingers well and truly burnt, he would never again be tempted to invest in a film. Andrews acknowledged that *No Minor Vices* helped seal the demise of Enterprise, but the real

clunker was *Arch of Triumph,* which according to the actor cost about four and a half million dollars, greatly exceeding its box office takings.

Andrews further claimed that *No Minor Vices'* poor box office showing was partly due to the fact that it had been released by MGM and not by United Artists. Because little of MGM's own money was in the film, Andrews felt that MGM didn't promote it as much as they could have, and that perhaps United Artists, who specialized in independent films, might have had more success with it. Andrews said of the film, "It was not a bad picture, it was a little ahead of its time."[1] He also recalled that insufficient time was given to preparing the script and that it was made hurriedly.

On face value, the director of *All Quiet on the Western Front* and Andrews's *A Walk in the Sun* and *The Purple Heart* seemed an odd choice to direct *No Minor Vices,* but Milestone was actually no stranger to comedy, having won the 1928

Academy Award for Best Comedy Director for *Two Arabian Knights*. Still recovering from his expensive flop *Arch of Triumph*, Milestone decided to play safe with *No Minor Vices*. In an attempt to keep audiences interested in the simple plotline, Milestone would occasionally cut to a little man in a window, making cigars and having different reactions that had nothing specifically to do with the scene. As summed up by the film's editor, Robert Parrish, "If a scene was lousy, he could cut to this little guy scratching his ear ... [O]bviously it wasn't enough to make the picture work."[2]

In addition to Andrews's measured performance, this quirky farce is lifted by Prussian-born Lilli Palmer (at her intoxicating best) and handsome Frenchman Louis Jourdan (the epitome of the suave Continental). Throw in a dash of warmth from Jane Wyatt and the heady concoction was complete, but perhaps a little too rich for audiences of the day.

Palmer studied drama in Berlin before fleeing to Paris when the Nazis came to power in 1933. In 1943, she married Rex Harrison and followed him to Hollywood where she made her mark, most notably in *Cloak and Dagger* (1946) and *The Four Poster* (1952) in which she starred with Harrison.

Born in Marseille, Jourdan joined the French Resistance when his father was arrested by the Gestapo. Like Palmer, he emigrated to Hollywood in the 1940s, where he made his American film debut in Hitchcock's *The Paradine Case* (1947). He is perhaps best remembered as the debonair romantic lead in the multi–Academy Award–winning *Gigi* (1958).

Jane Wyatt sealed her place in film history as Ronald Colman's love interest in the Frank Capra classic *Lost Horizon* (1937). An all–American girl, she was perfectly cast as Andrews's wife in *Boomerang!* (1947). The film also marked the screen debut of Beau Bridges as the ill-behaved child, Bertram.

Displaying smug complacency, Andrews is thoroughly convincing as the arrogant pediatrician Dr. Perry Aswell, a character very much in the mold of his self-centered Dan O'Mara from *Daisy Kenyon*. And when it comes to a "science knows best" mentality, the rational doctor is only matched by Andrews's unflappable, cynical psychologist John Holden from *Night of the Demon*. When confronted with young Bertram's rebellious behavior, he glibly offers the mother his diagnosis: "Fracture the parents and heal the children."

But rebellious kids are one thing, pretentious artists quite another. When Quaglini offers up his latest masterpiece ("born out of the truth of his emptiness"), the good doctor lets loose his artistic appreciation — with both barrels: "It's only a self-indulgent, childish glorification of a feeling of rejection — petulant precocious pyrotechnics. It's not art, it's not truth. Junk!"

The movie falls well short of hilarious, but Milestone nonetheless maintains a keen sense of fun throughout the proceedings, particularly in the memorable lobster-cooking sequence, with our erratic artist persuading April to share his compassion for their plight, in contrast to the good doctor who simply feels that they're cute enough to eat.

In another notable scene, Andrews reprises that hypnotic stare from *Laura* when his ravishing wife April slips on her black silk stockings. No need to hit the pause button here, guys, as the sexy pose is perfectly captured in freeze-frame.

With the movie's comedy neatly framed around the soliloquies of the three leads, *The New York Times* labeled it "cubist humor, spoofing *a la* Gertrude Stein." (Huh?) On the performances, the *Times* commented, "[T]hey were good — even though here they have a tendency to play it in the grand and sweeping style. The sets are nice, the music impish."

In addition to all that cubist spoofing, creatively interspersed with the voyeuristic little guy rolling cigars (I'm still scratching my head, too), this is well worth staying in your seat just to catch Andrews give that Quaglini wolf a well-deserved slug in the kisser. Boy, that right hook never fails to entertain.

The Forbidden Street
20th Century–Fox, 1949

Cast: Dana Andrews (Gilbert Lauderdale/Henry Lambert); Maureen O'Hara (Adelaide Culver); Sybil Thorndike (Mrs. Mounsey); Diane Hart (The Blazer); Anne Butchart (Alice Hambro); Wilfred Hyde-White (Mr. Culver); Fay Compton (Mrs. Culver); A.E. Matthews (Mr. Bly); Anthony Tancred (Treff Culver); Herbert C. Walton (The Old Un); Mary Matlew (Milly Lauderdale); June Allen (Adelaide Culver, as a Child); Susanne Gibbs (Alice, as a

Child); Heather Latham (Blazer, as a Child); Peter Hobbes (Fred Baker); Ernest Hare (Policeman); Gwynne Whitby (Miss Bryant); Scott Harrold (Benson); Anthony Lamb (Treff, as a Child); Neil North (Jimmy Hambro).

Credits: William Perlberg (Producer); Jean Negulesco (Director); Margery Sharp (Novel *Britannia Mews*); Ring Lardner, Jr. (Screenplay); George Perinal (Cinematography); Malcolm Arnold (Music); Muir Mathieson (Music Direction); Andrew Andrejew (Art Direction); George K. Benda (Costumes); Guy Hamilton (Assistant Director); Buster Ambler (Sound); Ben Hipkins (Sound Editor); Richard Best (Editor). Running time: 91 minutes

In Victorian London, Adelaide Culver, an aristocratic young woman, marries Henry Lambert (Dana Andrews), a struggling artist–puppet master, against the wishes of her family. Living in poverty with the artist, she also has to endure his alcoholism. When he dies in an accident, a street harridan, Mrs. Mousey, claims that Adelaide murdered him and begins blackmailing her. All is despair until young barrister Gilbert Lauderdale (Andrews in a second role), the image of her late husband, arrives on the scene to rescue the damsel with his legal advice and comforting nature. The two fall in love and together they revive the puppet show, which proves a great commercial success. This reunites Adelaide with her family and gives a new lease of life to the run-down Mews.

Tagline: "For herself alone — she must answer for what she was and did."

Forbidden Street was adapted from Margery Sharp's book *Britannia Mews* (also the film's UK title) which told the epic tale of Adelaide's life in Victorian England. Painter turned director Jean Negulesco made a reputation with the dramatic use of shadows, silhouettes and angled shots in his film work, qualities which were showcased in classic films such as *The Mask of Dimitrios* (1944) and *Johnny Belinda* (1948). This artistry is clearly evident in *The Forbidden Street* with the rich use of velvety blacks and glowing Victorian lamps that perfectly capture the fascination and mystery of the Mews. The atmosphere is vividly enriched by Malcolm Arnold's dramatic score.

Once voted one of the most beautiful women in the world, the red-headed Maureen O'Hara cornered the market on playing feisty heroines, usually opposite John Wayne and under the direction of John Ford; who can forget her Mary Kate Danaher from *The Quiet Man* (1952)? The

role of Adelaide gave her an opportunity to play a more restrained character, but as she recalled in her memoir *Tis Herself*, *The Forbidden Street* was one of several unmemorable films in her career. She added that the only reasons to watch this film today would be to see Dana Andrews do a nice job in a dual role, or to watch the fine character Sybil Thorndike steal the picture.[1]

For several reasons this is by far the oddest film on Andrews's résumé. For choice of film, one would not automatically associate the soft-spoken Southerner with Victorian melodrama. His casting as the poor artist, sporting bushy hair and a beard, is equally bizarre; the situation is compounded by a dubbed-in English-accented voice, usually out of synchronization, that comes over like a poor impression of Michael Wilding doing an equally poor impression of Ronald Colman. If this wasn't enough, he plays two unrelated characters, who both share, at different times, a love nest in the Mews with the lovely O'Hara, and who both have a great appreciation of marionettes, puppetry and the bottle. Minus the beard and the dubbed voice, his second character, mailroom clerk and would-be barrister Gilbert Lauderdale, is closer to the Andrews we know and admire, but even in this role, he manfully starts out attempting a clipped English accent before giving it up as a bad idea. Weird? You'd better believe it. But somehow these disparate strands do come together nicely in a way which makes you feel that watching this marvelous little curio was 91 minutes well spent.

Twentieth Century–Fox apparently made the film in London, probably to use up part of its frozen UK assets, but with all its Victorian set work it might as well have been shot in Hollywood. Lambert and Lauderdale would have ordinarily been played by two actors, but with a keen eye on the purse strings and struck by the neat halfway division of labor created by the death of the first character, Fox decided to take a chance and asked Andrews to undertake both personalities. Interviewed at the time, Andrews said that he accepted the film because he believed that superficially there was a wide enough difference in the two characters to give him a sporting chance of producing two distinct characterizations within the one film.[2]

The film was the first of a few occasions where Andrews was asked to play a character suffering a problem similar to his own — the "demon

Andrews's most bizarre film was the Victorian melodrama *The Forbidden Street* (20th Century–Fox, 1949). Here in the first of his two roles in the film, as the philandering, alcoholic artist Henry Lambert, he shares a love nest with doting wife Adelaide Culver, played by an unusually reticent Maureen O'Hara.

drink." Alcoholics were always meaty parts for actors to get their teeth into and they were usually a good bet in the Oscar sweepstakes as proved by Ray Milland's Academy Award–winning performance in *The Lost Weekend* (1945) and nominations for Bing Crosby in *The Country Girl* (1954) and Susan Haywood in *Smash-up, the Story of a Woman* (1947). *The Forbidden Street* was no Oscar contender, but if there was ever an award for the most bizarre casting, Andrews would certainly have won hands down with this feature.

While in London filming *The Forbidden Street,* Andrews admitted to influential Hollywood gossip columnist Louella Parsons that he had been cautioned by Sam Goldwyn about his drinking, which had landed him in trouble on several occasions: "Sam Goldwyn warned me to be careful of everything I say. I made a vow not to touch one drop of liquor while I'm here in Europe, and I like being on the wagon so much I may stay right on it."[3]

Abstinence, however, is clearly not on the mind of his movie character, drunken artist Henry Lambert, when he confesses to Adelaide, "If you walk through the Mews and listen to my enemies, they will tell you I drink like a fish." And if his drunken ways were not enough, he is also a brazen philanderer. In response to Adelaine's question whether he has had his wicked way with all his pupils, he unashamedly answers, "Certainly not. Some of them were positively repulsive."

However, we only have to endure this frightful caricature for the first part of the film before the more likable Gilbert Lauderdale arrives on the scene after Lambert's abrupt demise. And for those in need of a good prod, his equally intoxicated Gilbert Lauderdale drops a heavy hint about the switch when he first meets Adelaide: "I'm always reminding people of someone else. I guess I have no personality of my own."

A lack of personality is certainly not something that Andrews himself could be accused of, as *Picturegoer* magazine discovered during an interview with the star in between filming. Impressed by the incisiveness of his work and his pride and integrity as an actor, the interviewer commented, "Like all good American stars he is well schooled in handling people. But it is not solely an acquired technique that makes him unostentatiously charming to even the least important employee in the studios. It is an innate modesty, and philosophy of the man who has won success the slow hard way." The interview further revealed that after a day's work, Andrews sometimes traveled to London to relax with his wife and two of their four children, who came over from America to join him; and that when he had an early call, he usually stayed at Shepperton, spending the evening drifting around the riverside on a bicycle.[4]

With *The Forbidden Street* in the can, Andrews had little opportunity to do any sightseeing, on this his first visit to England. As he recalled, "The day that picture was finished, my ticket was waiting for me and I was rushed to a plane to get back to Hollywood to meet the starting date on my next film."[5]

Although today the bizarre and unique nature of this curio makes for compulsive viewing, the critics were less kind upon its release with the *New York Times* commenting, "In the role of the girl, Maureen O'Hara is a beautifully dressed automaton whose troubles with drunkenness and squalor make no mark whatsoever on her face. And in the role of her romancers, Dana Andrews is mechanical too." The 1949 *Film Review* was perhaps a little kinder with its overview: "Slow, halting, yet somehow strangely compelling..." *Variety Movie Guide* commented, "The main setting of Britannia Mews is a triumph for the art director as it captures the grim, degrading atmosphere necessary to indicate the gradual degradation of its inhabitants."

In his autobiography *Things I Did and Things I Think I Did*, director Jean Negulesco made it clear that this was a film he wished he hadn't done, calling it, "a disaster, insane casting. The critics murdered us." When he sent a note to Darryl Zanuck accepting all blame for the film, Zanuck revealed his sense of fair play when he also shouldered some of the blame for having approved the story, script, casting and final print. Having reassured Negulesco, Zanuck ended his note: "And try not to do it again."[6]

For those contemplating inner city regeneration, this film is certainly worth checking out, for it seems all you require to convert a derelict slum into a thriving middle-class area is to put on a puppet show.

Sword in the Desert
Universal, 1949

Cast: Dana Andrews (Mike Dillon); Marta Toren (Sabra); Stephen McNally (David Vogel); Jeff Chandler (Kurta); Philip Friend (Lt. Ellerton); Hugh French (Maj. Sorrell); Liam Redmond (Jerry McCarthy); Lowell Gilmore (Maj. Stephens); Stanley Logan (Col. Bruce Evans); Hayden Rorke (Capt. Beaumont); George Tyne (Dov); Peter Coe (Tarn); Paul Marion (Jeno); Marten Lamont (Capt. Fletcher); David Wolfe (Gershon); Campell Copelin (Sgt. Chapel); Art Foster (Sgt. Rummins); Gilchrist Stuart (Radio Operator); Emil Rameau (Old Man); Jack Webb (Hoffman); Paul Brinegar, George Dockstader (British Soldiers); Jerry Paris (Levitan); Shep Menken, Joe Turkel, Sam Resnik, Russ Kaplan (Haganah Soldiers); Robin Hughes (Soldier); Martin Garralaga (Ahmed the Great); Dennis Dengate (Driver); James Craven (Brig. Vincent).

Credits: Robert Buckner (Producer-Screenplay); George Sherman (Director); Irving Glassberg (Cinematography); Frank Skinner (Music); Bernard Herzbrun, Alexander Golitzen (Art Direction); A. Roland Fields, Russell A. Gausman (Set Decorations); Emile LaVigne, Bud Westmore (Makeup); Frank Shaw (Assistant Director); Nick Carmona (Special Effects); Glenn E. Anderson (Sound); Otto Ludwig (Editor). Running time: 100 minutes

The film is set in Palestine shortly after World War II, a few years before the formation of the state of Israel. Mike Dillon (Dana Andrews), a cynical American freighter captain, hopes to turn a quick profit by smuggling Jews into the Holy Land under the noses of the British occupation forces. But against his will he is drawn into the mounting hostilities between the Jews and the British. Foremost amongst the displaced persons are Sabra, a Jewish broadcaster who uses an underground radio to speak out against the British; her lover David Vogel; and Kurta, the Israeli rebel leader. Tensions escalate, and in the inevitable battle, Mike (trapped by the British) is forced to make a daring escape with the refugees.

Tagline: "THEIR NAMES WERE KNOWN ONLY IN WHISPERS but Their Deeds Made the Headlines of the World."

Publicity shot for the exciting actioner, *Sword in the Desert* (Universal, 1949), one of the first films to tackle the postwar struggles in Palestine. From left: Stephen McNally (as David Vogel), Andrews (as Captain Mike Dillon), Marta Toren (as Sabra), and, kneeling, Jeff Chandler (as Kurta) in his debut film.

Sword in the Desert was Hollywood's first attempt at dealing with the struggles in Palestine, but with a pro–Jewish screenplay by Robert Buckner it was hardly surprising that objectivity was overlooked, with the film making no effort to recognize the plight of the Palestinians in the conflict. As Jack G. Shaffeen's book *Reel Bad Arabs (How Hollywood Vilifies a People)* explains, "[T]his movie's Palestinians are practically invisible; they surface for about fifteen seconds."[1] The film was hastily put together to cash in on the headlines concerning the conflict, with filming taking a little over six weeks, commencing on February 28 and ending on April 15, 1949.

In addition to overlooking the Palestinians, the film also rubbed the British the wrong way, prompting demonstrations outside the New Gallery in London when it opened on February 2, 1950. *The Evening Telegraph* claimed that British audiences would be shocked to see the unwonted harshness with which British troops in the film treated Jewish civilians.

Due to accusations of bias, and to stop further disturbances, the film was withdrawn shortly after its initial release, which was unfortunate, because as an action film, it has been described as highly emotional and exciting. Its subject matter was certainly unusual for its time and as a precursor to the likes of *Exodus* (1960) and *Cast a Giant Shadow* (1966), it has been called one of the most interesting films directed by George Sherman. And once again it was another groundbreaking film for Andrews, who could never be accused of being trapped in a genre.

The roles of Captain Mike Dillon and Sabra were originally earmarked for Van Heflin and Ann Blyth before Andrews and Marta Toren took the parts. At an early stage, Robert Montgomery, Paulette Goddard and Burgess Meredith had also expressed an interest in the film.[2]

The film marked the screen debut of a young Jeff Chandler as the daring underground leader, Kurta. The critics were unanimous in their high praise of his performance, for which he was rewarded with an exclusive seven-year contract with Universal. With his premature gray hair and tanned features, Chandler was well-suited to outdoor adventures, particularly westerns, receiving an Oscar nomination for his role as Cochise in Fox's *Broken Arrow* (1950). His career was tragically cut short when he died at 42 from blood poisoning following an operation for a slipped disc.

Andrews also had to jostle for screen attention with another studio contractee, Stephen McNally, who took the role of David Vogel, Sabra's sweetheart and director of the immigrants. McNally gave up his career as a lawyer to take up acting in the 1930s and will be fondly remembered for many a fine western such as *Winchester '73* (1950) and *Tribute to a Bad Man* (1956). The excellent cast also included Liam Redmond as a former IRA man keen to take a pop at the British forces. Redmond worked with Andrews again in *Night of the Demon*.

After making the film, Swedish actress Marta Toren told *The Saturday Evening Post* that it was her favorite part to date, explaining, "It allowed me to play a woman of depth and purpose for the first time in my career." As evidence that Toren took the role seriously, she read books and watched films on Palestine as part of her preparation.

Due to the fact that most of the scenes in the film occurred at night, the studio made extensive use of infrared film as they shot day for night.[3]

With such a hot topic molded into a simple chase adventure, you'd expect Andrews's freighter captain to be the hero of the piece in typical John Wayne-*Blood Alley* vein. But you'd be wrong, as his Mike Dillon is once again a man of many layers, very much like the opportunist Eric Stanton from *Fallen Angel*. And, as with Stanton, once the tough, unfeeling layers are stripped away, the real heart of the man is revealed. From the early dialogue you are left in no doubt that Mike Dillon is a self-made man (he saved his last buck to pay for his own ship) who prefers to conceal his compassion for his fellow man. His initial reluctance to risk his own neck is quite apparent when he threatens to dump the refugees in the sea when, with the shore in sight, his ship's capture becomes a distinct possibility.

"Let's get this straight, mister, a few days ago you hired ship transportation from Italy, that's all. If I hadn't missed a load of fertilizer, I wouldn't have even listened to your deal," he snarls when Vogel pleads that this is their last hope.

To doubly ensure that Vogel gets the message that he doesn't give a hoot for the plight of the refugees, Dillon reminds him that, in his eyes, they simply stack up as a 120 bucks per head. And when accused by Vogel of having little faith in mankind, he spits out, "Why should I have? What's it ever done for me?"

Questioning Dillon's morals is one thing, but casting doubt on his navigational skills is quite another. When Vogel suggests that they might be off the shore of Egypt, not Palestine, Dillon makes it clear he doesn't make mistakes when he utters, "Maybe you'd like me to swim ashore and come back with a matzoh ball."

With weather-beaten face and deep, searching eyes that suggest too many a night scanning the distant horizon from a lonely bridge, Andrews slips into the role of the seafaring adventurer with his usual consummate ease. Complete with chip on the shoulder, his hard-headed sea captain would have been just at home sailing the seven seas aboard the *Red Witch* or the *Mary Deare*. But in all his years at sea, nothing has quite prepared him for his latest adventure — trapped on the beach with a dangerous cargo. And if the threat of prison, and the fate of his ship and his Master's ticket, aren't enough to contend with, he also has to shoulder attacks on his moral fiber from baiting IRA man McCarthy when he refuses to get involved in the conflict. In response to McCarthy's claim that he may be gun-shy, Mike barks back that having seen a good deal of action in the navy, he did his bit during the war, and that as an American, he'd be a sucker to get involved in somebody else's fight.

The conflict is succinctly summed up by the British commander: "This isn't a Jewish, British, or Arab problem. It's a problem for all mankind." The sense of compassion is picked up by Major Stevens in the closing scenes when he is asked by his sergeant, "What place is that?" as they both look out over the distant town. Stevens replies, "Bethlehem. Never again will we be here on Christmas Eve. This is where our faith began."

The Motion Picture Herald commented that the film, "will keep them on the edges of their seats." The *New York Times* said, "Dana Andrews is dourly truculent until his sudden transfiguring conversion through a pious coincidence...."

My Foolish Heart
RKO, 1949

Cast: Dana Andrews (Walt Dreiser); Susan Hayward (Eloise Winters); Kent Smith (Lewis H. Wengler); Lois Wheeler (Mary Jane); Jessie Royce Landis (Martha Winters); Robert Keith (Henry Winters); Gigi Perreau (Ramona); Karin Booth (Miriam Ball); Todd Karns (Miriam's Escort); Phillip Pine (Sergeant Lucey); Martha Mears (Nightclub Singer); Edna Holland (Dean Whiting); Jerry Paris (Usher at Football Game); Marietta Canty (Grace); Barbara Woodell (Red Cross Receptionist); Regina Wallace (Mrs. Crandall); Marcel De La Brosse (Waiter); Phyllis Coates (Girl on Phone); Edward Peil Sr. (Conductor); Neville Brand (Man in Football Stands); Sam Ash, Tom Gibson, Billy Lord, Kathy Marlowe, Robert Strong (Spectators); Roger Neury (Bartender); Bud Stark (Elevator Operator); Kerry O'Day (Bit Part); Arthur Tovey (Man at Train Station); Suzanne Ridgeway (Woman in Nightclub).

Credits: Samuel Goldwyn (Producer); Mark Robson (Director); J.D. Salinger (Story "Uncle Wiggily in Connecticut"); Julius J. Epstein, Philip G. Epstein (Screenplay); Lee Garmes (Cinematography); Victor Young (Music); Victor Young, Ned Washington (Song); Emil Newman (Music Direction); Richard Day (Art Direction); Julia Heron (Set Decorations); Mary Wills, Edith Head (Costumes); Marie Clark (Makeup); Ivan Volkman (Assistant Director); John P. Fulton (Special Effects); Fred Lau (Sound); Daniel Mandell (Editor). Running time: 98 minutes

This wartime, romantic tearjerker opens with Eloise Winters and her husband, Lew Wengler, looking to get a divorce. Guilt-ridden and resentful, she is contemplating revealing to Lew that he is not the father of their little girl Ramona. At this point, Mary Jane, a former schoolmate, drops in on the couple and prevents disclosure of the secret. Breaking away from the quarrel, Eloise packs to leave and comes across an old dress that transports her mind back to happier times.

In flashback we see Eloise meet Walt Dreiser (Dana Andrews) in 1941 at a Manhattan party. Walt, a "man about town," gate-crashes the party and gets acquainted with college girl Eloise after she has been snubbed by her date. The two start dating and eventually fall in love. Their romance is interrupted when America enters the war and Walt is called to duty in the Air Force. When Eloise discovers she is pregnant, she decides not to inform Walt, especially after her father confides that he and her mother married in haste after a similar affair in World War I and has always regretted it. Unaware of Eloise's condition, Walt is set to go overseas and doesn't propose marriage due to the uncertainties of the future. However, the next day he changes his mind and writes Eloise a letter asking her to marry him. Before Eloise receives the note, Walt is killed in a training accident.

With a baby on the way, a desperate Eloise marries Lew Wengler, the boyfriend of her best friend, Mary Jane. When the child is born, Lew believes he is the father, but the marriage is a hollow affair with Eloise still thinking of the real love of her life, Walt. In her mourning she takes to drinking, which puts a further strain on the marriage.

The story returns to the present with a guilt-ridden Eloise agreeing to a divorce which will allow Lew to take custody of Ramona. However, Mary Jane forgives Eloise for stealing the man she loves and persuades Lew to leave mother and child together. Lew agrees, and he and Mary Jane leave to begin a new life together, allowing Eloise to make a fresh start with Romana.

At the urging of twin brother screenwriters Julius and Philip Epstein, who had penned the likes of *Casablanca* (1942), Sam Goldwyn purchased the rights to a short story, oddly titled, "Uncle Wiggily in Connecticut," written by renowned author J.D. Salinger. The simple story concerned two former college mates, one an alcoholic who had entered into an empty marriage without revealing to her husband that the baby she was carrying was fathered by another man.

As director, Goldwyn signed up Mark Robson, who was the current talk of the town with his masterful direction of *Champion* and *Home of the Brave* (both 1949). Goldwyn was so impressed with his work that he contracted him to a three-picture deal starting with *My Foolish Heart*. The other two, *Edge of Doom* (1950) and *I Want You* (1951), also provided Andrews with leading roles. Robson's technique involved pre-production rehearsal.

To complement Robson's efforts, Goldwyn commissioned Victor Young to write the score. The composer had a big commercial hit with his popular song "My Foolish Heart," which he wrote with lyricist Ned Washington.

The film was Susan Hayward's most notable performance since *Smash-Up: A Story of a Woman* (1947), and her second outing with Andrews as co-star. Much of its success was due to Robson, who got Hayward to underplay her part. This kept her character fresh and believable, perfectly complementing Andrews's relaxed acting style. The director was also responsible for injecting some humor into the tragic tale, which prevented it from becoming a typical weepie for "ladies only." And as Andrews had admirably demonstrated in *Berlin Correspondent*, he was the ideal candidate to deliver witty one-liners when the occasion permitted. Such an occasion occurs when Eloise meets Walt for the first time in the lobby, and he explains that being in possession of a smart dinner jacket, he simply gate-crashes parties. When Eloise asks, "Always without a girl?" he answers "Oh, I couldn't afford a dinner jacket *and* a girl."

Having made a suitable impression with Eloise, Walt ratchets up his caustic wit to put down the chicest gal in college, Marian Ball. Unimpressed by her beautiful dress and her airs and graces, he informs her that her stunning gown reminds him of a mining town he passed through where every girl wore a similar one, as if it were some kind of uniform. (Meow!)

Walt may well give the impression that he's quite a ladies' man, but as we learn when he lures Eloise back to his apartment to listen to his latest Mendelssohn collection, he's not really the wolf type, confessing to Eloise, "You're looking at a guy with the lowest batting average in any major city."

Although they made a convincing couple on screen, Andrews and Susan rarely mixed when shooting was over, with Susan returning to the comfort of her suburban family life and Andrews preferring to hit the bottle alone in some downtown bar. But Andrews didn't bring his drinking problem to the set, always being on hand for the morning call. Because Andrews placed no social demands on Susan, she found him a most agreeable sort. Andrews, in turn, was intrigued by his co-star, commenting to a friend after meeting her husband Jess, "She's a strong woman with a steel will. If she ever marries an equally strong man, it might prove interesting to watch."[1]

With its story of Walt and Eloise having premarital relations, the film was deemed quite daring at the time, but attitudes had lightened by 1950 and the film went on to become the perfect "date movie" for young men and women. Although Andrews was excellent in the role of Walt Dreiser, the film did little to further his career. In contrast, Susan Hayward's performance struck a chord with women, which resulted in a huge increase in her fan base. It also earned her a second Academy Award nomination for Best Actress, but she lost out to Olivia de Havilland for *The Heiress*.

Bosley Crowther of the *New York Times* commented, "Every so often there comes a picture which is obviously designed to pull plugs out of the tear glands and cause the ducts to overflow. Such a picture is Samuel Goldwyn's latest romance, *My Foolish Heart*. "...[Dana] is very attractive as a suitor, very charming in a sentimental way, but we fear he is not quite consistent with the man he is meant to be." *Screen Guide* noted, "Susan Hayward and Dana Andrews are tops, and there is an unforgettable performance by Robert Keith. Women will love this picture."

With robust performances, a touching screenplay and a melodic music score constantly tugging at your heartstrings, this well-crafted tearjerker is undoubtedly one of Hollywood's finest "lost love" movies. And once again, as in *The*

Walt Dreisser (Andrews) and Eloise Winters (Susan Hayward) ponder how the war will affect their lives in the two-handkerchief tearjerker *My Foolish Heart* (RKO, 1949).

Ox-Bow Incident, Andrews brings the curtain down on his tragic part with a heart-rending letter, which Eloise reads shortly after his untimely death.

Where the Sidewalk Ends
20th Century–Fox, 1950

Cast: Dana Andrews (Detective Sgt. Mark Dixon); Gene Tierney (Morgan Taylor); Gary Merrill (Tommy Scalise); Bert Freed (Detective Sgt. Paul Klein); Tom Tully (Jiggs Taylor); Karl Malden (Detective Lt. Thomas); Ruth Donnelly (Martha); Craig Stevens (Ken Paine); Robert Simon (Inspector Nicholas Foley); Don Appell (Willie Bender); Tony Barr (Hoodlum); Neville Brand (Steve); Harry von Zell (Ted Morrison); Grace Mills (Mrs. Tribaum); Lou Krugman (Mike Williams); David McMahon (Harrington); David Wolfe (Sid Kramer); Steve Roberts (Gilruth); Phil Tully (Tod Benson); Ian MacDonald (Casey); John Close (Hanson); Lou Nova (Ernie); Oleg Cassini (Oleg, the Fashion Designer); John McGuire (Gertessen); Louise Lorimer (Mrs. Jackson); Lester Sharpe (Friedman); Chili Williams (Teddy); Robert Foulk (Fenney); Eda Reiss Merin (Shirley Klein); Mack Williams (Jerry Morris); Duke Watson (Cab Driver); Clancey Cooper (Lieutenant Arnaldo); Bob Evans (Sweatshirt); Joseph Granby (Fat Man); Harry Brooks, Anthony George (Thugs); Fred Graham (Attendant); Charles J. Flynn (Schwartz); Larry Thompson (Riley); Wanda Smith, Shirley Tegge, Peggy O'Connor (Models); Ralph Peters (Counterman); Robert B. Williams, John Marshall, Clarence Straight (Detectives); Bob Patten (Medical Examiner); John Trebach (Bartender).

Credits: Otto Preminger (Producer-Director); William L. Stuart (Story "Night Cry"); Victor Trivas, Frank P. Rosenberg, Robert E. Kent (Adaptation); Ben Hecht (Screenplay); Joseph LaShelle (Cinematography); Cyril J. Mockridge (Music); Lionel Newman (Music Direction); Lyle R. Wheeler, J. Russell Spencer (Art Direction); Thomas Little, Walter Scott (Set Decorations); Charles Le Maire, Oleg Cassini (Costume Design); Ben Nye (Makeup);

Henry Weinberger (Assistant Director); Fred Sersen (Special Effects); Alfred Bruzlin, Harry M. Leonard (Sound); Louis Loeffler (Editor). Running time: 95 minutes

Burdened with the memory of having a criminal father, police detective Mark Dixon (Dana Andrews) hates crooks and gradually builds an unsavory reputation for using unnecessary violence in his investigations. In an act of self-defense during a struggle, he accidentally kills a murder suspect, small-time crook Ken Paine. Unbeknownst to Mark, the man had a head wound which could prove fatal with the slightest blow. Worried that his track record might suggest something other than an accident, Mark disposes of the body to make it look like a gangland killing. He attempts to frame Scalise, a local gangster, for the murder, but all the circumstantial evidence points to Tully, a cab driver whose daughter, Morgan, was the wife of the murdered man. During the investigations, Mark and Morgan fall in love, and Mark uses his life's savings to pay for a lawyer to defend her father. When no one takes the case, Mark makes a written confession that incriminates him for the crime, which is only to be read in the event of his death. He then sets off to confront Scalise in a desperate attempt to put him back in the frame for murder, even if it means making the ultimate sacrifice by making himself the victim. In the inevitable shoot-out at the gangster's hideout, Scalise is killed and Tully is cleared. Back at the station, a guilt-ridden Mark asks his captain to read his incriminating letter, and as he is led away to a cell he gains comfort in the knowledge that Morgan will be waiting for him on his release from prison.

Tagline: "Only a Woman's Heart Could Reach Out for Such a Man!"

With the title sequence opening against a rain-washed sidewalk, while people walk along to the whistling of Alfred Newman's "Street Scene Theme," your journey into the murky underbelly of the big city gets underway. This urban jungle is far removed from the glitz and glamour of Manhattan high society depicted in Andrews's earlier noir classic *Laura*.

Indeed, the dark alleys, soulless basement apartments and menacing docklands of New York's low rent district are an ideal backdrop for Andrews's forlorn character, Mark Dixon, a bitter and twisted cop, trapped in a crumbling world by his one fatal weakness—a tendency to use violent, illegal methods in his one-man crusade against crime. His tactics do not endear him to his senior officers; reprimanded by Inspector Foley for the growing number of citizen complaints leveled against him for assault and battery, he snaps back, "From who?— Hoods, dusters, mugs—lotta nickel rats." His patience running thin, Foley figures him for an out-of-hand thug who simply likes to beat up hoodlums. And when Dixon returns to the station one day all battered and bruised, having been beaten up himself, Foley gives him the benefit of his best bedside manner, "Look at ya—all bunged up like a barrelhouse vag." (I simply love this line—but what on Earth is a barrelhouse vag?)

Reunited with leading lady Gene Tierney, Andrews delivers one of his most riveting performances in *Where the Sidewalk Ends*, taking full advantage of the opportunity to play a powerful leading character. His character, Mark Dixon, has more in common with his Eric Stanton from *Fallen Angel*, than his Mark McPherson from *Laura*. Essentially, both Stanton and Dixon are loners, emotionally detached from others and the world around them. But unlike Stanton, Dixon is a violent man who became a cop in an attempt to atone for the sins of his father, a crook killed in a jail shootout. During his criminal life, his father was a known associate of the main villain of the piece, Tommy Scalise, brilliantly played by Gary Merrill. Under Otto Preminger's deft direction the tension between Scalise and Dixon is tautly maintained to the final reel, adding to the gripping pace of the film. Preminger may well have been a tyrant on set, but he certainly knew how to tap into Andrews's raw energy, to enable the actor to deliver easily the most anguished performance in his career.

In an interview, Andrews described how Preminger gave some actors a hard time if he felt they were not up to the task, suggesting that it was not the role of the director to teach an actor how to act. But recognizing the fiery nature of the director, he further commented, "He will go into these tirades and I'm sure that he has bawled out very competent actors."[1] Preminger later claimed that Andrews, contrary to the actor's belief, was one of his favorite actors to work with.

One such fine actor, who experienced the full

Tough cop Mark Dixon (Andrews) contemplates his next move after accidentally killing murder suspect Ken Paine (Craig Stevens) in a tussle in the gritty noir *Where the Sidewalk Ends* (20th Century–Fox, 1950).

measure of Preminger's tempestuous personality, was Andrews's *Where the Sidewalk Ends* co-star Karl Malden. In his autobiography *When Do I Start*, Karl described how when he arrived in L.A from New York the film had already began shooting and that it was comforting to see two old pals on the set, Andrews whom he knew from *Boomerang!* and Gary Merrill who'd been in *Winged Victory* with him. Karl recalled, "They took me aside like concerned big brothers and told me, 'Don't let him throw you. He's mean when he's behind the camera.'" With his Broadway training, Malden felt he had nothing to worry about, but after several Preminger outbursts, he later confessed, "he had me so confused I didn't know whether I was in New York or Los Angeles. To top it off Andrews and Gary were grinning from ear to ear. They bit their tongues, but their 'I told you so's' came across loud and clear."[2]

In his autobiography *Bette, Rita and the Rest of My Life*, Gary Merrill recounted how he

sought out Preminger for some advice on how to play his part in the film. "I found him sitting in the tub having a shave. 'Otto, I've never played a gangster,' I told him. 'I'm having trouble getting into the part.'" Otto interrupted his shaving only long enough to say, "Don't tell me. Tell your psychiatrist."[3]

In addition to the expert direction and strong acting, the film also had great sets, memorable location shots (particularly those framed against the Brooklyn Bridge), and superb, shadowy black-and-white cinematography, courtesy of Joseph LaShelle. In this rich mix, Ben Hecht's gripping screenplay (from William L. Stuart's story "Night Cry") was simply the icing on the cake, providing Andrews and indeed all concerned with some hard-boiled dialogue:

> MARK DIXON: I don't like rats to grin at me.
> SCALISE: That's too bad.
> MARK DIXON: Maybe I'd better show you my hand, dream-boy.

MARK DIXON: What I think doesn't mean a row of nickels.

By now Andrews was used to playing the role of one of society's born losers (*The Best Years of Our Lives, Fallen Angel*) and through his honest performance he again gained the audience's sympathy. This ability to get under the skin of the viewer was greatly helped by Andrews's facial expressions and particularly his eyes, through which we fully explore his inner toil and anguish. Looking the business in his fedora and trenchcoat, his chiseled features are a natural haven for shadows, which perfectly frame the despair in his eyes — unquestionably representing "the face of noir."

But all is not total gloom, doom and despair with Mark Dixon as we learn in his tender encounters with Morgan and his humorous exchanges with Martha, the café owner who trades insults with Dixon, but can't conceal her concern and affection for him.

This was to be Andrews's fifth and final film with his consummate leading lady, the lovely Gene Tierney, after *Tobacco Road* (1941), *Belle Starr* (1941), *Laura* (1944), and *The Iron Curtain*

Andrews and Gene Tierney in a publicity shot from *Where the Sidewalk Ends* (20th Century–Fox).

(1948). During the making of the film, Andrews indulged his penchant for all-night drinking; this was amusingly recalled by Gene in her autobiography *Self-Portrait*. She described how one morning at five o'clock, as she was getting up to go to the studio, Andrews appeared on her doorstep, unshaven and weaving. When Gene's fashion designer husband, Oleg Cassini, answered the door and asked him the reason for his visit, Andrews replied in a thick voice that he wanted to share breakfast with them. They invited him to stay, as it was abundantly clear that he had not gone to bed.[4] (In addition to designing the costumes for the film with Charles Le Maire, Cassini also cameoed as a fashion designer in the movie.)

If at first Mark Dixon comes over as being just as ruthless and unpleasant as the criminals he is trying to put away, such thoughts are instantly dispelled when he redeems himself in the final scene, where his superior reads out a loud his sealed letter which should only have been opened in the event of his death. In it he confesses to the accidental killing of Ken Paine; the letter ends with his intention to get Scalise sent up for his own murder, a sacrifice which he hopes will atone for both his own sins and those of his gangster father. On its release, *Where the Sidewalk Ends* was highly praised by audiences and critics alike, with the film critic for *Variety* singling out Andrews for his "excellent performance." William K. Everson, in his book *The Detective in Film*, described *Where the Sidewalk Ends* as one of the best and least known detective films of the '50s, and also one of Preminger's best.

In *Film Noir — An Encyclopedic Reference to the American Style*, edited by Alain Silver and Elizabeth Ward, it is noted that *Where the Sidewalk Ends* reuses many elements of Preminger's earlier noir film *Laura*. However, under Hecht's influence, the decadent world of the corrupted upper class explored in *Laura* has been replaced by a gritty, naturalistic milieu.[5]

Andrews's role as the tough cop who takes the law into his own hands was clearly a forerunner of things to come, paving the way for Kirk Douglas in *Detective Story* (1951 — from the 1949 play), Robert Ryan in *On Dangerous Ground* (1952), and Glenn Ford in *The Big Heat* (1953), and culminating 20 years later in Clint Eastwood's snarling and unrepentant Dirty Harry character.

Edge of Doom
RKO, 1950

Cast: Dana Andrews (Father Thomas Roth); Farley Granger (Martin Lynn); Joan Evans (Rita Conroy); Robert Keith (Lieutenant Mandel); Paul Stewart (Craig); Mala Powers (Julie); Adele Jergens (Irene); Harold Vermilyea (Father Kirkman); John Ridgely, Douglas Fowley (Detectives); Mabel Paige (Mrs. Pearson); Howland Chamberlain (Mr. Murray); Houseley Stevenson (Mr. Swanson); Jean Inness (Mrs. Lally); Ellen Corby (Mrs. Jeanette Moore); Ray Teal (Ned Moore); Mary Field (Mary Jane Glennon); Virginia Brissac (Mrs. Dennis); Frances Morris (Mrs. Lynn); David Clarke (Drunken Seaman); Bess Flowers (Woman in Flower Shop); Robert Karnes (George, a Priest); Herbert Lytton (Apartment House Tenant); George Magrill (Policeman); Frank O'Connor (Detective at Murder Scene); Eddie Parker (Detective); Gil Perkins (Man Questioned at Police Headquarters); Charles Perry (Suspect); Eddie Borden, Mike Lally.

Credits: Samuel Goldwyn (Producer); Mark Robson (Director); Leo Brady (Story); Philip Yordan (Screenplay); Harry Stradling Sr. (Cinematography); Emil Newman (Music Direction); Richard Day (Art Direction); Julia Heron (Set Decorations); Mary Wills (Costumes); Robert Stephanoff (Makeup); Eddie Garvin (Assistant Director); Fred Lau (Sound); Daniel Mandell (Editor). Running time: 99 minutes

In this deft mix of social commentary and film noir, Martin Lynn, a sensitive young man holding down a low-pay job, becomes increasingly frustrated with the hopelessness of his existence in New York's poverty row, which provided the backdrop to his father's suicide. He cannot afford to marry his girl Julie or send his sick mother to a better area to improve her health. Frustration turns to anger when his mother dies and Father Kirkman, the local priest, is unable to meet the expenses of a lavish funeral for her. In a fit of rage, Martin kills the priest and in his rush to get home is picked up by the police on suspicion of another crime (a nearby robbery). A sympathetic priest, Father Roth (Dana Andrews), hears of the arrest and persuades the police to release Martin into his custody. Roth soon begins to suspect the boy of the murder and gradually gets him to repent and confess to the crime. From his prison cell, Martin, his faith restored, keeps in contact with Roth through writing letters.

As a lesson of how faith can prevail over despair, Father Roth recounts the story to a young priest who has also lost hope in the squalor of New York's slums.

Tagline: "The Devil need only whisper to those who listen...."

On the face of it, *Edge of Doom* is a rather odd entry in the Sam Goldwyn catalogue; his films usually display an upbeat quality, far removed from this grim slice of film noir. The truth of the matter is that the main impetus to have the film made didn't come from Goldwyn but from his wife, Francis. Seriously involved in Catholicism, Francis read Leo Brady's novel and was desperate to turn it into a film.[1]

Selecting the right director was no problem; Mark Robson was now on the payroll, and had already made a good impression with his directorial debut for Goldwyn, the tearjerker *My Foolish Heart*. The real challenge came with the novel's adaptation for the screen. Philip Yordan accepted the poisoned chalice, and stripped out so much of its psychological substance there was only "raw meat" left (as later described by newspaper columnist Walter Winchell).

With a director and screenwriter in place, Goldwyn set his two leading stars Andrews and Farley Granger to work, accompanied by Joan Evans and Robert Keith. *Edge of Doom* was Andrews's third film with Farley Granger following their previous successes *The North Star* (1943) and *The Purple Heart* (1944). Granger started out in theatre before Goldwyn put him under contract and was originally slated to play in *another* of Andrews's films, *The Best Years of Our Lives*.* During his term with Goldwyn, Granger begged the mogul to give him a split contract, similar to that enjoyed by Andrews, but his pleas fell on deaf ears. Granger was at his best as flawed heroes, giving probably his top performance in Hitchcock's *Strangers on a Train* (1951). His career faltered thereafter; after a long break in his film career, he returned to the screen in the 1970s in Italian exploitation films.

Trained as a stage performer, Joan Evans arrived in Hollywood in 1949 as Goldwyn's latest "discovery." She was named after (and was the goddaughter of) Joan Crawford. For publicity purposes Goldwyn tried to pair her with Granger

---

*Goldwyn considered casting Granger as a character with cerebral palsy, but changed his mind when filming started, replacing Granger with someone who had actual war injuries, veteran Harold Russell.

Worldly parish priest Father Roth (Andrews) and Police Lt. Mandel (Robert Keith, left) accompany priest killer Martin Lynn (Farley Granger, center) to the police station in the uncompromising noir *Edge of Doom* (RKO, 1950).

as the new romantic couple on the scene, featuring them both in *Roseanna McCoy* (1949) and *Edge of Doom*. However, when audience response to her failed to meet Goldwyn's expectations, he dropped her contract option. Thereafter, she freelanced, appearing in several noteworthy films such *The Outcast* (1954) with John Derek and the classic Audie Murphy western *No Name on the Bullet* (1959).

There is no doubt that with its daring subject matter, *Edge of Doom* qualified as another strong entry in Andrews's impressive repertoire of offbeat stories — *Tobacco Road, Swamp Water, The Ox-Bow Incident, Boomerang!* and *Sword in the Desert*. As a "man of the people" it was only a matter of time before he played the part of a priest, and it has to be said that as Father Roth he gives it his best shot. But the character sim-

ply wasn't given enough screen-time and was clearly secondary to that of Martin, played by Granger. Notwithstanding the limitations of the part, Andrews's presence registers as a beacon of light against the all-too-bleak urban landscape. He portrays Roth as a paragon of virtue, delivering his pearls of wisdom with warmth and sincerity. "I dislike sermonizing during my tea-time. God's warriors must always be ready for battle. Even over the tea cups," he tells a despairing young priest ready to throw in the towel. Anxious to restore the young man's faith in the wretched souls who make up the parish, he adds, "Priests believe it's their job to bring God to the people. Sometimes it's the people who bring God to the priest. That's what happened to me."

As purveyors of hope presiding over despair,

street-wise priests were popular leading character parts, and it would appear that no Hollywood tough guy's career was complete without a stint in cassock, with Andrews joining the ranks of Spencer Tracy (most notably *Boys Town*, 1938), Pat O'Brien (most notably *Angels with Dirty Faces*, 1938) and another tough guy turned cleric, Ward Bond (most notably *The Quiet Man*, 1952). This saintly fraternity swelled in later years with the addition of Humphrey Bogart (*The Left Hand of God*, 1955), William Holden (*Satan Never Sleeps*, 1962), and Robert Mitchum (*The Wrath of God*, 1972). Some of these subsequent entries were of course very tongue-in-cheek, with our tough guy usually concealing a shooter about his person. And in similar vein, there are moments with Father Roth where you feel that Mark McPherson (Andrews's flatfoot from *Laura*) looks likely to burst through, to deliver his own brand of righteousness. This is particularly true in the scene where Roth displays his prowess when it comes to the old fisticuffs with one of his violent parishioners.

It was no great surprise that audiences found the film to be "depressing" and "morbid" on its first sneak preview in Santa Barbara. On wider release, audience (and critical) response was much the same, which prompted Goldwyn to pull it out of circulation until he could figure out a way to salvage it. In much the same way that *Wuthering Heights* had been saved by adding narration, two new scenes were added to *Edge of Doom* to act as bookends, thereby turning the story into one about a priest who makes good, rather than a boy who went bad. This technique entailed inserting a prologue and epilogue into the story, making Father Roth's experience with Martin a flashback.[2] Within this new framework, Roth recounts Martin's plight to the disillusioned young priest. After recalling the details, Roth concludes, "I know now I saw God in Martin Lynn. Conscience had triumphed over fear and despair. I don't think I helped Martin as much as he helped me." These changes, penned by Ben Hecht and Charles Brackett, enlarged Andrews's role in the film and were just the "tonic" it required. Thereafter the reviews were more favorable, with the *Hollywood Citizen-News* terming it "an adult film with a believable message."

Even though Andrews's sincere portrayal of the priest does much to lift the film, it did little for his career or that of costar Granger, whose recollections of the film were less than affectionate ("*Edge of Doom*—That's where it brought all our careers," he once stated). Granger had never been particularly excited about the assignment, further declaring, "You can't breathe life into a stiff."[3]

The performances all round were good, including those of Virginia Mayo lookalike Adele Jergens and Paul Stewart playing Martin's fellow, desperate tenants—all trying to survive in a world devoid of compassion. When Martin tells Stewart's character that his (Martin's) mother has died, he replies, "Well, tough. Money, money, that's all that counts in this world."

With the public rushing into a brighter new world with the onset of the 1950s, it is not difficult to understand why they initially turned their backs on this uncompromising, ahead-of-its-time drama. Today, the film is more appreciated by noir fans who relish Mark Robson's taut direction and Harry Stradling's excellent camerawork, which nicely captures the dark cityscapes and claustrophobia of New York. This brooding city atmosphere was appreciated by the *New York Times* reviewer who noted, "Mark Robson's direction gives flashes of high tension to the film, for he has made effective use of street scenes and noises and has skillfully reflected the oppressive atmosphere of poverty and squalor...."

Andrews is possibly the only Hollywood actor to have two films under his belt concerning the murder of a priest (the other being *Boomerang!*). It is also one of the rare occasions where he gets an opportunity to use his fine voice for a spot of narration.

The Frogmen
20th Century–Fox, 1951

Cast: Richard Widmark (Lt. Comdr. John Lawrence); Dana Andrews (Jake Flannigan); Gary Merrill (Lt. Comdr. Pete Vincent); Jeffrey Hunter (Pappy Creighton); Warren Stevens (Hodges); Robert Wagner (Lt. Franklin); Harvey Lembeck (Canarsie); Robert Rockwell (Lt. Bill Doyle); Henry Slate (Sleepy); Robert Adler (Chief Ryan); Parley Baer (Dr. Ullman); William Bishop (Ferrino); Ed Donovan (Crew Officer); Harry Flowers (Kinsella); James Gregory (Chief Petty Officer Lane); Harry Hamada (Gunner); Russell Hardie (Capt. Radford); Ray Raike (Repairman); Peter Leeds (Pharmacist's

Mate); Norman McKay (Capt. Phillips); William N. Neil (Comdr. Miles); Robert Patten (Lt. Klinger); Fay Roope (Admiral Dakers); Sydney Smith (Gen. Coleson); Richard Allen, Frank Donahue, Ed Donovan, Jack Warden (Crew Members).

Credits: Samuel G. Engel (Producer); Lloyd Bacon (Director); Oscar Millard (Story); John Tucker Battle (Screenplay); Norbert Brodine (Cinematography); Cyril J. Mockridge (Music); Lionel Newman (Music Direction); Albert Hogsett, Lyle Wheeler (Art Direction); Thomas Little, Fred J. Rode (Set Decorations); Charles Le Maire, Sam Benson (Wardrobe); Ben Nye (Makeup); Fred Sersen (Special Effects); Richard Maybery (Assistant Director); Roger Heman Sr., Winston H. Leverett (Sound); William Reynolds (Editor). Running time: 96 minutes

This World War II action drama is a tribute to the daring exploits of the underwater demolition divers popularly known as frogmen. Lieutenant Commander John Lawrence is put in charge of a group of frogmen, but soon alienates the men

Clearing the way for a beach attack, frogmen Creighton (Jeffrey Hunter, left) and Jake Flannigan (Andrews) survey the risks ahead in a tribute to the navy's wartime underwater demolition teams, *The Frogmen* (20th Century–Fox, 1951)—Andrews's last film for the studio.

with his strict, unyielding manner. Instead, the men look up to senior diver Jake Flannigan (Dana Andrews), a tough and courageous character with the more relaxed leadership style of their former commander, who was killed in action saving one of his men. When this lack of discipline results in the serious injury of "Pappy" Creighton during a mission; Lawrence becomes even more unpopular when he places the blame on Flannigan, despite the fact that Pappy's injury resulted from his own recklessness. With everyone giving him a wide berth, Lawrence's only confidant is Lieutenant Commander Pete Vincent, who is in charge of the naval boats used to transport the men on their missions.

After a surprise submarine attack, Lawrence finally gets the opportunity to win the respect of the men when, assisted by Flannigan, he risks his life to deactivate a live torpedo lodged in the sickbay next to the wounded Pappy. The men realize that both courage and discipline are essential requirements in their dangerous work. These lessons are put into practice during their next mission to blow up a Japanese submarine pen. After hand-to-hand combat with some Japanese frogmen, in which Lawrence is stabbed, the base and its vessels are destroyed. The mission a success, Flannigan helps pull the wounded Lawrence back to safety, and the two put aside their differences and learn a new respect for one another.

Tagline: "The Thrilling Story of Uncle Sam's Underwater Commandos."

In the early 1930s, when Darryl F. Zanuck left Warner Brothers to form his own studio, Samuel G. Engel joined him and was responsible for naming the company 20th Century Pictures, which later merged with Fox Pictures to form 20th Century–Fox. Engel's most notable films as producer include the John Ford western classic *My Darling Clementine* (1946) and the noir *Night and the City* (1950). *The Frogmen* was his second film with Andrews, their first encounter being *Deep Waters* (1948).

Director Lloyd Bacon started his film career playing heavy roles in silent Lloyd Hamilton comedies before providing the perfect foil to Charlie Chaplin in many of his films. He went on to become a prolific film director; his precise timing, which he learned from Mack Sennett, is clearly evident in his action films, and particularly so in *The Frogmen*.

Richard Widmark joined Andrews in the hall of noir icons with his first movie appearance as the giggling sociopathic villain in *Kiss of Death* (1947) for which he received an Academy Award nomination for Best Supporting Actor (losing out to Edmund Gwenn in *Miracle on 34th Street*). For a short spell he continued to play similar villains before widening his range to include sympathetic heroes. From 1950, he carved a niche as unpopular commanders in memorable films such as *The Frogmen, Halls of Montezuma* (1950), *Destination Gobi* (1953) and *The Bedford Incident* (1965). In 1999, at the age of 84, Widmark married Susan Blanchard, who was Henry Fonda's third wife.

The story of men railing against their disciplinarian commanding officer was not a new one to Andrews, essentially relying on the same plotline used in *Wing and a Prayer* (1944). Once again Andrews would be the voice of the men having to confront a strict superior who on the face of it has little time for the individual. And as in *Wing and a Prayer* he received second billing on the cast list. But in this position he was in good company with Gary Merrill, his old pal from *Where the Sidewalk Ends* (1950). (Merrill's role as Pete Vincent was initially earmarked for Richard Conte.) Merrill had the makings of a real contender after the likes of *Twelve O'Clock High* (1949) and *All About Eve* (1950), but he was never able to get beyond supporting roles and is probably best remembered today for his marriage to Bette Davis and his affair with Rita Hayworth. To give him something to think about while filming *The Frogmen,* Davis rang to inform him that he was the proud father of a beautiful baby girl.[1]

The film also provided early roles for Jeffrey Hunter and Robert Wagner. Hunter, looking like an Adonis, puts in a memorable performance as Pappy, the wounded diver with an unexploded torpedo for company in sickbay. Blink and you'll miss Wagner. He enjoyed fifth billing, but only appears for a few seconds.

Although Widmark is clearly the star of the film, and a fine job he does, Andrews is excellent in support as the "nose out of joint" Flannigan who initially has no time or respect for his boorish commanding officer. Well and truly weary of Lawrence's "strictly by the book" manner, he grumbles, "He makes everything sound like a presidential directive." And when some things just have to be said face to face, Flannigan puts on his best scowl when he rattles off, "Oh, to heck with it. I'm gonna tell him. He can like it or lump it!"

But one can't accuse Flannigan of not putting the safety of his men first as we observe when the recovery launch explodes from a direct hit. With enemy shells raining in from all directions, he quickly advises his fellow frogman, "We'd better start paddling outta here, or they'll pick us up with a sieve, too."

Andrews's "average guy" persona made him the natural choice to play middle-ranking servicemen who gain the respect of the men through outward empathy. In Flannigan, Andrews expertly crafts a man of fortitude, prone to indignation and antipathy to his strict superiors, but with a strong sense of responsibility to duty and for his men. Although there is no question of his courage, he is a leader who instills little discipline in his team; as observed by Lawrence who is quick to castigate him when Pappy is wounded following a reckless prank ashore after a mission: "Your kind of bravery comes ten cents a dozen, and isn't worth a hoot more when the chips are down." (Ouch!)

Although this was a war movie through and through, with no romantic subplot, the female audiences of the time would have enjoyed watching some prime Hollywood beefcake going about covert missions in their swim trunks. Incidentally, in Andrews's case this was the first of two movies in which he bares his chest (the second was *Enchanted Island*). Apparently, all female roles were written out of the script because working conditions on set were deemed too "riotous." (A shame; you could just picture the likes of Virginia Mayo and Jeanne Crain as navy nurses, working up temperatures in their starched white uniforms.)

In addition to the guys flexing their pecs, the film also packs in some impressive camerawork which brilliantly captures the tension of the underwater scenes and the pace and excitement of the Underwater Demolition Teams operations as launches drop off and pick up frogmen at high speed. This basically entailed rolling off a rubber boat when the launch approached the target area and being yanked back into the boat when the mission was completed. Norbert Brodine's cinematography and Oscar Millard's story both received Oscar nominations.

The Navy was initially reluctant to have the story of their underwater demolition experts told because at the time of making the film, much of the organization's activities remained classified.[2] However, the assistant secretary of the Navy eventually gave his blessings and assistance to the project following a meeting with Sam Engel. The film acknowledges that the Navy's Underwater Demolition Teams were the unsung heroes of World War II, going in ahead of the Marines to remove from the water enemy obstacles which would have cost many Marines their lives during beach landings.

In addition to its pseudo-documentary style, showing how frogmen performed their missions, another distinguishing feature of the film was the final scene in which frogmen blow up a Japanese submarine base with a huge explosion lasting 62 seconds. Director Bacon recalled, "I have made eight pictures with a war background, but none of the others contained a sequence with so much concentrated fireworks and all the trimmings. When you see it on the screen it practically blasts you out of your seat."[3]

The *Saturday Review of Literature* commented that the story itself is never the movie's center of attention but is "simply an excuse to send the cameras below the waterline for some of the most remarkable and occasionally the most beautiful shots in a long time.... It's fascinating, exciting stuff...."

According to the *New York Times*: "The dauntless swimmers ... perform incredible feats. But the straight demonstration of their techniques as literal one-man submarines is utterly fascinating, and thus the picture is too.... With top-notch performances by all hands and action that is unusual. *The Frogmen* rates a position close to the top of superior movies inspired by the innovations and heroics of World War II. See it and be proud of your Navy."

The success of the movie provided the Navy with an excellent recruitment poster for its elite underwater team. This was to be Andrews's last film for Fox and, although he wasn't the star, he at least went out on a high note in a high-quality production.

Fox remade the film for television in 1957 under the title *Deep Water*, this time starring Ralph Meeker, James Whitmore and Richard Arleen. Having penned his own story entitled *Frogmen in Korea,* producer Engel had intended to make a sequel to *The Frogmen,* but the project never materialized.

Sealed Cargo
RKO, 1951

Cast: Dana Andrews (Pat Bannon); Carla Balenda (Margaret McLean); Claude Rains (Captain Skalder); Philip Dorn (Konrad); Onslow Stevens (Comdr. James McLean); Skip Homeier (Steve); Eric Feldary (Holger); J.M. Kerrigan (Skipper Ben); Arthur Shields (Kevin Dolan); Morgan Farley (Caleb); Dave Thursby (Ambrose); Henry Rowland (Anderson); Charles A. Browne (Smitty); Don Dillaway (Owen); Al Hill (Tom); Lee MacGregor (Flight Lt. Cameron); Steve Forrest (Holtz); Richard Norris (Second Mate); Kathleen Ellis, Karen Norris, Brick Sullivan, Harry Mancke (Villagers); Dick Crockett, Wesley Hopper, Bob Morgan (Nazis); Bruce Cameron, Ned Roberts (Nazi Machine Gunners); Whit Bissell (Schuster); Watson Downs (Ethan); Kay Morley (Wharf Official); Burt Kennedy (Old Seaman); John Royce, Bob Smitts (Nazi Sailors).

Credits: Warren Duff (Producer); Alfred Werker (Director); Edmund Gilligan (Novel *The Gaunt Woman*); Dale Van Every, Oliver H.P. Garrett, Roy Huggins (Screenplay); George E. Diskant (Cinematography); Roy Webb (Music); C. Bakaleinikoff (Music Direction); Albert S. D'Agostino (Art Direction); Darrell Silvera, William Stevens (Set Decorations); Michael Woulfe (Costume Design); Mel Berns (Makeup); Lloyd Richards (Assistant Director); Phil Brigandi, Clem Portman (Sound); Ralph Dawson (Editor). Running time: 89 minutes

On the Newfoundland coastline during World War II, fishing boat captain Pat Bannon (Dana Andrews) wants to join the Navy to do his bit for the war effort, but his requests are continually turned down because the Navy feels that he can better serve his country by catching halibut. Resigned to this role, he sets out on another fishing trip, this time carrying a beautiful passenger, Margaret McLean, who is looking to visit her father, a former naval captain living in Trebor, a remote harbor settlement with a population of 50 people. While at sea, Bannon comes to the aid of a badly damaged Danish square rigger. An air of mystery surrounds the ship with only Captain Skalder left on board following an alleged U-Boat attack. Bannon tows the ship to the isolated harbor, only to find himself in the midst of spies when he discovers that its cargo, concealed in a secret hold, consists of torpedoes. Far from being an innocent casualty of war, the schooner is really the supply ship for a wolf pack

of German submarines. Tensions are heightened when it's suspected that one of Bannon's crew members may be a spy. Bannon hatches a daring plan which climaxes with the destruction of the schooner and the wolf pack. Having saved the day, he finds safe harbor in the loving arms of Miss McLean.

Taglines: "CARGO THAT BLASTS THE SEA WIDE OPEN"; "Savage Passions aflame in the North Atlantic ... unleashed by treachery ... hate ... violence."

As we are informed in the foreword, "This is the story of one small victory in WWII." Set in 1943 and loosely inspired by true incidents, this wartime thriller serves as a tribute to the "little people" (fishermen and villagers) who gave their all to fight a common foe. Shot on a tight budget, this unique, absorbing tale is given the full RKO treatment, with director Alfred Werker skillfully weaving mystery and romance on the high seas with a hefty dose of film noir for good measure.

Werker began his career directing minor westerns in the 1920s before going on to direct in various film genres, usually on a medium budget, until his retirement in the late '50s. Although much of his work can rightfully be considered routine, several notable exceptions suggest a talent that was not fully exploited. Those films included *The House of Rothschild* (1934), *The Adventures of Sherlock Holmes* (1939 — one of the best in the Holmes series), and *Lost Boundaries* (1949). In the late '40s he went to work for the B-picture studio Eagle-Lion Films where he turned out some of his most notable work, including the excellent *Repeat Performance* (1947) and *He Walked by Night* (1948), both starring the much underrated Richard Basehart.

Having coached Basehart to perfection, Werker also worked his magic on Andrews in this taut and moody melodrama, which was based on Edmund Gilligan's novel *The Gaunt Woman.* With its suspense-laden storyline, eerie fogbound setting, mysterious *Marie Celeste*–type schooner and a wonderfully atmospheric Roy Webb score, this is a real hidden gem from the RKO vaults.

Unable to enter active service because the powers-that-be feel that he fulfills a more valuable war role as a fisherman, Andrews's Pat Bannon is an intelligent and resourceful man of the sea, itching for a piece of the action. With yet another bumper haul to add to his coffers, Pat's growing frustration with his essential occupation is summed up in his conversation with village friend Kevin Dolan (Arthur Shields):

"You've got four sons in the service and I get rich. Where does that leave us?" (Shields teamed with Andrews again seven years later in another nautical yarn, *Enchanted Island*.)

GW-Adv-46

Ship's skipper Pat Bannon (Andrews) on the scent of Nazi spies, accompanied by Margaret McLean (Carla Balenda), in the thrilling actioner *Sealed Cargo*. (RKO, 1951).

Pat's resigned attitude soon gives way to wily cunning and steely-eyed determination when the enemy presents itself in the guise of the deliciously sinister Claude Rains and his gang of Nazis passing themselves off as Danes. Reinvigorated, Pat pits his wits against this nest of vipers when he discovers that their schooner's secret hold stores a huge arsenal of torpedoes and explosives. (With the inner dimensions of the ship's hull as apparently limitless as Doctor Who's TARDIS, there was ample scope to stretch the imagination a mite further and squeeze in a couple of submarines.)

With the safety of Atlantic shipping in his hands and perhaps the fate of mankind, Pat also finds time to romance the beautiful nurse Margaret McLean, played by Carla Balenda. But with Nazis on his mind instead of halibut, he is a little too preoccupied in their early exchanges to give her his full attention. When she questions the cost of a boat ride to Trebor, he flippantly informs her that his boat would simply be used as target practice by the hundreds of Nazi subs lurking in the Grand Bank.

And if that wasn't enough to send her packing, he does a slick marketing job on the only remaining cabin — a small closet-type space full of junk, which he describes as a coffin. However, the fiercely independent Miss McLean is not easily deterred, proving that it would take more than the ancient mariner's grimace and a dozen or so deadly wolf packs to prevent her from taking tea with her father.

But when both are faced with adversity, such initial frostiness inevitably blossoms into unbridled love, prompting Pat to wax lyrical to a starry-eyed Miss McLean about his other great love — that of the dear old briny. "We have an old saying that the sea is only good to sailors that are afraid of her."

With the exception of Marta Toren, who co-starred with Andrews in *Sword in the Desert* (1949), most of his leading ladies up to this point in his career were established household names — Gene Tierney, Susan Hayward, Joan Crawford, Merle Oberon, etc.; but with the virtually unknown Carla Balenda at his side he would have certainly been carrying the full weight of the film on his shoulders were it not for the robust support given by Claude Rains as the "villain of the piece." This was the second time that Andrews starred with an up-and-coming actress straight out of the Hughes–RKO stable, the first being Jean Peters in *Deep Waters* (1948). Like many of the tycoon's starlets-in-waiting, Balenda was given a lot of dramatic training, but nothing in the way of a film role, and it was only after a nine-year wait and countless heated arguments about her stalled career that she eventually got to star in four RKO movies, the other three being *Hunt the Man Down* (1950), *The Whip Hand* (1951) and *The Pace That Thrills* (1952).

Sealed Cargo was the first and only time Andrews worked with the great character actor Claude Rains. Born in London in 1889, Rains served in the First World War and was involved in a gas attack that left him almost blind in one eye for the rest of his life. Having established his credentials in the theatre, he arrived in Hollywood late in life and, although he was nominated four times for the Best Supporting Actor Oscar, he was never the winner. His most memorable films include *The Invisible Man* (1933), *The Adventures of Robin Hood* (1938), *Casablanca* (1942), *Mr. Skeffington* (1944) and *Caesar and Cleopatra* (1945). Quite remarkably, within his busy work schedule he managed to fit in six marriages.

In terms of screen presence, Andrews and Claude were from the same mold, both gifted with memorable voices and the skillful ability to convey great expression through their eyes. Having Rains in a supporting role certainly gave the film a seal of quality, and with both actors in top form vying for the most penetrating stare, the tone was set for some crackling dialogue and noir laden intrigue.

Pat to Captain Skalder: "You'll forgive me for mentioning it, captain, but for a Dane you have little accent."

(More to the point: for a fully paid-up Nazi, he has even less of an accent.)

Drifting into film noir mode, Pat later dispenses with the niceties where Captain Skalder's concerned: "Keep him here. If he bats an eye, blow it out of his head."

Sporting sideburns, courtesy of RKO, and kitted out in wind-battered sea cap and slicker, Pat Bannon is very much a seagoing cousin of Andrews's Mark McPherson from *Laura*. Sure, he's a worldly tough guy, but his real strength, like Mark's, lies in his rational and intuitive mind, which enables him to get to the truth of the matter with little recourse to his fists. This is Andrews at the top of his game, with the RKO treatment and style making the most of the nuances in his screen persona. It is therefore perhaps a little disappointing that he didn't make more film noirs with the studio in the early '50s when both actor and genre were at their peak. Of course, this window of opportunity was fully exploited by RKO's leading star Robert Mitchum, who deservedly became noir's undisputed king. Andrews challenged the noir throne again with RKO in the mid–1950s with the Fritz Lang classics *While the City Sleeps* and *Beyond a Reasonable Doubt,* but unfortunately at this juncture, both the studio and the genre were looking a bit tired and would shortly be consigned to the past.

Sealed Cargo is one of my personal favorites, ticking all the boxes on the entertainment front, and indeed providing a shining example of what can be achieved on a tight budget with a little ingenuity, imagination and of course that essential ingredient — a credible leading actor.

The *New York Times* reviewer wrote, "Alfred Werker has made some of the unbelievable sequences taut and exciting.... Dana Andrews ... is a grim, determined sailor who is willing to risk his own neck as well as those of his crew.... Call *Sealed Cargo* a fairly exciting package for the action fans, but it is hardly a superior consignment." (A kiss for one cheek and an undeserved slap for the other, methinks.)

I Want You
RKO, 1951

Cast: Dana Andrews (Martin Greer); Dorothy McGuire (Nancy Greer); Farley Granger (Jack Greer); Peggy Dow (Carrie Turner); Robert Keith (Thomas Greer); Mildred Dunnock (Sarah Greer); Ray Collins (Judge Turner); Martin Milner (George Kress, Jr.); Jim Backus (Harvey Landrum); Marjorie Crossland (Mrs. Turner); Walter Baldwin (George Kress Sr.); Walter Sande (Ned Iversen); Peggy Maley (Gladys); Jerrilyn Flannery (Anne Greer); Erik Nielsen (Tony Greer); James Adamson (Train Porter); Jean Andren (Secretary); Johnny Arthur (Draftman); Ralph Brooks (Albert); Dee Carroll (Woman); Don Hayden (Candidate); Harry Lauter (Art Stacey); Melodi Lowell (Girl); Charles Marsh (Mr. Jones); David McMahon (Taxi Driver); Roland Morris (Sergeant); Al Murphy (Man); Jimmy Ogg (Soldier); Ann Robinson (Gloria); Carol Savage (Caroline Krupka); Frank Sully (Bartender); Lee Turnbull (Fat Boy); Paul Birch (Bit Role).

Credits: Samuel Goldwyn (Producer); Mark Robson (Director); Edward Newhouse (Story); Irwin Shaw (Screenplay); Harry Stradling Sr. (Cinematography); Leigh Harline (Music); Richard Day (Art Direction); Howard Bristol (Set Decorations); Mary Wills (Costume Design); Pat McNalley (Makeup); Ivan Volkman (Assistant Director); Fred Lau (Sound); Daniel Mandell (Editor). Running time: 102 minutes

The story depicts the trials and tribulations of small-town family life following the outbreak of hostilities in Korea. Martin Greer (Dana Andrews), a family man and World War II veteran, struggles with his conscience and his wife Nancy's misgivings about his re-enlisting. Kid brother Jack Greer is more concerned that the draft will disrupt his romance with his girl Carrie Turner, the daughter of the draft board chairman. When the board sign him fit for duty, Jack becomes angry in the belief that her unfriendly father used it as an opportunity to break up his plans to marry Carrie. Jack's mother Sarah, having already lost one son in action, resents her husband Thomas's glorification of warfare and his pro-war stance. For another young man, George Kress, Jr., the main problem is his possessive father, George Kress Sr., who, frightened at the prospect of losing his son, concentrates his energies on keeping him from being drafted. When Martin, a building contractor and the lad's employer, refuses to label him "indispensable," his father's anguish turns to despair and he takes to the bottle when his son sets off to war and is killed in action. Nancy, realizing that in fighting for his country her husband will be protecting his family, finally consents to his enlistment. Jack, eventually overcomes his anger and accepts his part in the war when Carrie agrees to marry him.

Tagline: "No three words ever meant so much to so many people."

And no other film cleverly depicted how the ordinary American viewed the Communist threat building momentum on the other side of the world during the early months of the Korean War. From its opening shots, the pro-interventionist stance of the film is clearly stated with Andrews's voiceover, as we view his comfortable, middle-class home town from the air. In a sobering tone he says, "This is how it might look to a bird, or to a bomber pilot straightening out for his run over the target...."

With the Korean War gathering pace, army reservist and family man Martin Greer considers his call-up with loyal wife Nancy (Dorothy McGuire) showing equal concern in Andrews's last Goldwyn film, *I Want You* (RKO, 1951).

Goldwyn found the main inspiration for *I Want You* in his only son, Sammy, who had served in Europe during World War II. Initially the film (then tentatively titled *No Time Like the Present*) was to tell the story of an American soldier in postwar Allied-occupied Germany, who befriends a family there. However, this "pet project" quickly became out-of-date when North Korean troops invaded South Korea in the summer of 1950. With the UN entering the conflict, army reservists such as Sammy were called up, which sparked a new idea in Goldwyn's mind. Just as *The Best Years of Our Lives* had told the story of the lives of returning servicemen, *I Want You* would describe the effect of America's rearming on the lives of the average American family.[1] After several years in the wilderness, Goldwyn was confident that this project would put him back on top. Irwin Shaw, fresh from the success of his first publication *The Young Lions*, wrote the screenplay, borrowing

the title from the Uncle Sam enlistment poster caption. With a cast that included his two leading men, Andrews, Farley Granger, plus Dorothy McGuire borrowed from Selznick, Goldwyn was pinning his hopes on emulating the artistic and commercial success of *Best Years*. But the preview of the film coincided with ceasefire negotiations in Korea and the audience response to the film was lukewarm.

I Want You was Andrews's last film under his Goldwyn contract, and from now on he would have to face the uncertain world of being an independent star. Despite its modest box office return, *I Want You* at least provided him with a high-quality feature to end his successful run under the studio system, which in itself was in its final years.

Andrews had played the part of a married man on several occasions, but this was the first time his character was happily married with a family. The part of Martin Greer, a loving husband and father, could perhaps be seen as an older version of his Fred Derry character from *The Best Years of Our Lives*. Conceivably, in the immediate post–World War II years, Fred works hard to build a business and starts a family, morphing into Martin Greer along the way. With his reserved manner, Andrews seamlessly slips into the role of the conscientious parent, but no family would be perfect without the inclusion of the actress who chalked up numerous successes in many motherly roles, the wonderful Dorothy McGuire. A sincere and versatile actress, McGuire expertly engaged audiences' emotions in many memorable films including *Claudia* (1943), its sequel *Claudia and David* (1946), *The Spiral Staircase* (1946), *Gentleman's Agreement* (1947), for which she received an Oscar nomination, and *Friendly Persuasion* (1956).

The natural warmth and honesty that Andrews brings to his part is noticeably conveyed in his scenes with his family and particularly in the very touching finale where he bids farewell to his children before re-enlisting. Although all the performances are excellent, it is arguably Andrews's solid presence that anchors the film and provides its heartfelt qualities.

The song "My Foolish Heart" (from Andrews's earlier film of the same title) is skillfully put to good use as background music in two scenes, perfectly complementing the mood in these moments. In the first, Martin ponders how, in perhaps ten years' time, he will respond when his son asks, "What were you doing, Daddy, when the world was shaking?" A question he answers himself after a brief pause: "I built a hotel for 200 guests." It's heard again in the bar scene when Martin tries, unsuccessfully, to buy 19-year-old George Kress, Jr., a farewell drink before he sets off for boot camp, prompting Martin to growl, "Old enough to hold a gun, to kill and be killed, but not old enough to buy a drink."

To recreate small town America, Goldwyn hired Richard Day, who had also designed the sets for Andrews's *My Foolish Heart* and *Edge of Doom*. *Newsweek* commented that Day's work "has all the exaggerated realism of a painting by Norman Rockwell."

The film was described in a *Los Angeles Times* article as "a picture that tells the story of the effect of America's rearming on the lives of an American family today ... in terms of the loves,

the aspirations, the disappointments, the tears and the joys of real people — not cardboard characters — in times of stress...."

A recent review went even further, commenting, "The screenplay is excellent, and the performances ring touching and true. This is very much a period artifact, fascinating to watch today."

In defense of the subject matter, Philip T. Hartung, writing in *Commonweal*, wrote, "At times *I Want You* is raw and grim in putting over its points, and at times it approaches the sentimental; but it is never just a recruiting poster for our white-bearded Uncle Sam or for Sam Goldwyn's business. It is a well-made human drama to which attention must be paid."[2]

Although not quite in the same league as *Best Years*, *I Want You* is nonetheless a strong, unusual film that has been described as one of Goldwyn's most trouble-free productions. Undeterred by its poor reception from critics and audiences alike, Goldwyn went that extra mile to help its promotion, proclaiming at every opportunity that it was not a mere movie, but more a statement of national importance.[3] Its lack of success is possibly down to the simple fact that *Best Years* was a drama of World War II, a war that touched the lives of all people, whereas *I Want You* was set against the Korean War, which only affected certain families, and is sometimes referred to as "The Forgotten War."

Assignment Paris
Columbia, 1952

Cast: Dana Andrews (Jimmy Race); Marta Toren (Jeanne Moray); Herbert Berghof (Prime Minister Andreas Ordy); Ben Astar (Minister of Justice Vajos); George Sanders (Nicholas Strang); Sandro Giglio (Grisha); Audrey Totter (Sandy Tate); Willis Bouchey (Biddle); Earl Lee (Dad Pelham); Leon Askin (Franz); Peter J. Votrian (Jan Czeki); Georgina Wulff (Gogo Czeki); Joseph Forte (Barker); Pal Javor (Laslos Boros); Paul Hoffman (Kedor); Jay Adler (Henry, the Bartender); Hannelore Axman (Secretary); Paul Birch (Colonel in Charge of Prisoner Exchange); Mari Blanchard (Wanda Marlowe); Maurice Doner (Victor); Paul Frees (Narrator/Radio Budapest Announcer); Don Gibson (Phone Operator); Don Kohler (Bert); Fay Roope (American Ambassador); Victor Sutherland (Larry); Andre Simeon (Waiter); Harold Stiller (American Sergeant); Vito Scotti (Italian Reporter); Ken Terrell (Military Aide); Robert Stevenson (Medical Officer at Prisoner Exchange).

Credits: Samuel Marx, Jerry Bresler (Producers); Robert Parrish (Director); Paul & Pauline Gallico (Story "Trial of Terror"); William Bowers (Screenplay); Walter Goetz, Jack Palmer White (Adaptation); Burnett Guffey, Ray Cory (Cinematography); George Duning (Music); Morris Stoloff (Music Direction); John Meehan (Art Direction); Frank Tuttle (Set Decorations); Jean Louis (Costume Design); Clay Campbell (Makeup); Carter DeHaven (Assistant Director); Jack A. Goodrich (Sound); Charles Nelson (Editor). Running time: 85 minutes

In this Cold War conspiracy thriller set against the backdrops of Paris and Budapest, ace reporter Jimmy Race (Dana Andrews) works for editor Nick Strang at the Paris office of the *New York Herald Tribune*. Also on the payroll is French journalist Jeanne, who has just returned from Budapest with a top story she is unable to substantiate, about a plot to overthrow the communist puppet dictator with the help of Tito. When the *Tribune*'s Budapest correspondent is taken ill, Race is dispatched to take his place with the hope of establishing the facts behind the story. Strang also sees this as a good opportunity to get Race out of the way, leaving the field clear to pursue the beautiful Jeanne. During the course of his investigations, Race becomes embroiled in a dangerous hotbed of communist spies and censors; he is arrested as a suspected spy after discovering photographic proof of the connection between Tito and the plotters. Through the intervention of another man wanted by the communists, Race, a little worst for wear after his incarceration, finds his freedom and returns to the love of Jeanne.

Taglines: "PARIS.... A City Made for Excitement.... Excitement on a Night Made for Murder"; "The Last Time He Saw Paris—he had a girl in his arms and a gun in his back."

To further whet our appetites, the press coverage excitedly informed us,

In covering his *Assignment Paris*, Andrews travels from the boudoirs and bistros of this

Ace reporter Jimmy Race (Andrews) reviews the evidence concerning a potential political conspiracy in Hungary with fellow reporter Jeanne Moray (Marta Toren) and editor Nicholas Strang (George Sanders, right) in *Assignment Paris* (Columbia, 1952).

world capital of intrigue to the back alleys of Budapest, following a hunch and a girl in a plunging neckline. Andrews gets himself tangled with such varied characters as a girl whose figure has a French accent; a rough tough editor in a soft, silky town, and a Paris manikin looking for a man to make her forget the man on her mind. He makes love between bulletins, and he makes history between bullets ... and his biggest story is one that can't be printed![1]

The film was based on a serialized *Saturday Evening Post* yarn entitled *Trial of Terror* and the real-life experiences of Robert A. Vogeler, an American citizen who was arrested in Hungary in 1949 and sentenced to 15 years imprisonment on charges of espionage and sabotage. He was released in 1951 after long negotiations between the U.S. and Hungary.

After two credible performances based on true-life characters in the docu-dramas *Boomerang!* and *The Iron Curtain*, Andrews was a fitting choice to play the imprisoned American, even though Columbia's interpretation of the actual character and the incidents surrounding him were loose to say the least.

The movie places the star back in the world of journalism: Andrews's Jimmy Race is very much an older version of his quick-witted Bill Roberts from *Berlin Correspondent*, who would eventually grow into the world-weary but equally humorous reporter Edward Mobley from *While the City Sleeps*. Like Roberts, the brash Jimmy Race also uses coded messages to outwit the bad guys in his quest to broadcast the truth to the outside world. And in the face of death or torture, he is a man you can depend on to hold his nerve to the bitter end. Luckily our intrepid hero survives the rough treatment by his commie captors, but there is no romantic kiss to mark the finale in this story, with our Jimmy being driven off to safety in a brainwashed daze with leading lady Marta Toren in tow.

Shot in Paris and Budapest, *Assignment Paris* was Andrews's second outing with the sultry Swedish actress Marta Toren following their successful first pairing three years earlier in *Sword in the Desert* (1949). A close friend of fellow Swedish beauty Ingrid Bergman, Toren started her Hollywood career with Universal-International, who signed her up to a seven-year con-

tract in 1947. She was cast in a number of action adventure movies in the late '40s and early '50s including *Spy Hunt* (1950) and *Sirocco* (1951), but these roles did little to advance her career and she returned to Europe in 1952. When she was first considered for the part of Jeanne in *Assignment Paris*, Columbia asked her to make a test, to which she sensibly replied, "Why make a test? I already made a picture here with [Humphrey] Bogart [*Sirocco*]. Why waste time and money when you know what I can do?" In 1957, Toren was stricken with a brain hemorrhage while on stage in Stockholm and died in hospital at the age of 31. Among the many wreaths at her funeral was one with a simple message: "Farewell, dear Marta. Your friend, Ingrid."

Throughout his movie career, Andrews enjoyed good support from many highly acclaimed character actors and *Assignment Paris* was no exception, with the suave and sophisticated George Sanders included in the cast line-up. Born in Russia of British parents, Sanders traveled to Britain with his family at the age of eleven on the outbreak of the Russian Revolution in 1917. Starting in British films before moving to Hollywood, he made his name with *The Saint* and *Falcon* film series in the late 1930s and early 1940s. In his supporting capacity he will be best remembered for his part in the likes of *Rebecca* (1940), *The Picture of Dorian Gray* (1945) and *All About Eve* (1950), in which his performance as the venomous drama critic earned him an Academy Award for Best Supporting Actor. Married four times (two of his wives were sisters Zsa Zsa and Magda Gabor), he committed suicide with an overdose of barbiturates in 1972, leaving a note that attributed his suicide to boredom with life.

Perhaps a little uncertain as to the artistic merits of *Assignment Paris*, Sanders was overheard on set asking fellow co-star Audrey Totter, "Whatever are we doing this tripe for?"[2]

The movie is clearly no masterpiece, but such a barbed estimation was perhaps a trifle harsh and undeserved for a feature that did at least attempt to present a new angle on the typical spy formula, with our innocent hero falsely accused of spying and forced by torture to make a public confession. The film was also noteworthy for its fair depiction of the difficulties of a free press working under the strict censorship of Communist countries.

Notwithstanding the rather mixed reviews, the film did provide Andrews with another opportunity to showcase his natural talent for light humor. This is neatly captured in an early scene where love-smitten reporter Jimmy Race gives it his best shot in an attempt to date the ice cool Jeanne: "I'm an extremely grateful feeder, hostesses fight over me. Husbands even ask me back." Eventually arriving at first base, he and Jeanne discuss what he did during the war, with the former paratrooper explaining that fighting was nothing new to him having been brought up in New York's East Side. His keen sense of fun shines through even when the chips are down; when interrogated by the Reds, he protects his contact by declaring himself the lone wolf type. And in answer to the remark that his sense of humor is somewhat out of place considering his predicament, he delivers the best line in the picture when he nonchalantly observes, "I don't know, I think this place could use a couple of laughs."

Equal amusement was to be found in a French interview. Unable to speak a word of French, Andrews memorized his answers phonetically prior to the chat. However, the interview turned into an amusing farce when the French interviewer asked the questions in the wrong order. As a result, when Andrews was asked whether he had any children, he replied, "Yes, Samuel Goldwyn and Darryl Zanuck." And when asked who were his favorite producers, he responded with the names of his two favorite actresses, Myrna Loy and Irene Dunne.[3] A series of other questions and answers which failed to synchronize followed.

The *New York Times* noted, "[T]he film emerges as a standard display piece for some palpitating star heroics against a provocative but mildly effective background of totalitarian intrigue." James Robert Parish and Michael R. Pitts commented in their excellent book *The Great Spy Pictures II*, "Dana Andrews does the best he can with the difficult role of an ace reporter, who cannot figure out that he is being set up both by his boss and the Reds."[4]

Having tried once, those darn Reds get another opportunity to scramble his brains when they catch up with Andrews again in the 1958 feature *The Fearmakers*.

Elephant Walk
Paramount, 1954

Cast: Elizabeth Taylor (Ruth Wiley); Dana Andrews (Dick Carver); Peter Finch (John Wiley); Abraham Sofaer (Appuhamy); Abner Biberman (Dr. Pereira); Noel Drayton (Atkinson); Rosalind Ivan (Mrs. Lakin); Barry Bernard (Strawson); Philip Tonge (John Ralph); Edward Ashley (Gordon Gregory); Leo Britt (Chisholm); My Lee Haulani (Rayna); Jack Raine (Norbert); Victor Millan (Koru); Norma Varden (Mrs. Beezley); Carlos Rivero (Thomas the Chauffeur); Delmar Costello (Native Patient); Santini Pualoa (Foreman); Leslie Sketchley, Charles Heard (Planters); Reginald Lai Singh, Rodd Redwing (Servants); Madhyma Lanka Nritya Mandala Dancers (Themselves).

Credits: Irving Asher (Producer); William Dieterle (Director); Robert Standish (Story); John Lee Mahin (Screenplay); Loyal Griggs (Cinematography); Franz Waxman (Music); Hal Pereira, J. McMillan Johnson (Art Direction); Sam Comer, Grace Gregory (Set Decorations); Edith Head (Costume Design); Wally Westmore (Makeup); John P. Fulton, Paul K. Lerpae (Special Effects); Francisco Day (Assistant Director); John Cope, Gene Merritt (Sound); George Tomasini (Editor). Running time: 103 minutes

Shortly after World War II, tea plantation owner John Wiley, visiting England to look for a wife, meets the beautiful Ruth and wins her hand in marriage. He returns home with his bride to the ancestral mansion in Ceylon known as Elephant Walk. (By all accounts it took its name from a malicious act of John's father in building it in the middle of a route taken by the local elephant population — an act that the elephants have not forgotten.) Ruth's excitement about moving to a new world soon gives way to despair when she realizes that her husband is obsessed with keeping the memory of his father alive through heavy drinking and childish games with the neighboring British planters. Feeling lonely and isolated, she begins to spend more time in the company of the plantation manager, Dick Carver (Dana Andrews). The two fall in love, but before they can run off together there is a cholera outbreak and Ruth stays behind to help her husband by ministering to the sick. Adding to the drama, the elephants go on the rampage and stampede through the mansion with Ruth trapped inside. As the walls come crashing down around her, John arrives on the scene and rescues her from certain death. With John having exorcised the memory of his dead father, he and Ruth see things in a new light, and decide to give their marriage another try.

Tagline: "One man claimed the land. Two men claimed the woman who lived there."

From the chic streets of Paris, Andrews's next assignment took him into the steamy wilds of Ceylon, once again propping up an all-too-familiar love triangle. This time Andrews nearly succeeds in winning the hand of the fair maiden, but is thwarted by a cholera outbreak and a herd of thirsty elephants. It is fair to say that in this romantic melodrama, all the leads do their professional best with their stock characters, but just as the ants and our feathered friends stole the show in *The Naked Jungle* and *The Birds,* respectively, the real stars of *Elephant Walk* were the elephants themselves, proving the W.C. Fields observation that one should "never work with children or animals" (or indeed, seriously unhinged birds). Although Andrews took the role of "the other man," it did at least provide him with an opportunity to play perhaps his most debonair and carefree character to date, and one who should have won the gal, hands down, if audiences had been given the vote.

Producer Irving Asher initially thought that the role of the tea planter's wife would be ideally suited to the talents of Elizabeth Taylor, whom he hoped to borrow from MGM, but with the actress's unavailability due to pregnancy he turned his attentions to real-life husband-and-wife team Laurence Olivier and Vivien Leigh for the roles of the newlyweds.[1] Although Vivien was available, Olivier had theatre commitments for the entire year. However, he suggested that Asher offer the part of the tea planter to his protégé, a new talent named Peter Finch. The British actor was virtually an unknown at an international level, but Paramount decided to give him a chance to prove his worth and in the company of Leigh he flew to Ceylon to begin filming.[2]

Although Paramount was an American company, Technicolor United Kingdom had an agreement with Technicolor Hollywood that any film made in the British Commonwealth (which included Ceylon) would use British technicians. The film therefore became very much an Anglo-American project. Nationalities tend to stick together, which was noticeable on set with Leigh, Finch and the British crew forming one camp, and the Americans under the leadership of Andrews and director William Dieterle forming another.[3]

German-born Dieterle was noted for wearing a large hat and white gloves on set and will be fondly remembered for directing the likes of *A Midsummer Night's Dream* (1935), *Juarez* (1939) and *The Hunchback of Notre Dame* (1939). In the 1940s his films were more infused with a lush, romantic expressionism which bore fruit in the shape of two classic love stories starring Joseph Cotten and Jennifer Jones, *Love Letters* (1945) and *Portrait of Jennie* (1948).

Cut very much from the same cloth as Richard Burton, Finch was without doubt one of the greatest actors of his generation, but alas, like Burton, his film roles rarely provided the opportunity to reveal his real talent. In his hell-raising days he enjoyed well-publicized affairs with Vivien Leigh, Kay Kendall and Mai Zetterling. *A Town Like Alice* (1956) was one of his most popular films, followed closely by his last film *Network* (1976). He died a few months before being awarded his sole Oscar for his performance in *Network* and was the first actor to have received the award posthumously.

To the Brits on set, the old colonial ways of Ceylon were taken for granted, but for Andrews they were a constant source of bemused frustration. Talking about the hotel where crew and cast stayed, he recalled, "The waiters are all called 'boy,' no matter what their age, and they in turn call all white people 'Master.' I tried to get my room-boy to use my name, but he didn't dig me, and continued calling me Master." Andrews also said that the frenetic atmosphere of the place made it difficult to relax after a day's shoot: "At the hotel we were met by barefoot bellhops who moved around like the place was on fire."[4]

In addition to the heat and humidity, which most of the company found overpowering, Andrews also discovered that sleep in Ceylon was near impossible with squawking crows and the general cacophony of city sounds all kicking off at dawn: "I wouldn't recommend Ceylon unless you want your nervous system shattered."[5]

Aside from the separate Anglo-American camps, the questionable hotel accommodation and noisy birds, the filming of *Elephant Walk* went relatively smoothly, until the harmony on set was disrupted when Leigh suffered a nervous breakdown during the early stages of production and was quickly replaced by the director's initial choice for the part, MGM's top

Looking suitably pensive, plantation manager Dick Carver (Andrews) and Ruth Wiley (Elizabeth Taylor) share precious moments together in Paramount's most expensive feature of 1954 *Elephant Walk.*

star Elizabeth Taylor, who had since given birth, and was now available at a loanout cost of $150,000.[6]

Fortunately for the filmmakers, in many of the location scenes already shot, Leigh was unrecognizable as a distant figure, or had her back to the camera, which enabled Taylor to smoothly make the substitution as both actresses shared a similar height. However, in the wardrobe department, 20 of the 26 costumes made for Leigh had to be let out to accommodate Taylor's somewhat fuller figure.

The arrival of the fun-loving Taylor on set helped to unite the Anglo-American camps and, together with fellow hell-raisers Andrews and Finch, they formed the "Fuck You Club" back in the States and ate a noisy daily lunch at Lucy's El Adobe, the restaurant across the street from Paramount.[7]

At the time of *Elephant Walk*, Taylor was at the height of her popularity, with a long list of credits to her name, but her Oscar-winning performances in *Butterfield 8* (1960) and *Who's Afraid of Virginia Woolf?* (1966) were still ahead of her. During a publicity shoot for *Elephant Walk*, a tiny sliver of metal was blown into her eye by a wind machine; she bravely had it surgically removed without anesthetic. "A foreign body," the doctor remarked. "Anybody I know?" she joked.[8]

In addition to sharing a passion for hard-drinking off set, Andrews and Finch were also excellent horsemen. Once while out riding together, Andrews admiringly complimented his riding partner by exclaiming, "By Christ, you ride like the man in the Marlboro ad!"[9]

Out on location, away from the clatter of the hotel and the city din, Andrews regarded Ceylon as one of the most beautiful and interesting places he had ever seen; he told an interviewer: "Ceylon is a land of color, from the bright saris of its people, the glow of their skin, the greens of the jungles and its flamboyantly colored birds, to the contrasting soft grays of the elephant herds."[10]

Andrews's recollection of a jungle trip he made with Leigh and Finch revealed his fascination for the indigenous peoples of the country:

[W]e found aborigines who speak an entirely different language from the other Ceylon inhabitants. We had a government man as a guide. The natives did a dance for us; it was the most fantastic primitive thing I have ever seen. Most of the people there are Sinhalese or Tamils, but these were neither. They were all that remained of a tribe that lived in those parts for thousands of years.[11]

Although filming in Ceylon was certainly a memorable experience, as "the other man" in this love triangle, the newly freelancing Andrews could have been forgiven for thinking his career had turned full circle (he played "the other man" 14 years earlier at the beginning of his career in *Kit Carson*). But even though he was no longer the leading character, he could at least be cheered by the fact *Elephant Walk* was certainly an "A" status film. In fact, because of going over schedule, retakes, and the costly replacement of Vivien Leigh, *Elephant Walk* cost $3,000,000 and was the most expensive Paramount film of 1954.

Despite losing out in the love sweepstakes, Andrews's Dick Carver is infinitely more likable than Finch's John Wiley. Not prone to the same schoolboy games and drunkenness as Wiley, Carver is a more refined, cultured man, preferring to tap out a mean Chopin tune on the piano than to indulge in bicycle polo while intoxicated. In fact, Wiley's ace card in winning back his wife is an unexpected cholera epidemic, which reveals his sensitive, caring side when he tries to save the locals from being wiped out. (After all, someone's got to pick the tea — and it ain't those drink-sodden jokers on bicycles.)

Determined to stop the spread of the epidemic, Wiley floors a fleeing stretcher bearer with a shot to the leg, prompting Dick to comment, "That's one way of stopping an epidemic — shoot the people!" And as a parting note, when his first real love slips back into the arms of her husband, he sighs, "Looks like I get to Paris one boat or less."

One critic described *Elephant Walk* as a variation on the *Rebecca* theme relocated to the tea plantations of Ceylon. It is possibly for this reason that Franz Waxman, who composed the romantic score for *Rebecca*, was given the *Elephant Walk* assignment. Taylor's theme from *Elephant Walk* was popularized by the song "Many Dreams Ago." The film also has strands of *Giant*, with Taylor reprising the role of the outsider in a man's world.

One critic called Andrews' work "his strongest performance in several years." In contrast, Bosley Crowther of the *New York Times* commented, "Miss Taylor's performance of the young wife is petulant and smug, Mr. Andrews is pompous as the manager. And Mr. Finch as the husband is just plain bad." Although reactions to the various performances were mixed, the film was noteworthy for Waxman's beautiful score, some excellent photography of Ceylon from the lens of Loyal Griggs, lavish sets and a climactic elephant stampede, which through clever trick photography gave the illusion of the characters rubbing shoulders with the rampaging beasts as they bring the house down (clearly proving that hell hath no fury like an elephant in need of a stiff drink).

Duel in the Jungle
Warner Bros., 1954

Cast: Dana Andrews (Scott Walters); Jeanne Crain (Marian Taylor); David Farrar (Perry Henderson and Arthur Henderson); Patrick Barr (Supt. Roberts); George Coulouris (Capt. Malburn); Charles Goldner (Martell); Wilfrid Hyde-White (Pitt); Mary Merrall (Mrs. Henderson); Heather Thatcher (Lady on the Niagara); Michael Mataka (Vincent); Paul Carpenter (Clerk); Mary Mackenzie (Secretary); Alec Finter, Bee Duffell, Patrick Parnell, John Salew, Walter Gotell, Charles Carson, Bill Shine, Robert Sansom, Irene Handl, Bill Fraser, Simone Silva.

Credits: Martin Hellman, Tony Owen (Producers); George Marshall (Director); S.K. Kennedy (Story); Sam Marx (Screenplay); Erwin Hiller (Cinematography); Mischa Spoliansky (Music); Louis Levy (Music Direction); Mischa Spoliansky, Norman Newell (Song); Terence Verity (Art Direction); Nell Taylor (Makeup); Tony Kelly (Assistant Director); Harold V. King (Sound); Edward B. Jarvis (Editor). Running time: 102 minutes

In Rhodesia, American insurance investigator Scott Walters (Dana Andrews) looks into the mysterious death of diamond broker Perry Henderson, who was insured for one million pounds. Henderson was reportedly drowned after falling overboard during a sea journey off the African coast, but no body was found. A suspicious Walters follows the dead man's fiancée Marian Taylor, with whom he has fallen in love, on a dangerous safari into the Dark Continent. Their wanderings ultimately lead them to the hideout of Henderson, who faked his death for the insurance payout, which would have financed his plans for the underwater mining of diamonds. With the local natives under his command, Henderson plans the death of Walters, who escapes in the nick of time with Marian and their loyal jungle guide Vincent. Making their getaway down river in a canoe, they successfully evade their pursuers, and in a tussle in the white waters, Scott gets the better of Henderson, who is delivered into the custody of the local constabulary. Having wrapped up the case, Scott heads off into the sunset in the arms of the beautiful Marian.

Tagline: "Through screeching jungle haunts, across the veldt of violence, past lion fang and boa coil…. They shadowed the "Dead man of the Transvaal" they had to bring back alive!"

Hooked? You should be, for this is a fine jungle romp that pushes all the right buttons. Expertly directed by veteran George Marshall, this exciting and taut action-adventure has all the ingredients to serve up a veritable jungle feast — scary natives, even scarier wild animals, excellent photography, a solid, square-jawed hero, a voluptuous heroine and a scene-stealing villain. It's top drawer, and certainly up with the best of the Dark Continent yarns such as *King Solomon's Mines* (1950) and *Trader Horn* (1931).

Prolific Marshall started his career as an actor before becoming one of the most successful of Hollywood directors with a natural flair for comedies and westerns. In a career than spanned more than 50 years, he directed the great comics including Laurel and Hardy, W.C. Fields, Bob Hope and Jerry Lewis. He is perhaps best remembered for the classic comedy western *Destry Rides Again* (1939), *The Ghost Breakers* (1940), *The Blue Dahlia* (1946) and *The Sheepman* (1958).

Duel in the Jungle was Marshall's first foray into the world of freelancing after his break from Paramount Studios, and in Andrews he found the consummate lead to inject a subtle sense of fun into the action. For the most part, it is expressed through his character's tongue-in-cheek attempts to woo Marian Taylor, deftly played by the beautiful Jeanne Crain. Diamonds are certainly beautiful, but according to Scott they will never match the sparkle in Miss Taylor's eyes. When she initially proves resistant to such flattery, Scott has another crack at it during their London sightseeing tour when he asks, "Why should we look at castles when we only have eyes for each other?"

If his pitches sound familiar, they should, with Andrews's equally brash man about town from his previous film *Assignment Paris* trying a similar form of flattery on Marta Toren. And for the source of this "silver tongue," look no further than *State Fair*, where Andrews practiced such lines for the first time in his debut encounter with a 20-year-old Miss Crain.

In addition to being a charmer, Andrews's intrepid insurance investigator is also a man of the world, with an outlook tempered by too many

Out on a big game hunt, wily insurance investigator Scott Walters (Andrews) pits his wits against the ruthless Perry Henderson (David Farrar) in the excellent "boys adventure" *Duel in the Jungle* (Warner Bros., 1954).

turns around the block. At Arthur Henderson's office we learn that he has met a lot of wealthy people in his line of work, but no matter how rich, they always want more. His world-weariness also extends to some old flames. When Arthur Henderson handles a rough diamond and comments, "Not much to look at in this rough state — pretty cold," Scott replies "Like some girlfriends I've met."

Away from the office, out in the jungle, Scott proves that he's just as good with a gun as he is with a sharp line, but there is little you can do with a rifle that has been tampered with, particularly when confronted with a ferocious lion looking for a midday snack. Saved in the nick of time by Marian's loyal guide and his handy spear, Scott inspects Perry Henderson's favorite weapon and sees that the firing pin is missing. Looking suitably puzzled, Henderson mutters, "I see," to which Scott indignantly replies, "Too bad you didn't see it before."

Marshall's eagerness to make the film was shared by co-producer Tony Owen, who regarded the trip to Africa as a great adventure, much to the frustration of his wife, celebrated actress Donna Reed, who was left at home to look after the family.[1] If circumstances had permitted, Reed could have easily slipped into the Jeanne Crain role as both actresses projected a similar screen image as the tough, no-nonsense "girl next door type." Reed got the chance to accompany her husband a few years later on another jungle actioner, *Beyond Mombasa* (1956), which was also directed by George Marshall. Andrews and Reed had the opportunity to work together in his next film *Three Hours to Kill.*

David Farrar's role as the villain of the piece was one in a long line of bad guys the British-born actor played in his career. Powell and Pressburger successfully tapped into his talent in three of their most noteworthy productions, *Black Narcissus* (1947), *The Small Back Room*

(1949) and *Gone to Earth* (1950). Having saved a few bob with Andrews taking on two roles in his earlier British film *The Forbidden Street*, the British film studios went on a similar economy drive in *Duel in the Jungle*, with Farrar playing both Perry Henderson and his cousin Arthur. Farrar was also the dialogue director on set, schooling Jeanne Crain towards an English accent.

Continuing the lineup, we receive an excellent turn from Wilfrid Hyde-White as Andrews's shipboard companion on a voyage which conjures up memories of *Journey into Fear*. And to make up the quota of eccentric Brits, we are later introduced to Henderson's scatterbrain mother, convincingly played by Mary Merrall, who leaves you with the distinct impression that she might burst into a verse of "Cherry Ripe, Cherry Ripe" at the slightest provocation (definitely on the same daffy Richter scale as Karswell's mother from *Night of the Demon*).

Cast and crew endured nearly two months of rigorous location shooting in South Africa and Rhodesia before moving on to London to shoot interiors at Elstree Studios. This was Andrews's second visit to London, but once again his tight filming schedules gave him little opportunity to explore the capital. He recalled, "I used to leave the Dorchester, where I was staying, every morning before daylight for the studios, and it was dark when I got back again in the evening. I never had time for sightseeing or shopping, and this is a repetition of what happened when I was in England five years before when Maureen O'Hara and I were making [*The Forbidden Street*]."[2]

In Africa, sequences were filmed at Johannesburg, Pretoria and the romantic part of the Transvaal known as Derdepoort, which means "Third Gateway to the North" (made famous three hundred years ago when the Voortrekkers decided to move northwards). After Pretoria, they made their headquarters just inside Kruger Park Game Reserve. Light goes early in this part of Africa, which meant that during the five days of filming here, everyone had to be up ready for filming at six and, because of wild animals, had to be back in camp before sunset. This presented few problems because after working from six in the morning, cast and crew thought only of a quick dinner in the camp restaurant before taking to their beds.[3]

During filming, several incidents occurred which highlighted the everpresent dangers of location shooting in Africa. While en route through Kruger Park, a bush fire engulfed the truck convoy, setting light to the camera truck, which Andrews helped to put out, saving thousands of dollars of equipment. On another occasion, Jeanne Crain casually posed with a lion which later in the week attacked and killed its trainer.[4]

From Kruger Park they returned to Pretoria to take a few more shots before traveling a thousand miles north to Livingstone, Northern Rhodesia, location of the famous Victoria Falls, where more scenes were taken. One of these included a shot with publicity stillsman Bob Hawkins demonstrating to Andrews a pose on a brink that wasn't there. Luckily, Andrews grabbed Hawkins in the nick of time, saving him from a 300-foot drop to certain death.[5]

Several days later, assistant director Tony Kelly disappeared when his boat, a 14-foot outboard motor dinghy, overturned in the Zambezi River when he was out testing the rapids for safety in advance of a canoeing shoot planned for Andrews and Jeanne on this part of the river.[6] The other two crew members made it to shore; it was believed that Kelly disappeared while trying to save the camera equipment. His body was never found and the most likely explanation was that he was taken by crocodiles.

Against this backdrop of tragic incident, filming continued, although the mood in camp must have been quite somber. But the show must go on as they say, and having lost the girl to the blue-blooded Brit in his last tropical excursion *Elephant Walk*, Andrews doesn't repeat the mistake in *Duel in the Jungle*, this time winning the hand of Miss Crain in the final reel, after having saved her from snakes, stampeding elephants and a snarling David Farrar. This was Crain's first film since leaving Fox, and her smoldering performance leaves you in no doubt that she had finally escaped her wholesome "girl next door" tag. On her experiences during filming, Jeanne humorously remarked, "Africa is simply movie land with baboons instead of wolves."[7]

There were times when Andrews also thought that he was enjoying a home-away-from-home experience, commenting, "While in Africa we managed one night in Johannesburg, a thoroughly modern city, with its cosmopolitan air. In its nightclubs we saw orchestras, in South American costumes, playing the mambo and the samba. It seemed strange to be in faraway Africa, yet in exactly the same atmosphere as if we were at home visiting a nightclub on the Sunset Strip."[8]

Although the film was seen as little more than a routine jungle romp by the critics of the day, it did provide some memorable photography which was noted by the *New York Times*: "Some of the glimpses of lusty tribal dancing, canoes plying perilous waterways and a shot or two of what would appear to be Victoria Falls, are stunning."

On an amusing note, the *Times* further commented, "One scene, for good measure, has Miss Crain spellbound by a bongo-bongo campfire chant that could pass for 'Deep in the heart of Texas.' At any rate, the three principals have a tough time of it and they perspire freely."

Like good wine, "boys own" adventure yarns such as *Duel in the Jungle* have improved with time, particularly with modern reviewers who, like me, appreciate these gems for their innocent simplicity. Sharing my enthusiasm, the *Radio Times Guide to Films* described the film as "immensely entertaining."

P.S. It took me two years to track down a copy of this rarity — easily my most difficult Andrews film acquisition. It arrived all the way from Australia in the form of a battered old ex-rental video.

Three Hours to Kill
Columbia, 1954

Cast: Dana Andrews (Jim Guthrie); Donna Reed (Laurie Hendricks); Dianne Foster (Chris Plumber); Stephen Elliot (Ben East); Richard Coogan (Niles Hendricks); Laurence Hugo (Marty Lasswell); James Westerfield (Sam Minor); Richard Webb (Carter Mastin); Carolyn Jones (Polly); Charlotte Fletcher (Betty); Whit Bissell (Deke); Felipe Turich (Esteban); Arthur Fox (Little Carter); Francis McDonald (Vince); Paul E. Burns (Albert); Edward Earle (Rancher); Frank Hagney (Cass); Hank Mann, Syd Saylor (Townsmen); Robert Paquin (Storekeeper); Buddy Roosevelt (Drunk); Reed Howes, Ada Adams, Eslie Baker.

Credits: Harry Joe Brown (Producer); Alfred Werker (Director); Alex Gottlieb (Story); Richard Alan Simmons, Roy Huggins (Screenplay); Charles Lawton, Jr. (Cinematography); Paul Sawtell (Music); George Brooks (Art Direction); Frank Tuttle (Set Decorations); Sam Nelson (Assistant Director); John P. Livadary (Sound); Gene Havlick (Editor). Running time: 77 minutes

Falsely accused of a murder he didn't commit, stagecoach driver Jim Guthrie (Dana Andrews) narrowly escapes a lynching and is run out of town by an angry mob. After several years of living off the land, he returns to the town, hell-bent on tracking down the real killer. He is given three hours by the sheriff to clear his name, but in his search he has to contend with the townsfolk, who are fearful that he may be out to exact some form of revenge for the noose scars around his neck — the result of their previous attempt to lynch him. He finds little compassion or support from his former fiancée, Laurie Mastin, as the murder victim was her brother. Unbeknownst to Guthrie, she had been left pregnant by him at the time of the murder and had married another man on the rebound. With the assistance of sympathetic saloon gal Chris Plumber, Guthrie captures the real murderer, who turns out to be one of the few helpful characters in the town. Having cleared his name, Guthrie turns his back on Laurie and the town and heads out to make a fresh start with the plucky Miss Plumber in tow.

Tagline: "The Man with the Rope Scar ON HIS NECK!"

Andrews, like many of the noir icons of the late 1940s such as Fred MacMurray, Alan Ladd and Ray Milland, exchanged his fedora for a Stetson when the genre of the western went through a major revival in the 1950s. *Three Hours to Kill* was the first of four westerns Andrews made in the mid–50s with *Smoke Signal* (1955), *Strange Lady in Town* (1955) and *Comanche* (1956) following in quick succession.

It was also Andrews's second film under the direction of Alfred Werker, the pair having worked together three years previously in *Sealed Cargo*. Although he was not rated as one of the top directors of his day, Werker was responsible for some interesting and taut westerns including *The Last Posse* (1953), *Devil's Canyon* (1953) and *At Gunpoint* (1955). All these films shared a common theme of the individual sacrificed by the very community they helped to build.[1] With all the townsfolk set against the vengeful Guthrie, *Three Hours to Kill* continued this theme in a very tense and bleak manner. Phil Hardy in his *Aurum Film Encyclopedia of the*

Embracing Laurie Hendricks (Donna Reed), the girl he left behind, a vengeful Jim Guthrie (Andrews) sets out to find the man who framed him for murder in *Three Hours to Kill* (Columbia, 1954).

Western noted, "[A]lthough *Three Hours to Kill*, like *At Gunpoint*, was quite clearly influenced by *High Noon* (1952), it has a bitter edge to it that *High Noon* lacks."[2] This edge was partly provided by Andrews's gritty performance, as he spits out his lines like a rivet gun. When the sheriff asks Guthrie why he chose to return with the town clearly against him, he snaps back that he got tired of hiding under rocks. Weary of being a patsy and bursting with a lust for revenge against the "good townsfolk" who tried to string him up, he warns the sheriff, "I want to see them sick with fright. I want to see them at the end of a rope."

Welker's taut direction cranks up the tension and suspense as the story unfolds like a film noir, with the plight of our troubled hero Guthrie told through a series of flashbacks, one of which requires Andrews to act drunk at the town shindig. (Up to this point, even though Andrews had a drinking problem his film char-

acters rarely over-indulged). In another memorable scene, Guthrie makes the classic movie mistake of being discovered standing over a dead body with a gun in his hand (he looks guilty—fetch a rope). To add to the film's realism, Andrews looks as if he went that extra mile in the scene where he escapes the lynch mob in a runaway wagon with the trailing rope still around his neck, and judging by his pained expression it appears like he was genuinely experiencing each and every tug of the rope as it wrapped around just about every protrusion the town has to offer. And if rope burns weren't enough, his character has to suffer the ultimate agony when he discovers that his intended bride (deftly played by Donna Reed) and son belong to another man.

The film is regarded as one of the best of the several westerns in which Donna Reed appeared following her Oscar-winning (Best Supporting Actress) performance in *From Here to Eternity* (1953). Nevertheless, in his Reed biography, Jay

Fultz commented, "*Three Hours to Kill* received so little promotion that not even her children have heard of it."[3]

For the most part, 1950s westerns provided ample work for actresses such as Reed, but offered little in the way of career development, which must have been quite frustrating and disappointing for the actress following her success in *It's a Wonderful Life* (1946) and *From Here to Eternity* (1953). In 1958, she turned to television in her own show which was a huge success for eight years. In the 1984–85 season of *Dallas*, she took the role of Miss Ellie when Barbara Bel Geddes decided not to return to the part after undergoing open heart surgery. Reed was fired from the show for no apparent reason; she was in the process of suing the producers when she died of pancreatic cancer in 1986 at the age 65.

With his incredible performance in *The Ox-Bow Incident* (1943), Andrews was no stranger to playing a character who has to contend with the frenzied nature of a lynch mob. In the role of the victim, Andrews once again fires on all cylinders in a powerhouse performance, which quite literally drives this film from beginning to end. And what an ending it is—I doubt if anyone enjoying this little gem for the first time would have identified the real killer. It also came as a bit of a shock when he rode off into the sunset minus old flame Donna Reed. But don't despair for our troubled hero, with saloon gal Dianne Foster more than happy to share his saddle blanket. Foster was another one of those actresses with pin-up looks who never quite fulfilled her film potential after a promising start with features such as *The Kentuckian* (1955), *Night Passage* (1957) and *The Last Hurrah* (1958). Today she is an accomplished pianist and painter living in California.

The *New York Times* commented, "In this timid, one-dimensional view of a community beset by fear and conscience, the actors, as we say, acquit themselves respectively. Mr. Andrews, for instance, is bedraggled bitterness personified."

Smoke Signal

Universal, 1955

Cast: Dana Andrews (Brett Halliday); Piper Laurie (Laura Evans); Rex Reason (Lt. Wayne Ford); William Talman (Capt. Harper); Milburn Stone (Sgt. Miles); Douglas Spencer (Garode); Gordon Jones (Corp. Rogers); William Schallert (Pvt . Livingston); Robert J. Wilke (First Sgt. Daly); William Phipps (Pvt. Porter); Pat Hogan (Delche); Peter Coe (Ute Prisoner); Lee Bradley.

Credits: Howard Christie (Producer); Jerry Hopper (Director); George F. Slavin, George W. George (Story and Screenplay); Clifford Stine (Cinematography); Irving Gertz, William Lava, Henry Mancini (Music); Joseph Gershenson (Music Direction); Alexander Golitzen, Richard H. Riedel (Art Direction); Russell A. Gausman, James M. Walters (Set Decorations); Bill Thomas (Costume Design); Bud Westmore (Makeup); Joseph E. Kenny (Assistant Director); Leslie I. Carey, Robert Pritchard (Sound); Milton Carruth, Eddie Broussard (Editors). Running time: 88 minutes

Cavalry deserter Brett Halliday (Dana Andrews) is regarded as a renegade because his sympathies are with the Ute Indians; he feels that they have been harshly and cruelly treated by certain white officers, including Major Evans, commander at the local fort. A cavalry patrol led by Captain Harper enters the fort shortly after an Indian attack in which Evans is killed. Amongst the survivors he finds Evans' daughter Laura, her admirer Lieutenant Ford, and a prisoner awaiting sentence, Brett Halliday. Of the opinion that Halliday was responsible for the recent Indian troubles which led to the death of his brother, Harper is determined to get him back to headquarters to face a court martial. However, with an all-out Indian attack imminent, the group must first make their escape via the only route available — the uncharted rapids of the Colorado River. En route, Laura begins to sympathize with Halliday's predicament, which angers Harper and Ford. However, with all the perils of the river and the everpresent Indians to contend with, Halliday and Harper are forced to pull together to ensure the survival of the group. Having made it through to safety, Laura finally convinces Harper that it was her father who wanted war and not the peace-loving Halliday, who lost his Indian wife during the conflict. Realizing that Halliday is the only man who can stop the needless bloodshed, Harper sets him free, to the joy of Laura, who knows he will return to her one day when the troubles are over.

Andrews forcefully played a vengeful character in *Three Hours to Kill*; his next western outing *Smoke Signal* saw him as the object of someone else's vengeful quest. But that's the least of his worries in this thrilling oater in which all the characters contend with Injuns meaner than a grizzly b'ar chewing a wasp.

Universal's original choice for the part of Brett Halliday was Charlton Heston, but his fee was too high so the studio offered the role to Andrews. Like other freelancing actors in the 1950's Andrews had to compete with many other actors in the quest for good roles. Most of the studios still had their old reliable big stars under contract (Power, Holden, Cooper, Gable, etc.) and their priority more than ever was to find vehicles for these stars. The period also witnessed the growth of a new breed of independents with the likes of Kirk Douglas and Burt Lancaster and the emergence of a new type of actor such as Marlon Brando, Paul Newman and Heston. With this competition, chasing good roles would have been difficult for all concerned, but Andrews still managed to hold his own.

His star may well have lost some of its luster, but in *Smoke Signal*, Andrews's presence still packs a punch at the head of an excellent cast, which has to compete with the spectacular Grand Canyon and the mighty Colorado River. Veteran action director Jerry Hopper, who used a young Heston to excellent effect in *Pony Express* (1953) and *Secret of the Incas* (1954), strikes a fine balance here between adventure and characterization. The tense plot, based on an excellent screenplay by George W. George and George F. Slavin, was superbly complemented by Clifford Stine's deft cinematography.

And no matter how unusual the plot or setting, no western was complete without the obligatory love interest, here provided by Piper Laurie, who incidentally was a replacement for Allison Hayes (star of the 1958 cult film *Attack of the 50 Foot Woman*).

By the mid–1950s, Laurie was also experienc-

Buckskin-clad Brett Halliday (Andrews) is the only man who can avert all-out war with the Utes in the exciting western *Smoke Signal* (Universal, 1955).

ing a dearth of substantial roles in her career, which prompted her to leave Hollywood shortly after making *Smoke Signal* and head to New York City to study acting in a more serious manner. Laurie had been signed by Universal when she was only 17 and spent several years usually playing Casbah spitfires alongside Universal's other young contract star, Tony Curtis. When she eventually returned to Hollywood, she was finally able to prove herself as a dramatic actress, giving three memorable performances that earned her Oscar nominations: *The Hustler* (1961), *Carrie* (1976) and *Children of a Lesser God* (1987).

By contrast, Andrews had nothing to prove on the acting front, playing his part with his customary relaxed and well-paced reticence. As Brett Halliday, he is stoicism personified in the type of role he excelled at: a man alone, fighting against the odds. Questioned by Captain Harper as to whether he is aware of the charges leveled against him, he casually remarks that nobody's taken the trouble to put him in the picture. Clearly, Halliday is a man of few words, but get him in the right mood with the right subject matter, and he will obligingly wax lyrical, particularly on the subject of Injun drums and impending danger: "They want us to know what's up ahead — they want us to sweat — they want to tie us up in knots. When they have a reason to hate you, they have a way of letting you feel it."

And as Andrews's characters demonstrated in *Wing and a Prayer* and *The Frogmen*, his Brett Halliday has no time for uptight officers who do things strictly by the book. After beating up love rival Lieutenant Ford, he informs Harper that Ford at least has the guts to do his own killing without having to resort to a trumped-up court martial.

In his previous western outing, *Three Hours to Kill,* Andrews's character had the whole town against him, and the odds are no better in *Smoke Signal* with our hero having to contend with marauding Indians out for his blood, a vengeful army captain hell-bent on his court martial, a jealous suitor, an ice-cold heroine — and on top of all that, the treacherous white waters and rapids of the Colorado River. Surprisingly, the use of the river as a means of escape from pursuers was rarely used in westerns, but when is was, it made for a thrilling ride as experienced in *Smoke Signal* and Otto Preminger's 1954 hit with

Marilyn Monroe and Robert Mitchum, *River of No Return.*

Although *Smoke Signal* was regarded as just another western, there was nothing ordinary about the solid supporting cast, which included the excellent William Talman, who went on to television fame as the DA who lost every case to Perry Mason in the last reel. Talman's best remembered film role is, without doubt, as the escaped killer in the classic film noir *The Hitch-Hiker* (1953). Just as Andrews would make a dramatic TV appearance on the perils of being an alcoholic, Talman was the first actor to do a TV commercial on the danger of smoking when he knew he was dying of lung cancer.

As jealous love rival, Rex Reason was also in top form with his excellent impression of a jilted Stewart Granger, as was Douglas Spencer as the "skin man" Garode who, kitted out in buckskins, coon hat and muzzle loader, looked like he might well have been making his way to the Alamo before he bumped into Harper's patrol.

The *New York Times* commented, "Though the plotline of *Smoke Signal* is pedestrian, the film's action highlights are well-worth the price of admission." In *Western Films: A Complete Guide*, Brian Garfield noted, "Ordinary Indian-fighting plot is well acted by a good cast and well directed with fine location scenery."[1] Other critics also praised the spectacular setting, one commenting that with the benefit of glorious Technicolor, the Colorado River's Grand Canyon looked more inviting than the most elaborate travel brochure.

In his *The Encyclopedia of Westerns*, Herb Fagen struck a similar upbeat note with his review, "Piper Laurie adds the female equation to this zesty adventure, and like Andrews and Talman, she turns in a first-rate performance."[2]

Rather bizarrely, *Smoke Signal* was released in London on a double bill with *Garden of Eden*, the first-ever nudist film. (Bye, Honey — I'm off to catch the afternoon western. Oh, and the latest skin flick to boot!)

Strange Lady in Town
Warner Bros., 1955

Cast: Greer Garson (Dr. Julia Winslow Garth); Dana Andrews (Rourke O'Brien); Cameron Mitchell (David Garth); Lois Smith (Spurs O'Brien); Walter Hampden (Father Gabriel Mendoza); Pedro Gonzalez-Gonzalez (Trooper Martinez-Martinez); Joan

Rourke O'Brien (Andrews) passes the red-haired Julia Garth (Greer Garson) off as his wife to avoid the attentions of Geronimo in *Strange Lady in Town* (Warner Bros., 1955).

Camden (Norah Muldoon); Jose Torvay (Bartolo Diaz); Adele Jergens (Bella Brown); Robert J. Wilke (Karg); Frank DeKova (Anse Hatlo); Russell Johnson (Shadduck); Gregory Walcott (Scanlon); Douglas Kennedy (Slade Wickstrom); Nick Adams (Billy the Kid); Anthony Numkena (Tomascito); Marshall Bradford (Sheriff); Joey Costarello (Alfred); Robert Foulk (Joe); Joe Hamilton (Mr. Harker); Antonio Triana, Lusita Triana (Flamenco Dancers); Jack Williams (Rebstock); George Wallace (Curley); Helen Spring (Mrs. Harker); Ralph Moody (Gen. Lew Wallace); Louise Lorimer (Mrs. Wallace).

Credits: Mervyn LeRoy (Producer-Director); Frank Butler (Story & Screenplay); Harold Rosson (Cinematography); Dimitri Tiomkin (Music); Dimitri Tiomkin, Ned Washington (Songs); Gabriel Scognamillo (Art Direction); Emile Santiago (Costumes); Russ Saunders, William Kissel (Assistant Directors); Folmar Blangsted (Editor). Running time: 117 minutes

Julia Garth, a pioneering Boston doctor, arrives in Santa Fe, New Mexico, in 1880 to set up practice, but must first overcome the ignorance and social prejudices of the townspeople, who have never experienced a female physician. On arrival, she is befriended by local tomboy Spurs O'Brien, who is in love with Julia's brother Lt. David Garth, stationed at the nearby fort. Spurs's widower father, Dr. Rourke O'Brien (Dana Andrews), also proves resistant, but when the two become romantically involved, he learns to respect her ways. Nora sets up shop next to a mission church run by Father Gabriel Mendoza, her practice getting underway with a toothache case brought in by Billy the Kid, an Indian boy with glaucoma and the treatment of Nora, a physically abused mental patient. Julia's wayward brother turns outlaw, which results in the death of Father Gabriel following a failed bank raid. The townsfolk threaten to force her out of town, blaming her for his crimes. On the day of her departure, an angry crowd gathers to make sure she leaves, but she is persuaded to stay by the timely intervention of Rourke, who shames the crowd for their cruel behavior. Betrothed to Rourke, she remains in town to pursue her promise to Father Gabriel to build the best hospital in Santa Fe.

Tagline: "She was the one woman Rourke didn't want in Santa Fe ... but he'd kill anybody who'd try to make her leave...."

The screenplay for *Strange Lady in Town* developed out of a chance meeting between Warner Brothers screenwriter Frank Butler and Greer Garson at a Hollywood dinner party, when the screenwriter learned of the actress's passionate interest in the early days of Santa Fe.[1] Frank Butler's script tells the story of a female medical doctor who arrives in Santa Fe from Boston in 1880 hoping to leave behind the prejudices against female physicians which had plagued her career in the East. Studio mogul Jack Warner approved the script, but was very concerned that in times of falling revenues the production could prove too costly. To improve its chances of turning a profit, the mogul insisted that the film be photographed in CinemaScope and WarnerColor.

The film was the one and only time that Andrews worked with Greer Garson and director Mervyn LeRoy. With Garson quite clearly the star of the movie, Andrews was once again playing a robust supporting role, which would not in any way steal the limelight from the leading lady. This was particularly important to Garson at this point in her career because, as with Andrews, her most notable performances were back in the 1940s. Discovered in London by MGM's Louis B. Mayer, Garson came to Hollywood where her first film was *Goodbye, Mr. Chips* (1939), for which she was nominated for an Oscar, losing out to fellow British actress Vivien Leigh for *Gone with the Wind*. In company with Bette Davis, Garson holds the record for the most consecutive Oscar nominations for an actor running from 1941 to 1945 — winning the award in 1942 for the role she is best remembered for, *Mrs. Miniver*.

Director LeRoy was also highly acclaimed in his field, with a number of classics under his belt including *Little Caesar* (1930). *I Am a Fugitive from a Chain Gang* (1932) and *The Wizard of Oz* (1939), which he produced and partly directed.

Andrews's casting as Dr. Rourke O'Brien in the summer of 1954 had been a relatively straightforward affair. Several young actors including

Richard Egan, Tab Hunter and Robert Stack had been considered for the role of Julia's brother David, before the role was offered to Cameron Mitchell. Today Mitchell is best remembered for the part of Buck Cannon in the successful television western *The High Chaparral.*

Garson offered Warner Brothers her Fork Lightning Ranch home for location filming, but the studio chose instead a western set in Old Tucson, Arizona, where carpenters built an additional 34 buildings on the 150-acre site.[2] Cast and crew set off for Tucson in August 1954 for five weeks of location shooting. With the arrival of the cast, movie mania ensued in the city with the local newspapers reporting that 750 people jammed the Santa Rita Hotel lobby when a request was made by Mervyn LeRoy for movie extras.

To insure that there were no nasty surprises on set, each morning a "snake patrol" was sent to clear the area. On one occasion a large tarantula got rather close to Greer and Andrews; the actress nonchalantly flicked it away with a twig without batting an eyelid.[3] While on location, Garson became life threateningly ill with appendicitis, but she refused to be operated on until shooting was over. Garson had fond memories of the film, which she described as "a richly corny period story" that allowed her to indulge in an outdoor role.

Andrews has a costume change for each of his scenes (could those wardrobe fellas have possibly been handed the script for *Beau Brummell* by mistake?). His churlish performance provides the requisite edge to what is essentially "Mrs. Miniver Goes West." His physician's views on a "woman's place" in society would certainly have feminists in an uproar today. These opinions are conveyed to his daughter Spurs when he first learns of Julia's arrival in town. Since Julia is quite a looker and a success in her profession, he can only surmise she must be kinda screwy for not having a ring on her finger. Taking on the role of matchmaker, Spurs continues to whet his appetite, only to elicit the terse response, "What man would like to come home to a woman that's been rolling pills all day or working about in people's insides?"

And if his attitudes about the fairer sex are stuck in the Middle Ages, his opinions on new medical advancements are positively prehistoric, as we learn from his first confrontation with Julia. Questioned as to whether he is aware of Lister's scientific breakthrough, his response blatantly reveals that he is undoubtedly a man who must have partnered up with Barney Rubble at Med School. "Oh, I've heard of him all right. Wash it off Lister, keep it clean Lister, carbolic acid Lister, antisepsis Lister. Why didn't everyone die before Dr. Jacob Lister came along. He's a charlatan and a crackpot."

Rourke may be an old dinosaur, with his general outlook on life clearly soured by the premature death of his wife, but when staring at danger he is a man to be reckoned with. We first witness this side to his character on a riding trip with Julia, which is interrupted by a confrontation with a band of Apaches who are understandably intrigued by her red hair (has she been sent by the gods?). During these tense moments, Rourke remains calm and collected, passing Julia off as his woman to avoid any trouble. This "knight in shining armor" image is reinforced when he uses his fists to stop an abusive boyfriend from removing his mentally ill girlfriend from Julia's surgery. In addition to Billy the Kid and Geronimo's Apache gang, the script also included a slot for the governor of the territory, General Lew Wallace, who went on to write the novel *Ben-Hur*.

The film premiered on April 12, 1955, in Austin, Texas—Andrews's home state. Commercially it proved a big hit, with the returns exceeding its $3 million cost. The *Los Angeles Herald-Examiner* commented, "Go see it and have some un-arty, un-depressing, important fun." The Southern California Motion Picture Council proclaimed it "a delight to all." Penned by Dimitri Tiomkin and Ned Washington, the song from the film also proved a commercial hit for Frankie Laine, who also recorded it on the Columbia label. According to *The Aurum Film Encyclopedia of Westerns*, "LeRoy's direction is heavy handed and Butler's script too cute by far, but Garson and Andrews make a likable pair and Rosson's cinematography makes the most of the Tucson locations."[4] Recognizing the secondary nature and limiting confines of Andrews's role as the stereotypical male chauvinist, the *New York Times* mused, "Dana Andrews plays the leading doctor with an air of acknowledged defeat."

Comanche
United Artists, 1956

Cast: Dana Andrews (Jim Read); Kent Smith (Quanah Parker); Linda Cristal (Margarita); Nestor Paiva (Puffer); Henry Brandon (Black Cloud); Stacy Harris (Art Downey); John Litel (Gen. Nelson Miles); Lowell Gilmore (Commissioner John Ward); Mike Mazurki (Flat Mouth); Tony Carbajal (Little Snake); Reed Sheman (2nd Lt. John French); Iron Eyes Cody (Medicine Arrow); Caetana Paiva, Joseph Paiva, Carlos Muzquiz, Carlos Rivas, Jorge Martinez de Hoyos, Jose Angel Espinosa "Ferrusquilla," Fanny Schiller.

Credits: Carl Krueger (Producer-Screenplay); Henry Spitz (Associate Producer); George Sherman (Director); Jorge Stahl, Jr. (Cinematography); Herschel Burke Gilbert (Music); Lindsley Parsons, Jr. (Assistant Director); Manuel Topete (Sound); Charles L. Kimball (Editor). Running time: 87 minutes

Comanche is set against the majestic beauty of the Mexican landscape and allegedly based on a true story. Frontier scout Jim Read (Dana Andrews), ably assisted by his loyal sidekick Puffer, tries to stem rising tensions between white men and Comanches in order to avert all-out war. To appease the whites, Read must persuade the Comanches to end their age-old fight with their neighbors, the Mexicans—a mission made difficult by the fact that a number of white settlers, led by Art Downey, a hunter of Indian scalps, and Indian Commissioner John Ward would prefer to see the Comanches defeated through show of force. The peace talks are also threatened by renegade Comanche Black Cloud, who is also in favor of going on the warpath. Only one Indian holds the key to peace, Antelope Comanche chief Quanah Parker—son of a Comanche chief and a white woman taken captive during an Indian raid, who is also Read's cousin by virtue of the fact that their two mothers were sisters. In his search to find Parker, Read comes across pretty Mexican girl Margarita wandering dazed and alone in the desert, having escaped her Comanche captors. Accompanied by the girl, Read and Puffer meet up with Parker at his camp and convince him that peace is preferable to hostilities. However, before peace can be brokered, there is one final encounter between the U.S. cavalry, under the command of General Nelson Miles, and the hostile Indians led by Black Cloud, who in defiance of Quanah Parker kills Commissioner Ward. During the pitched battle,

Indian scout Jim Read (Andrews) has his work cut out with renegade Comanche Red Cloud (Henry Brandon), who is after his scalp in George Sherman's western *Comanche* (United Artists, 1956).

Read kills the murderous Downey and the hot-headed Black Cloud, paving the way for peace and a happy reunion with his love, Margarita.

Tagline: "The Never-Before–Told Epic of the Last Great Indian Battle ... Filmed in the All-the-Earth-Spanning Power of Cinemascope."

"Epic" is an appropriate description for Andrews's fourth and final western entry in the 1950s. This time he was supported by one of the largest gatherings of Indians to grace a '50s screen, all lavishly conveyed in glorious CinemaScope and De Luxe Color.

Filmed entirely near Durango in Old Mexico, *Comanche* was the second time Andrews worked under the direction of George Sherman following their successful collaboration on the action thriller *Sword in the Desert* seven years earlier. Sherman was no stranger to the action genre with his earlier experiences directing B-westerns including the *Three Mesquiteers* series starring a young John Wayne. (Sherman's last film re-

united him with Wayne in the kidnap western *Big Jake* [1971].) *Comanche* also marked the second occasion that Andrews starred alongside Kent Smith, who in a similar fashion to Andrews had initially been groomed by Hollywood to play solid and dependable types. Although he played in some of the most popular cult movies of the '40s including *Cat People* (1942) and *The Curse of the Cat People* (1944), most of his work was in the B-movie category, with a few exceptions like *The Fountainhead* (1949) and his first outing with Andrews, the commercially successful weepie *My Foolish Heart* (1949).

As well as furthering the 1950s tendency to show the North American Indian in a more sympathetic light, *Comanche* also continued the Hollywood trend of featuring real-life historical Indians alongside fictitious screen cowboys. Whereas *Indian Uprising* (1952), *Hondo* (1953), *The Great Sioux Uprising* (1953) and *Sitting Bull* (1954) had focused on Geronimo, Vittorio, Red

Cloud and Sitting Bull respectively, *Comanche* took Quanah Parker as its central Indian character. Parker was the son of a Comanche war chief and Cynthia Ann Parker; she had been captured during a Comanche raid in 1836 (her capture and rescue formed the basis of John Ford's 1956 western classic *The Searchers*). For several years in the 1860s Parker's Quahadis (Antelopes) held the Texas plains, and as shown in the film the U.S. Cavalry's inability to find their secret encampment Blanco Canyon was a source of great frustration. With the end of the Indian Wars, Parker helped his tribe to adjust to reservation life and through some shrewd investments he became one of the wealthiest Indians in America.

With Andrews having portrayed most of the usual, clichéd western "good guy" types it was only a matter of time before he tried his hand at playing an army frontier scout, and as the tough, fearless Jim Read, he is suitably impressive in a role that pits him against two adversaries, scalphunter Art Downey (Stacy Harris) and renegade Indian Black Cloud (Henry Brandon). With these two hot-heads causing mayhem against the backdrop of an impending Indian war, he is clearly the only man who can save the day, even if it means risking his own life in the process. When General Miles commends him for his prompt arrival, Read explains, "We traveled at night, mostly. Comanches hole up at night. It's bad medicine for them."*

As well as being tough, Read is also a man of great composure, particularly when provoked:

> DOWNEY: They say you're pretty good with a gun, Read. Now, just how good?
> READ: I manage to stay alive.
> DOWNEY: I asked you a question, Read! How good?
> READ: That's your gamble.

Not one for heavy theorizing about the hostilities, the rational Read tells it plain and simple: "So that's the way it is. Comanches kill Mexicans to get even with the Spanish. And Mexicans kill Comanches in revenge for that. It's become a way of life."

Read is very much a carbon copy of Andrews's Brett Halliday from *Smoke Signal*, with both

men sharing a great empathy and compassion for the plight of the Indians, memorably represented in *Comanche* by Kent Smith, Henry Brandon and Mike Mazurki. If at first Smith must have seemed an odd choice to play the Comanche chief Quanah Parker, the same could not be said of Henry Brandon in the role of Black Cloud. With his sharp features, the German-born actor was a natural when it came to playing Indians, notching up 26 appearances in the role, including a stint as Quanah Parker in the John Ford western *Two Rode Together* (1961).

No Hollywood western would be complete without an injection of humor, which in *Comanche* came courtesy of Read's sidekick Puffer, played by Nestor Paiva, who at times comes over as a tribute act to Gabby Hayes and Walter Brennan. Staked out awaiting their fate from the hostile Comanches, our heroes are saved by Puffer's hairpiece as explained by Read: "Your wig scared them. They think it's your scalp. Take it off."

The film also featured a young Linda Cristal, who reprised the role of the beautiful, aristocratic Mexican lady many years later as Victoria Montoya in the television western series *The High Chaparral*. Coincidentally, she also played another Comanche captive in *Two Rode Together* alongside Brandon's Quanah Parker. By riding off into the sunset with the lovely Cristal, Andrews's frontier scout rigidly stuck to the golden Hollywood rule that the white guy sent to make peace with the Indians, and who usually didn't speak with a forked tongue, should have his pick of the prettiest woman in the village for his troubles. (Small wonder those frisky young Indian bucks were always slapping on the war paint!)

To complement the superb outdoor cinematography, the film employed a catchy theme song by the Lancers, so catchy in fact, I still can't get it out of my head. Apparently the mint American pressing of this soundtrack is a rare collector's item (a must buy, if you're into Disneyesque type themes).

One critic commented, "Purportedly based on fact (at least that's what the producers claim in the opening credits), *Comanche* is just as entertaining as any fictional film on the subject." Leonard Maltin mused, "Andrews is staunch as

---

*According to Hollywood, there were only three things you needed to know to get the better of Indians: They don't fight at night; one whiff of whisky and they plunge into drunken revelry; and they will happily trade a shed-full of gold "from them thar hills" for a horse blanket and some shiny beads.

an Indian scout in this pat western."[1] Halliwell trod a similar line, describing the film as a "[c]heerful action western, satisfying to the easily pleased."[2]

While the City Sleeps

RKO, 1956

Cast: Dana Andrews (Edward Mobley); Rhonda Fleming (Dorothy Kyne); George Sanders (Mark Loving); Howard Duff (Lt. Burt Kaufman); Thomas Mitchell (John Day Griffith); Vincent Price (Walter Kyne); Sally Forrest (Nancy Liggett); John Drew Barrymore (Robert Manners); James Craig (Harry Kritzer); Ida Lupino (Mildred Donner); Robert Warwick (Amos Kyne); Mae Marsh (Mrs. Manners); Ralph Peters (Gerald Meade); Sandy White (Judith Felton); Larry J. Blake (Tim, Police Sergeant); Celia Lovsky (Miss Dodd); Ed Hinton (Mike O'Leary); Pitt Herbert (Carlo, Bartender at the Dell); Vladimir Sokoloff (George Pilski); David Andrews (Bar Pianist); Ralph Brooks (Waiter); Carleton Young (Police Interrogator); Leonard Carey (Steven, Walter's Butler); Joe Devlin (Newspaper Teletype); Mike Lally (Bartender in Biscayne's Cocktail Bar); Andrew Lupino (Jim Leary); Mickey Martin (Bellhop); Charles Sherlock (Detective); Bert Stevens (Newsman).

Credits: Bert E. Friedlob (Producer); Fritz Lang (Director); Charles Einstein (Novel *The Bloody Spur*); Casey Robinson (Screenplay); Ernest Laszlo (Cinematography); Herschel Burke Gilbert (Music); Carroll Clark (Art Direction); Jack Mills (Set Decorations); Norma Koch (Costume Design); Robert Martien, Jackie Spitzer (Wardrobe); Gustav Norin (Makeup); Ronnie Rondell (Assistant Director); Verna Fields, Buddy Myers (Sound); Gene Fowler, Jr. (Editor). Running time: 100 minutes

Following the death of his father, spoiled playboy Walter Kyne inherits the *Sentinel*, one of the city's major newspapers. The city is being terrorized by the sex murderer Robert Manners, who preys on beautiful women at night and is known as the Lipstick Killer. With little idea of running a newspaper, Kyne offers the editor-in-chief position to the executive who can uncover the identity of the killer. Newspaper editor John Day Griffith, a hard-drinking Irishman who has his sights on the extra money the position

pays, enlists the help of a friend, a streetwise reporter and Pulitzer Prize winner, Edward Mobley (Dana Andrews). Ruthless cad Mark Loving, head of the wire service, motivated by the higher social standing that comes with the job, uses his mistress, resourceful columnist Mildred Donner, to extract information from Mobley using her seductive charms. The photo editor, Harry Kritzer, exploits his romantic link with Kyne's wife Dorothy in his attempt to secure the position. Mobley is persuaded to use his girlfriend, Nancy Liggett, as bait to catch the killer, which nearly results in her becoming another victim when he enters her apartment. A climactic chase ensues; Mobley pursues the killer through the streets down into the subway, where the two slug it out, narrowly avoiding on coming trains. Manners is finally apprehended by the police.

Tagline: "Suspense as startling as a strangled scream!"

The much underrated *While the City Sleeps* was Fritz Lang's second favorite film after his 1936 masterpiece *Fury*, which like Andrews's *The*

Burning the midnight oil, Pulitzer-winning journalist Edward Mobley (Andrews) sets his type to catch "The Lipstick Killer" in *While the City Sleeps* (RKO, 1956).

Ox-Bow Incident tackled the subject of lynch mob violence.

Born in Vienna, Lang enlisted in the Austrian army in 1915 and was wounded four times in action during the First World War. He worked in the German cinema throughout the 1920s and early '30s, directing two of his most celebrated films, *Metropolis* (1927) and *M* (1931). In 1935 he moved to Hollywood, where he spent the next 20 years producing classics such as *Ministry of Fear* (1944), *The Big Heat* (1953) and his last two American films, both starring Dana Andrews, *While the City Sleeps* and *Beyond a Reasonable Doubt*. The latter two were part of a low-budget package deal put together by producer Bert E. Friedlob.

Based on Charles Einstein's novel *The Bloody Spur* and newspaper accounts of an actual Chicago murder case, the independent production *While the City Sleeps* was originally scheduled for release through United Artists, but RKO ended up with the distribution rights. (The studio was shortly to be consigned to the pages of cinematic history.)

Two themes are cleverly explored in this multilayered thriller. The main subject matter, delving into the methods and motivation of the serial killer, is closely intertwined with the ruthless nature of the journalists, who readily expose other people to danger for their own purpose. Lang had originally explored the idea of the sexual psychopath killer in the memorable *M*, which gave Peter Lorre his first prominent film role. And just as Otto Preminger had given Andrews's career a huge boost in the 1940s with his trilogy of film noirs (*Laura, Fallen Angel* and *Where The Sidewalk Ends*), Lang revitalized the actor's career in the 1950s with *While the City Sleeps* and *Beyond a Reasonable Doubt*.

This movie's large, star-studded cast was unusual for a film noir. The film gave Andrews another opportunity to work with Vincent Price (*Laura*) and George Sanders (*Assignment Paris*). In addition to these veterans, valuable support was provided by the marvelous character actor, Thomas Mitchell, James Craig, the beautiful Rhonda Fleming, and husband-and-wife Howard Duff and Ida Lupino. Renowned for her acting, the tough-minded Lupino was one of the few women to achieve success as a director in the 1950s. The youngsters in the film included former dancer Sally Forrest, who starred in several films directed by Ida Lupino; and John Drew Barrymore, father of actress Drew Barrymore and the son of stage and screen legend John Barrymore and actress Dolores Costello. As the Lipstick Killer, Barrymore was very much on top form. Marvelously skulking around the corridors of New York's apartment blocks, he looks as mad as the proverbial Hatter and at certain angles registers as a cross between a young, psychotic Stewart Granger and a skittish Sean Penn. His career was ruined by drug and alcohol abuse, and in later life he became a reclusive derelict.

In addition to some excellent lighting by Ernest Laszlo, the film enjoyed a superb Herschel Burke-Gilbert film score. By way of trivia, Andrews's son David makes an appearance in the film, playing the piano in the barroom scene. Friedlob persuaded the U.S. government to use the film as a weapon against the corrupting force of comic books on young minds: In the film, the killer is depicted as an avid comic-book fan.[1]

The film shows Andrews at his most relaxed and laid-back; his Pulitzer Prize–winning journalist Ed Mobley doesn't really care who wins the top *Sentinel* job, as long as he can still indulge in his favorite pastime of propping up the local bar and making eyes at Sally Forrest or Ida Lupino, depending upon who comes through the door first. Plastered or suffering a hangover, Mobley is a warm and likable character, whom you'd half-expect to see exiting the bar in the company of a six-foot white rabbit. At least he is honest to himself; on the way home in a cab alongside drooling gossip columnist Mildred, he says, "I'm so plastered. The movement of this cab is slightly inimical to me. The fact I can say 'inimical' proves how drunk I am." Mobley soon discovers that one's little flirtatious indiscretions the night before have a habit of kicking you in the teeth when the office drums start beating the next morning, prompting him, with an almighty hangover, to proffer resignedly, "If I'm gonna be hung — don't hang me for a sheep."

But when it comes to catching the killer, Mobley shakes out the cobwebs and kicks into action, and down at the police station his genius for criminal deduction comes into play when the only suspect is revealed. Unimpressed by the efforts of the local flatfoots, who clearly learned their trade off the back of a cereal box, he exclaims to Griffith over the phone, "The janitor!

If that old boy did it, I'll sit on the hot seat for him." And, after baiting the real killer through a memorable TV broadcast, he proves he is also good at the old fisticuffs in the nail-biting climax.

Great stuff—but if vintage noir, Lang-style, isn't your bag, the sight of the statuesque Rhonda Fleming doing her exercises in a two-piece swimsuit is certainly worth the entrance fee alone.

Shot quickly in the summer of 1955, the film was favorably reviewed as a good suspense film by most of the critics and Andrews's performance was included in the sweeping praise of the principal characters.

THE NEW YORK TIMES: "A tight and sophisticated script by Casey Robinson and a clutch of professional performances make *While the City Sleeps* a diverting and workmanlike fiction...."

LIBRARY JOURNAL: "...An excellent cast and good direction keep the threads of the plot at an entertaining level throughout...."

THE HOLLYWOOD REPORTER: "Fritz Lang has directed it astutely in tabloid style, with short vignettes keeping the action going at a good clip, and the cast is studded with fine troupers...."

VARIETY: "A top-flight job."

Beyond a Reasonable Doubt
RKO, 1956

Cast: Dana Andrews (Tom Garrett); Joan Fontaine (Susan Spencer); Sidney Blackmer (Austin Spencer); Arthur Franz (Bob Hale); Philip Bourneuf (Roy Thompson); Ed Binns (Lt. Kennedy); Shepperd Strudwick (Jonathan Wilson); Robin Raymond (Terry Larue); Barbara Nichols (Dolly Moore); William F. Leicester (Charlie Miller); Dan Seymour (Greco); Rusty Lane (Judge); Joyce Taylor (Joan Williams); Carleton Young (Allan Kirk); Trudy Wroe (Hatcheck Girl); Joe Kirk (Clerk); Charles Evans (Governor); Wendell Niles (Announcer); Benny Burt, Myron Cook (Reporters); Tony De Mario (Doctor); Phillip Barnes (Policeman); Dorothy Ford (Blonde); Joey Ray (Eddie); Larry Barton (Customer); Frank Mitchell (Waiter); Harry Strang (Warden); Hal Taggart (Court Clerk); Ralph Volkie (Photographer); Carl Sklover (Cab Driver); Frank Farnum (Spectator at Electrocution); John George (Newspaper Vendor); Dorothy Gordon (Secretary); Billy Reed (Emcee); Eric Wilton (Clergyman); Baynes Barron (Higgens, the Fingerprint Man); Jeffrey Sayre (Jury Foreman); Frank Mills (Burlesque Patron); Dave Wiechman (Condemned Man); Bob Whitney (Bailiff).

Credits: Bert E. Friedlob (Producer); Fritz Lang (Director); Douglas Morrow (Story & Screenplay); William Snyder (Cinematography); Herschel Burke Gilbert (Music); Herschel Burke Gilbert, Alfred Perry (Song); Carroll Clark (Art Direction); Darrell Silvera (Set Decorations); Lou LaCava (Makeup); Maxwell O. Henry (Assistant Director); Terry Kellum (Sound); Gene Fowler, Jr. (Editor). Running time: 80 minutes

After witnessing an execution, writer Tom Garrett (Dana Andrews) discusses capital punishment with his prospective father-in-law, crusading newspaper publisher Austin Spencer. The two devise a plan to prove that a man can be tried and convicted of murder based on flimsy circumstantial evidence; this will also expose conviction-happy district attorney Roy Thompson, who has built a successful career convicting suspects on such evidence. Garrett plants clues that will incriminate him in the murder of a burlesque stripper; once he is tried and convicted, it is the intention that Spencer will step in to reveal the hoax and provide the evidence to prove him innocent. All goes according to plan until Spencer is killed in a car accident and all the evidence exonerating Garrett is destroyed. With the date of execution looming, Garrett's fiancée Susan focuses on securing a pardon, which is eventually forthcoming when Spencer's lawyer discovers a letter from the dead man, which sets out the ruse, providing the evidence to free Garrett. However, just before being pardoned, Garrett accidentally reveals to Susan that he *is* the killer after all. It transpires that Garrett, the long-lost husband of the murder victim, took advantage of the scheme to rid himself of his wife, freeing him to marry the wealthy Susan and enter high society. Feeling betrayed, Susan reveals this to the authorities and Garrett is led back to his cell to await his fate.

Tagline: "What Kind of Man would frame himself for MURDER?"

Andrews was tailor-made for the role of the scheming novelist, but the part was originally intended for that other fine minimalist actor, Joseph Cotten,[1] who had shown in Hitchcock's *Shadow of a Doubt* that he, too, could surprise audiences by playing the bad guy when the occasion demanded. Cotten was earmarked for the role when Ida Lupino and then-husband Howard Duff were attempting to secure the story rights, but producer Bert E. Freidlob beat

Society gal Susan Spencer (Joan Fontaine) is anxious to get her man, talented writer Tom Garrett (Andrews), but all is not as it seems in Fritz Lang's engrossing thriller *Beyond a Reasonable Doubt* (RKO, 1956).

them to it, paving the way for Andrews to take on one of his most intriguing roles: a calculating murderer who at times gains our sympathy as a consequence of Fritz Lang's skillful direction and Andrews's sincere performance.

Beyond a Reasonable Doubt was Lang's second film for Friedlob and his last American film before retiring from filmmaking in Hollywood. It was prepared simultaneously with *While the City Sleeps* to enable Lang to divide his time with Douglas Morrow, who wrote the story and the screenplay for both films. Morrow was inspired to write *Beyond a Reasonable Doubt* by a 1955 Gallup poll that indicated that Americans were evenly divided on their views on capital punishment.

Andrews's romantic interest in the film was played by celebrated screen actress Joan Fontaine. Younger sister to Olivia de Havilland, Fontaine specialized in vulnerable, innocent heroines, which rewarded her with an Academy Award nomination for *Rebecca* (1940) and Oscar gold a year later for *Suspicion*. Interestingly, she is the only star to win an Academy Award for a performance in a film directed by Alfred Hitchcock. As Susan Spencer, the elegant socialite in *Beyond a Reasonable Doubt*, she is a little bit more forward than we would normally expect, in a role that requires her to do all the running where her man's concerned. Keen to get him alone, all to herself, she brazenly informs him that she has never checked out his apartment, prompting Tom to comment, "Aren't we a little mixed up? That's supposed to be my line."

The character of writer, Tom Garrett, marked a complete departure from Andrews's previous roles, in that for the first time he was playing a genuine villain. As the protagonist, his duplicity is contrary to the actions of the acknowledged flawed noir hero, whose circumstances are usually beyond their control. This is clearly not the case with Garrett, whose premeditated scheming permeates throughout the entire story. Andrews's compelling performance prompted one critic to comment, "The deviousness works well here, thanks in part to the cold-eyed, dead-voiced, deliberately wooden persona which Andrews creates." Another wrote, "Andrews' peculiarly distant screen personality is admirably suited to the role of the rather calculating hero, and makes plausible the twist that reveals him as a murderer." The *New York Times* noted, "Dana Andrews is forceful as the fellow who plants clues on himself."

Andrews's characters in his Preminger noirs *Fallen Angel* and *Where the Sidewalk Ends* were clearly blighted heroes, but they were not capable of premeditated murder. Tom Garrett is a different kettle of fish and by far Andrews's most complex and multi-faceted character. On face value he is the perfect prospective son-in-law — a compassionate, talented writer who is prepared to go that extra mile to see that justice is served, very much like his crusading district attorney in *Boomerang!* But as we learn, Tom Garrett is no Henry Harvey, for scrape away at the surface, and a cold character is revealed — one capable of murder if his happiness and social progression are concerned.

Lang suggested in an interview that Garrett's actions were understandable, suggesting that perhaps the murder was "a crime out of despair," stemming from a loveless first marriage that made his life unhappy."[2] Intriguingly, suspicion has always surrounded Lang's first marriage; his wife died under mysterious circumstances, apparently a gunshot suicide from a revolver owned by the director. This incident strongly affected Lang, which many suggest influenced the nature of his films thereafter.

Lang's relationship with Freidlob broke down while the film was in production due to the producer's interference with the direction. When Garrett is revealed as the real murderer, Friedlob wanted to show his execution by electric chair, but Lang refused, preferring that the character die off-screen. Lang eventually got his way, but after the last scene was shot he walked off the set never to return, leaving his friend Gene Fowler, Jr., to complete the editing. This feuding clearly encouraged Lang's retirement and possibly influenced his opinion of the film:

"I hate it , but it was a great success. I don't know why?"[3]

During filming, Lang had to contend with an inebriated Andrews, who according to Fowler "was really on the sauce," turning up most mornings "with the most god-awful hangover in the world." Fowler added, "We couldn't get a shot out of him until eleven o'clock, when he was fed gallons of coffee." Eventually, Lang got Andrews to promise to quit the bottle, and just to make sure, put a tail on him one day after filming. Andrews gave the man the slip, turning up the next day with the usual hangover.[4]

The film's memorable twist ending was reminiscent of Agatha Christie's novel *The Murder of Roger Ackroyd*. RKO decided to keep the outcome a closely guarded secret, with the actors receiving the scripts for that scene on the day of filming. It was shot behind locked doors, and only nine people knew how the story ended. The film also had two openings, with one showing Garrett and Spencer watching the execution of a murderer, and another shot for the more censorious English market, in which the characters simply discuss what they have witnessed.

Even though the film was favorably reviewed, Andrews had reservations concerning the unexpected twist in the story, and in particular the way it fooled the audience; he felt that they should have been presented with a clue or two to enable them to arrive at their own conclusions.[5] (I have to say, the final twist sure had me fooled, but then again, I was still trying to figure how Andrews's Tom Garrett could possibly resist Susan's amorous "take me to bed" advances without breaking into a cold sweat.)

Spring Reunion
United Artists, 1957

Cast: Dana Andrews (Fred Davis); Betty Hutton (Maggie Brewster); Jean Hagen (Barna Forrest); Sara Berner (Paula Kratz); Robert F. Simon (Harry Brewster); Laura La Plante (May Brewster); Gordon Jones (Jack Frazer); James Gleason (Mr. Collyer); Irene Ryan (Miss Stapleton); Richard Shannon (Nick); Ken Curtis (Al); Herbert Anderson (Edward); Richard Benedict (Jim); Vivi Janiss (Grace); Florence Sundstrom (Mary); Mimi Doyle (Alice); Sid Tomack (Caterer); Shirley Mitchell (Receptionist); George Chandler (Zimmie); Dorothy Neumann (Roseanne); Barbara Drew (Verna); Richard Deacon (Sidney); Don Haggerty (Pete); Leon Tyler (Teenager in Car).

Credits: Jerry Bresler (Producer); Robert Pirosh (Director); Robert Alan Aurthur (Story); Robert Pirosh, Elick Moll (Screenplay); Harold Lipstein (Cinematography); Herbert Spencer, Earle Hagen (Music); Johnny Mercer, Harry Warren (Song "Spring Reunion," sung by the Marty Kaye Trio); Paul Groesse (Art Direction); Don Loper (Costume Design); John Burch (Assistant Director); Sylvia Lewis (Choreography); Leon Barsha (Editor). Running time: 79 minutes

In their Midwestern town, 33-year-old spinster Maggie Brewster meets up with old high school flame Fred Davis (Dana Andrews) during the "Class of '41" reunion at Carson High School. It has been 15 years since they last met, but the old chemistry is still there. Once regarded as "the boy most likely to succeed," ex-football star Fred has become a drifter since leaving high school and has returned to town to sell his house before taking a job in San Francisco. During their earlier courting days, Fred had proposed marriage to Maggie, but was turned down. Maggie's decision was heavily influenced by her wealthy and domineering father, who feels that no one is good enough for her. In the years since Fred left town, Maggie has found success with her real estate career, but her love life has been empty. While Maggie is getting reacquainted with Fred, her best friend Barna Forrest, who is happily married with four children, contemplates a fling with ex-athlete Jack Frazer, who still lives on campus and whose wife is conveniently out of town. With feelings of unfulfillment and a longing to make up for lost years, Maggie is encouraged by her compassionate mother Mary to leave her possessive father and make a fresh start with Fred.

Tagline: "This is real ... this is a man ... these are his arms, his lips ... this may be my last chance.... THIS TIME I CAN'T AFFORD TO LET LOVE PASS ME BY!"

Off the top of your head, how many lost love stories, set against the backdrop of a school reunion, can you think of? Precisely — a big fat zero! So squeeze into that old high school

Former high school sweethearts Maggie Brewster (Betty Hutton) and Fred Davis (Andrews) get together to discuss old times in *Spring Reunion* (United Artists, 1957).

sweatshirt, treat yourself to some popcorn and enjoy.

This was producer Jerry Bresler's second project featuring Andrews, Bresler having co-produced the 1952 spy thriller *Assignment Paris*. His later productions were varied in their subject matter, ranging from the epic costume drama *The Vikings* (1958) to the gritty Sam Peckinpah western *Major Dundee* (1965) and the James Bond spoof *Casino Royale* (1967).

Spring Reunion also reunited Andrews with director Robert Pirosh, who had worked with the actor on the 1944 Danny Kaye vehicle *Up in Arms*. Pirosh earned an Academy Award for his script for the World War II drama *Battleground* (1949), which like Andrews's earlier war classic *A Walk in the Sun* (1945) concentrated on the life of the ordinary G.I. in the battlefields of Europe. Pirosh would go on to help create the successful World War II television series *Combat!*

Andrews was no stranger to the love story theme with *Night Song* (1947) and the cult weepie *My Foolish Heart* (1949) under his belt, but his excursions into the romantic arena usually saw him propping up a love triangle of some description, and more often than not he would end up losing the girl. He lost Lynn Bari to Jon Hall in *Kit Carson* (1940), Gene Tierney to Randolph Scott in *Belle Starr* (1941), Anne Baxter to Tyrone Power in *Crash Dive* (1943), Joan Crawford to Henry Fonda in *Daisy Kenyon* (1947), and Elizabeth Taylor to Peter Finch in *Elephant Walk* (1954). He just about hung on to wife Lilli Palmer in *No Minor Vices* (1948), although it was a "close run thing" with Louis Jourdan on the prowl.

No such triangle featured in *Spring Reunion*, with Andrews disappearing into the sunset with Betty Hutton, who on the face of it appeared an odd match for the actor. Renowned for her brassy, exuberant style, Hutton, on paper, seemed the complete antithesis to the more laid-back Andrews. But fortunately for all concerned, and as noted by the *New York Times*, "Miss Hutton is a restrained heroine unlike the ebullient songstress she has portrayed on screen in the past ... turns in a low-voltage portrayal that is marked by sincerity, if not passion."

Andrews's Fred Davis is very much in the same mold as his Eric Stanton (*Fallen Angel*) and Walt Dreiser (*My Foolish Heart*)—all of them loners, aimlessly drifting from job to job, and through

life, with little aim or purpose—searching for something, but not entirely sure what. If they have little time to contemplate the future, they have even less time to mull over the past. Contemptuous of life and his empty existence, Fred's humor is soured, particularly where college reunions are concerned: "I can see it now, Maggie. A bald-headed classmate comes in—somebody's bound to say, 'Hi ya Curly.' 'Hey, any of you see Carlotta? Boy was she stacked—weighed in at 185 pounds this morning.'" Finding it all rather too much when the big day arrives, he resignedly suggests to Maggie, "Why don't we crawl out of this swamp of nostalgia and find a nice bar?" Not wishing to lose her man for the second time, Maggie finally acquiesces and joins Fred for an evening saunter around the college football field, where we learn the reason for his air of despondency: a broken leg in his first high school football match, which ended a promising future (using football as a platform).

And as our former sweethearts get reacquainted with one another, we learn more about their empty existence over the past 15 years through Fred's plaintive soul-searching:

FRED: You're thirty-three years old, you've never been married and at night there just isn't much to do. Oh, you call up people, go for a drive, take in a movie, find something else to do , like...

MAGGIE: Like babysitting.

FRED: Like babysitting, but none of it's very fun, none of it.

MAGGIE: How do you know so much about me?

FRED: I was just describing myself Maggie, except I don't baby-sit.

...

MAGGIE: You have the longest nights in New York.

FRED: You know what I do at night ? Wander around from one bar to another, looking for something—I dunno what—bump into a lot of people looking for the same thing.

Spring Reunion marked Hutton's return to the big screen after a four-year break. Originally the role of the spinster had been conceived for Judy Garland. This was the second time that Hutton had replaced Judy in a film role: In 1949, she took over from an exhausted Judy to star in the classic film musical *Annie Get Your Gun*, which became a smash hit. Most of her subsequent roles didn't provide any real opportunity to reveal her acting ability and her career faded. *Spring Reunion* was Hutton's final film before concentrating on television and the stage, and it allowed her to showcase her singing skills with the standard "That Old Feeling." In 1970, Hutton, suffering from alcohol and substance abuse, attempted suicide after losing her singing voice.

Betty looks stunning in this film, comfortably handling her role with great tenderness and sincerity. Her moonlight scene on the sailboat, in the arms of Fred, is as romantic as they come; you can almost imagine Andrews crooning Crosby's "True Love" as they merrily slice through the waves.

At the age of 48, Andrews just about gets away with playing a man in his early 30s (Hutton was only 36); Hollywood always had an ample supply of black shoe polish to take away the gray. Incidentally, at 55, Crosby was nearly twice Grace Kelly's age when they teamed in *High Society.*

In company with many of the 1950s soap operas, and in particular the mother of all potboilers *Peyton Place* (1957), *Spring Reunion* provided an ideal opportunity for many a character actor and aging star to remind us of their talents: The film boasted Jean Hagen, who is best remembered as Lina Lamont, the silent-film star in *Singin' in the Rain* (1952), and real-life silent star Laura La Plante, who like Hutton was also making a return to the screen after a long retirement (this was her last film appearance). Other roles went to the consistently brilliant character actor James Gleason, who had worked with Andrews in *Crash Dive* (1943), and Irene Ryan, who would become a household face as Granny on TV's *The Beverly Hillbillies.* Those with good memories will also recognize Robert Simon from *Where the Sidewalks Ends* (Andrews's boss Inspector Foley) in the role of Maggie's possessive father.

Spring Reunion was made by Kirk Douglas's production company, Bryna Company, which he founded in 1955. Many of the 19 films produced by the company starred Douglas but not their several low-budget films, which included *Spring Reunion.* According to Douglas, he was badly advised that for tax reasons the company had to make movies in which he didn't appear. Douglas later learned that his trusted financial adviser had collateralized his company's profitable first picture *The Indian Fighter* (1955) with the non-

profitable *Spring Reunion*, which meant that *The Indian Fighter* didn't make a penny when aired.[1]

On the lost love front, *Spring Reunion* is no *Casablanca,* and admittedly the problems of two lonely old high school sweethearts "don't amount to a hill of beans in this crazy world," but it is nonetheless an entertaining piece, that will have you wallowing in nostalgia and digging out that old high school yearbook when the final credits begin to roll.

Zero Hour!
Paramount, 1957

Cast: Dana Andrews (Lt. Ted Stryker); Linda Darnell (Ellen Stryker); Sterling Hayden (Capt. Martin Treleaven); Elroy "Crazylegs" Hirsch (Capt. Bill Wilson); Geoffrey Toone (Dr. Baird); Jerry Paris (Tony Decker); Peggy King (Janet Turner); Charles Quinlivan (Harry Burdick); Patricia Tiernan (Mrs. Wilson); Steve London (Co-pilot Stewart); Jo Ann Wade (Treleaven's Babysitter); Raymond Ferrell (Joey Stryker); John Ashley (TV Singer); Willis Bouchey (British Army Doctor); Robert Stevenson (Air Traffic Controller); Maxine Cooper (Sick Woman); Mary Newton (Mrs. Purty, Landlady); David Thursby (Whitmond the Argo Fan); Will Sage (Vancouver Radar Controller); Noel Drayton (Vancouver Control Man); Will J. White (Vancouver Policeman); Fintan Meyler (Mrs. Treleaven); Hope Summers (Mrs. Summers); Larry Thor (Vancouver Radio Dispatcher); Richard Keith (Station Manager); Russell Thorson (Vancouver Flight Dispatcher); Arthur Hanson (Reporter); Roy Gordon (Frank Graham); Woody Chambliss (Whitmond's Drinking Buddy); William Conrad (Narrator); S. John Launer (Vancouver Switchboard Operator); Duane Grey (Plane Passenger); John Zaremba (Passenger with Sick Wife).

Credits: John C. Champion (Producer); Hall Bartlett (Director); Arthur Hailey (Teleplay "Flight into Danger"); Arthur Hailey, Hall Barlett, John C. Champion (Screenplay); John F. Warren (Cinematography); Ted Dale (Music); Ross Dowd (Set Decorations); Eddie Armand (Costume Design); John P. Fulton, Norman O'Skeete (Special Effects); Lyle Figland, Charles Grenzbach (Sound); John C. Fuller (Editor). Running time: 81 minutes

During the flight of a Canadian passenger airliner, the pilots and some of the passengers are struck down with food poisoning brought on by the in-flight meal. With the crew rendered incapable of flying and landing the plane, all hope rests upon passenger Ted Stryker (Dana Andrews), a former World War II Battle of Britain ace who, traumatized by his wartime experiences, is terrified of flying again. Helping him overcome his fear is his wife Ellen, who boarded the flight with son Joey to escape their failed marriage not knowing that Ted would pick up the scent and board the plane just before take-off. With the marriage having gone cold due to Ted's inability to put the past behind him, their airborne ordeal provides the impetus to rekindle their love. Ground controller Treleaven has steel-nerved resolve and convinces Stryker to pull himself together and make a safe landing.

With lives at stake, including his own son, traumatized ace Ted Stryker (Andrews) lines up for a bumpy landing with wife Ellen (Linda Darnell) manning the radio in Hall Barlett's airborne suspenser *Zero Hour!* (Paramount, 1957).

Tagline: "It Builds to the Tensest 50 Minutes in the History of the Screen!"

And that's no idle boast, for this is a corker of a movie, if you enjoy suspense-laden drama, 1950s style.

Zero Hour! was adapted from Arthur Hailey's 1956 Canadian television play "Flight into Danger," which also formed the basis of his novel *Runway Zero-Eight.* If the plot sounds familiar, it should, because it went on to be successfully spoofed in the hilarious movie *Airplane!* (1980).

Against-the-odds landings were the flavor of 1950s airplane disaster movies, with John Wayne taking the controls in William Wellman's hugely successful *The High and the Mighty* (1954), Doris Day landing safely in *Julie* (1956) and Andrews overcoming his flying phobia in *Zero Hour!* The role of the heroic aviator was, in fact, the most popular in Andrews's film career, the actor having donned flying garb on six occasions: *The Purple Heart* (1944), *Wing and a Prayer* (1944), *The Best Years of Our Lives* (1946), *Zero Hour, The Crowded Sky* (1960) and *Airport '75* (1974). Sticking with the airplane disaster theme, Andrews also appeared in *The Pilot* (1979), directed by and starring Cliff Robertson.

In *Zero Hour!*, great play would once again be made with Andrews's ambivalent persona — the flawed hero who finally makes good. Like his ex–USAF bombardier character Fred Derry from *Best Years of Our Lives,* Andrews's ex-fighter pilot Ted Stryker experiences great difficulty readjusting to civilian life due to his wartime trauma, which is explained in the opening sequence when the RAF fighter squadron, under his command, crashes in the fog during a risky low level attack on a German supply depot. Badly wounded, Stryker is the only survivor, but the real suffering kicks in with his recurring flashbacks of the incident. Holding himself responsible for the death of his men, Stryker's mental anguish makes it difficult for him to settle into a job after the war and eventually leads to the breakdown of his marriage. When his wife takes her leave with their son Joey, Stryker catches up with them after they board Flight 417 and, with all the passengers strapped in, the white-knuckle ride begins.

In contrast to John Wayne's equally traumatized aging pilot in *High and the Mighty*, who remains defiantly cool with disaster looming, Andrews's Stryker sweats profusely throughout the proceedings as the violent flashbacks continue to haunt him. His edgy, heartfelt performance helps to maintain the brisk pace of the film which, unlike, *The High and the Mighty*, doesn't overly dwell on passenger subplots.

Zero Hour! is unique in that it works perfectly well on two different levels depending on your mood. As a taut suspense drama they don't come any finer, but if you're in the mood for laughs this can actually be a funnier treat than the film that spoofed it, *Airplane!* Some of the memorable lines resurfaced in *Airplane* to great comic effect:

> DR. BAIRD: Our survival hinges on one thing—finding someone on board who can not only fly this plane, but who didn't have fish for dinner.
>
> …
>
> CAPT. TRELEAVEN: I guess I picked the wrong week to give up smoking.

Director Hall Barlett set up his own production company in 1952, winning many awards that same year for his first project (*Navajo*, a contemporary docudrama set on a reservation). He was married to Rhonda Fleming from 1966 to 1971, but he never featured her in any of his films. The beautiful actress would, however, star with Andrews in his next airborne drama *The Crowded Sky.*

The romantic interest in the film was Linda Darnell, who as the tart Stella had been the object of lust for Andrews's character Eric Stanton in *Fallen Angel* (1945). After *Zero Hour!* was "in the can," she took a seven-year break from filmmaking. But in common with many actresses who had entered their thirties, her return to the big screen proved difficult with many of the studios looking for a fresh face to promote.

Matching the stoicism of Andrews's central character was that other master of dry monotone delivery, Sterling Hayden, who provided excellent support as airport controller Treleaven (the role comically reprised by another Hollywood stalwart, Lloyd Bridges in *Airplane!*). Hayden was perhaps the only other star who could give Errol Flynn a run for his money when it came to leading an adventurous life: He had sailed around the world by the age of 20, married Hollywood beauty Madeleine Caroll, served in the Marines, and as a OSS undercover agent ran guns through German lines to Yugoslav partisans during World War II. Hayden disliked acting, claiming he only did it to fund his life on the ocean waves. He tended to specialize in westerns and noirs with his most notable roles in *The Asphalt Jungle* (1950), *The Killing* (1956) and *Dr. Strangelove* (1964). His seagoing adventures formed the basis of his autobiography *Wanderer,* published in 1963.

Even though *Zero Hour!* was shot on a low budget, it was acknowledged by one critic that Barlett's direction cleverly sustained the tension contained within the screenplay and that Andrews did a commendable job of conveying fear as the trauma-stricken pilot. This sense of dread is clearly etched on Andrews's face when he scans the myriad of gauges on the plane's instrument panel after the doctor candidly informs him that he is the only one on board who stands any sort of chance of landing the plane.

In fact, the tension was deemed almost unbearable during editing, which prompted the moviemakers to insert a musical interlude to break it up. This took the form of a nightclub scene with flaming hot music supplied by ace trumpeter Billy Regis, who sealed his fame with the Perez Prado recording of "Cherry Pink and Apple Blossom White."[1]

Also included in the cast were Geoffrey Toone, Jerry Paris, perky singer Peggy King and the famous American football player Elroy "Crazylegs" Hirsch, who had previously starred as himself in Hall Bartlett's romanticized tribute to his life *Crazylegs* (1953). When Hirsch asks Stryker's little boy if he's ever been in a cockpit before, it's extremely difficult not to crease up with laughter. And just when you're recovering from one unintended hilarious line, out pops another :

GROUND CONTROL: How's she handling?
STRYKER: Sluggish, like a wet sponge.

But all sense of comic relief disappears when Stryker, with Ellen alongside him in the cockpit handling the radio, decides to land the plane in the fog against Treleaven's orders. (Due to their troubled history with one another dating back to the war, Treleaven thinks Stryker will crack when the going gets tough.) With sick passengers requiring immediate hospitalization, Stryker has no time for Treleaven's order to circle the field until the weather breaks; determination is written all over his face when he shouts into the mike, "Listen, Treleaven, I'm coming in, do you hear me? I'm coming in right now. We have people up here, including my own son, who will die in less than one hour.... I may bend your precious airplane, but I'll bring it down. Now, get on with the landing check."

He comes in too fast on the final approach, and the undercarriage is destroyed on touchdown, but luckily for all on board, the plane comes to a halt mostly intact, which prompts Ellen to coo, "Ted ... I'm very proud." Equally relieved and impressed, Treleaven concedes, "Ted, that was probably the lousiest landing in the history of this airport, but there are some of us here, particularly me, who would like to buy you a drink and shake your hand."

With Andrews's close association with airplane disaster movies, people were amusingly advised to take another flight if Andrews's name appeared on the passenger list. Coincidently, according to the film's pressbook, Andrews and Peggy King had first-hand experience of airborne near-crashes, with Andrews once making an emergency landing in Greenland and Peggy surviving a traumatic flight during the war (the plane nearly ditched in the Pacific).[2]

The *New York Times* noted, "Dana Andrews as the hero and Sterling Hayden as the captain are first rate in these roles, keeping them hard and unrelenting."

Having impressed the usually hard-to-please *New York Times*, *Zero Hour!* continued to get good notices.

MOTION PICTURE HERALD: "An extraordinary powerful melodrama."

THE HOLLYWOOD REPORTER: "Exciting, gripping drama ... one of the most exciting pictures in some time."

INDEPENDENT FILM JOURNAL: "Climax that will keep audiences on the edge of their seats...."

MOTION PICTURE DAILY: "Absorbing suspense ... ably acted!"

BOXOFFICE: "Certain to generate enthusiastic word-of-mouth reactions."

A competent TV remake of *Zero Hour!* was produced in 1971 under the title *Terror in the Sky.* The role of the reluctant substitute pilot was taken by Doug McClure and the character was updated to that of an ex–Vietnam helicopter pilot suffering delayed trauma.

Night of the Demon
(Curse of the Demon)
Columbia, 1957

Cast: Dana Andrews (Dr. John Holden); Peggy Cummins (Joanna Harrington); Niall MacGinnis (Dr. Julian Karswell); Maurice Denham (Prof. Henry Harrington); Athene Seyler (Mrs. Karswell); Liam Redmond (Prof. Mark O'Brien); Reginald Beckwith (Mr. Meek); Ewan Roberts (Lloyd Williamson); Peter Elliot (Prof. K.T. Kumar); Rosamund Greenwood (Mrs. Meek); Brian Wilde (Rand Hobart); Richard Leech (Inspector Mottram); Lloyd Lamble (Detective Simmons); Peter Hobbes (Superintendent); Charles Lloyd Pack (Chemist); John Salew (Librarian); Janet Barrow (Mrs. Hobart); Percy Herbert (Farmer); Lynn Tracy (Air Hostess); Ballard Berkeley, Michael Peake (Reporters); Shay Gorman (Narrator); John Harvey (Hobart's Brother); Walter Horsburgh (Bates, the Butler); Leonard Sharp (Ticket Collector).

Credits: Hal. E. Chester (Producer); Jacques Tourneur (Director); Montague R. *James* (Story "Casting the Runes"); Charles Bennett, Hal E. Chester (Screenplay); Ted Scaife (Cinematography); Clifton Parker (Music); Muir Mathieson (Music Direction); Ken Adam (Production Designer); Peter Glazier (Assistant Art Director); Betty Lee (Hair Stylist); Basil Keys (Assistant Director); George Blackwell, Wally Veevers, S.D. Onions, Bryan Langley (Special Effects); Arthur Bradburn, Charles Crafford (Sound); Michael Gordon (Editor). Running time: 95 minutes

Renowned American psychologist John Holden (Dana Andrews) travels to England to assist his colleague Professor Harrington in his attempt to expose Dr. Julian Karswell, head of a black magic cult. The day before Holden's arrival, Harrington pays Karswell a visit and on his return home is killed by a towering demon which materializes out of the dark of night. Upon arrival at the airport, Holden is shocked to learn of his friend's death, which is reported as the result of a car accident. Holden is skeptical of the powers

In search of the truth about all things supernatural, disbelieving Dr. John Holden (Andrews) pays a visit to Stonehenge in Jacques Tourneur's horror classic *Night of the Demon* (Columbia, 1957).

of the supernatural and decides to continue the investigation with the assistance of Harrington's niece Joanna, who alerts him to her fears and suspicions concerning Karswell. During a chance meeting at the British Museum Library, Karswell secretly slips a parchment containing runic symbols into Holden's papers and predicts that he will die in four days. For Holden to avoid this fate, the parchment, which is similar to one given to Harrington, must be passed back to Karswell. As the days pass, Holden's investigations involve him in a séance, hypnotism, a trip to Stonehenge and a narrow escape from the demon in the woods surrounding Karswell's mansion. Holden is finally convinced that his life is in danger and that he must return the parchment. With time quickly running out, he catches up with Karswell and a hypnotized Joanna on a train from London to Southampton. As Karswell tries to make his escape, Holden manages to slip the parchment into his coat pocket. The occultist, chasing the windblown slip of paper along the railway tracks, becomes the demon's next victim.

Taglines: "Who will be the next in line to defy the curse?"; "Horror! Most terrifying story the screen has ever told!"; "Chosen ... singled out to die ... victim of his imagination or victim of a demon?"; "Skeptical? Don't make up your mind till you see this masterpiece of the macabre!"; "Terrifying!! All the Dark Forces of Black Magic ... Hurled Against a Man and a Woman Who Dare to Scoff!"; "What horrific fate will befall those who defy the Night of the Demon?"

If none of those grab you, you shouldn't be reading this book. Now let's remind ourselves of that superb opening scene with its eerie introductory narration, read against the backdrop of a windswept Stonehenge and a thrilling Clifton Parker score:

It has been written since the beginning of time, even unto these ancient stones, that evil, supernatural creatures exist in a world of darkness. And it is also said Man, using the magic power of the ancient runic symbols, can call forth these powers of darkness: the demons of Hell. Through the ages men have feared and worshipped these creatures. The practice of witchcraft, the cults of evil, have endured and exist to this day.

With such an introduction you know you're in for an edge-of-your-seat ride, and at no stage of the proceedings are you disappointed.

Night of the Demon was adapted from M.R. James's supernatural short story "Casting the Runes," which tells the tale of an academic, George Dunning, who tries to escape the hex placed upon him by Karswell, an Aleister Crowley–type figure with mysterious powers. James, a Cambridge scholar, brought the ghost story to new prominence in 1904 with the publication of his *Ghost Stories of an Antiquary*. One of Hitchcock's screenwriters, Charles Bennett, owned the rights to "Casting the Runes" and adapted it into a script entitled *The Haunted,* which initially sparked some interest with the likes of Robert Taylor and Dick Powell before independent producer Hal E. Chester sealed the deal for the film rights.[1]

Chester was one of the Dead End Kids in the '30s and '40s before turning to production, initially with low-budget Monogram. He was responsible for *The Beast from 20,000 Fathoms* (1953), *The Bold and the Brave* (1956) and *School for Scoundrels* (1960).

Director Jacques Tourneur accepted the job of director and returned to the genre in which he had made his reputation in the '40s with *Cat People* and *I Walked with a Zombie* (both Val Lewton productions). Andrews and Tourneur were good friends, having worked together previously in the western *Canyon Passage,* so it took little encouragement for Andrews to join the cast when Tourneur discussed the script with him. Andrews recalled how Tourneur called him from England where he was searching for locations and convinced him that together they could make something of the story: "Witchcraft in England was at the time — and still is — a big thing there, and Tourneur had talked to a lot of people involved and come up with some exciting ideas. He was so enthusiastic that I just couldn't turn him down."[2]

Andrews was joined by Irish character actor Niall MacGinnis (as Karswell) and petite Welsh beauty Peggy Cummins (as Joanna Harrington). MacGinnis had played a variety of supporting roles and occasional villains up to this point in his career and in Julian Karswell he found the perfect character to demonstrate his talents as an actor. Cummins began her career in the London theatre before moving to Hollywood, where she arguably gave her best performance in *Gun Crazy* (1949).

In *The Cinema of Nightfall,* an essential read

on Tourneur's work, author Chris Fujiwara saw Holden as a tailor-made role for Andrews: "It belongs to the type of role for which he was best suited: one in which his customary impassivity betrays a moral weakness, a fatal flaw (as in *Fallen Angel*, *Where the Sidewalk Ends* and *Beyond a Reasonable Doubt*), and in which his self-control is the telltale sign of narcissism (as in *Daisy Kenyon* and *While the City Sleeps*)."[3]

Although the film is unique and is probably one of the best supernatural thrillers ever made, many people, including the director, were critical of Chester's revisions that resulted in close-ups of the demon appearing at the beginning and end of the film, which greatly undermined Tourneur's attempts to convey fear and suspense through understatement. (That approach had been the key to success of his earlier horror classics.)

Andrews made clear his angry feeling that putting the demon in after the film had wrapped was a big mistake, arguing that the script left it to the audience to decide whether the strange occurrences were the result of a demon or pure coincidence. To support this opinion, Andrews recalled his last line in the film when he said to Peggy Cummins, "Maybe it's better not to know."

Chester's tampering and interference throughout the production were an additional annoyance to Andrews, who recalled, "He would come up and start telling Jacques how to direct the picture. Jacques would say, 'Now, now, Hal,' and try to be nice. But I just said, 'Look, you little son of a bitch! You want me to walk off this picture? I didn't come all this way over here to have the producer tell me what he thinks about directing the film. I came because Mr. Tourneur asked me. Let the director direct the film!'"[4]

Whatever your views on the inclusion of demon close-ups, there is no denying the film's all-pervading sinister atmosphere conjured up by Clifton Parker's powerful score and some particularly chilling scenes (including Holden's dart through the wood chased by an invisible beast, a gripping séance and a windstorm summoned up by Karswell at a children's party). I was 12 on first viewing and it certainly had me hiding behind the sofa, feverishly assembling my "demon stopper" crucifix with two lolly sticks and a lackey band.

However, there's no spooking Andrews's Dr.

Holden, with his churlish dialogue throughout the proceedings clearly demonstrating a hard-nosed skepticism (he'd give Dana Scully a run for her money on the disbelieving front). Plugging his latest book, he jams his dubitation down the throat of his colleague O'Brien: "Myths, demonology and witchcraft have been discredited since the Middle Ages, O'Brien. I wrote a book about it; that's why I'm here." Very much a rational man, he does at least concede that mankind might as well throw in the towel now if the world is at the mercy of demons and the like. And, having studied superstitions from an early age, he explains to Joanna why he took up the quest to debunk them, "Maybe just to prove one thing — that I'm not a superstitious sucker like ninety percent of the population."

However, when finally convinced that things beyond comprehension do exist, he admits to Karswell in the penultimate scene, "You've sold your bill of goods too well, because I believe you now. I believe that in five minutes something monstrous and horrible is going to happen. And when it does, you're going to be here so that whatever happens to me will happen to you."

In between scoffing at his learned colleagues, Karswell and all things pertaining to the supernatural, Holden also finds time to romance Harrington's niece Joanna, played by the fine actress Peggy Cummins. Andrews and Peggy had become good friends since her early days as a Fox contract player in the 1940s, and they remained good friends right up to his death in 1992. In 2001 Peggy heaped praise on her *Night of the Demon* co-star: "Dana was a remarkable actor — brilliant, absolutely brilliant." As well as being in awe of his photographic memory with dialogue, Peggy also acknowledged that he possessed a great voice.[5]

These thoughts were echoed by Brian Wilde (*Porridge*, *Last of the Summer Wine*), who played the part of Rand Hobart in the thrilling hypnosis scene: "I liked Dana Andrews although I didn't have much to do with him. He was brilliant on set. He didn't chuck his weight about. He was humble and well behaved."[6]

Shortly after arriving in England, Andrews accompanied a number of stars at a Royal Command Film Performance in Leicester Square; this provided him with an opportunity to shake hands and indulge in a brief conversation with the queen. As fondly recalled by Andrews, when he informed her that he was in England making a film about witchcraft, she looked at him in a funny way and wrinkled her nose before saying, "Good heavens! Don't bring that back again."

At the press launch for the film, Andrews met Dr. Margaret Murray, a 93-year-scholar on witchcraft. When he was introduced to the most senior witch in England, he grabbed her and kissed her on the cheek, with the alcohol-fueled greeting "You old son of a witch."[7] (Priceless!)

On another amusing note, Hal E. Chester recalled that during the last night of location filming (a bitterly cold November night), Tourneur and Andrews were both behind a trailer boozing, with Tourneur offering the explanation that it was their way of keeping warm.

Although the film enjoys a cult following today, it was not a box office hit on first release, with the critics mostly indifferent. In England it was released on a double-bill with *20 Million Miles to Earth* and in America, where it was renamed *Curse of the Demon* it variously accompanied *The True Story of Lynn Stuart* and *The Revenge of Frankenstein*.

Variety commented, "Directed with a supernatural touch by Jacques Tourneur, it abounds in magic, hypnotism, séances, strange aberrations and profuse delving into the occult." In recent times the film has been described as "Tourneur's most distinguished horror movie since his RKO days, providing an abject lesson in atmospheric horror."

As a sign of the film's lasting appeal, Maurice Denholm's lines, "It's in the trees! It's coming!" was featured in the Kate Bush track "Hounds of Love" from her 1985 album. The film was also referenced in the song lyrics of the *Rocky Horror Picture Show*.

Continuing on the trivia trail, did you notice that Joanna Harrington's license plate includes the numbers "666," the traditional "Mark of the Beast"?

The original story "Casting the Runes" was given a modern makeover in Yorkshire Television's 1979 production starring Iain Cuthbertson as Karswell and Jan Francis filling in for Andrews as the recipient of the runic parchment.

The Fearmakers

United Artists, 1958

Cast: Dana Andrews (Alan Eaton); Dick Foran (Jim McGinnis); Marilee Earle (Lorraine Dennis); Mel Torme (Barney Bond); Veda Ann Borg (Vivian Loder); Kelly Thordsen (Harold Loder); Roy Gordon (Senator Walder); Joel Marston (Rodney Hillyer); Dennis Moore (Army Doctor); Oliver Blake (Dr. Gregory Jessup); Robert Fortier (Col. Buchane); Janet Brandt (Walder's Secretary); Fran Andrade (TWA Stewardess); Robert Carson (Conference Room Speaker); Lyle Latell (Police Sergeant).

Credits: Martin H. Lancer (Producer); Jacques Tourneur (Director); Leon Chooluck (Associate Producer); Darwin L. Teilhet (Novel *The Fear Machine*); Elliot West, Chris Appley (Screenplay); Sam Leavitt (Cinematography); Irving Gertz (Music); Serge Krizman (Art Direction); James Roach (Set Decorations); Dave Grayson (Makeup); Eugene Anderson, Jr. (Assistant Director); John Kean (Sound); J. R. Whittredge, Paul Laune (Editors). Running time: 83 minutes

In this Cold War propaganda drama, Korean war veteran Captain Alan Eaton (Dana Andrews), who was brainwashed as a POW and still suffers dizzy spells and headaches, returns home to Washington D.C. to find that his public relations firm has been taken over by Jim McGinnis. Eaton is informed by McGinnis that his (Eaton's) partner sold the business to him and the next day was killed by a hit-and-run driver. Eaton discusses the mysterious death with his old friend Senator Walder and learns that the Senator suspects McGinnis of using the PR firm to promote communist-backed organizations in the hope of undermining the American government. In search of evidence, Eaton takes up the offer of a consultant job with the firm and initially tries to enlist the help of chief statistician Barney Bond; he soon realizes that Barney is in with the crooks. He becomes romantically involved with McGinnis's secretary Lorraine, and with her assistance he gains access to confidential files which expose the conspiracy to back the communists by fixing polls to swing public opinion. With the truth revealed, the villains are captured by Eaton near the Lincoln Memorial, following a patriotic speech by Senator Walder.

Tagline: "You have nothing to fear but the Fearmakers."

With its unusual subject matter, combining crooked pollsters with the "Red Menace," *The Fearmakers* was another exciting entry in Andrews's growing list of offbeat tales involving a topical theme. And in common with the likes of *The Rack* (1956) and *Time Limit* (1957), it was one of only a handful of films which attempted to explore the psyche of Korean War POWs attempting to readjust to civilian life on their return to the States.[1]

Based on a 1945 novel by Darwin L. Teilhet, and shot in a fortnight, *The Fearmakers* was one of the last films directed by Jacques Tourneur. The director accepted the assignment at the request of Andrews, who informed producer Martin H. Lancer that he would only star in the film if Tourneur was appointed as director.[2] In between filming, both Andrews and Tourneur indulged their passion for sailing, and together with friends they made frequent trips aboard the director's yacht, *The Shearwater*. French critics have noted that Tourneur always encouraged his actors to underplay their roles, which possibly explains his preference for minimalist actors such as Andrews and Robert Mitchum.[3]

Teilhet's anti–Nazi novel *The Fear Machine*

was adapted into a anti-communist tale set at the height of the Cold War. What makes this movie different from the majority of "Red Scare" movies is that the baddies are not Communists, but simply a gang of crooks who are willing to offer their services to the highest bidder, whatever their ideology.

The *Fearmakers* was Andrews's third film with a Cold War theme following *The Iron Curtain* (1948) and *Assignment Paris* (1952). It was also his third and final film under Tourneur's direction. Whereas Andrews's collaboration with other great directors were usually associated with a particular genre (war with Milestone and noir with Preminger and Lang), his output with Tourneur was notable for its diversity — western (*Canyon Passage*), supernatural shocker (*Night of the Demon*), and Cold War thriller (*The Fearmakers*).

In the thick of skullduggery, Korean War vet Alan Eaton (Andrews) seeks the help of Lorraine Dennis (Marilee Earle) and office statistician Barney Bond (Mel Torme) in *The Fearmakers* (United Artists, 1958).

Maintaining his iconic noir image, Andrews looks the business in trenchcoat, as he tackles the bad guys, while dealing with recurring headaches and blackouts courtesy of those Chinese Commies, who according to Jim McGinnis's sympathetic medical diagnosis "must have really scrambled your marbles."

To compensate for this slight handicap, Eaton, in the fine tradition of all movie Korean War vets, is an expert in both karate and judo, which he proves to excellent effect in two set pieces: First with the hulking Loder back at the guest house, and next in the final tussle with McGinnis at the Lincoln Memorial. Prior to this showdown, our hero, following a blackout, is brutally worked over by the menacing Loder, with McGinnis looking on. Absorbing the blows like a well-used punch bag, Eaton sneers at McGinnis, "Your boy is an amateur. I've been worked over by professionals."

As well as being the only Andrews film where his character is adept at karate, *The Fearmakers* also provided a rare opportunity, in the opening prisoner of war scene, to catch the actor sporting a wild and woolly beard. (It must have been kicking around the wardrobe department since *The Forbidden Street*).

Playing the role of his chief adversary is Dick Foran, who started his film career as a band singer before going on to become Warner's only singing cowboy. Andrews's love interest is nicely played by Marilee Earle, whose very short film career included only one notable entry, the unusual western *Terror in a Texas Town* (1958). Effective in the role of chief statistician Barney Bond is singer Mel Torme, making his return to the silver screen after an eight-year absence. Watch out for Torme's scene-stealing Coke bottle glasses and his mean impression of Edmond O'Brien going through the sweats.

In his autobiography *It Wasn't All Velvet* Torme explained that one of the joys of being in *The Fearmakers* was working with Andrews: "I had always admired Andrews's work and was delighted to find he was a friendly, gregarious guy who didn't take himself too seriously and who was professional to a fault. Those were his drinking days, but his fondness for the grape never interfered with his ability to perform, and he did so perfectly under the direction of Jacques Tourneur."[4]

The subject of brainwashing really came to prominence with the outbreak of the Korean War, where Chinese Communist interrogators employed a range of disorientation techniques (including drugs plus physical and mental torture) to manipulate the minds of their victims. With Andrews portraying a Korean War veteran suffering from Communist torture and brainwashing, *The Fearmakers* was a forerunner of John Frankenheimer's masterpiece on the subject, *The Manchurian Candidate* (1962). In 1954, Andrews's brother Steve Forrest, playing alongside Ronald Reagan, was subjected to similar treatment by Communist captors in the Korean War feature *Prisoner of War*.

In addition to brainwashing Chinese-style, Andrews's character Eaton is also subjected to another form of mental torture, that of being stuck alongside an incessant talker, Dr. Jessop, during his flight to Washington. The good doctor's boorish opinions on the plight of mankind are enough to induce a self-imposed coma if Eaton's expression is anything to go by. Prompting the first yawn, he informs Eaton, "Science has brought us to the brink of world extermination and the delights of Washington." And in a last ditch effort to keep Eaton awake, he hypothesizes whether the French architect ever realized that in laying out Washington he had designed the perfect target with its circular streets and radiating avenues.

Back on the ground, and having been clearly advised by his doctors to take it easy and avoid stress, our traumatized hero is soon up to his eyeballs in pulse-racing skullduggery, spurred on by his old friend Senator Walden, who wants him to risk his neck trying to expose the racketeers (some friend). Convinced that sinister forces are at large, exploiting the power of lobby over the postal polling system, Eaton remarks, "If money talks, Senator, the little three-cent stamp must have a hard time being heard." And mindful of the threat at large, back at the office he lectures Barney Bond that packaging politicians for wholesome consumption through manipulative polling is different from promoting a packet of soap.

In his riveting *Korean War Filmography*, Robert J. Lentz commented that although Andrews is appropriately sincere as Eaton, the film was perhaps made a little too late to be taken seriously, hence the fact that it was barely released, and never found an audience. He concludes,

"[T]he film tries to responsibly relate an area of threat while remaining hopeful and patriotic. The result is a very uneven, but oddly satisfying mixture of rhetoric and entertainment."[5]

Chris Fujiwara shared this mixed view in his book on Tourneur's work *The Cinema of Nightfall*: "*The Fearmakers* isn't a failure — most viewers would probably find it the most acceptable of the five late films — but neither is it a film strongly marked by the director's personality."[6] On Andrews's contribution, he noted, "Because Andrews is so ambiguous a hero, our attitude to the outcome of the story remains uneasy, and the film's sense of potential disaster lingers even at the end...."[7]

It is a real irony that the manipulation of data and news by pollsters and PR firms to market and elect politicians, which is deplored as the work of conspirators in *The Fearmakers*, is accepted as common practice in the world of modern politics.

Enchanted Island

Warner Bros., 1958

Cast: Dana Andrews (Abner Bedford); Jane Powell (Faraway); Don Dubbins (Tom); Arthur Shields (Jimmy Dooley); Ted de Corsia (Capt. Vangs); Friedrich Ledebur (Chief Mehevi); Augustine Fernandez (Kory); Francisco Reiguera (Medicine Man); Les Hellman (1st Mate Moore); Eddie Saenz, Paul Stader, Dale Van Sickel (Sailors); The Four Lads (Singers).

Credits: Benedict Bogeaus (Producer); Allan Dwan (Director); Herman Melville (Novel *Typee*); James Leicester, Harold Jacob Smith (Screenplay); George Stahl, Jr. (Cinematography); Raul Lavista (Music); Robert Allen (Song); Hal Wilson Cox (Art Direction); Georgette (Wardrobe); Albert M. Simpson, Lee Zavitz (Special Effects); Nacio Real (Assistant Director); Weldon Coe (Sound); James Leicester (Editor). Running time: 94 minutes

In the South Seas in the 1840s, whalers Abner Bedford (Dana Andrews) and Tom are tired of the sadistic treatment of Captain Vangs and decide to jump ship when their vessel puts in at a tropical island. As they explore the island they come across the settlement of the local inhabitants, who still indulge in cannibalism. The sailors are treated well by the natives and Abner falls in love with the chief's granddaughter, Faraway. During a surprise attack on the village by a neighboring tribe, Abner saves Chief Mehevi's life and in return receives his consent to marry Faraway. But their happiness is curtailed when Tom, still fearful of the cannibalistic habits of the natives, escapes into the jungle. Later Abner learns that Tom was caught and killed to keep the Typee safe from the outside world. Angered by the loss of his friend, Abner attacks the medicine man responsible for Tom's death and is sentenced to die with Faraway. The two lovers make their escape in a canoe and head for Captain Vangs' ship, pursued by a flotilla of angry Typee. As they close in, Faraway is wounded by a spear thrown by the medicine man, who is in turn speared by Chief Mehevi; filled with remorse, the chief now calls off the chase, allowing Aber and Faraway to continue towards the ship.

Tagline: "Captured by Cannibals! Slave to the blue-eyed princess of the dread 'Typee' Headhunters ... and to her savage code of love and taboos."

Enchanted Island was loosely based on Herman Melville's first book *Typee*, a semi-autobiographical account of his life in the South Seas in the 1840s. In search of adventure, Melville went to sea as a cabin boy and in his subsequent travels spent some time among the Typee cannibals in the Marquesas Islands. His romanticized account of his adventures influenced many of the writers on the Pacific, including Jack London and Robert Louis Stevenson.

Director Allan Dwan read *Typee* and thought if he stuck rigidly to the story it might work as a film. Before embarking on this project, Dwan was aware that the filming of *Typee* had been started once before by Allied Artists, but he claimed it was stopped for running out of hand.[1] Dwan was no stranger to action adventure stories having directed many classics including Douglas Fairbanks in the 1922 *Robin Hood* and John Wayne in the 1949 *Sands of Iwo Jima*. In 1950, he entered into a partnership with real-estate salesman turned producer Benedict Bogeaus, and together the two were responsible for several highly acclaimed low-budget westerns and film noirs usually starring the much underrated John Payne. *Enchanted Island* was Dwan's penultimate film in a career spanning nearly half a century.

According to Dwan, *Typee* was public domain so Bogeaus grabbed it with a view to producing something only loosely based on the book. Due to an agreement with the Producers Association,

Restless sailor Abner Bedford (Andrews) finds love with blue-eyed native girl Faraway (Jane Powell) in *Enchanted Island* (Warner Bros., 1958).

Borgeaus couldn't call it *Typee* so the film version was changed to *Enchanted Island*.[2]

The film was shot on a low budget, with Acapulco, Mexico, filling in for the South Seas. It was initially scheduled for release through RKO, but when that studio closed its distribution arm, Bogeaus was forced to distribute through Warner Brothers.

Singing star Jane Powell took the part of the native girl who falls in love with Andrews's character. This was a significant departure from her previous roles (she was usually cast as a starry-eyed teenager in MGM musicals of the '40s and '50s). Her most notable success came in 1954 with the release of *Seven Brides for Seven Brothers*. Her blue eyes in *Enchanted Island* were explained away by the rogue Jimmy Dooley: "Her father was a gallant son of the old sod, who swam ashore from a tramp freighter. He probably ended up in the cooking pot."

Although generally entertaining as an outdoor adventure, *Enchanted Island* was not a commercial success. Several reasons could be put forward for this, including the low budget and loose adherence to the original story, but possibly the main problem lay in the casting. Andrews had signed up to do the movie in November 1957, but now in his late forties, he was simply too old to do justice to his character, whose exploits were based on Melville's adventures when he was a young man. The fresh-faced Andrews who had wooed audiences with *Swamp Water* and *The Ox-Bow Incident* in the early 1940s might have been better suited to the part, but alas that fresh-faced persona had long been replaced by a look of world-weary cynicism.

To compound the problem, Jane Powell was equally wrong in the role of the native girl. Dwan would later comment, "She looked like a little girl pretending. If we had a real native girl or even a young Mexican girl it would have been fine."[3]

Such miscasting did not go unnoticed by the *New York Times*, who wryly commented, "In a film that has little to do with Melville's best-selling novel, Andrews seems like a dislocated insurance executive, and Powell, a girl in search of a prom dress."

To add to Andrews's woes he was served with a breach of contract in 1958 by Waverley Productions and producer Benedict Bogeaus, who sought $157,769 from the actor, citing that his drinking problem had interfered with his work during filming. Andrews responded that the charges were "ridiculous" and the lawsuit was eventually dropped, but the damage to his career had already been done.[4]

In her autobiography "The Girl Next Door," Jane Powell recalled that she felt that both Andrews and Dwan had no interest in making the film and said that her only positive memory was the location shooting, which provided her and the family with a wonderful vacation in Acapulco ("vacation with pay" as she aptly described it).[5]

Also enjoying the sun was Don Dubbins as Abner's sidekick Tom, who constantly thinks he's the next item on the cannibal menu. Dubbins came to prominence when James Cagney featured him in his films *These Wilder Years* (1956) and *Tribute to a Bad Man* (1956).

One of the best villains in the business, Ted de Corsia, took the role of Captain Vangs, playing the part like a cross between Captain Bligh and Captain Ahab — great stuff! Arthur Shields, younger brother of Barry Fitzgerald, is also in fine sneering form as the booze-sodden island rogue, Jimmy Dooley. And let's not forget the imposing presence of Friedrich Ledebur as Chief Mehevi. A count in real life, Friedrich served in the Austrian Cavalry during World War I and is remembered for his impressive performance as another cannibal, the tattooed harpooner Queequeg in John Huston's stunning 1956 adaptation of Melville's classic novel *Moby Dick.*

In Andrews's modest opinion, the film would have fared better if the role had been given to a bigger box-office star (Marlon Brando immediately came to my mind, but then I came to my senses when I remembered his South Seas clunker *Mutiny on the Bounty*). Of course, were it not for the constraints of Melville's true story, we might have been treated to a conveniently well-timed life-threatening hurricane or erupting volcano to bring things to a climax.

And to prove that at 49 he was not beyond

baring a bit of flesh, Andrews stripped to the waist for the marriage ceremony scene, displaying his manly chest for the second time in his career (*The Frogmen* was the first). He also frolics in the surf with Powell and gets an ocean bath from half a dozen native girls. To get you further into the mood, the idyllic scenery is underpinned by a lush tropical music score by Raul Lavista and the song "Enchanted Island" by Robert Allen. And in keeping with all of Andrews's movies, the great one-liners come thick and fast. Having brushed up on the idiots' guide to cannibalism, Abner advises his sidekick, "Better to please them, Tom. Nobody eats a pet." And later, when discussing one of the potential "bone crushers," Abner allays their fears when he informs Tom, "She has to be Happar. You don't get cannibals that pretty."

In an effort to rustle up trade, the pressbook synopsis tries to put some sort of Romeo and Juliet slant on this salty tale by claiming that the two lovers are united forever when they both die by the spear.[6] In my copy of the movie, Faraway is indeed wounded by a spear at the end, but both she and Abner make it back to the ship, to no doubt plan the wedding of the year with Captain Vangs presiding. This departure was explained by Jane Powell, who looked forward to doing *Enchanted Island* with Andrews because she didn't have to sing and was originally down to die at the end. But because her loyal fans wouldn't allow it, at the last minute the script was changed and she lived to start a new life with Abner,[7] which moves Captain Vangs to comment as he watches the approaching lovers, "I haven't performed a marriage on a ship of mine in over twenty years. A married man makes a docile hand."

And for all the talk about cannibalism, there is very little evidence of it throughout the film, which is simply a love story between a restless sailor and a native girl, who in time-honored fashion learns to speak English after a handful of lessons from our ancient mariner. The pressbook also tries to make some connection between the film and Andrews's love of sailing.[8]

To be fair, although Andrews was clearly past his best, *Enchanted Island* is no better or worse than any other of the South Seas offerings that were served up in the '50s such as *Hurricane Smith* (1952), *Return to Paradise* (1953), *His Majesty O'Keefe* (1953) and *Fair Wind to Java*

(1953). It was only when *Lord Jim* was brought to the screen in 1965 that this sort of "lost in paradise" hokum was lifted to another level. Although for the most part I appreciate the serious merits of *Enchanted Island*, I have to confess that somewhere along the jungle trek I half-expected Abner and Tom to bump into Hope and Crosby with an amorous gorilla in tow.

Andrews met up with Jane Powell again in 1981 when they joined a number of other film stars in a class-action suit against the major film studios, seeking television residuals for their pre–1960 films.

The Crowded Sky

Warner Bros., 1960

Cast: Dana Andrews (Dick Barnett); Rhonda Fleming (Cheryl Heath); Efrem Zimbalist, Jr. (Dale Heath); John Kerr (Mike Rule); Anne Francis (Kitty Foster); Keenan Wynn (Nick Hyland); Troy Donahue (McVey); Joe Mantell (Louis Capelli); Patsy Kelly (Gertrude Ross); Donald May (Norm Coster); Louis Quinn (Sidney Schreiber); Ed Kemmer (Caesar); Tom Gilson (Robert Fermi); Hollis Irving (Beatrice Wiley); Paul Genge (Samuel N. Poole); Jean Willes (Gloria Panawek); Frieda Inescort (Mrs. Mitchell); Nan Leslie (Bev); Sam Harris, Harold Miller, Charles Sullivan, Douglas Grange (Airline Passengers); S. John Launer (Police Officer); Chet Stratton (Male Nurse in Asylum).

Credits: Michael Garrison (Producer); Joseph Pevney (Director); Hank Searls (Story); Charles Schnee (Screenplay); Harry Stradling Sr. (Cinematography); Leonard Rosenman (Music); Eddie Imazu (Art Direction); William L. Kuehl (Set Decorations); Howard Shoup (Costumes); Gordon Bau (Makeup); Paul Mantz (Technical Advisor); Chuck Hansen (Assistant Director); M.A. Merrick (Sound); Tom McAdoo (Editor). Running time: 105 minutes

An airborne disaster drama with two aircraft set on a collision course. Captain Dale Heath and junior officer McVey, on a spot of leave, take off in their navy jet for a short flight when they realize that their radio and navigation equipment has failed. With no idea of his altitude or course, Heath is aware that a midair collision threatens and is terrified that history is repeating itself because he has been in this predicament before, and on that occasion he saved himself at the expense of the other plane and pilot. Flying in the opposite direction is a commercial airliner with Captain Dick Bennett (Dana Andrews) at the controls. As the inevitable disaster approaches, the troubled lives of passengers Kitty Foster, Gloria Panawek, Nick Highland and Gertrude Ross are revealed in a series of flashbacks. The pilots of the two planes also find moments to reflect, with Captain Bennett dealing with his delinquent son in flashback and Captain Heath mulling over his marriage to the flirtatious Cheryl. But as time passes, Heath becomes increasingly anxious as he struggles to solve the equipment problem. When the commercial airliner finally comes into view, Heath, not wishing to repeat the past, puts the jet into a rapid dive to avert a head-on collision. But contact is made with the airliner's fuselage and the jet explodes, killing Heath and Ross. One of the liner's engines is damaged, threatening the lives of everyone aboard. With another engine catching fire on the final descent, Barlett summons up all his courage and flying skills to safely land the stricken airliner.

Tagline: "The most fascinating people the gods of chance ever swept up into high adventure!"

If "fascinating," means highly emotional and neurotic, then I would tend to agree, for if there's one thing that this movie delivers in spades, it's a rollercoaster of soap opera dramatics that will have you making a grab for that oxygen mask long before the two planes collide.

The second installment in Andrews's trilogy of airborne disaster movies came with *The Crowded Sky*. Shot in widescreen and Technicolor and with a stellar cast, the film was Warner Brothers' attempt to lure people away from their television sets and back into the theatres. Andrews and Rhonda Fleming were on hand to draw in the older audience members, while the youngsters had Efrem Zimbalist, Jr., Troy Donahue, John Kerr and Anne Francis to ogle.

Rhonda and Andrews first worked together in *While the City Sleeps*, which had also made use of a large cast to boost its appeal (although one could argue that Fleming's radiant beauty was enough in itself to draw in the crowds). Indeed, in one of her films, a cameraman was so taken by her looks that as a joke, he deliberately tried to photograph her badly, but no matter how hard he tried she always came out looking stunning. In both of Andrews's encounters with Fleming, there was no question of any romantic entanglement with their characters as the redhead's smoldering, uninhibited persona was

Captain Dick Barnett (Andrews) makes pre-flight preparations with his air crewmembers Mike Rule (John Kerr), Louie Capelli (Joe Mantell) and Kitty Foster (Anne Francis) in *The Crowded Sky* (Warner Bros., 1960).

probably a little too rich for the morally upright Andrews, who was more at home with wholesome girls typified by Gene Tierney, Jeanne Crain and Teresa Wright. This absence of romantic chemistry also applied to another regular in Andrews's latter films, Anne Francis, who was groomed by MGM to replace Lana Turner as a blonde sexpot. In fact, the closest Andrews got to the sex kitten type was perhaps Virginia Mayo in *The Best Years of Our Lives*, but as we recall she dumps him for a slick hoodlum character played by a young Steve Cochran, and Andrews in turn walks off with girl-next-door type Teresa Wright. Of course we mustn't forget Linda Darnell from *Fallen Angel*, but once again, no deal, for when her Stella character winds up on the slab, he takes up with the prim and proper Alice Faye.

With its rich combination of drama and suspense, *The Crowded Sky* was a valiant big-screen attempt to stem the advance of television, but its battle was simply a rearguard action. With good film roles becoming rarer than hen's teeth

in the late '50s and early '60s, many stars turned their attention to television — a change of direction which rescued Efrem Zimbalist, Jr., from a second-lead film career and put him in the spotlight with the successful shows *77 Sunset Strip* (1958–1964) and *The F.B.I.* (1965–1974). In a similar fashion, Anne Francis notched up a handful of promising film roles in the 1950s, most notably *Bad Day at Bad Rock* (1955) and *Forbidden Planet* (1956), but it was in television where she found her niche, particularly in her role as the Emma Peel–type detective in the cult series *Honey West* (1965–1966). John Kerr also pursued television before taking up a full-time career as a Beverly Hills lawyer in the late 1960s. However, no such lifeline was thrown to teenage heartthrob Troy Donaghue, whose career began promisingly with *A Summer Place* (1959) and *Parrish* (1961), then went into decline in the early 1960s. In 1966, at the age of 30, he became an alcoholic after his contract was terminated by Warner Brothers.

Returning to the plot: In *The Crowded Sky*,

Zimbalist's navy jet is on a collision course with the airliner piloted by Andrews. Fourteen years later, *in Airport '75,* these roles are reversed when Andrews, as a businessman, pilots a small light aircraft on a collision course with an airliner piloted by Zimbalist. To keep the ghoulish happy, both films feature dispensable flight crews being sucked out into space. For those who enjoy a good soap, we are also treated to a heady brew of sex lives and personal problems in *The Crowded Sky,* which leaves one thrice-married passenger wondering how long it will take for the guy sitting next her to realize that they were once lovers (they must have met and parted with the lights off). And if you think she's got problems, they're nothing compared to Captain Barnett's hang-ups. Carrying the heavy emotional burden of a delinquent son who hates him, widower Barnett is one of the colder characters in Andrews's repertoire. The coldness cuts to the bone when he sourly reflects on Junior's mixed-up ways: "I'll be dammed if I'll feel sorry for myself. I have no son and have only me. Make that do."

His lack of emotion and compassion also compels him to block the promotion of his co-pilot, Mike Rule, purely on the grounds that he has a strong penchant for art, which Barnett feels will get in the way of his flying (sure, if he's got the oils and canvas out in the cockpit — but if not, can't a man have a hobby?). The tension between Barnett and Rule is captured in an early scene when Barnett growls to the co-pilot, "If you have to call me captain, just say it, not spit it." In another confrontational scene, Barnett's thought bubble complains: "He's needling me using a long, thick needle." And when the needling really gets under his over-sensitive skin, he scowls, "You slugged me once and I didn't slug back. Don't tempt me now."

Compounding his many problems and hang-ups, he has to ensure that the passengers, who are affectionately referred to as "the geese," have no disruptions when taking a snooze or enjoying their mid-flight meal. When Mike Rule informs him that he's flying 500 feet too high, Barnett pipes back, "I'm flying just above the clouds to keep out of the rough — so the geese back there can eat in peace."

However, as in *Where the Sidewalk Ends,* Andrews's true colors are revealed at the end, when against all odds he skillfully lands the disabled plane, much to the relief of all on board, and shortly afterwards makes good with both his son and nose-out-of-joint co-pilot. A neat wrap, it prompts Barnett's final analysis, "Without mistakes, there's no forgiving and without forgiving, there's no love."

In between Barnett and Rule bitching at each other, *The Crowded Sky* makes efficient use of a series of flashbacks which recount the backgrounds of the crew and passengers. By today's standards, this technique of focusing in on a character by dimming the surrounding lights and allowing their thoughts to be heard may seem a little heavy-handed, but it was groundbreaking at the time, serving as template for the blockbuster disaster movies of the 1970s and 1980s.

To insure that he looked convincing in the part, Andrews spent 25 hours in a mock-up cockpit of a DC-7 actually used to train commercial pilots. The time was divided into half-hour slots, during which Andrews learned about the operation of commercial airliners and all the measures taken in emergency situations. It was only when he had totally familiarized himself with the bewildering panel of controls that he felt ready to take on the role.[1]

Variety commented, "Dana Andrews handles his role in his affably level-headed fashion."

Madison Avenue

20th Century–Fox, 1962

Cast: Dana Andrews (Clint Lorimer); Eleanor Parker (Anne Tremaine); Jeanne Crain (Peggy Shannon); Eddie Albert (Harvey Ames); Howard St. John (J.D. Jocelyn); Henry Daniell (Stipe); Kathleen Freeman (Miss Thelma Haley); David White (Brock); Betti Andrews (Katie Olsen); Jack Orrison (Mayor of Bellefield); Yvonne Peattie (Miss Malloy); Arlene Hunter (Miss Horn); Doris Fesette (Blonde); Grady Sutton (Dilbock); Leon Alton (Maitre d'); William H. O'Brien (Waiter); Cosmo Sardo (Brock's Barber); Jack Mower (Man at Bistro); Harry Carter (Man at Bar); Fred Aldrich (Man in Audience).

Credits: Bruce Humberstone (Producer-Director); Jeremy Kirk (Novel *The Build-Up Boys*); Norman Corwin (Screenplay); Charles G. Clarke (Cinematography); Harry Sukman (Music); Harry Harris (Song); Duncan Cramer, Leland Fuller (Art Direction); Walter M. Scott, John Sturtevant (Set Decorations); Ben Nye (Makeup); Jack R. Berne (Assistant Director); Warren B. Delaplain, Don McKay (Sound); Betty Steinberg (Editor). Running time: 94 minutes

This film depicts the high-powered world of advertising. Shrewd account executive Clint Lorimer (Dana Andrews) is sacked from his job in a big ad agency when his boss, T.C. Jocelyn, grows tired of his inflated ego. With no regrets, Lorimer heads off to make a name for himself and prove that he is superior to his former employers. Lorimer will stop at nothing to achieve his objectives including the alienation of his friends. One potential sacrifice is girlfriend Peggy Shannon, whose relationship with the egomaniac Lorimer is strained when he starts romancing Anne Tremaine, an advertising agent for a milk company run by eccentric Harvey Ames. Lorimer transforms Anne from a dowdy failure into a stunningly chic but spiteful businesswoman, and uses her and the dim-witted Ames to help him muscle his way into a position of strength in the cut-throat world of advertising. Witnessing the rapid rise of his former employee, Jocelyn realizes that he has lost a valuable asset and offers him back his job. Having fulfilled his objectives, Lorimer finally develops a conscience and realizes that the love he enjoys with Peggy is more important than his portfolio of accounts.

Tagline: "I Can Make Anybody."

And you'd better believe it, with Andrews cutting a dash as slick advertising man Clint Lorimer — ready to take on the corporate giants and beat them at their own game. If you need to build up a nobody into a somebody, Clint's definitely your man. More about PR and hype than advertising, *Madison Avenue* sits comfortably alongside those other entertaining swipes at corporate America such as *Executive Suite* (1954), *Woman's World* (1954) and *Patterns* (1956). In *The Fearmakers*, Andrews's PR man Alan Eaton was up to his neck in subversives, but in *Madison Avenue* the machinations of corporate America provide the intrigue and thrills. Clint Lorimer is perhaps a shrewder operator than Alan Eaton, but his morals leave a lot to be desired, for in his quest to build and promote an image, he will quite happily overlook the facts — a tendency that the more principled Alan Eaton would have found abhorrent. But that said, Andrews again turns in another flawed character who is more likable than not, which will have you rooting for him all the way.

Based on Jeremy Kirk's novel *The Build-Up Boys*, the glossy, modest-budgeted *Madison Avenue* explored the ruthless nature of New York's advertising jungle, and was the last major feature made by prolific film director Bruce Humberstone. Expertly shot in black and white (which gave it an early 1950s feel), the film was completed in less than a month on November 28, 1960, but its release was delayed until March 1962. Harry Sukman's lush score fuses well with the Manhattan setting, particularly in the opening montage sequence with New Yorkers heading to work amidst the mighty skyscrapers.

For romantic support, Andrews's PR character finds himself in the enviable position of having two of the silver screen's most beautiful actresses chasing him — Jeanne Crain and Eleanor Parker. It had been 17 years since Andrews had first worked with Crain in the hit musical *State Fair*, made at the peak of both their careers in the mid–1940s. In 1954, they sparkled again in the African actioner *Duel in the Jungle*. By 1962, Crain was reaching the end of her career and she and Andrews only made one more film together, *Hot Rods to Hell* (1967). Both Crain and Parker still looked as fresh-faced and trim as they did in the previous decade, which is a testament to their natural beauty when considering that at the time of filming, Crain was the mother of six children and Parker the mother of four. Parker was another of those accomplished, versatile actresses who never won an Oscar, although she was nominated on three occasions. Her most notable credits include *Caged* (1950) and *The Man with the Golden Arm* (1955), but she will probably be best remembered as the baroness in *The Sound of Music* (1965).

Twentieth Century–Fox contractees Joan Collins and Suzy Parker were the first choices for the Crain and Parker roles, but they both preferred to take a studio suspension rather than participate in the production.[1] This rejection annoyed Andrews; he put it down to the inflated egos of younger stars who choose to turn down roles that co-star them because they don't appear in every scene. He added, "Their psychology is all wrong — some of the best roles from a dramatic standpoint aren't the longest ones by any means."[2]

Director Humberstone, best known for his Charlie Chan films, managed to draw efficient performances from the cast which also included Eddie Albert, who had served as a Marine during World War II and was awarded a Bronze Star

Shrewd PR man Clint Lorimer (Andrews) gives Anne Tremaine (Eleanor Parker) and milk company owner Harvey Ames (Eddie Albert) a lesson in advertising in *Madison Avenue* (20th Century–Fox, 1962).

for rescuing up to 70 wounded Marines while under enemy fire. He enjoyed a long film career as a popular character actor, in notable films such as the 1956 war drama *Attack* (incidentally playing a coward in total contrast to his real nature), before going on to television fame in the hugely successful series *Green Acres*. He died in 2005 at the age of 99.

Amongst the cast line-up, television buffs will spot David White, who became a familiar face as Larry on *Bewitched*, which coincidentally was also set in the world of advertising. And in an early piece of dialogue, he delivers a line that sounds like it came from the show: "Milk is actually a solid and should be sipped and chewed."

Andrews's role was an interesting contrast between scheming promoter and a "Henry Higgins" type. As the doe-eyed girlfriend left behind, waiting for her lover, Crain's character was exposed to the former (how could anyone regularly stand up this beauty?), while Parker as an "Eliza Doolittle" type enjoyed the latter. As

Anne's mentor, smooth-talking Andrews remarks on their first meeting, "You look like a refugee from a nursing school, or a novel by Louisa May Alcott.... You could moor a tugboat with that braid."

Quite apart from Crain and Parker, Andrews has so many gals batting their eyelids at him I thought for a while I was viewing a Matt Helm movie. But when he makes with the clever "big city" sarcasm, you know you're back in the corporate jungle. Lecturing Ann on the state of her business, and starting off with the dowdy receptionist, he's not a man to mince his words: "She greets people as if they are stepping into an open coffin.... This is not a whole business, only a corpse of one — I'll give it six months." But there's no denying that, with all his faults, Clint certainly knows his business as we learn when he explains the art of advertising and PR to Ann and millionaire milkman Harvey Ames: "A great man is like a great book or a great invention — he needs to be exploited. He should become the symbol of all human accomplishment — however small, however great...." Clint is certainly one smart cookie, and he knows well the ruthless nature of the ad business, informing J.D. in the cab after learning of his skullduggery: "You might want to wipe the blade after you pull it out of my back."

As the film unspools, we learn that Clint is essentially an honest man, perhaps too honest for cut-throat Madison Avenue, but he is still a self-serving character, a "type" which Andrews had honed to perfection following his earlier roles as Eric Stanton the PR drifter in *Fallen Angel* and newspaperman Edward Mobley in *While the City Sleeps*.

Although the cast did well with an ungainly script, the reviews were generally lukewarm with the *New York Times* commenting, "*Madison Avenue* is the best advertisement for farming in years. By that we mean simple, honest hand toil in fresh air and sunshine."

Today the film is viewed more favorably, with one critic musing, "Dana, Jeanne and Eleanor shine as though they knew this was going to be one of the last gasps of the once beloved Fox studio system."

Crack in the World

Paramount, 1965

Cast: Dana Andrews (Dr. Stephen Sorenson); Janette Scott (Dr. Maggie Sorenson); Kieron Moore (Dr. Ted Rampion); Alexander Knox (Sir Charles Eggerston); Peter Damon (John Masefield); Jim Gillen (Rand); Gary Lasdun (Markov); Mike Steen (Steele); Sydna Scott (Angela); John Karlsen (Dr. Reynolds); Todd Martin (Simpson); Ben Tartar (Indian Ambassador).

Credits: Bernard Glasser, Lester A. Sansom (Producers); Andrew Marton (Director); Jon Manchip White (Story); Jon Manchip White, Julian Zimet (Screenplay); Philip Yordan (Executive Producer); Manuel Berenguer (Cinematography); John Douglas (Music); Eugene Lourie (Production Design); Alex Weldon, Eugene Lourie, Charles-Henri Assola (Special Effects); Laure Lourie (Costumes); Jose Maria Ochoa (Assistant Director); Kurt Hernfeld (Sound); Derek Parsons (Editor). Running time: 96 minutes

A group of scientists seek a new energy source at the core of the Earth. Dr. Stephen Sorensen (Dana Andrews) is determined to prove his theory that the heat from the molten magma near the Earth's center can be harnessed as a major energy source for all the world to enjoy; the only problem is, how to get to it? Assistant Ted Rampion is fearful that Sorenson's plans to drill to the crust using a thermonuclear device could cause the Earth to crack. Sorenson suffers from a terminal illness which he keeps secret from the team and wife Maggie. With his life draining away, he is not prepared to pursue a cautious approach and decides to go ahead with the drilling. Rampion's predictions become real when a crack appears, causing earthquakes and tidal waves around the world. In a desperate attempt to stop the crack spreading, the scientists explode a nuclear bomb in its path, but this only serves to alter its direction and cause a large part of the Earth to break off, creating a second moon for the planet. As they try to help humanity, former lovers Rampion and Maggie get romantically reunited, still unaware that Sorensen only has a short time to live. With nothing to lose, the dying scientist lowers a second bomb into the crack, sacrificing his life in the process. The explosion stops the crack and the world is saved.

Taglines: "Thank God It's Only a Motion Picture!"; "Science miscalculates ... underground Atom Bomb explodes Earth's core ... and the world totters on the brink of destruction!"; "Today's terrifying look into what might happen tomorrow!"

The year 1965 was not only one of Andrews's busiest, it also marked a turning point in his film career. He was well into middle age, his days as a romantic lead were for the most part behind him, and his film schedule was now filled with a variety of character parts and cameos. *Crack in the World* was perhaps one of his most notable film releases in that year (six in total), providing him with a strong part to get his teeth into after a long absence from the big screen (his previous film *Madison Avenue* was produced in 1960).

The end-of-the-world scenario was a popular film theme in the sixties with two British films topping the list — Val Guest's impressive *The Day the Earth Caught Fire* (1961) and Andrew Marton's thrilling *Crack in the World* (1965).

Marton began his film career working as a editor with Ernst Lubitsch in Germany, then made his name in Hollywood as a second unit director specializing in action scenes like the chariot race in *Ben-Hur* (1959). In 1950, he replaced an ailing Compton Bennett as the director of *King Solomon's Mines* (1950) and was also the director

With the pressure mounting to prove his scientific theories correct, dedicated Dr. Sorenson (Andrews) looks suitably anxious in the intelligent science fiction tale *Crack in the World* (Paramount, 1965).

behind many a TV adventure series including *Daktari, Flipper* and *Sea Hunt*. His ability to bring the screen alive in a colorful and exciting way was given full rein in *Crack in the World*, his first science fiction film.

Andrews had worked in most of the different film genres in his long career, and *Crack in the World* was his baptism into the world of science fiction. The complex character of Dr. Sorenson provided an opportunity to project a harder screen image useful for his future characters. Although usually well-meaning, these characters would be tainted with a distinctive surliness which made them generally less likable than his previous leading man roles.

In *Crack in the World* the tight-lipped Andrews sure had a lot to grimace about, what with the end of the world nigh (cue footage of earthquakes, tidal waves, volcanoes and stampeding animals), a funding crisis threatening to close down his project, and the presence of his wife's former lover creating uncertainty in his marriage. If that wasn't enough, the good Dr. Sorenson has to cope with a terminal illness that puts him in bandages and dark glasses.

Andrews's ready acceptance of this new direction in his career was summed up in his comments to a newspaper: "The romantic phase is now over; my roles are good, meaty ones, the kind I like at this time in my life."[1]

With Andrews taking a back seat, the film's main romantic interest (a low-key subplot) was ably provided by real-life husband-and-wife, Janette Scott and Kieron Moore. The daughter of character actress Thora Hird, Scott enjoyed success as a child star, most notably appearing in *No Place for Jennifer* (1949) before moving into medium budget melodramas and comedies in adult life. Scott's character was also romantically entwined with Irish-born Kieron Moore in another science fiction classic, *The Day of the Triffids* (1962). *Crack in the World* was her last film before retiring from the screen upon her marriage to Mel Torme in 1966.

The multi-faceted Dr. Sorenson was quite a rare find in the science fiction genre, which tended to depict scientists as mad egomaniacs. The doctor's character is clearly shaped by the pressures and tensions in both his professional and personal life, and it is a testament to Andrews's versatility that he was able to portray the part so convincingly. His soul-searching eyes and pained expression clearly convey the plight and tragic nature of his character, particularly in the scenes when he realizes what he has unleashed on the world through his scientific vanity and subsequent fallibility. But Sorenson is redeemed when in true sci-fi disaster movie style, "he goes down with the ship" after discovering a way to save the world from disaster.

Despite all his weaknesses, we are left in no doubt that Dr. Sorenson is essentially a good man who has dedicated his life in the pursuit of science. "Someone once said, if a man had a chance to spend his life fishing, making love and watching things grow and didn't choose to do it, he was mad. I made that choice a long time ago."

He is also a brilliant man stressed by funding constraints and besieged by government officials (excellently represented by the wonderfully reserved and much undervalued Canadian actor Alexander Knox in the role of Sir Charles Eggerston). Questioned by his wife as to whether the big wigs are bothered by Rampion's theory, Sorenson replies, "No, it's the budget. I could blow up the whole world with their blessing, if I did it cheaply enough."

Many of Sorenson's lines perfectly lend themselves to Andrews's temperate delivery, particularly in the scene where he explains what will happen to the circle cut out of the Earth by the intersecting cracks, and his thoughts on whether the world will survive: "No man has ever observed the birth of a moon, Masefield."

As well as superb performances from all concerned, the film is also notable for its excellent special effects courtesy of Alex Weldon and Eugene Lourie, and a thrilling soundtrack by John Douglas.

One has to marvel at the way the use of nuclear weapons is casually accepted by all concerned (with the exception of Masefield) as a good way to access a new energy source. This blasé approach is further evidenced in the scene where the scientists watch an atomic explosion at close range with no protective clothing and only a piece of darkened glass to shield their eyes.

Several years after the release of the film, the science of plate tectonics became readily accepted, proving once and for all that due to the fluid nature of the Earth's crust the planet was already heavily cracked and not the solid mass as described in this film. Although the science in the film was subsequently found to be flawed, it was presented in a clear and logical manner which appealed to audiences without talking down to them. The film was also well received by the critics, who for the most part heaped on the praise for its intelligent approach and solid special effects. The *New York Times* commented, "Andrew Marton's direction is brisk, so is the acting and, until that climax — a surprise, in any case — the whole thing is intelligent, compact and tingling. Good show. Go."

The Satan Bug
United Artists, 1965

Cast: George Maharis (Lee Barrett); Richard Basehart (Dr. Gregor Hoffman); Anne Francis (Ann Williams); Dana Andrews (General Williams); John Larkin (Dr. Leonard Michaelson); Richard Bull (Eric Cavanaugh); Frank Sutton (Donald); Ed Asner (Veretti); Simon Oakland (Tasserly); John Anderson (Agent Reagan); John Clarke (Lt. Raskin); Hari Rhodes (Lt. Johnson); Martin Blaine (Henchman posing as Henry Martin); Henry Beckman (Dr. Baxter); Harry Lauter (Fake SDI Agent); James Hong (Dr. Yang); Tol Avery (Police Captain); Russ Bender (Mason); William Bryant (SDI Agent); James Doohan (Hoffman's Henchman); Harold Gould (Dr. Ostrer); John Hubbard (Guard); Naom Pitlik (Motel Clerk); Carey Loftin (Agent).

Credits: John Sturges (Producer-Director); Alistair MacLean as Ian Stuart (Story); James Clavell, Edward Anhalt (Screenplay); Robert Surtees (Cinematography); Jerry Goldsmith (Music); Herman A. Blumenthal (Art Direction); Chuck Vassar (Set Decorations); Wesley Jeffries (Costumes); Emile LaVigne (Makeup); Paul Pollard (Special Effects); Jack N. Reddish (Assistant Director); Harold Lewis (Sound); Ferris Webster (Editor). Running time: 113 minutes

This science fiction mystery thriller is set in a top secret military research base in the California desert. When several flasks of a killer virus are stolen and a scientist is killed, former government agent Lee Barrett is called in to help the general (Dana Andrews) track down the culprit.

The big fear is that a particularly virulent strain known as the Satan Bug may have fallen into the wrong hands. With the help of the general's daughter Ann, Barrett determines that insane scientist Dr. Hoffman as the thief. Hoffman, who worked in the original experiments in developing the virus, is angry with the American government for their involvement with germ warfare and, with the help of his two henchmen, threatens to unleash a deadly dose on LA by way of protest. To show that he means business, the virus is first released in a small Florida community, killing the entire population. Barrett reaches Hoffman before he can expose LA to the killer virus, and the two fight it out in an airborne helicopter. Hoffman falls to his death and Barrett takes over the controls and makes a safe landing.

Tagline: "The Price for Uncovering the Secret of the Satan Bug Comes High — Your Life."

Andrews may well have relinquished his romantic leading man credentials in *Crack in the World*, but he still retained top billing in the film. In *The Satan Bug* he was able to show, for the first time, that he could comfortably slip into small character parts and still make a strong contribution. Andrews once commented: "I've played detective stories, and I've played lawyers. During the war, I was in every branch of the service, I think ... I played everything but a general."[1] Starting with *The Satan Bug*, the role of a general or some other high-ranking service officer would become his "stock in trade" character part for the rest of his film career.

Whereas the majority of the "end of the world" films of the '60s saw the threat coming from nuclear annihilation, *The Satan Bug* was unique in showing that an uncontrollable virus could present an equally horrific threat. Germ warfare had featured in RKO's 1951 release *The Whip Hand*, but the world had to wait until *The Satan Bug* before accepting the threat as an all-too-chilling reality. This biological menace would resurface in later years in *The Andromeda Strain* (1971), *Rage* (1972), *The Cassandra Crossing* (1977), *Plague* (1978), *Warning Sign* (1985) and *Outbreak* (1995).

Although the subject matter was a complete departure from his usual film fare, Andrews was again blessed with an intelligent screenplay. Adapted by James Clavell (of *Shogun* fame) and Edward Anhalt from an Alistair MacLean novel,

The Satan Bug was very much a "thinking man's" spy thriller contrary to the light entertainment style popularized by the Bond films. The film also marked a new direction for director John Sturges, who had risen to fame with the likes of *Bad Day at Black Rock* (1955) and his blockbusters *The Magnificent Seven* (1960) and *The Great Escape* (1963). To focus the mind on the story rather than the star, Sturges cleverly put a relatively unknown actor in the leading role, George Maharis, who effectively played the hero part with more reliance on the use of his brains than on his fists. Although Maharis was a popular TV star with *Route 66* to his credit, film success evaded him. Interestingly, in *Sylvia* (1964), filmmakers tried to emulate the success of *Laura* with Maharis playing an Andrews-type private detective on the trail of Carroll Baker. To enhance the atmosphere, *Laura* composer David Raksin was assigned to write the score. Unfortunately, the film was a disappointment.

Solid performances were also provided by veteran screen actor Richard Basehart and the alluring Anne Francis. Neither the archetypal hero or villain, Basehart was a difficult star to cast and tended to give his best performances playing introverted characters usually suffering from some form of mental anguish. He made his mark in the gritty film noir *He Walked by Night* (1948), *Fourteen Hours* (1951), Fellini's masterpiece *La Strada* (1954) and *Moby Dick* (1956), in which he played Ishmael. Andrews shared many characteristics with Basehart: Both could play subdued, slightly flawed characters and they were both gifted with distinctive, sonorous voices which perfectly complemented their square-jawed, rugged looks. It doesn't require too much a stretch of the imagination to see Andrews in the Admiral Nelson role on TV's *Voyage to the Bottom of the Sea*.

In addition to its taut direction, *The Satan Bug* was also driven by a suspenseful Jerry Goldsmith score, set against the backdrop of some stunning location photography of the Palm Springs desert. Although this chilling thriller is highly rated today, it failed at the box office upon its initial release.

Looking very distinguished with his silver-gray hair, Andrews brings a great deal of authority to his role, his furrowed brow and deeply searching eyes leaving us in no doubt that the world is threatened with complete annihilation unless the deadly flasks are safely recovered. We

All eyes are on the general (Andrews) in a desperate race to save the world in *The Satan Bug* (United Artists, 1965). Background left to right, George Maharis, John Larkin, Anne Francis and Richard Bull.

only see a faint relaxation of this worried look in the final scene when Lee informs him from the helicopter that Hoffman has fallen to his death and the flask is now in his possession. Relieved, his general responds, "Take it nice and easy and for God's sake make a good landing." (And let's hope it's not handling like a wet sponge!)

Although the film is starkly serious in its ap-

proach, which is borne out by Andrews's constantly worried expression, there is one scene where we slip precariously close to *Man from U.N.C.L.E.* territory: When Lee and his two colleagues (including James "Scotty" Doohan from *Star Trek*) are locked in a shack, Hoffman's henchmen, including a young Ed Asner, decide to silence them by tossing a deadly flask of the serum in through a hole in the roof, when it would have been so much easier to have simply shot them and have done with it. Scotty and his expendable sidekick bite the dust as a consequence but our hero Lee survives to tell the tale and track down the deranged Hoffman.

The *New York Times* said: "The cast ... is a sturdy, competent one...." Other reviewers also acknowledged the solid supporting cast and the subtle treatment of the plot, with the *Variety* critic commenting, "*Satan Bug* is a superior suspense melodrama and should keep audiences on the edge of their seat, despite certain unexplained, confusing elements which tend to make the plot difficult to follow." *Kine Weekly*'s critic wrote, "For the serious-minded patron, here is another excellent example of a world at the mercy of a scientific invention in this day and age. The scientific jargon, of which there is more than an ample supply, may confuse some folk, but there is hectic action to follow. A tense and thought-provoking effort."

In Harm's Way

Paramount, 1965

Cast: John Wayne (Capt. Rockwell Torrey); Kirk Douglas (Paul Eddington); Patricia Neal (Lt. Maggie Haynes); Tom Tryon (Mac McConnell); Paula Prentiss (Bev McConnell); Brandon De Wilde (Jere Torrey); Jill Haworth (Annalee); Dana Andrews (Vice Admiral Broderick); Stanley Holloway (Clayton Canfil); Burgess Meredith (Commander Egan Powell); Franchot Tone (Admiral Kimmel); Henry Fonda (Admiral Chester Nimitz); Patrick O'Neal (Commander Neal Owynn); Carroll O'Connor (Lt. Commander Burke); Slim Pickens (C.P.O. Culpepper); James Mitchum (Ensign Griggs); George Kennedy (Colonel Gregory); Bruce Cabot (Quartermaster Quoddy); Barbara Bouchet (Liz Eddington); Tod Andrews (Capt. Tuthill); Larry Hagman (Lt. J. G. Cline); Stewart Moss (Ensign Balch); Richard LePore (Lt. Tom Agar); Chet Stratton (Ship's Doctor); Soo Yong (Tearful Woman); Dort Clark (Boston); Phil Mattingly (PT-Boat Skipper); Hugh O'Brian (Air Force Major); Yankee Chang (Mortuary Clerk); Christopher George (Sailor); Jerry Goldsmith (Piano Player).

Credits: Otto Preminger (Producer-Director); James Bassett (Novel); Wendell Mayes (Screenplay); Loyal Griggs (Cinematography); Jerry Goldsmith (Music); Lyle Wheeler (Production Design); Al Roelofs (Associate Art Director); Morris Hoffman, Richard Mansfield (Set Decorations); Hope Bryce, Gordon T. Dawson (Wardrobe); Lawrence W. Butler, Farciot Edouart (Special Effects); Michael Daves, Howard Joslin, Daniel McCauley (Assistant Directors); Harold Lewis, Charles Grenzbach, Don Hall (Sound); Richard Carruth (Music Editor); Hugh S. Fowler, George Tomasini (Editors). Running time: 167 minutes

A World War II naval epic set in the immediate aftermath of the Japanese attack on Pearl Harbor. On the fateful morning of December 7, 1941, a heavy cruiser commanded by Captain Rockwell Torrey is one of several ships at sea that escape the attack. With his loyal friend and executive officer Paul Eddington at his side, Torrey is ordered to gather his small task force and engage the enemy. Torrey is injured when he attempts a daring maneuver, which results in his ship being seriously damaged. Having disobeyed orders, he is reprimanded and assigned to a desk job. At this juncture a number of subplots are introduced: Torrey's romance with Navy nurse Lt Maggie Haynes; his attempts to build bridges with Ensign Jere, his estranged son from a long-ended marriage; Eddington's bitterness brought on by the death of his wife during the Japanese attack and his subsequent interest in Jere's girlfriend, young Navy nurse Annalee, which culminates in her suicide. Inadvertently, through his opportunist son, who is looking to land a cushy staff job, Torrey learns of a top secret offensive called Skyhook. When the operation is stalled by the indecisiveness of Vice Admiral Broderick (Dana Andrews), Torrey's friend Commander Egan Powell convinces Admiral Chester Nimitz that Torrey is the right man to spearhead the mission. Promoted to rear admiral, Torrey sets sail to intercept the enemy fleet whose whereabouts is unknown. On board, Eddington, tortured with guilt over his rape of Annalee which drove her to suicide, tries to redeem himself in a certain death mission. Disobeying orders, he takes off alone in a reconnaissance plane to locate the Japanese fleet. Before he is shot down, he radios the location and size of the enemy force. In the sea battle that follows, Jere is killed and Torrey is injured when his ship is sunk. Although there are heavy American casualties, Operation Skyhook, the first major naval engagement of the Pacific, proves successful when the much larger enemy fleet retreats in disarray.

Tagline: "Stripped of everything — they lived and loved and fought as if there were no tomorrow...."

The title of the film derives from a statement made by America's first well-known naval hero, the Revolutionary War's John Paul Jones: "I wish to have no connection with any ship that does not sail fast, for I intend to go in harm's way."

Based on a novel by James Bassett, *In Harm's Way* was Andrews's last film under the direction of Otto Preminger, and on this occasion he found himself working alongside two screen giants, John Wayne and Kirk Douglas. Even though Andrews had not been able to work for some time due to his ongoing struggle with alcoholism, Preminger personally selected him for the part of Admiral Broderick. Hope Bryce, the film's costume coordinator, who married Preminger in 1971, recalled her husband's admiration for his old friend: "Otto, who hated scenery chewers, always appreciated Andrews's underplaying, and in the Fox days had also liked him very much personally. He had only a short part for Andrews, but was delighted that he accepted, and when Andrews showed up in Hawaii looking fit and healthy Otto was so pleased."[1]

Like Henry Fonda's cameo, Andrews's was small but pivotal. However, in contrast to Fonda, who once again reprised his familiar mild-mannered but firm type, Andrews broke new ground in his repertoire with a more questionable character. By convincingly portraying Broderick as a fearful, manipulative procrastinator, Andrews helped to define the contrasting heroic nature of Wayne's character, Captain Rockwell Torrey. Playing a weak man who puts his political ambitions before the lives of his men was a significant departure from Andrews's usual types. In the past, his characters may have been ambiguous, and as time moved on, more surly as his looks hardened, but they were usually men with some level of inner courage and integrity, unlike the timorous, patronizing Broderick (the sort of leader you would have preferred to have serving on the other side when the chips were down). The self-serving nature of his character is laid bare in the briefing room scene when confidential facts about the enemy movements come to light. Putting his political image first when the press are in attendance, he dismisses Rock's request for a private session to discuss the news, smugly claiming, "Oh, Rock — the press is *with* us, they're not against us. Let's give them a break!"

Andrews would reprise this self-important senior officer type that same year in *Battle of the Bulge* with his Colonel Pritchard, who like Broderick was certainly a "Doubting Thomas." But there was no doubting Pritchard's courage as a soldier, unlike the fearful admiral.

The filming of *In Harm's Way* was not a pleasant experience for many of the actors who regarded Preminger as a tyrant, but Wayne and Douglas (who were both known to be less than willing to take orders from temperamental directors) got on with their jobs in a professional manner. Like Wayne, Andrews respected the fact that Preminger called the shots on set, but he did recognize that the director had a terrible reputation for bawling out actors. According to Douglas, poor Tom Tryon bore the brunt of Preminger's tirades throughout the production.[2]

It is widely believed that John Wayne underplays the film due to the fact that he was seriously ill with lung cancer at the time. Healthwise, 1965 was also a bad year for leading lady Patricia Neal, who went into a coma for 21 days following complications during childbirth. The following year she had a series of strokes from which she made a remarkable recovery. She will always be remembered for her smoldering role in *The Fountainhead* (1949) and for her 1963 Oscar-winning performance in *Hud*. If there was ever a female voice that matched the richness of Andrews's, it was Patricia Neal's.

The film was superbly shot in black and white by Loyal Griggs, who was nominated for a Best Cinematographer Academy Award for his work. The film also benefits from a memorable score by Jerry Goldsmith.

The U.S. Navy gave Preminger its full cooperation, including the use of two of their ships and permission to film at the U.S. Pacific Command HQ at Pearl Harbor. Even years after the Japanese surprise attack, Pearl Harbor residents were still very sensitive about large explosions. As a consequence, arrangements had to be made for Honolulu radio to broadcast reassuring messages that any fire, smoke and large bangs were purely down to filming.

One of the criticisms leveled at the film was Preminger's insistence on using model ships in the battle scenes; they did little to convey the reality of naval combat. Admittedly, they look like little toy boats on a studio sea, but at least there was nobody noticeably poking them along with a stick.

This aside, the film was generally praised by

most critics. *Time* felt that with "half a dozen plots to juggle, Preminger keeps all of them interesting for at least two of the three hours spent *In Harm's Way.*" *Variety* commented that it contained "a full, lusty slice of life in a time of extreme stress, which Preminger had artfully guided so that incidents of adultery, rape, suicide, opportunism and stupidity in high command ... come across naturally, making their intended impression without battering the audience."

Happy for the work, Andrews regarded the film as "just an action type of picture...."[3]

Brainstorm

Warner Bros., 1965

Cast: Jeffrey Hunter (Jim Grayam); Anne Francis (Lorrie Benson); Dana Andrews (Cort Benson); Viveca Lindfors (Dr. Elizabeth Larstadt); Stacy Harris (Josh Reynolds); Kathie Browne (Angie DeWitt); Phillip Pine (Dr. Ames); Michael Pate (Dr. Mills); Robert McQueeney (Sergeant Dawes); Strother Martin (Mr. Clyde); Joan Swift (Clara); George Pelling (Butler); Victoria Paige Meyerink (Julie); Stephen Roberts (Judge); Pat Cardi (Bobby).

Credits: William Conrad (Producer-Director); Larry Marcus (Story); Mann Rubin (Screenplay); Sam Leavitt (Cinematography); George Duning (Music); Robert Smith (Art Direction); Hoyle Barrett (Set Decorations); Rose Brandi, Ken Laurence (Wardrobe); Gordon Bau (Makeup); Howard Grace, Monty Masters (Assistant Directors); M.A. Merrick, Ben Sad, William Thompson (Sound); William Ziegler (Editor). Running time: 110 minutes

In this 1960s film noir, young scientist James Grayam stops Lorrie Benson from committing suicide and subsequently they fall in love. Lorrie is unhappily married to Grayam's employer, the powerful industrialist Cort Benson (Dana Andrews), whose sadistic ways lie at the heart of Lorrie's depression. When Benson becomes aware of his wife's affair, he hatches a plan to split up the pair and also destroy Grayam's career. He discovers from the personnel files that Grayam once had a nervous breakdown and orchestrates a series of incidents to give the impression that Grayam is still mentally unstable.

The ruthless industrialist Cort Benson (Andrews) has little time for his wife Lorrie (Anne Francis) and even less time for her lover James Grayam (Jeffrey Hunter) in the compelling noir *Brainstorm* (Warner Bros., 1965).

In retaliation, Grayam and Lorrie conspire to commit the perfect crime by using the claim of his insanity to their advantage. Grayam publicly murders Benson with the hope of receiving a light sentence by pleading insanity. Aware that Grayam is perhaps faking, psychiatrist Elizabeth Larstedt nonetheless testifies to his insanity at the trial and he is committed to an institution. At this point, Lorrie leaves him. With no one to turn to for support in the harshness of his new surroundings, Grayam's mental health suffers. Escaping from the institution, he seeks out Dr. Larstedt and tries to convince her that he is not insane, but his explanation of the truth falls on deaf ears and she sends him back to the nightmare world of the asylum.

Tagline: "The Most Fiendish Idea Ever Conceived by the Human Brain!"

If you figured Andrews for a cold fish with a fiendish plan in *Beyond a Reasonable Doubt,* you ain't seen nothing yet, with *Brainstorm* providing him with an opportunity to play a real nasty piece of work. In the villainy department, Andrews delivered in spades with wealthy industrialist Cort Benson.

Regarded as a minor psychological masterpiece of the 1960s, *Brainstorm* was directed by William Conrad, who played one of the gunmen in *The Killers* (1946) and went on to become a household face as the TV detective *Cannon* in the 1970s. *Brainstorm* has much in common with Billy Wilder's noir classic *Double Indemnity* (1944) with the male leads in both stories seduced into unhealthy and doomed love affairs with married women.

With *Brainstorm,* Andrews moved back into familiar noir territory, but on this occasion he took the part of a villain with *no* redeeming features—a role he played to chilling effect. A handful of his past characters had shown a darker side, but overall they were generally well-meaning types. Eric Stanton in *Fallen Angel* was a self-seeking drifter, but love helps him learn the error of his ways. Mark Dixon in *Where the Sidewalk Ends* is a bit fast and free with his fists when the bad guys turn up on the scene, but he too is reformed by the love of a good woman. Sure, Tom Garrett got rid of his first wife in *Beyond a Reasonable Doubt,* but one never gets the feeling that he is bad to the core. Cort Benson in *Brainstorm,* however, is a different kettle of fish, for they don't come any meaner, with perhaps

the exception of Jack Palance's Wilson in *Shane*—but even he had a mother. By playing such a cold and ruthless character, Andrews once again showed his great versatility.

We get our first taste of Benson's evil ways in his confrontation with his wife after her failed suicide attempt. Playing on a mother's love for her child, he menacingly threatens that if she humiliates him again through her behavior, their young daughter's innocent cries in the night will go unanswered for as long as she lives. Lorrie tries to comprehend how the tyrant's evil can also embrace his only child; she is enlightened by Benson's explanation that as his wife, she is a mere possession that gives him pleasure. Such inherent evil surfaces again when Cort discovers that Grayam suffered a mental breakdown as a young man, a revelation he is quick to use to his advantage, coldly reminding Grayam, "Shall we call it your days of wine and neuroses. A nervous breakdown, they called it. Isn't that just a polite name for insanity?"

And in a scene reminiscent of *The Fearmakers* when Andrews's traumatized character is accused of having scrambled brains by the villain of the piece, he taunts, "Tell me, Mr. Grayam, what goes on in the head of a crazy man? Are there explosions, color flashes, or is it just a slow, paralyzing blackness that creeps over your mind like an eclipse of the sun?"

In the role of Grayam, Jeffrey Hunter is also in fine form, playing his slightly unhinged character with great intensity. Like Andrews, he was able to do this, with a minimum of effort, through the use of his penetrating eyes. The two stars had previously worked together in *The Frogmen* (1951).

In common with John Wayne, Hunter's rise to stardom was very much down to director John Ford, who coached some memorable performances out of the actor in *The Searchers* (1956), *The Last Hurrah* (1958) and *Sergeant Rutledge* (1960). However, with the end of the studio contract system in the early 1960s, his film career (like that of another handsome '50s heartthrob, Tab Hunter) went into decline, and he died at an early age in 1969 from a skull fracture sustained in a fall. Trekkies will always remember him as the first Captain Kirk, a role he gave up after *Star Trek*'s pilot episode to concentrate on such film projects as *Brainstorm.*

The film marked Andrews's third outing with

Anne Francis (after *The Crowded Sky* and *The Satan Bug*) and their doomed marriage was the closest their characters ever got to any romantic entanglement. And as in *Crack in the World*, Andrews was again destined to lose his beautiful wife to the handsome hunk in his employ.

Fueling the paranoia, the leads are excellently supported by Viveca Lindfors as an attractive psychoanalyst and Strother Martin and Richard Kiel as mental patients. The eagle-eyed will also spot Robert Mitchum's brother John as another ward psycho. The Swedish-born Lindfors came to Hollywood in 1946, making her mark in such films as *Adventures of Don Juan* (1948) and *Dark City* (1950), but for the most part her talent was never fully tapped in the movie capital. Strother Martin is remembered as Paul Newman's sadistic prison captain in *Cool Hand Luke* (1967), uttering the immortal line: "What we got here is ... failure to communicate." Martin once described the characters he played in western films as "prairie scum." Richard Kiel made his debut in the *Laramie* western series in 1960 and is best known for his role as the steel-toothed Jaws in the James Bond movies.

Silver and Ward rated *Brainstorm* as one of the best examples of the 1960s counterpart of the 1940s film noir. With its complex and compelling plot, the review went on, the film was a minor masterpiece of the 1960s.[1]

Town Tamer

Paramount, 1965

Cast: Dana Andrews (Tom Rosser); Terry Moore (Susan Tavenner); Bruce Cabot (Riley Condor); Lon Chaney, Jr. (Mayor Charlie Leach); Lyle Bettger (Lee Ring); Richard Arlen (Dr. Kent); Barton MacLane (James Fenimore Fell); Richard Jaeckel (Deputy Johnny Honsinger); Philip Carey (Jim Akins); Sonny Tufts (Carmichael); Coleen Gray (Carol Rosser); Pat O'Brien (Judge Murcott); DeForest Kelley (Guy Tavenner); Jeanne Cagney (Mary Donley); Don "Red" Barry, Robert Ivers (Hired Killers); James Brown (Davis); Richard Webb (Kevin); Roger Torrey (Mike Flon); Bob Steele (Ken, a Vigilante); Dale Van Sickel (Bartender); Dinny Powell (Cook); Frank Gruber (Hotel Clerk). Running time: 89 minutes

Credits: A.C. Lyles (Producer); Lesley Selander (Director); Frank Gruber (Novel & Screenplay); W. Wallace Kelley (Cinematography); Jimmie Haskell (Music); Jimmie Haskell, William D. "By" Dunham (Song); Hal Pereira, Al Roelofs (Art Direction); Claude E. Carpenter (Set Decorations); Wally West-more (Makeup); Howard Roessel (Assistant Director); Paul K. Lerpae (Special Effects); Hugo Grenzbach, John Wilkinson (Sound); George A. Gittens (Editor). Running time: 89 minutes

When his wife is killed by a bullet meant for him, lawyer Tom Rosser sets out to find perpetrators Riley Condor and Lee Ring. In his search he becomes a hired gun, exacting revenge on all lawbreakers. After two years he finally tracks the killers to a town, where Condor runs the saloon and Ring is the marshal. Rosser soon realizes that as corrupt town leaders the two men exert a powerful hold over the townsfolk, including Mayor Leach, Dr. Kent and businessman James Fenimore Fell. In their quest for wealth and power the evil pair are assisted by sadistic Deputy Honsinger. Rosser sets out to clean up the town, which culminates in a showdown with the bad guys. Emerging victorious from the shoot-out, Rosser has had his revenge and won the respect of the townsfolk for liberating their town.

Tagline: "Triggers All the Excitement of the Violent West!"

Lots of good old-fashioned "good vs. evil" excitement is generated by Andrews as a revenge-seeking lawman, as he takes on a prime crop of western bad guys headed by Bruce Cabot and he of the crooked menacing smile, Lyle Bettger. Frank Gruber (who played the hotel clerk in the film) adapted his own novel to write the screenplay for *Town Tamer*, which provided Andrews with another opportunity to get his teeth into a western character driven by revenge. In *Three Hours to Kill* his character is hell-bent on getting even with the bad guys who tried to string him up — and after what happened in *The Oxbow Incident*, who could blame him? In *Town Tamer*, he is equally motivated in his quest to exact his own brand of justice on the men who murdered his wife. In both films, Andrews proved that he could do "embittered and twisted" with the best of them and it's a shame that he wasn't featured in any of the Anthony Mann westerns of the '50s which successfully explored these themes, and in so doing provided James Stewart's career with a new lease on life in classics such as *Bend of the River* (1952) and *The Man from Laramie* (1955). I can just see Andrews's Mark Dixon (*Where the Sidewalk Ends*) decked out in western attire, chewing up the scenery *and* the bad hombres in both these Mann classics.

Town Tamer was director Lesley Selander's first film for producer A.C. Lyles and it is rightfully rated as one of his best westerns for years. The cast line-up is well worth the entrance fee alone. Lyles produced a stream of mid–'60s westerns which featured many veteran actors, and *Town Tamer* was no exception, with Andrews "shooting it out" with a "Who's Who" of western oldtimers, including Cabot, Bettger, Lon Chaney, Jr., Richard Arlen, DeForest Kelley

Looking for his wife's killers, the vengeful Tom Rosser (Andrews) shows his disdain for corrupt town leaders Lee Ring (Lyle Bettger, center) and Riley Condor (Bruce Cabot, right) in the taut little western *Town Tamer* (Paramount, 1965).

and Richard Jaeckel. The film also provided Pat O'Brien with a small role as Judge Murcott, marking his return to the big screen at the age of 66 after a six-year absence. Incidentally, during the making of *Laura* 18 years earlier, Zanuck suggested that Andrews should base his character Mark McPherson on the type of cops played by Pat O'Brien.

Some cast trivia: Did you know....

Bruce Cabot tested for the role of The Ringo Kid in *Stagecoach* (1939). John Wayne got the part and went on to become a living legend. And for those of you, like me, whose memory is in occasional need of a good set of jump leads, Cabot was the unlucky patsy who suffered a brutal interrogation at the hands of Charles Bickford's sadistic cop in Andrews's *Fallen Angel* (1945).

Lon Chaney, Jr., is the only actor to have played all of four of the classic movie monsters—the Wolf Man, the Frankenstein Monster, the Mummy and the son of Dracula. (Okay, the last one stretches it a bit, but he did have sharp teeth and there is a bloodline.)

DeForest Kelley was offered the part of Mr. Spock in *Star Trek* before accepting the role of Dr. McCoy.

Philip Carey played a regular role as a Texas Ranger captain in the successful NBC television series *Laredo* which ran from 1965 until 1967. He also starred as Philip Marlowe in a 1959 television series of the same name.

Richard Jaeckel, who went from playing baby-faced teenagers to hired killers, ended his successful film and television career with a three-year stint on *Baywatch* from 1991 to 1994 (very little persuasion was required to get him to take on that part, I bet). Jaeckel's second screen role saw him as an under-aged flight gunner in Andrews's torpedo plane squadron in the 1944 flag waver *Wing and a Prayer*.

Sonny Tufts was considered for the role of Jim Bowie in the John Wayne epic *The Alamo* (1960) before the part went to Richard Widmark.

Pat O'Brien chose acting after considering a career in the priesthood, but made up for it at Warners by appearing several times as a priest, most notably as Father Connelly in *Angels with Dirty Faces* (1938).

To get pulses racing, Howard Hughes's girlfriend Terry Moore was also included in the star line-up. A former child model, Moore made her mark in films such as *Mighty Joe Young* (1949) and *Peyton Place* (1957), and received an Oscar nomination for *Come Back, Little Sheba* (1952). Andrews was no stranger to the girls in Hughes's life, having starred with two of his other protégées: Jean Peters in the salty sea tale *Deep Waters* (1948) and Carla Balenda in the equally salty *Sealed Cargo* (1951).

Like other western characters played by Andrews, Tom Rosser is a resilient man of few words who goes about his task with steely determination. Unlike his Jim Guthrie (*Three Hours to Kill*), Tom is not entirely alone in his battle against the bad guys, this time finding able support from town seniors Barton MacLane, Lon Chaney, Jr., and Richard Arlen, who are all keen to see violence removed from the streets in order to attract new immigrants to the territory.

And if you thought Andrews had his work cut out when he came to blows with the huge brute Honey Bragg in *Canyon Passage,* check out Flon, the murderous giant lug he tangles with in *Town Tamer*. Badly bruised after their first encounter, Rosser coolly dispenses with him, Indiana Jones style, in their rematch, when Flon threatens him with a big knife, after sadistically carving up his horse.

In his determination to plug the guys responsible for the murder of his wife, Tom Rosser will happily go up against the odds, rendering justice in true dime novel style. "I've tamed a lot of towns, Mr. Fell. This will be the first time I had to go against a lawless element and the law." (The lawless element is in desperate need of a few lessons about the finer aspects of bushwhacking after two bungled attempts are made on Rosser's life.)

Rosser has little time for vigilantes, explaining to the marshal that he once passed through an outlaw-infested town, in which several guilty and innocent men were hung.

> TOM ROSSER: Now, I'm going to do what I came here to do, my own way.
> DR. KENT: ... Don't try it alone, they'd kill ya.
> TOM ROSSER: That's my job, Doc—killing and getting killed.

In a rare departure from the norm, this is one of the very few films where the husky-voiced Bettger shows a hint of remorse for his treacherous ways, killing fellow bad guy Honsinger in the final shootout.

Leonard Maltin aptly summed it up: "Andrews cleans up the community, and among the rubble are some veteran actors. Routine Western has minor nostalgia value, in light of the cast."[1]

The Loved One
MGM, 1965

Cast: Robert Morse (Dennis Barlow); Jonathan Winters (Wilbur Glenworthy/Henry Glenworthy); Anjanette Comer (Aimee Thanatogenos); Rod Steiger (Mr. Joyboy); Dana Andrews (Gen. Buck Brinkman); Milton Berle (Mr. Kenton); James Coburn (Immigration Officer); John Gielgud (Sir Francis Hinsley); Tab Hunter (Guide); Margaret Leighton (Mrs. Helen Kenton); Liberace (Mr. Starker); Roddy McDowall (D.J., Jr.); Robert Morley (Sir Ambrose Abercrombie); Barbara Nichols (Sadie Blodgett); Lionel Stander (Guru Brahmin); Bernie Kopell (Guru Assistant); Ayllene Gibbons (Joyboy's Mother); Roxanne Arlen, Pamela Curran, Claire Kelly (Whispering Glades Hostesses); Robert Easton (Dusty Acres); Don Haggerty (Haggerty); Chick Hearn (Announcer); Asa Maynor (Nikki, Secretary to D.J., Jr.); Alan Napier (English Club Official); Edwin Reimers (Minister); Reta Shaw (Zomba Café Manager); Paul Williams (Gunther Fry).

Credits: John Calley, Haskell Wexler (Producers); Neil Hartley (Associate Producer); Tony Richardson (Director); Evelyn Waugh (Story); Terry Southern, Christopher Isherwood (Screenplay); Haskell Wexler (Cinematography); John Addison (Music); Rouben Ter-Arutunian (Production Designer/Costumes); James W. Payne (Set Decorations); Emile LaVigne (Makeup); Kurt Neumann (Assistant Director); Stan Fiferman (Sound); Hal Ashby, Brian Smedley-Aston (Editors). Running time: 119 minutes

In this pointed satire on the Southern California funeral business, naive English poet Dennis Barlow arrives in Hollywood to visit his uncle Sir Francis Hinsley, a fussy art director, who hangs himself when he loses his job. Head of the Hollywood Community of British Talent, Sir

Scheming partners the Rev. Wilbur Glenworthy (Jonathan Winters) and General "Buck" Brinkman (Andrews) plan their next move in the wickedly surreal comedy *The Loved One* (MGM, 1965).

Ambrose Abercrombie persuades Dennis to have his uncle buried at Whispering Glades Memorial Park, run by Wilbur Glenworthy. While making the funeral arrangements, Dennis takes a job at a pet cemetery run by Wilbur's twin brother Henry Glenworthy. Dennis falls in love with sultry funeral home cosmetician Aimee Thanatogenos, who is also sought after by Wilbur and a fussy funeral director, Mr. Joyboy. When Aimee's ideals are shattered by Wilbur's attempt at seduction, she commits suicide by injecting herself with embalming fluid. In this bizarre world, a number of other unusual characters emerge, including General Brinkman (Dana Andrews), who in collusion with Wilbur is planning to send all the Memorial Park bodies into space so that the cemetery can be developed into a lucrative luxurious spa for retired folk. Their plans are dashed by Dennis who, having exposed the pair, returns home to England.

Tagline: "The motion picture with something to offend everyone!"

Need someone to play a general — get Dana Andrews on the blower. For Evelyn Waugh's glorious send-up of the California funeral business, Andrews found himself back in uniform, this time in a cameo part. And the two films couldn't have been more of a contrast — from traditional "shoot 'em up" oater to scathing satire. Moving on from *Town Tamer* with its large cast of familiar western veterans, Andrews was now in the thick of an equally large, star-spangled line-up of comic actors, interspersed with a fine assortment of serious British and American thespians, and they don't come any finer than Robert Morse, Jonathan Winters, Rod Steiger, Liberace, James Coburn, Anjanette Comer, Robert Morley and John Gielgud.

Tony Richardson was representative of the British "New Wave" of directors generally referred to as the "Angry Young Men." Before forsaking the British film industry in 1965 to make *The Loved One* in Hollywood, Richardson had been responsible for some of *the* landmark films of the last decade including *Look Back in Anger* (1959), *A Taste of Honey* (1961), *The Loneliness of the Long Distance Runner* (1962) and *Tom Jones* (1963), for which he received two Academy Awards (for Best Director and Best Picture).

Richardson chose the Waugh novel as a follow-up to the immensely successful *Tom Jones*.

In his hands the film version was not only a dark satire on the funeral business but also a wickedly funny and surreal commentary on Hollywood and America. To enhance the wacky flavor, Terry Southern was brought in as one of the screenwriters. Southern had proved his credentials with *Dr. Strangelove* (1964) and would go on to pen *Barbarella* (1967).

The Loved One was billed as "the motion picture with something to offend everyone," and they weren't kidding, with its hilarious anti-establishment swipes at '60s values. Although it is possibly one of the funniest black comedies ever made, it is definitely not for those that are easily offended; in particular, the scenes depicting the eating habits of Mr. Joyboy's bedridden overweight mother may leave you cold.

In keeping with the film's surrealist edge, the intentionally campy acting from all concerned is superb, with Andrews's General "Buck" Brinkman playing like a close relative of George C. Scott's General "Buck" Turgidson and Sterling Hayden's Brigadier General Jack D. Ripper from *Dr. Strangelove*. But, unlike these two characters, Andrews's general has precious little screen time to make any significant impact. This is a missed opportunity, because with his thin-lipped, grimly determined expression and deadpan persona, Andrews would have been the ideal actor to send himself up with the right material. We get a hint of the possibilities in his one meaningful scene with the blessed reverend. Scotch in hand, he wickedly delivers a line straight out of the George Wallace speech manual (during his presidential campaign, Wallace often railed at "the left-wing pinko press" and at "pseudo-pinko intellectuals"):

REVEREND WILBUR GLENWORTHY: Tell me, Buck, what about clearance from the Space Agency? Think we'll have any trouble there?

GENERAL "BUCK" BRINKMAN: I'll tell you frankly, Will — I don't trust those civilian eggheads — too much of the old "Pinko Prevert" influence to suit me. No, I think I'll go straight to Mr. Big with this one.

Brinkman is by far the most shallow, one-dimensional character in Andrews's film career. Who knows? If the timing had been right, and with the appropriate material, he could have reinvented himself and begun specializing in spoofy roles the way Lloyd Bridges did several years later with the *Airplane!* and *Hot Shot!* series.

Although today the film is hailed as a minor surreal masterpiece of the 1960s, second only to *Dr. Strangelove*, it was generally regarded as a fiasco on its initial release and the box office receipts proved disappointing. It is very likely that the film simply went over the heads of most people in 1965, for *Dr. Strangelove* received a similar response upon its release.

The reviews at the time were succinctly summed up by *The New Yorker* critic, who commented, "This sinking ship only makes it to port because everyone on board is too giddy and self-obsessed to panic."

As an indication that he could be "hip as well as the next guy," Andrews once commented in an interview that for a period he felt that none of his later films were outstanding with the exception of *The Loved One*, which he described as being out of the rut. He further added that in the United States they substantially cut his biggest scene, an orgy sequence, because the exhibitors thought it would be too rich for the general public.[1]

Battle of the Bulge
Warner Bros., 1965

Cast: Henry Fonda (Lt. Col. Daniel Kiley); Robert Shaw (Col. Martin Hessler); Robert Ryan (Gen. Grey); Dana Andrews (Col. Pritchard); George Montgomery (Sgt. Duquesne); Ty Hardin (Lt. Schumacher); Pier Angeli (Louise); Barbara Werle (Elena); Charles Bronson (Maj. Wolenski); Hans Christian Blech (Corp. Conrad); Werner Peters (Gen. Kohler); James MacArthur (Lt. Weaver); Karl-Otto Alberty (Maj. von Diepel); Telly Savalas (Sgt. Guffy); Steve Rowland (Eddy); Robert Woods (Joe, Kiley's Pilot); Charles Stalmaker (Maj. Burke); Janet Brandt (Mother Superior); Quinn Donoghue (Nun); Carl Rapp (MP).

Credits: Milton Sperling, Philip Yordan (Producers); Ken Annakin (Director); Milton Sperling, Philip Yordan, John Melson (Screenplay); Jack Hildyard (Cinematography); Benjamin Frankel (Music); Benjamin Frankel, Kurt Wiehle (Song); Eugene Lourie (Art Direction); Laure Lourie [as Laure DeZarate] (Costume Design); Charles Simminger (Wardrobe); Alex Weldon (Special Effects); Jose Lopez Rodero, Martin Sacristan, Julio Sempere, Luis Garcia (Assistant Directors); Kurt Hernfeld, Alban Streeter, David Hildyard, Gordon McCallum, Otto Snel (Sound); Derek Parsons (Editor). Running time: 167 minutes

This World War II epic is based on the breakthrough of the German army in the Ardennes,

Belgium, in the winter of 1944 — a counter-offensive known as the "Battle of the Bulge." With the Allied armies poised to invade Germany, Hitler orders a last desperate offensive to halt the American advance. The plan consists of a rapid tank assault on five points in the American line, which he hopes will divide the Allied forces in the West and allow the Germans to recapture the port city of Antwerp. Commanding a secret Panzer division is brilliant tank officer Colonel Hessler. Taking advantage of a weather front that has grounded Allied aircraft, the Germans break through with little opposition, but in order to continue their advance it is crucial that they capture American fuel supplies. Over in the Allied camp, only one American officer foresees this audacious attack, intelligence specialist Lt. Colonel Kiley, but his opinion is rejected by his immediate superior intelligence chief, Colonel Pritchard (Dana Andrews), and commanding officer, Major General Grey. A policeman in civilian life, Kiley is determined to follow up his hunch and flies behind enemy lines seeking out the enemy, and eventually sights them through the heavy mist as the tanks advance. As the drama unfolds, several additional characters enter the fray, including black marketeer Sergeant Guffy and his beautiful cohort Louise; battle-wise old soldiers Sergeant Duquesne and Major Wolenski; greenhorn officer Lieutenant Weaver; English-speaking German infiltrator Lieutenant Schumacher; Third Reich General Kohler, and Hessler's war-weary aide, Corporal Conrad. With the ever-advancing German attack forcing the Allies into full retreat, Kiley saves the day when he discovers that the one flaw in the German plan is their fuel supply. Armed with this knowledge, he and a group of American soldiers led by Lt. Weaver beat Hessler to the crucial fuel depot. They roll gasoline drums into the approaching Panzers, setting the depot and tanks ablaze.

Taglines: "The last desperate fight that changed the course of history"; "The Epic Adventure of the Clash that Turned the Tide of World War II"; "Unlike anything you have seen before, as Cinerama hurls you into the most extraordinary days of World War II!"

Andrews — your mission for 1965 is to appear in as many films as possible, covering all the major genres, without compromising on quality. The outcome — seven bumper movies, with the

Men-at-arms Lt. Col. Kiley (Henry Fonda) and Colonel Pritchard (Andrews, right) eventually see eye to eye in the sprawling World War II epic *The Battle of the Bulge* (Warner Bros., 1965).

action-packed *Battle of the Bulge* providing a memorable wrap-up:

Crack in the World: science fiction
The Satan Bug: spy thriller
In Harms Way: war (naval)
Brainstorm: film noir
Town Tamer: western
The Loved One: comedy (satire)
Battle of the Bulge: war (Army)

It's a pity he missed out on a musical, but Christopher Plummer already had his marker down for *The Sound of Music* that year.

Although Andrews and fellow noir icon Robert Ryan enjoyed significant roles in *Battle of the Bulge*, each competing for the most furrowed military brow, the film was really a battle of wills between Henry Fonda, as the former policeman

who relies on his hunches, and Robert Shaw as the heroic German tank commander Hessler (a role initially offered to Stanley Baker).

In the film, Andrews stepped down from his usual role of general to play a colonel, but he still outranked that other heavyweight contender for general roles, Henry Fonda, who had to settle on this occasion for lieutenant colonel. The part saw Andrews mustached for the fourth time in his film career (previously in *Kit Carson* , *Belle Starr* and *Berlin Correspondent*). With his charming 1940s persona, Andrews just about got away with the mustache routine, but in this, his surly middle years, it certainly looked like a 'tache too far.

British director Ken Annakin* was no stranger to epic war films having directed the British seg-

*On the trivia front, Ken Annakin's name inspired his friend George Lucas to use the character name Anakin Skywalker in *Star Wars*.

ments of the film which set the standard for all combat spectaculars, *The Longest Day* (1962). Following the successful model set by this masterpiece, the story of *Battle of the Bulge* unfolds as a series of star-studded individual soldier vignettes, ably enacted by George Montgomery, Telly Savalas, Ty Hardin, Charles Bronson, James MacArthur, and Werner Peters. Pier Angeli and Barbera Werle provided the female interest.

Annakin recalled in his autobiography that he required little coaxing to accept the film assignment when he discovered that three of Hollywood's finest (Andrews, Henry Fonda and Robert Ryan) were already signed up. In addition to being word perfect with their lines, the three veterans earned Annakin's respect when they used their strong acting instincts and long theatre experience to improvise in scenes where the scripted dialogue was poor.[1]

Like Andrews, Robert Ryan was often cast as embittered men, and with his gritty acting style could play hardened heroes or ruthless villains with equal ease. He made his mark as the anti–Semitic killer in *Crossfire* (1947), for which he received an Oscar nomination. Actor-novelist Robert Shaw is remembered as the dangerous secret agent Red Grant in *From Russia with Love* (1963), for his Oscar-nominated performance in *A Man for All Seasons* (1966) and for *Jaws* (1975).

For practical reasons the film was shot on location in Spain. The major financial backers had most of their money there, and due to financial restrictions they could only spend it in that country. In addition, the Spanish Army made available its men and equipment, including a fleet of World War II American and German tanks.[2] For the more technically minded, the King Tigers in the film are played by M47 Pattons and the M4 Shermans by M24 Chaffees.

Andrews turned in a strong performance, conveying his character in a very forthright manner which perfectly blended with the distinctive acting styles of Ryan and Henry Fonda. With all the big stars in the film pretty much playing characters they were familiar with, Andrews is the only headliner who plays against type. As the military "stuffed shirt," his skepticism is all-pervasive, typified in his verbal attacks on Kiley's hunch-driven theories: "I have ten other officers in my section. We see the same information, get the same facts as you, Kiley. All of us come up with one answer, and you come up with the complete opposite. When ten men tell you you're drunk, you'd better lie down."

Even with evidence of a German attack building up, Pritchard is not easily swayed. When General Grey asks him whether the tank in a reconnaissance photo is a Tiger, he stubbornly responds, "So it appears. But one tiger doesn't make a jungle, sir!"

Andrews's Pritchard was clearly not an older version of his Sergeant Tyne from *A Walk in the Sun*, but it is conceivable that if you took his John Holden from *Night of the Demon*, penciled on a mustache, added a dash of surly sarcasm, and ladled on the skepticism threefold, hey presto!—you'd have Colonel Pritchard. And there's no doubting that in the role of this gruff, strictly by-the-book officer, Andrews was the perfect foil for Fonda's laid-back, quietly dignified Kiley.

Although the film was a box office success, it was criticized at the time for its historical inaccuracies. The climax, with German tanks facing American on a vast flat plain, was pure artistic license, since there was no such terrain in that battle. For the real purists, the dusty plains of Spain, with the glimpse of the odd palm tree, were no substitute for the evergreen of the Ardennes. However, it is quite apparent that having invested millions in the Cinerama process (its original release format), the makers of the film were simply more interested in dramatic visual effect than a recreation of history.

To keep military historians happy, the factual elements included the rapid German advance through the Ardennes, the massacre at Malmedy, and the German attack on Bastogne resulting in General McAuliffe's "Nuts" rebuff to the German ultimatum to surrender. The escapist fun included Andrews's mustache, Robert Ryan's squint, and the grand finale where Danno from *Hawaii Five-O* (James MacArthur) helps to blow up the fuel depot. In fact, the only American fuel dumps in the battle area were to the north; the Germans bypassed them because they were unaware of their existence.

Sure, *Battle of the Bulge* plays fast and loose with the facts, but what the heck, it's still a great war picture, with some truly memorable action set pieces, more tough guy stars than you can shake a stick at, and a particularly rousing Benjamin Frankel film score which will have you merrily singing along, in harmony with the square heads, to the Panzer March.

Lawrence J. Quirk remarked in his book *The Great War Films*, "Dana Andrews is thoughtful and compelling as another of Ryan's senior officers whose main objective is to think through — and act through — the campaign dilemmas posed."[3]

Johnny Reno

Paramount, 1966

Cast: Dana Andrews (Johnny Reno); Jane Russell (Nona Williams); Lon Chaney, Jr. (Sheriff Hodges); John Agar (Ed Tomkins); Lyle Bettger (Jess Yates); Tom Drake (Joe Connors); Richard Arlen (Ned Duggan); Robert Lowery (Jake Reed); Tracy Olsen (Marie Yates); Regis Parton (Bartender); Rodd Redwing (Indian Brave); Charles Horvath (Wooster); Dale Van Sickel (Ab Conners); Paul Daniel (Chief Little Bear); Chuck Hicks (Bellows); Edmund Cobb (Townsman).

Credits: A.C. Lyles (Producer); R.G. Springsteen (Director); Steve Fisher (Story & Screenplay); Hal Stine (Cinematography); Jimmie Haskell (Music); Jimmie Haskell, William A. "By" Dunham (Song); Hal Pereira, Malcolm Brown (Art Direction); Robert Benton, Jerry Welch (Set Decorations); Edith Head (Costumes); Louis Haszillo, Wally Westmore (Makeup); Jim Rosenberger, Bob Jones (Assistant Directors); Paul K. Lerpae (Special Effects); Regis Parton (Stunts); Harold Lewis, John H. Wilkinson (Sound); Bernard Matis (Editor). Running time: 83 minutes

Riding toward Stone Junction, Kansas, U.S. Marshal Johnny Reno (Dana Andrews) is fired upon by Joe Connors and his brother Ab, who mistakenly believe he is after them. In the shootout, Ab is killed and Joe is captured by Reno. Arriving in town with his prisoner, Reno learns that Joe is wanted for the murder of Ed Little Bear, son of Chief Little Bear. Joe fiercely maintains that he is being framed. To see that Joe gets a fair trial, Reno has to confront the lynch law mentality of the townsfolk, who are ruled by corrupt Mayor Jess Yates with the support of Sheriff Hodges. The only welcoming face in town is Reno's ex-fiancée Nona Williams, owner of the local saloon. Anxious to see the back of Reno, town leaders Ned Duggan, Ed Tomkins and Jake Reed offer him $10,000 to leave without his prisoner. Reno refuses and ends up in a fistfight with Yates. With the angry mob ready to pounce, Joe knocks out Reno and

agrees to surrender if they let the marshal leave town alive. Yates agrees but immediately breaks his word, ordering the mob to hang Joe and Reno. Chief Little Bear rides to the rescue with a band of Indians, having learned from Tomkins that Yates had his son killed because he was courting his (Yates') daughter. In the ensuing gun battle, Reno shoots Yates, ridding the town of its corrupt leader. His mission accomplished, Reno rides out of town to start a new life with his true love, Nona.

Taglines: "On the trail of justice"; "The hard-fisted Texan with the easy-loving way."

From the introduction, which featured the Jimmie Haskell title song sung by Jerry Wallace, we learn that "U.S. Marshals quietly and with conscience and compassion opened up new frontiers from the Mississippi to the Pacific. One of these men was Johnny Reno. This is a chronicle of but two days in his two-fisted fight to establish truth and justice."

If there was ever a call for a seasoned actor to play a veteran U.S. Marshal quietly, with conscience and compassion, Dana Andrews — 57 years old and still remarkably fit — was your man. This was his third western that featured a lynching theme (after *The Ox-bow Incident* and *Three Hours to Kill*), but in this instance he was protecting the victim rather than assuming the role himself. A popular theme in westerns, lynching in America was usually instigated by unsolved crime and racism and it is estimated that there were 4,743 lynch victims between 1882 and 1968 (official statistics exist only for this period). The practice declined sharply after 1935, and there have been no reported incidents of this type since the late 1960s.

As the world-weary lawman Johnny Reno, Andrews is at his most nonchalant and dignified, and very much his own man. His composure is maintained throughout the proceedings, even with warring Indians and the whole town against him. The irate locals are led by one of the best psychos in the business, Lyle Bettger.

In the film's pressbook, Andrews explained how regular theatre assignments enabled him to retain a sense of individual characterization in his film work: "I believe that periodic stage appearances help to keep the actor from being typed. I know that after a play, I return to films refreshed and with increased enthusiasm." Practicing what he preached, Andrews began 1965 by starring in the play *A Man for All Seasons* in Palm Beach, Florida. Then after making some films in Europe, he appeared in summer stock in a new play, *Remedy for Winter*, just before returning to Hollywood for *Johnny Reno*.[1]

For those who like to play spot the star in good old-fashioned, cliché-ridden shoot 'em-

ups, *Johnny Reno* is a gold mine courtesy of that veteran filmmaker A.C. Lyles, who produced the film in answer to the pleas from theatre owners for more good clean motion pictures. Andrews is ably supported by Lyles' reliable stalwarts Bettger, Lon Chaney, Jr., and Richard Arlen (all three carry-overs from *Town Tamer*), this time

With the whole town against him, Marshall Johnny Reno (Andrews) can always depend on former love Nona Williams (Jane Russell) to back him when the chips are down in the lively "spot the veteran" western *Johnny Reno* (Paramount, 1966).

joined by the shapely Jane Russell and John Agar. This was one of the last Lyles Westerns (the final entry was made in 1968).

Russell rose to fame on the back of her ample front in Howard Hughes' western *The Outlaw* (1943) and was one of the few actresses who could match Marilyn Monroe curve for curve, as she demonstrated in the classic musical *Gentlemen Prefer Blondes* (1953). It took all of Lyles's powers of persuasion to get the happily married Russell to star in the movie, after the glamour queen had turned down many previous film offers. Lyles explained, "She's been missed, and after audiences see her in *Johnny Reno* I believe she'll find it difficult to turn down future offers. There is a built-in audience for established favorites; they are like old friends with which people can readily identify."[2]

With Russell's screen presence and stature it usually required a Robert Mitchum type to square up to her, and Andrews proved that he was more than up to the task. Aged 57 and 45, respectively, Andrews and Russell showed in their scenes together that they still had what it takes to light up the screen. One scene has Russell in an old bathtub happily soaping herself when Andrews pays a surprise visit to her ranch house. Lyles saw the bathing scene as added insurance for the success of *Johnny Reno*. (Cecil B. DeMille was the first filmmaker to successfully introduce the tub scene in his 1918 production *Old Wives for New*. The soap suds also reappeared, to good effect, in Andrews's *Kit Carson*).

Looking very much the part of one of the town's sharp-suited business leaders, John Agar is a welcome addition to the usual A.C. Lyles line-up. As well as being Shirley Temple's first husband, Agar is perhaps best remembered for his strong performances in the John Wayne films *Fort Apache* (1948), *She Wore a Yellow Ribbon* (1949) and *Sands of Iwo Jima* (1949). Thereafter, he made his mark as a B movie icon in sci-fi movies such as *Tarantula* (1955) and *Hand of Death* (1962).

Lyles always reserved a slot for Lon Chaney, Jr., who always seemed to play the sort of ambling, burned-out sheriff you'd rather have standing in front of you than behind you when it came to a showdown.

As well as its superb supporting cast, the familiar plot is lifted by Andrews's understated performance, which greatly emphasizes the composed but slightly offhand nature of his character. In response to Joe's gripe that his life isn't worth two cents at Stone Junction where he will stand trial, Reno growls, "Indians get you — it'll be worth even less." When the Indians do catch up with them on the way to town, they are none too pleased that Reno got to Ab first, claiming it was their right to kill him. Unperturbed by the threat at hand, Reno responds, "Pity he didn't know that before he started shooting at me."

Low-budget shoot-'em-ups don't come any finer than this entry, which incidentally also provides a rare opportunity to see the Indians ride to the rescue in the penultimate scene, enabling our hero and villain to shoot it out in the final confrontation. You'd have thought that those bad guys would have learned their lesson by now: You don't pursue the "old necktie" game when Andrews's in town, as you're liable to end up on Boot Hill.

While promoting *Johnny Reno*, Lyles claimed, "Westerns are ageless; ten years from now they will be as timely as they are today."[3] Sad to say, he was proved wrong, when a few years later the genre became virtually extinct in all media.

Berlino—Appuntamento per le spie
(Spy in Your Eye)
American International, 1965

Released in the U.S. in January 1966

Cast: Brett Halsey (Bert Morris); Pier Angeli (Paula Krauss); Dana Andrews (Col. Lancaster); Gastone Moschin (Boris); Tania Beryl (Madeleine); George Wang (Ming); Alessandro Sperli (Karalis); Marco Guglielmi (Kurt); Renato Baldini (Belkeir); Mario Valdemarin (Willie); Luciana Angiolillo (Miss Hopkins); Luciano Pigozzi (Leonida); Tino Bianchi (Dott. Van Dongen); Massimo Righi (Lavies); Franco Beltramme (Serghey); Yui Chang Pio Tou (Pio); Giulio Maculani (Stanko); Aldo De Francesco (Seaton); Abdul-Rahim Bazin (Ibrahim).

Credits: Fulvio Lucisano, Luciano Marcuzzo (Producers); Louis M. Heyward (Executive Producer); Vittoria Sala (Director); Lucio Marcuzzo (Story); Romano Ferrara, Adriano Baracco, Adriano Bolzoni. Louis M. Heyward (Screenplay); Fausto Zuccoli (Cinematography); Riz Ortolani (Music); Luciano Del Greco (Art Direction); Ugo Pericoli (Costume Design); Stefano Rolla (Assistant Director); Robert & Renato Cinquini (Editors). Running time: 88 minutes

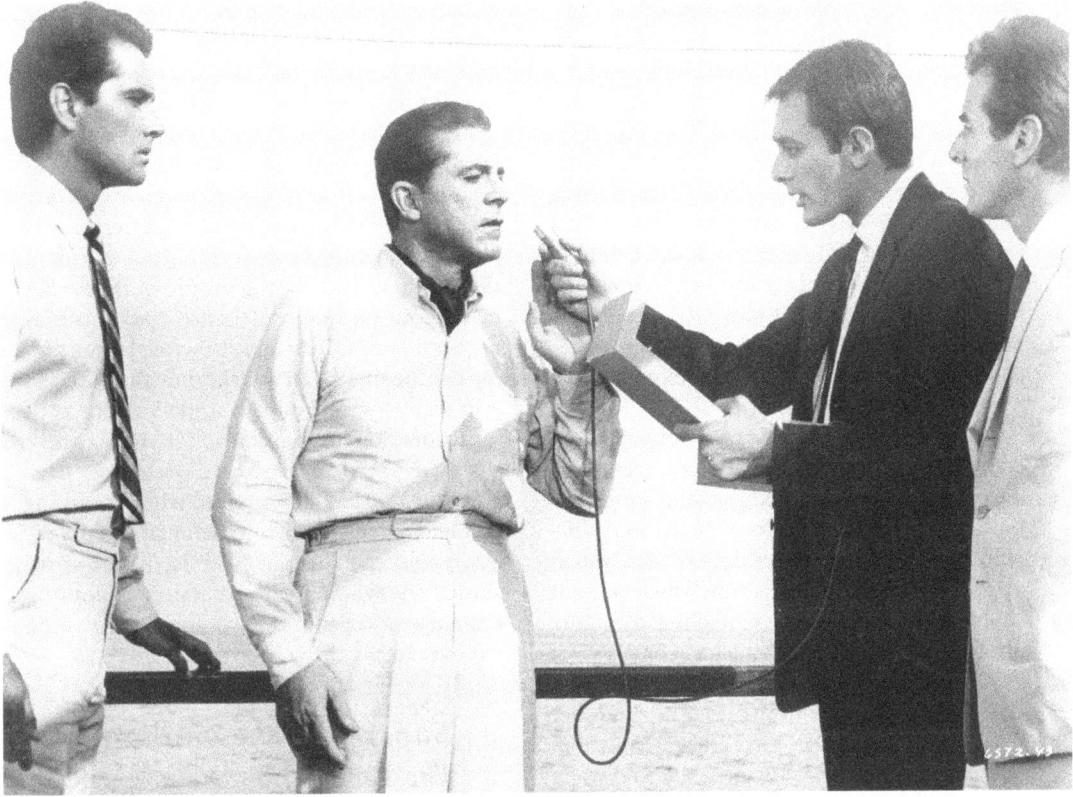

U.S. Intelligence chief Colonel Lancaster (Andrews, center), unknowingly snoops for the Reds who have implanted a mini-camera in his eye in the Euro spy-thriller *Spy in Your Eye* (American International, 1965).

U.S. Intelligence chief Colonel Lancaster (Dana Andrews) unknowingly becomes a spy for the Russians when they implant a mini-tele-camera in his eye during an operation to replace his glass eye with an "all-seeing" upgrade. Both the Americans and the Russians are after the secrets of a death ray developed by a now deceased Nobel Prize–winning scientist, and the suspicion is that he passed the formula on to his daughter Paula, before he died. With their spy camera advantage, the Russians hope to kidnap Paula, who is unaware that her father had the formula tattooed on her scalp to prevent it from falling into enemy hands. U.S. agent Bert Morris is dispatched to tail Paula and a romantic relationship soon develops. When the Americans discover the secret camera, they turn it to their own advantage by feeding false information back to the Russians. With the two superpowers preoccupied with trying to outdo each other, Bert and Paula steal away to safety.

Tagline: "DANA ANDREWS as Secret Agent Z.3 who has to try harder 'cause he's not No. 1... But a Blend is better than a Bond — when he has sexier gals ... groovier gimmicks and much more gall!"

Quick!, get me trade descriptions on the line! The film may well be a spy flick, but any comparison with Bond is purely a delusion. This is more like a bargain basement *Man from U.N.C.L.E.* which in turn was a cheap and cheerful Matt Helm, who at the very best was a poor distant relative of Bond. However, the film is still great fun and should be available on prescription for anyone looking to "kick the blues," as it is so unintentionally funny it's guaranteed to raise a smile. Whether the gals are sexier than Bond's, it's hard to say as they appear all too briefly (they must have been on double-time), but "groovier gimmicks" — that's a hoot ! The gadgets looked liked they were improvised in between coffee breaks. In the gimmick box, apart from Andrews's eye camera, we have a hunchback's hump that conceals a radio transmitter and a large flick knife, and a zoom camera that doubles as a gun for some dodgy-looking Chinese agents dressed in suits and bowler hats.

Aside from the "mind-blowing" gadgets, the film also boasts some memorable set pieces including a bulldozer charging towards a border watch tower with its tilted bucket deflecting gunfire (John Wayne, eat your heart out), a training camp for fit chicks to practice judo in skimpy outfits, and a chase through a warehouse bursting with props that look left over from a *Scooby Doo* movie. It's the sort of film where anything is possible — I half expected Fu Manchu to make an entrance.

The plot runs at a frantic pace jumping from continent to continent, and in one scene Andrews sports an Arab's headgear which looks almost as bizarre as his stick-on beard from *Forbidden Street*. The brisk pace doesn't allow you to dwell too long on the lazy script, which is about as sharp as a pig's snout. Cue obligatory cute nurse offering Col. Lancaster a hand on his short walk to the operating theatre for an eye operation. Clearly a man with two feet, he shoos her away, mumbling, "It's the eyes that are missing, not the legs. I can move by myself." And when the job is done, he exclaims, "Congratulations, doctor, you've done a fine job. A thing of beauty is a joy forever." (Bond scriptwriters beware.)

Described by one critic as an interesting voyeuristic spy movie, *Spy in Your Eye* was Andrews's first venture into the world of Italian-made movies. The film required little effort on the travel front as Andrews was already in Europe, having crossed the Atlantic to appear in *Battle of the Bulge* in Spain. Andrews was not alone in his foray into European productions as lean pickings in the American film industry had prompted many Hollywood veterans to follow the overseas trail, among them Stewart Granger, Van Heflin, George Nader, Lex Barker, Steve Reeves, Henry Fonda, Audie Murphy, and of course the most successful Hollywood export of them all, Clint Eastwood.

The male lead in *Spy in Your Eye*, handsome beefcake Brett Halsey, started his Hollywood career in juvenile delinquent films before appearing in better quality films such as *Return of the Fly* (1959) and *Return to Peyton Place* (1961). However, in common with many of the young actors of the day such as Efrem Zimbalist, Jr., Jeffrey Hunter, and Ty Hardin, who incidentally

had all worked with Andrews, he was born ten years too late to enjoy a full-fledged Hollywood film career, and in the 1960s he packed his bags to make his mark in Italian action films.

Leading lady Pier Angeli suffered a similar fate. After a promising start with such films as *The Silver Chalice* (1954) and *Somebody Up There Likes Me* (1956), she ended her career in sexploitation pictures before committing suicide at the age of 39 with a drug overdose. Before her marriage to Vic Damone, she had a passionate affair with James Dean and she wrote before taking her life that Dean was the only man she had ever really loved. Andrews worked with Angeli in his previous film *Battle of the Bulge*, where she played Telly Savalas's love interest.

Spy in Your Eye was directed with serious intent and given a wide international cinema release, but I can't help but feel that Andrews regarded the whole Euro-excursion as nothing more than a series of paid vacations with a little left over to pay the grocery bill.

Supercolpo da 7 miliardi
(The Ten Million Dollar Grab)
(The Ten Thousand Carat Diamond)
Italian, 1966

Cast: Brad Harris (Robert Colman); Elina De Witt (Gaby); Dana Andrews (George Kimmins); Arrigo Peri (Lucas Bol); Franco Andrei, Fernando Poggi, Gilberto Galimberti, Marisa Traversi, Antonio Corevi, Antonietta Fiorito, Giuseppe Lighissa, Giovanni Ivan Scratuglia, Danlio Turk, Giorgio Valletta.
Credits: Bitto Albertini (Director, Story & Screenplay); Emilio Varriano (Cinematography); Nico Fidenco (Music); Adriana Spadaro (Costumes); Franco Schioppa (Makeup); Anna Gruber (Assistant Director); Attilio Nicolai (Sound); Jolanda Benvenuti (Editor). Running time: 105 minutes

A Euro caper-heist movie very much in the *Rififi* tradition: Thieves steal a diamond insured for $10 million and George Kimmins (Dana Andrews), the billionaire owner, manages to recover it, but he keeps it hidden while he claims the insurance money.

In his next Italian production, Andrews found himself playing second fiddle to another piece of prime U.S. beefcake, Brad Harris. Starting his film career as a stunt man, Harris traveled to Europe in the late '50s to work as a stunt coordinator which eventually led to a starring role in *Goliath Against the Giants* (1962). With his muscular good looks, Harris was at home with sword-and-sandal movies before moving into spaghetti westerns and spy thrillers. Andrews was quite fortunate that when he arrived in Europe, spy-caper movies were in vogue; they were more suited to his type of character than the costume actioners. A few years earlier and he might have gone the way of fellow noir icon Alan Ladd, who was disastrously miscast as a Roman warrior in the Italian production *Duel of Champions* (1962). Such bad film choices in European productions would blot the copybook of several veteran Hollywood stars, particularly when sexploitation films became popular in the 1970s.

Other successful U.S. imports to the Euro spy-caper genre included George Nader, Lex Barker, Gordon Scott and Stewart Granger. The spy mania was clearly influenced by the success of 007, whereas the caper movie drew most of its inspiration from Jules Dassin's *Rififi* (1955). More often than not, these small-budget films were usually international co-productions, churned out quickly to meet the insatiable demand for low-grade filler material that the big studios were no longer making.

The film marked the debut of director Bitto Albertini, who had previously enjoyed great success as cinematographer. His most successful project as director was the film noir-ish gangster hit *L'uomo piu velenoso del cobra* (1971). He would go on to make many exploitation movies including the Black *Emmanuel* series in 1975 and '76. The raunchy soundtrack came courtesy of Nico Fidenco.

The film was known as *The 1000 Carat Diamond* in the UK. The English-dubbed version has only been shown on U.S. television. Chances are, you'll probably discover The Lost City of Atlantis before tracking down a copy of this movie, but I'm still on the lookout.

I diamanti che nessuno voleva rubare
(The Diamonds Nobody Wanted to Steal/No Diamonds for Ursula)
Italian, 1966

Cast: Jeanne Valerie (Ursula); Salvo Randone (Spiros); Dana Andrews (Maurizio); John Elliot (Fangio); Kathy Baron (Maurizio's Wife); Aldo Giuffre (Marcos); Mario Brega (Sansone); Bruno Piergentili (Giorgio); Roger Beumont (Charlie); Aymo (Edison); Lilly Mantovani, Giovani Petrucci, Ignazio Spalla, Thomas Walton, Nino Vingelli, Attilio Dottesio, Giovani Ivan Scratuglia, Raniero Gonnella.

Credits: Gino Rossi (Producer); Gino Mangini (Director); Sergio Pisani (Story); Sergio Pisani, Gino Mangini, Hannes Schmidhauser, Fiorella Ricciardello (Screenplay); Angelo Filippini (Cinematography); Carlo Rustichelli (Music); Gabriele Crisanti (Production Design); Emilio Zago (Set Decorations); Vera Poggioni (Costume Design); Leandro Marini (Makeup); Roberto Giandalia (Assistant Director); Pietro Ortolani (Sound); Alberto Gallitti (Editor). Running time: 85 minutes

While looking after the store for her employer, her uncle Spiros, the beautiful Ursula is assaulted by a brute of a sailor on shore leave. In the struggle, she fatally shoots the rapist with his own gun, but is then blackmailed into a life of servitude by Spiros, who witnessed the killing. Flash forward, and Spiros is living a life of luxury with Ursula, who despises him, and another beautiful young girl who came under his control following a gang rape in Hong Kong. To add to his fortune, the wheelchair-bound Spiros uses blackmail to assemble a team of criminals (a couple of heavies, a forger named Carbon Copy, a safecracker and a getaway driver named Fangio) to pull off a diamond heist. Spiros has information on each of the villains which will put them behind bars if they don't do his bidding. The gang also includes Charlie (who deserted from the French Army after killing his colonel and is now involved in the murky world of espionage) and the lecherous Stephanopolis (who was caught on camera in compromising positions with a 16-year-old). Their objective is a high-class jewelry store in Rome owned by Maurizio (Dana Andrews) and his voluptuous young wife, who on behalf of a rich client are trying to sell a prized diamond collection.

After much double-crossing by all concerned, Spiros is bumped off by the gang, who then pull off the robbery only to discover that the diamonds in their possession are fake. Unbeknownst to all, Maurizio employed the services of Ursula's secret young lover, Giorgio, to pull a diamonds switch after the robbery, the idea being that Maurizio can keep the diamonds *and* the insurance money. Maurizio is in turn double-crossed by his wife who, accompanied by the jewelry store assistant, takes off with the diamonds. The criminal gang members are machine-gunned by Spiros's other young female slave, as an act of revenge for killing her master; Maurizio's wife and lover are arrested by Interpol, and Ursula and new love Fangio make their escape to start a new life together.

It seems that everybody's double-crossing someone in this caper movie, which culminates, rather bizarrely, in the death of most of the criminal gang following a commando-style attack by Spiros's maid, who up to this point in the film had done little more that serve cups of tea. Still, we are talking '60s Euro plot antics, so close scrutiny is optional.

American tough guys Brett Halsey, Brad Harris, and Peter Martell were around to flex their muscles in Andrews's other Euro excursions, but in *No Diamonds for Ursula* he is very much on his own amongst a complete European cast and crew. As Maurizio, the jewelry store owner, Andrews has surprisingly little to do except zip up the dress of his wife and, in the shower, sing his own version of the Sinatra standard "The Lady Is a Tramp."

In true Euro dubbing style, deep voices abound in this film, with one character in particular, Fangio (who incidentally looks like a cross between Sean Connery and Randolph Scott), occasionally sounding like a poor version of Andrews. The sound is such that Andrews even sounds like he is doing a poor imitation of himself.

This may well be a strong candidate for Andrews's worst film and is a complete waste of his talent, but at the very least, as the dodgy and rather seedy-looking Maurizio, he does get the opportunity to lay on the charm thicker than farm-sliced ham, particularly where the selling of diamonds is concerned.

When Ursula buys a wristwatch from his store, she comments on its beauty, to which Maurizio replies, "It looks even more beautiful on you, madam." And going in for the clincher, he pitches, "They are also lucky if the woman is beautiful." To top it all, Maurizio explains to his assistant, "Always remember one thing: It's the beautiful women in this world who keep us in business."

In tandem with the spy genre, the European caper movie genre came to an end in the early 1970s when the psychedelic "anything goes" climate of the 1960s gave way to a harsher reality which expressed itself in violent crime and horror films.

Hot Rods to Hell
(52 Miles to Terror)
MGM, 1967

Cast: Dana Andrews (Tom Phillips); Jeanne Crain (Peg Phillips); Mimsy Farmer (Gloria); Laurie Mock (Tina Phillips); Paul Bertoya (Duke); Gene Kirkwood (Ernie); Jeffrey Byron (Jamie Phillips); George Ives (Lank Dailey); Hortense Petra (Wife at Picnic); William Mims (Man at Picnic); Paul Genge (Highway Patrol Officer); Peter Oliphant (Little Boy at Picnic); Harry Hickox (Bill Phillips); Charles P. Thompson (Charley); Jim Henagan (Youth); Mickey Rooney, Jr. (Combo Leader); Liz Renay (Hazel); Christopher Riordan (Student); Arthur Tovey (Man Seated at Bar).

Credits: Sam Katzman (Producer); John Brahm (Director); James Curtis Havens (Assistant Director); Alex Gaby (Story); Lloyd Ahern (Cinematography); Fred Karger (Music); George W. Davis, Merrill Pye (Art Direction); F. Keogh Gleason, Henry Grace (Set Decorations); William Tuttle (Makeup); Ben Lewis (Editor). Running time: 92 minutes

All-American family Tom Phillips (Dana Andrews), his wife Peg and their two children, Tina and Jamie, set off to start a new life in California. Tom, who is disabled from a car accident, is looking to make a new living as the owner of a desert motel. While en route the family is terrorized by hot-rodding teenagers: Gloria and her malicious boyfriends Duke and Ernie. Shaken by the ordeal, the family arrives at their destination, only to discover to their horror that the motel is run-down and is being used by the local delinquents for illicit drinking. To make matters worst, Duke sets his sights on Tom's inexperienced daughter Tina and tries to entice her with promises of fast cars and fast fun — a temptation, to which she nearly succumbs. To escape the unfolding nightmare, Tom decides to take the family to his brother's house 52 miles away. During the journey, the youths launch another vicious attack on them. Stretched to breaking point, Tom eventually snaps and, bringing the car to an abrupt halt, he aims his headlights at the oncoming hoodlums. Blinded by the light, Duke swerves at the last minute and crashes his hot rod. Hauling the hoodlums out of the car, Tom forces them to give up their delinquent ways or

Terrorized by hot-rodding punks, Tom Phillips (Andrews) keeps a firm set of hands on the wheel to ensure the safety of his family in *Hot Rods to Hell* (MGM, 1967). From the left: wife Peg (Jeanne Crain), teenage daughter Tina (Laurie Mock) and son Jamie (Jeffrey Byron).

face a prison sentence. Valuing their freedom, the youths promise to reform, and Tom returns to the motel with his family, having decided to make a go of the business.

As the PR boasted:

Hotter than Hell's Angels! The motorcycle gangs take a back seat, when these young animals clear the road for excitement.

Too bad easy chairs don't come with seat belts. You might need 'em for *Hot Rods to Hell*.

Based on a *Saturday Evening Post* story, *Hot Rods to Hell* was originally intended for television under the title *52 Miles to Terror*. The producers were so pleased with the finished product that they changed the title and released the film theatrically. With its rebellious teenagers and roadsters, the film was perhaps a bit too rough for television audiences of the day, but it was perfect fodder for the drive-in circuits, and over the years it has garnered a cult following. Despite its modest budget, it grossed over a million dollars at the box office, and there is now a website dedicated to it.

This type of movie was "bread and butter" to producer Sam Katzman, who made his mark with low- to medium-budget productions, starting out in the 1930s with Tim McCoy westerns and the East Side Kids series, before churning out sci-fi films and teenage musicals in the 1950s, followed by hippie and biker films and Elvis Presley musicals in the 1960s. He is credited with having coined the term "beatnik." Director John Brahm was the man behind some of the classic *Twilight Zone* episodes and was also responsible for some memorable films including *The Lodger* (1944), *Hangover Square* (1945), and *The Locket* (1946).

The shooting of *Hod Rods from Hell* was wrapped up in about two weeks on the MGM backlot and in the area surrounding Palmdale, California. With its roadsters and rebellious teenagers, the film really belongs to the '50s and not the hippie acid-tripping '60s in which it was set. The camp atmosphere of the period is richly fuelled by the background roadhouse music, which is supplied by Mickey Rooney, Jr. and His Combo.

With Andrews growling great lines such as, "What kind of animals are these?" and "Can anyone sleep with that awful music?" you know you're in for a fun, bumpy ride; and like many of Andrews's '60s B-movies, to be fully relished they should *not* be taken too seriously. For memorably funny lines, this film is only pipped by Andrews's *Zero Hour!* and *The Frozen Dead*. In fact, *Hot Rods* would have made a great double bill with *The Frozen Dead*. At the time of release, it was sometimes shown as a double-feature with *For a Few Dollars More*.

Joining Andrews on this hazardous journey was fellow veteran star Jeanne Crain, who still looked as fresh as when she first appeared with Andrews in *State Fair* 22 years previously. This was their fourth and last film together (the other two being *Duel in the Jungle* and *Madison Avenue*). Noted for her humor, Jeanne once remarked, "Frankly, I wouldn't go to a picture named *Hot Rods to Hell*...."[1] Joking aside, Jeanne enjoyed making the film, commenting, "I love both my children and my profession and I have always prided myself on neglecting neither. This is probably one reason why I was enthusiastic over my role in *Hot Rods to Hell*, in which I play a wife and a mother who has to give moral support to her husband and children when the family is terrorized by hoodlum teenagers on a lonely stretch of desert highway.... I am firmly convinced that confused youngsters are strongly influenced for either evil or good as a result of family relations. If they feel rejected by their parents, they often take out their frustrations by becoming such savages as the youthful terrorists of our picture. If we want our sons and daughters to grow up into happy adults, we must give them close family ties and all the love and understanding that these ties can bring."[2] (Amen!)

The film is also a historical snapshot of the fears of the postwar middle class, seeing their safe, moral and conservative society under threat from rebellious teenagers. With Andrews and Crain righteously representing the "old guard," the beatnik youth made their presence felt through the likes of Mimsy Farmer, who tended to specialize in "party-girl types." Having mastered the low-budget actioner in the U.S. with films such as *Hot Rods to Hell* and *Riot on Sunset Strip* (1967), she continued her film career in Europe where such movies were held in high esteem.

Andrews was in almost every scene of the film, but he insisted that the length of a part isn't always the most vital factor: "The actor who turns down offers because he is not in every scene is unwise. While Jeanne Crain and I have the adult leads, the very nature of the story about a youth cult, dedicated to danger and a menace to everyone with whom they come into contact, puts its emphasis on the characterizations played by such talented young performers as Mimsy Farmer, Laurie Mock, Paul Bertoya and Gene Kirkwood.... There were times when the young actors and actresses in our picture came close to stealing the scenes right from under Jeanne's and my nose. But we were glad to share the honors. We had our innings. It is what an actor has a chance to do, not how much footage he fills that is important."[3]

Andrews's Tom Phillips is another addition to his repertoire of traumatized, vulnerable characters, which kicked off with his airman in *The Best Years of Our Lives* (like Fred Derry, Tom suffers from recurring nightmares) and who were then put through their paces in *Zero Hour!* and *The Fearmakers*. However, on this occasion he also has to take on the hoodlums with a bad back that resulted from a car accident; the injury has made him reluctant to get back behind the wheel of a car. However, as we witnessed in *Zero Hour!*, when the safety of his family is threatened, it's only a matter of time before he overcomes his nerves. But not before he nearly reduces wife Peggy to a nervous wreck, when in a moment of panic during the road ordeal he grabs the steering wheel from her, offering the feeble excuse, "I had to do something—even if it was wrong. I just can't sit here like a stick." Looking suitably aggrieved and stony-faced after the incident, he snarls, "Running people off the road with those souped-up sardine cans. Nowhere to go—but want to get there at 150 miles per hour."

Shaken after their first brush with the roadsters, the family finds refuge in a lush green picnic area that seems to appear out of nowhere in the parched desert. And while we're on the subject of puzzlers, where do the punks live?; there appear to be no houses on view. One can only assume that they, too, vaporize at night and reappear out of the morning mist for the sole purpose of running squares off the road. And with the exception of Homer Simpson, they don't come any squarer than Tom Phillips.

I had hoped that, when the chips were down, Andrews would do his take on Spencer Tracey's disabled war vet from *Bad Day at Bad Rock*, by dispensing lethal karate chops. Instead we are treated to justice *Mad Max* style with a final game of chicken on the dusty highway. This could also be seen as the road version of *Rocky*, with Tom making a strong comeback in his attempt to rid the open highway of jerks.

With the roadster wrecked in the ditch, Tom gives it a few extra dents for good measure with a tire iron (eat your heart out, Basil Fawlty) before snarling at the bruised and shaken Duke and Ernie, "Punks—the both of you. I could have killed you, that's what I just found out, any time today, I could have killed you, but you see, I didn't know that until you dirty punks made me know it." Not a man to bear a grudge, Tom describes the incident as an accident when the police arrive, which no doubt sends Duke and Ernie to the nearest church to repent their wicked ways (yeah, like). Suitably reinvigorated by the whole experience, Tom exclaims, "I'm not going to run any more, I'm going back to my motel and I'm gonna clean up all the slop and garbage and the smell and it's gonna be like it should be." (A dreary little motel in the middle of nowhere?)

And as a parting gesture to the audience before the credits roll, he tells his doting wife: "Peg—I wouldn't even mind if you drove now."

The *New York Times* commented, "This is a well-intentioned, but lumpy little picture. Two postwar favorites, Dana Andrews and Jeanne Crain, act professionally as the agonized parents."

Recognizing its unique appeal, one later critic noted, "Unintentionally funny delinquent picture that has developed something of a cult following in recent years."

The Frozen Dead
Warner Brothers–Seven Arts, 1967

Cast: Dana Andrews (Dr. Norberg); Anna Palk (Jean Norberg); Philip Gilbert (Dr. Ted Roberts); Kathleen Breck (Elsa Tenney); Karel Stepanek (General Lubeck); Basil Henson (Dr. Tirpitz); Alan Tilvern (Karl Essen); Anne Tirard (Mrs. Schmidt); Edward Fox (Norberg's Brother); Oliver MacGreevy (Joseph the Butler); Tom Chatto (Inspector Witt); John Moore (Bailey the Stationmaster); Charles Wade (Alfie the Porter).

Credits: Robert Goldstein (Executive Producer); Herbert J. Leder (Producer-Director-Screenplay); Tom Sachs (Associate Producer); Davis Boulton (Cinematography); Don Banks (Music); Scott MacGregor (Art Direction); Mary Gibson (Wardrobe); Eric Carter (Makeup); Douglas Hermes (Assistant Director); Jim Roddan (Sound); Tom Simpson (Editor). Running time: 95 minutes

Twenty years after the end of World War II, insane German scientist Dr. Norberg (Dana Andrews) attempts to resurrect the Third Reich by thawing out a small army of Nazis, who were voluntarily frozen when Hitler was defeated. Secluded now in his English countryside retreat, Norberg conducts defrosting experiments that prove successful; the soldiers, who have been stored in a deep freeze locker, soon regain their ability to move, but unfortunately their brains do not function correctly. In a desperate attempt to rectify the problem, his colleague Karl cuts the head off Elsa, a visiting female friend of Norberg's niece, Jean. Resigned to this brutal murder, which was committed without his knowledge, Norberg carries on with his experiment by attaching the head to some electrical apparatus in the hope that Elsa's telepathic powers will help them gain control of the zombie men. To explain away the disappearance of the young girl, Norberg tells his niece that she left with little notice on the early morning train. Unfortunately for Norberg and some visiting Nazi bigwigs, Elsa

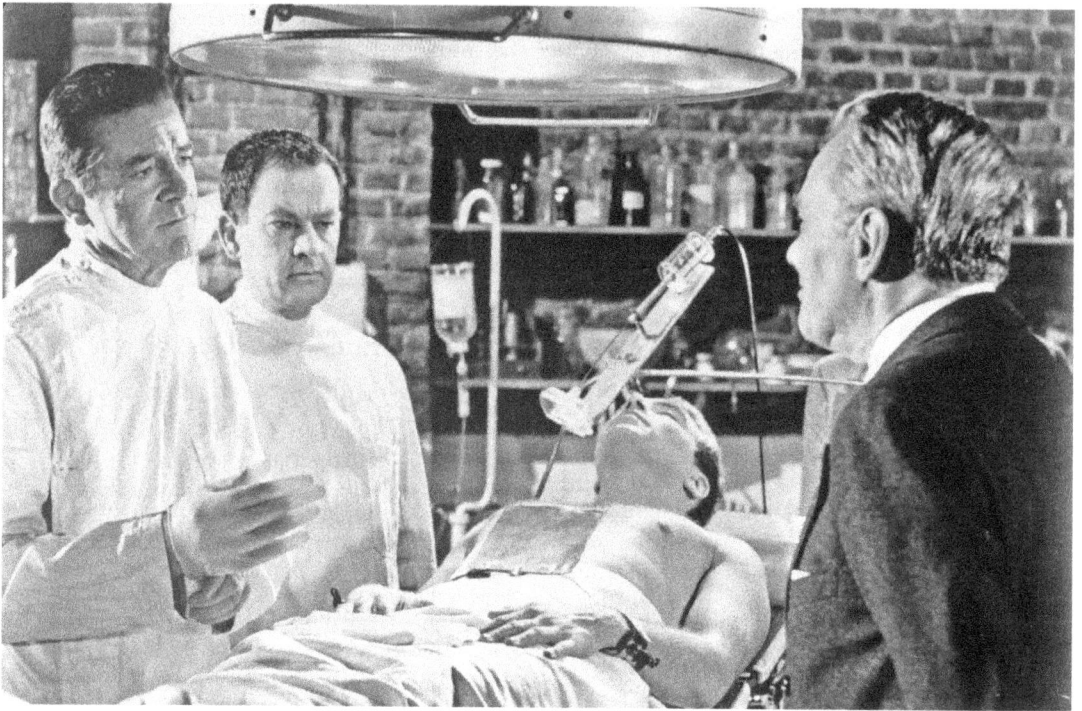

Under the watchful eye of General Lubeck (Karel Stepanek, right), Dr. Norberg (Andrews) and his assistant Karl Essen (Alan Tilvern) make another attempt to resurrect the Third Reich in *The Frozen Dead* (Warner Bros., 1967).

refuses to cooperate in the experiments, instead using her telepathic powers to mobilize a wall of disembodied arms which strangle the Nazis to death.

Tagline: "Frozen alive for 20 years! Now they return from their icy graves to seek vengeance."

If Nazis on ice and a dismembered talking head, cut the mustard for you, then you're in for a treat with this offering. Personally, I prefer my Nazis at the receiving end of Audie Murphy's rifle butt; and as for talking heads, they're okay as long as Steve Martin features somewhere in the plot. But let's see what Andrews got up to in England in 1967 when the bankroll must have been looking a bit thin.

As well as producing, Herbert J. Leder also directed and wrote the screenplay for *The Frozen Dead,* which appeared on a double bill with his other low-budget horror offering for 1967, *It!,* starring Roddy McDowall. Formerly a college professor, Leder produced *The Loretta Young Show* and wrote the screenplay for the classic sci-fi horror *Fiend Without a Face* (1958).

A Gold Star Production, *The Frozen Dead* was shot in England in Eastman Color, but did the American circuits in black and white. Cashing in on the popularity of bizarre horror flicks in the '60s, the film plays like a combination of *Revenge of the Zombies* (1943), *Donovan's Brain* (1953), *The Brain That Wouldn't Die* (1963) and *They Saved Hitler's Brain* (1963). So, disengage your own brain and enjoy, for this is the type of film that readily qualifies for one of those "it's so bad, it's actually good" awards. With this one in the can, Andrews's career had clearly been seen both ends of the spectrum from the multi–Oscar winning *The Best Years of Our Lives* to *The Frozen Dead* in a little over 30 years.

However, when it comes to having at least one trashy '60s–'70s horror flick on your CV, Andrews was at least in good company. Remember Bette Davis in *The Anniversary* (1968), Joan Crawford in *Trog* (1970) and *I Saw What You Did* (1965), Laurence Harvey in *Welcome to Arrow Beach* (1974) and of course the best of all, Ray Milland in *The Thing with Two Heads* (1972)?

As the story evolves, it is quite evident that

Andrews's character, Dr. Norberg, is every bit as tragic as Baron Frankenstein in his attempts to breathe new life into human Popsicles. At first sight this might appear as a dreadful piece of miscasting, but it is not necessarily so, because playing disillusioned, rather tragic characters was by now second nature to Andrews. However, his performance is marred by having to speak with a German accent and the low production values of the film.

Although Norbeg's actions cannot be condoned, it is quite clear that the real villain of the piece is his assistant Karl, played by the British character actor Alan Tilvern, who towards the end of his career appeared in *Who Framed Roger Rabbit* (1988) as cartoon producer R.K. Maroon.

Andrews was also ably supported by convent-educated Anna Palk, playing his niece Jean, and Canadian actor Philip Gilbert as Dr. Ted Roberts. The eagle-eyed out will spot a young Edward Fox as one of the zombies in the basement. Six years later, he would go on to make his mark in the excellent thriller *Day of the Jackal* (1973).

Notwithstanding its low budget, the film does have some memorable scenes, particularly the wall of severed, electronically operated arms and the disembodied head which is shot to chilling effect in a sinister blue-green light. Kathleen Breck's performance as the head is particularly noteworthy, fully conveying the agony and helplessness of the character (definitely Oscar potential). The climactic scene showing Norberg's death at the hands of his own creation hits the right notes, but the only image that will linger in the mind long after the credits have gone, is that of the severed head whispering the chilling words, "Bury me." As final words go, they are definitely up there with David Hedison's heart-rending "Help meeee! Help meeee!" from *The Fly* (1958).

A detached head uttering "Bury me" is certainly a difficult act to top, but Andrews manfully does his best with the poor script. With the Nazi bigwigs eager for results, Norberg has to explain to them that the human brain is a little more complicated than that of a frog, and after shrugging off these dummkopfs for the time being, he gets back to the lab to devise the next Martell Christmas toy for budding young scientists, boasting, "I plan to keep an ape's head alive. I will remove the skull and replace it with one that is plastic and transparent. Then I can study the brain's functions in detail."

The *New York Times* commented, "The key role of the doctor — not a Nazi fanatic but simply a fatherland patriot — is played by Dana Andrews. He grapples with a guttural accent manfully, professionally and sadly."

When making *Crack in the World* Andrews rose to the challenge of playing his first mad scientist, but with *The Frozen Dead* it appears that he was simply going through the motions, and one gets the impression that he was possibly thinking, "Sure I know it sucks, but they can't all be *Best Years.*"

Il cobra (Cobra)
American International, 1968

Credits: Dana Andrews (Captain Kelly); Peter Martell (Mike Rand); Elisa Montes (Corinne); Anita Ekberg (Lou); Jesus Puente (Stiarkos); Peter Dane (Hullinger); Luciana Vincenzi (Ulla); George Eastman (Crane); Omar Zolficar (Sadek); Giovanni Petrucci (King); Ehsane Sadek Karter (Gamel); Guido Lollobrigida (Killer); Jacques Stany (Journalist Agency Man); E. Chang (Li Fang); Claudio Ruffini (U.S. Agent); Pietro Torrisi (Cobra Gang Member); Conrado San Martin, Lidia Biondi, Aldo Cecconi, Franco De Rosa.
Credits: Fulvio Lucisano (Producer); Mario Sequi (Director); Adriano Bolzoni (Story); Cumersindo Mollo (Screenplay); Enrique Toran, Claudio Racca (Cinematography); Anton Garcia Abril (Music); Stefano Rolla (Assistant Director); Pedro del Ray (Editor). Running time: 93 minutes

When a member of the American Secret Service is murdered by the operatives of an international drug smuggling gang headed by "The Cobra," her brother, ex–CIA agent Mike Rand, is brought into the case. Although Rand was initially dismissed from the Service for gross insubordination, Chief Kelly (Dana Andrews) believes he is the only man for the job. As a team, the two set off around the world to track down "The Cobra," who wears a black nylon mask to protect his identity. Along the way they enlist the help of the amorous Lou, a junkie who runs a women's spa. In Beirut, they encounter Stiarkos, a night club owner (who is really The Cobra) and his crazy Chinese sidekick. From a coded Chrysanthemum chart, which is revealed at this encounter, the agents learn that the drugs are being smuggled in from China, dropped into

Keeping in the thick of the action, Secret Service chief Kelly (Andrews) joins Mike Rand (Peter Martell, center) and Lou (Anita Ekberg) in *The Cobra* (American International, 1968).

Beirut by parachute and then shipped to America. Captain Kelly believes that it is vital that the trade is stopped because it is really a fiendish Red Chinese plot to control the minds of the world's youth through the use of heroin. After much flexing of muscles and bullet-dodging, "The Cobra" is finally unmasked in Istanbul and the drug ring is smashed. Rand decides to stay in Istanbul and sample its delights, after turning down Kelly's offer to return to his job on a full-time basis.

Taglines: "Danger, Dames and Sudden Death! These are the fangs of the Cobra"; "With Guts and a Gun and a Babe for Bait he laid a trap for the Cobra."

With attention-grabbing lines such as these, who could fail to get excited? Alas, as with many of these '60s Euro spy movies, the shoestring budget, dodgy music, cardboard acting, dubbed dialogue, poor editing, and faded color tend to

make them an acquired taste these days. But if you're in the right frame of mind they can still be a barrel of laughs.

Andrews turns in another respectable performance as a Service head (what else?) and this time he's joined by "action man" Peter Mandell who cropped up in many spaghetti westerns. Mandell didn't comfortably fit into the spy genre, with one reviewer describing him as a swarthy brute with John Wayne delivery, who is always getting the gun kicked out of his hand.[1] Perhaps to make up for this, the multi-national producers pulled in good old reliable Andrews and Sweden's top heavy Anita Ekberg, who delighted audiences by cavorting in Rome's Trevi fountain in Fellini's *La dolce vita* (1960). For the most part, the film roles that came Ekberg's way provided little opportunity to develop her acting skills—and *The Cobra* was no exception. After a stint of modeling, Ekberg signed a contract with RKO where she claimed that Howard Hughes wanted to marry her (was there a female that he didn't use the old marriage line on?). Russ Meyer described her as the most beautiful woman he had ever photographed, and with her 39DD breasts she easily dwarfed her biggest rivals Jayne Mansfield and Sabrina.

Il cobra was an Italo-Spanish co-production which continued the European trend of using American stars to improve its international market. Stylishly directed by Mario Sequi, the film is very much in the spy mold, but occasionally drifts into the gangster genre. Typically, many locations are used to drum up international intrigue, which was usually associated with countries with an uncertain future — China, Lebanon and Istanbul in this instance. To keep a tight rein on the budget, many of these locations were reconstructed in the studio.

Despite being one year off 60, Andrews still gets involved in many of the film's action scenes; firmly at the controls of a helicopter one minute (without a hint of a flying hang-up) and shooting it out with the bad guys, in the next. Taking a breather in between deadly encounters, his Captain Kelly warns us of the Chinese plan to flood the market with opium which will destroy the moral fiber of our nation: "The future of our country and the whole free world is at stake," he declares. But when the going gets tough, the tough get going, with Rand and Kelly working in perfect harmony to rid the world of the evil Cobra. Keeping in the thick of it, Kelly is on hand to unmask the archvillain in the final reel, to reveal a character that will have you yelling "Who the hell is he?" Despite indulging our appetite for "Danger, Dames, and Sudden Death," those pesky scriptwriters made the classic mistake of giving the real face behind the Cobra precious little screen time to register with the audience. But who cares? You made it to the end, so give yourself a well deserved slap on the back. And as for Andrews, he may well have had reason to smile, for *Il Cobra* marked the end of his '60s Euro-trash excursion.

The Devil's Brigade
United Artists, 1968

Cast: William Holden (Lt. Col. Robert T. Frederick); Cliff Robertson (Maj. Alan Crown); Vince Edwards (Maj. Cliff Bricker); Michael Rennie (Lt. Gen. Mark Clark); Dana Andrews (Brigadier General Walter Naylor); Andrew Prine (Pvt. Theodore Ransom); Gretchen Wyler (Lady of Joy); Jeremy Slate (Sgt. Maj. Patrick O'Neill); Claude Akins (Pvt. "Rocky" Rockman); Jack Watson (Cpl. Wilfrid Peacock); Richard Jaeckel (Pvt. Omar Greco); Bill Fletcher (Pvt. "Bronc" Guthrie); Richard Dawson (Pvt. Hugh MacDonald); Tom Troupe (Pvt. Al Manella); Luke Askew (Pvt. Hubert Hixon); Jean-Paul Vignon (Pvt. Henri Laurent); Tom Stern (Capt. Cardwell); Harry Carey, Jr. (Capt. Rose); Carroll O'-Connor (Maj. Gen Hunter); Norman Alden (MP Lieutenant); Don Megowan (Luke Phelan); David Pritchard (Corp. Coker); Paul Busch (German Captain); Patric Knowles (Lord Louis Mountbatten); James Craig (American General); Wilhelm von Homburg (Fritz); Paul Hornung (Lumberjack); Gene Fullmer (Bartender); Maggie Thrett (Millie); Rita Rogers (Miss Kliensmidt); Alix Talton (Gen. Cullen's Secretary).

Credits: David L. Wolper (Producer); Theodore Strauss, Julian Ludwig (Associate Producers); Andrew V. McLaglen (Director); Robert H. Adleman, Colonel George Walton (Story); William Roberts (Screenplay); William H. Clothier (Cinematography); Alex North (Music); Al Sweeney, Jr. (Art Direction); Morris Hoffman (Set Decorations); Ed Lossman, Gene Martin, Ted Tetrick (Wardrobe); Donald W. Robertson (Makeup); Logan Frazee (Special Effects); Terry Morse, Jr., Newt Arnold, Dennis Donnelly (Assistant Directors); Al Overton, Clem Portman (Sound); Jack K. Tillar (Music Editor); William Cartwright (Editor). Running time: 131 minutes

In this war tale adapted from a factual account, a Special Service force is created in the early days of World War II for the purpose of engaging the Germans in Norway through commando raids, in the hope of diverting their attention until American troops enter the war. The force, made up of Canadian soldiers and American GIs, is led by pen-pusher Lieutenant Colonel Robert T. Frederick in his first field command. Overseeing operations at HQ are Brigadier General Walter Naylor (Dana Andrews), Lieutenant General Mark Clark and Major General Hunter. The efficient, well-trained Canadians are headed by Major Alan Crown while their American counterparts (mainly Army misfits just out of military jail) come under the command of Major Cliff Bricker. After an initial period of conflict between the two groups, Frederick turns them into a well-disciplined fighting force. With the men ready for action, Frederick is informed, much to his disappointment, that the Norway mission

Brig. Gen. Walter Naylor (Andrews, right) gives friend and fellow officer Lt. Col. Robert T. Frederick (William Holden) some helpful advice in *The Devil's Brigade* (United Artists, 1968).

has been cancelled. After Frederick appeals to Washington, and impressing Major General Hunter with his confidence and determination, the brigade is given another equally dangerous assignment: patrolling the German lines in southern Italy. In this role they capture an enemy village and are then given the seemingly impossible mission of taking a fortified mountain position. Scaling the mountain, the men overthrow the enemy, but sustain heavy losses along the way, among them Major Crown. As a mark of respect, the men are designated "The Devil's Brigade."

Tagline: "What they did to each other was nothing compared to what they did to the enemy!"

Normally associated with westerns and adventure films, director Andrew V. McLaglen (son of Victor) made his first major foray into the epic war genre with *The Devil's Brigade*. Andrews had little to do in the film, but it did give him an-

other opportunity to don the general's outfit before finally sending it back to wardrobe. Unlike his senior ranking officers from his other war epics (*Battle of the Bulge* and *In Harm's Way*) Andrews's Brigadier General Walter Naylor is quite a likable character, fully prepared to support William Holden's junior officer, even though at times he is exasperated by his friend's stubbornness: "Why do I help you ? Why do I bother even talking to you ? It's your funeral, Bob — enjoy it!"

Of all the stars with whom Andrews had worked over the years, leading man William Holden was perhaps the closest to his own screen character, in that both men played a series of roles that combined their square-jawed good looks with a world-weary, cynical detachment. However, whereas Andrews made his most notable films in the 1940s, Holden (affectionately known as "The Golden Boy") had to wait until the 1950s before really making his mark. And what a legacy he left behind — *Sunset Blvd.* (1950), *Stalag 17* (1953), for which he won an Oscar, *The Bridge on the River Kwai* (1957) and *The Wild Bunch* (1969).

Andrews once described Holden as "a very fine actor and a very charming man, one of the top men in the business." He clearly acknowledged that Holden's star appeal had outstripped his own in the 1950s, which prompted him to further comment, "If I had played in *The Bridge on the River Kwai* the part Bill Holden played, I think the picture would have been less box office than it was, because at the time he played, Bill Holden was at the top."[1] In common with Andrews and many other veteran actors of that period, Holden suffered from a drinking problem which led to his untimely death in 1981, following a fall while intoxicated.

Although Holden heads the all-star cast, the real acting honors go to Cliff Robertson as Canadian career soldier Major Brown and Vince Edwards as his witty American counterpart Major Bricker. Edwards, a potential Olympic swimmer before an appendectomy operation cut short that career, became a household name in the 1960s as the confrontational young doctor in the *Ben Casey* television series. In supporting roles, Jack Watson and Claude Akins are also impressive as warring rivals who eventually become close friends after they team for a good old-fashioned barroom punch-up with some obliging lumberjacks.

Although *The Devil's Brigade* throws out clichés by the dozen, it is nonetheless an entertaining war film. Unlike *The Dirty Dozen* (1967), with which it is sometimes unfairly compared, it actually has some basis in fact. The Devil's Brigade, or the First Special Service Force (FSSF) as it was officially known, was an elite unit of Canadians and Americans formed in 1942 to work behind enemy lines as saboteurs. Churchill called the Force's leader, U.S. Major General Robert Frederick (Holden's character), "the greatest fighting general of all time." The force's nickname "Devil's Brigade" was inspired by the blackened faces of the members when they were on patrols and in action. The film is memorable because it shows the influence the Canadian army had on the formation of such an elite fighting unit. Unfortunately, the film came out during the Vietnam War when war films were out of vogue.

The film has some impressive scenery as it was shot near the actual battle site in Italy and in the mountains of Utah. Like many films shot in Europe at the time, it made full use of the armed forces and World War II equipment which countries such as Spain, Italy and Austria were more than willing to rent out. In Utah, the film received the assistance of the National Guard, who bulldozed a road to the mountain used in recreating the actual assault and helped in the construction of the fortress.[2]

Despite the film's entertainment value, the reviews were generally negative. The *New York Times* noted, "You have a pretty good idea of the predictability of all the confrontations when you hear a German officer say evilly of a Yank prisoner 'Maybe he can be persvaded.'" *Time* commented: "After nearly three decades of World War II films, it is hardly surprising that Hollywood is beginning to suffer from combat fatigue." *Variety* called it "[a]n uneven combination of the worst of *The Dirty Dozen* and the best of *What Price Glory*.... Strong production values and a few good performances will maintain some audience interest."

Innocent Bystanders

Paramount, 1972

Cast: Stanley Baker (John Craig); Geraldine Chaplin (Miriam Loman); Dana Andrews (Blake); Donald Pleasence (Loomis); Sue Lloyd (Joanna Benson); Derren Nesbitt (Andrew Royce): Vladek Sheybal (Aaron Kaplan); Warren Mitchell (Omar); Cec Linder (Mankowitz); Howard Goorney (Zimmer); J.G. Devlin (Waiter); Ferdy Mayne (Marcus Kaplan); Clifton Jones (Hetherton); John Collin (Asimov); Aharon Ipale (Gabrilovitch); Yuri Borionko, Tom Bowman (Guards); Cliff Diggings (Harry Bigelow); Frank Maher (Daniel); Michael Poole (Zheikov).

Credits: George H. Brown (Producer); Peter Collinson (Director); James Mitchell (Story & Screenplay); James Munroe (Novel); Brian Probyn (Cinematography); John Keating (Music); Maurice Carter (Art Direction); Laura Nightingale (Wardrobe); Wally Schneiderman (Makeup); Pat Moore (Special Effects); Clive Reed (Assistant Director); Gordon K. McCallum, Bill Daniels (Sound); Alan Pattillo (Editor). Running time: 111 minutes

Burnt-out British espionage agent John Craig is assigned one last mission; to track down and capture eminent Russian scientist Aaron Kaplan, who has escaped from a Siberian prison. With the suspicion that Kaplan was allowed to escape

Ruthless British spy chief Loomis (Donald Pleasence, left) meets his match with American spy chief Blake (Andrews) in *The Innocent Bystanders* (Paramount, 1972).

in order to spy on the West, Craig has to make the difficult choice whether to bring in the scientist or to kill him. As the action unfolds, Craig's travels take him to London, New York and Turkey, where he comes in contact with several characters who are possibly double agents: American spy chief Blake (Dana Andrews), Turkish innkeeper Omar, the mysterious Miriam Loman, and fellow spies Royce and Joanna Benson.

Tagline: "You don't turn your back on anyone. Especially the partner who's backing you up."

And they're not kidding, with more double-crosses and triple-crosses in this spy romp than you can shake a stick at. And if Stanley Baker's bushy mustache gives you the faint impression, at times, that you are watching a '70s porn flick don't worry, it will pass.

James Mitchell's fast-paced screenplay (based on a novel by James Munroe) was given a realistic feel under Peter Collinson's taut direction.

Although Collinson's personal style was ill-defined, it certainly displayed originality, with *The Penthouse* (1967), *Up the Junction* (1967) and *The Long Day's Dying* (1968) to his credit.

In *Innocent Bystanders*, Andrews found himself working with the crème da la crème of British film and television actors. Welsh actor and film producer Stanley Baker was one of the few British actors then capable of slugging it out with the best of the U.S. crop on the tough guy front. With his strong build, commanding presence and natural ability to play both heroes and villains, he was perhaps Britain's equivalent to U.S. tough guy Robert Ryan. Equally impressive in supporting roles are TV stalwart Warren Mitchell, everyone's favorite psycho villain Derren Nesbitt, and two memorable characters from the 007 stable, Vladek Sheybval from *From Russia with Love* (1963) and Donald Pleasence from *You Only Live Twice* (1967).

The girls were also solidly represented by the versatile Geraldine Chaplin (Charlie's daughter) and an English model turned actress, glamorous Sue Lloyd, who kept many a pulse racing as the sexy Cordelia Winfeld, alongside Andrews's younger brother Steve Forrest, in the cult 1960s TV show *The Baron.*

The film marked Andrews's last foray into the murky world of the spy genre. And having played a good guy on each prior occasion, it was fitting that he should bow out of the genre playing a cold and merciless character. Head of the American Secret Service, his Blake is as sinister as his British counterpart Loomis, expertly hammed by the king of British villains, he of the fixed hypnotic gaze — Donald Pleasence.

Competing for character cliché of the year, their early scene together in a private gentleman's club is a belter, with Pleasence turning his nose up in complete disgust when our Andrews asks for a martini. This utterly disdainful look is magnificently matched by Andrews's indignant expression when he is instead offered a sherry. A sequel focusing on just these two characters would have been a beaut — not so much "The Odd Couple," but more a case of "The Deadly Duo."

In a press release, Baker commented that he felt that his role was a strong, important one because it revealed the foolishness of society in regarding middle-aged men as being over the hill: "This film is going to do a lot for the ego of the over-forties, and it should teach the youngsters a lot, too."[1] (What? Like how to kill someone with one karate chop, without flinching, super-spy style?)

At this point in his life, Andrews was making regular trips to Washington to work with the Secretary of Transportation in his campaign against drunk driving, appearing in commercials where he freely discussed his struggle to get away from the bottle. So in the same press release, Andrews candidly discussed his battle with the John Barleycorn: "You've got to have been over the brink, to the point of total self-destruction, before you can really find within yourself the strength to solve your own drink problem.... The drinking problem haunted me all during my starring years in the '40s and '50s and it almost destroyed me and ruined my career."[2]

Geraldine Chaplin described *Innocent Bystanders* as a "slam bang spy thriller in the tradition of James Bond." Although the film was clearly another variation on the well-trodden 007 theme, it arrived too late to breathe any new life into the espionage genre; 1972 audiences had grown weary of war, double agents, traitors and international unrest. The film indulged in a certain amount of violence and sex, but neither was explicitly exploited, with much being left to the imagination. As Collison himself put it, "Our intent is to have the first fully violent, bloodless film."

In the press release, Geraldine commented upon a sado-masochistic scene in the film where she is roughly interrogated by Nesbitt's character: "I was suspended from an iron stable and was stiff all over for days."[3]

Andrews's character Blake shows that he is not above using rough stuff when he interrogates Craig with the threat of electric shock treatment, mercilessly commenting, "Do yourself a favor, Craig. Eunuchs make lousy heroes."

As part of the film's promotion, Andrews's contribution to cinema was saluted through a special newspaper, radio and TV contest which acknowledged his place as one of Hollywood's most versatile and durable actors having portrayed an amazing variety of characters throughout his career — army generals, detectives, big game hunters, adventurers, western heroes, slick Madison Avenue executives and brilliant scientists. To win a free pass to *Innocent Bystanders*, readers were asked to fill in the missing word in a list of ten of Andrews' s most famous films.[4]

1. The ... Incident
2. The Best ... of Our Lives
3. A Walk in the ...
4. Strange ... in Town
5. My Foolish ....
6. ... in the Desert
7. The ... One
8. ... in the World
9. ... Bystanders (this one had me stumped)
10. The ... Day

I bet you were scratching your heads to number 10, their answer being *The Longest Day*— which Andrews didn't appear in, unless he was disguised as a tree or took the part of an uncredited German storm trooper (or perhaps John Wayne's shadow).

Although *Innocent Bystanders* is well-paced, the labyrinth of double-crossing and constant scene shifts between many colorful locations in Europe and America tended to make the story hard to follow. Viewers' reaction to the film was summed up by the *New York Daily News*: "It will keep the uncritical intrigued for a while."

The *New York Times* had seen it all before: "Almost everything in the movie seems to come from some other movie—from *One Day in the Life of Ivan Denisovich*, from a whole generation of hard-nosed disillusioned spy films, perhaps even from *North by Northwest* with its own elusive Mr. Kaplan." A *Films and Filming* critic opined, "When a project is connected in cinematic terms, and graced with a first rate team of actors, as in *Innocent Bystanders*, the effect makes for taut and gripping entertainment."

Having successfully completed his assignment, Craig (Baker) sends Miriam (Chaplin) away because Innocent Bystanders have no place in his kind of world; they simply get hurt. Hence the title.

Airport 1975

Universal, 1974

Cast: Charlton Heston (Alan Murdock); Karen Black (Nancy Pryor); George Kennedy (Joe Patroni); Gloria Swanson (Herself); Efrem Zimbalist, Jr. (Captain Stacy); Susan Clark (Helen Patroni); Helen Reddy (Sister Ruth); Linda Blair (Janice Abbott); Dana Andrews (Scott Freeman); Roy Thinnes (Urias); Sid Caesar (Barney); Myrna Loy (Mrs. Devaney); Ed Nelson (Major John Alexander); Nancy Olson (Mrs. Abbott); Larry Storch (Glenn Purcell); Martha Scott (Sister Beatrice); Jerry Stiller (Sam); Norman Fell (Bill); Conrad Janis (Arnie); Beverly Garland (Mrs. Scott Freeman); Linda Harrison (Winnie); Guy Stockwell (Colonel Moss); Erik Estrada (Julio); Kip Niven (Lieutenant Thatcher); Charles White (Fat Man); Brian Morrison (Joseph Patroni, Jr.); Amy Farrell (Amy); Irene Tsu (Carol); Ken Sansom (Gary); Alan Fudge (Danton); Christopher Norris (Bette); Austin Stoker (Air Force Sergeant); John Lupton (Oringer); Gene Dynarski (Friend); Aldine King (Aldine); Sharon Gless (Sharon); Laurette Spang (Arlene).

Credits: Jennings Lang (Executive Producer); William Frye (Producer); Jack Smight (Director); Inspired by the film *Airport* which was based on the Arthur Hailey novel; Don Ingalls (Screenplay); Philip H. Lathrop (Cinematography); John Cacavas (Music); Helen Reddy, R. Burton (Songs); George C. Webb (Art Direction); Mickey S. Michaels (Set Decorations); Edith Head (Costumes); Ben McMahon (Special Effects); Alan Crosland, Jr. (Assistant Director); Joe Canutt (Stunt Coordinator); Roger Sword, James Troutman, Melvin M. Metcalfe, Sr., Robert Hoyt (Sound); J. Terry Williams (Editor). Running time: 107 minutes

When a 747 is diverted from Los Angeles airport to Salt Lake City due to adverse weather conditions, it collides with a small private plane piloted by business executive Scott Freeman (Dana Andrews). (Just moments before the collision, Freeman suffered a heart attack and with his hands locked on the controls the plane rapidly ascended into the nose of the jumbo's flight deck.) Freeman is killed instantly, as are the 747's steward, co-pilot, and navigator; the pilot, Captain Stacy, is blinded. Head stewardess Nancy takes over the controls, guided by instructions from the tower. On the ground, the airline's president Joe Patroni and Nancy's fiancé, former jet pilot Alan Murdock, try to devise a rescue plan. As the tension racks up, the spotlight falls on the fears and thoughts of the passengers, among them Patroni's wife and son, singing nun Sister Ruth, Mrs. Abbott and her ailing daughter Susan, inebriated old lady Mrs. Devaney, non-stop talker Barney and old movie star Gloria Swanson. Patroni and Murdock decide to attempt the seemingly impossible feat of lowering a pilot into the plane via the hole using a jet helicopter. Major John Alexander volunteers for the mission and is nearly successful before part of the plane catches his tether release, and he plummets to his death. Watching helplessly in the rescue helicopter, Murdock ignores Patroni's orders and attempts the mid-air transfer himself. The second attempt is successful and Murdock lands the plane safely, much to the relief of all concerned.

Taglines: "Something hit us.... The crew is dead.... Help us, please, please help us!"; "Star-studded cast trapped in a plunging airplane.... And only a death-defying rescue mission can save them!"; "ALL NEW screen excitement inspired by the novel *Airport* by Arthur Hailey"; "A mid-air collision leaves a 747 without a pilot...."

Cliché-riddled, hammy and corny, without doubt, but one can't deny *Airport 1975*, its pure-camp entertainment value. It was the first of three sequels to the successful 1970 hit *Airport* (followed by *Airport '77* and *The Concorde: Airport '79*), and also completed Andrews's airplane disaster trilogy (after *Zero Hour!* and *The Crowded Sky*). Not a single miniature airplane model was used in the film. All stunts involving the aircraft were real, entailing some daring and spectacular stunt work above the Rockies by flamboyant stunt man Joe Canutt.[1]

In time-honored disaster movie fashion, the film crammed in as many Hollywood veterans and '70s stars as possible. The master of the epic disaster genre, Charlton Heston, topped the star-studded cast, proving once again that he was the perfect selection for any crisis situation. To get into character, Heston practiced flying a 747 in an American Airlines simulator before actually taking the controls of an airborne 747 for an hour and a half.[2] (I wonder if Myrna Loy got repeatedly sozzled to get herself into character.)

After nearly a 30-year gap, the film reunited Andrews with *Best Years of Our Lives* co-star, the ever-glamorous Myrna Loy; she was sadly wasted in the film playing a passenger with a drinking problem. Although it was good to see them together on the castlist, they shared no scenes; apart from their being on different planes, Andrews made one of his earliest film exits when his plane collides with the 747 in the first reel.

You just instinctively know that when a U.S. salesman has to make that vitally important trip to clinch the deal that you're in for a one-way ride, and Andrews's Scott Freeman is no exception. (If he'd gone by train, he probably would have been thrown together with an insufferable traveling companion, or if by automobile, he'd more than likely be the hapless guy with the faceless psychotic trucker on his tail.) Concerned that he might be flying into trouble, his wife asks him over the phone to cancel his business meeting. But our Scott is clearly having none of that. With nearly six months' sales commissions at stake, he tells her "No way. These guys only come out once a year. I'll find a hole in this weather and be there as soon as I can."

Unfortunately, Andrews makes his exit from the film before he can get in on the act with some of the great one-liners that come our way. When Bill asks Joe Patroni how much damage the collision caused, he barks back, "Oh, not a great deal — there's just a big hole where the pilots usually sit." And by the time you've put your false teeth back in, they're at it again, when one of the passengers pipes up, "You mean the stewardess is flying the plane?"

The film reunited Andrews with Efrem Zimbalist, Jr., who took the part of the 747 pilot blinded by the impact. In their first airborne encounter in *The Crowded Sky*, Zimbalist's jet fighter was on a collision course with Andrews's commercial passenger plane.

Helen Reddy took the part of a singing nun*; Linda Blair (of *Exorcist* fame) played a child in need of a kidney transplant; and Gloria Swanson spoofed herself as an aging silent film star. This was Swanson's first film in 22 years; it also turned out to be her last. Huffing and puffing throughout the proceedings was another old reliable, George Kennedy, as ground controller Joe Patroni. Kennedy certainly made his mark in the role, appearing in all four of the *Airport* films.

Despite the high production values and all-star cast, executive producer Jennings Lang managed to keep the production cost at less than $3,000,000, mainly by hiring television technicians to work on the film. Don Ingalls' script was initially earmarked for Universal's television division, but Lang was confident it had the makings of a feature film. Although the critics gave the film a rough time on its release, it proved popular with audiences, grossing $25 million for Universal.

In a tragic coincidence, the Beech Baron light aircraft that Andrews flew to his doom in the film was involved in a real-life mid-air collision in 1989, which resulted in the death of both pilots.

Take a Hard Ride
20th Century–Fox, 1975

Cast: Jim Brown (Pike); Lee Van Cleef (Kiefer); Fred Williamson (Tyree); Catherine Spaak (Catherine); Jim Kelly (Kashtok); Dana Andrews (Morgan); Barry Sullivan (Kane); Harry Carey, Jr. (Dumper); Robert Donner (Skave); Charles McGregor (Cloyd); Leonard Smith (Cangey); Ronald Howard (Halsey); Ricardo Palacios (Calvera); Buddy Joe Hooker (Angel); Robin Levitt (Chico).

Credits: Harry Bernsen (Producer); Antonio Margheriti [as Anthony M. Dawson] (Director); Eric Bercovici, Jerry L. Ludwig (Screenplay); Riccardo Pallotini (Cinematography); Jerry Goldsmith (Music); Julio Molina (Art Direction); Carmen Martin (Makeup); Luciano D'Achille, Antonio Molina (Special Effects); Scott Maitland, Pepe Lopez Rodero (Assistant Directors); Juan Majan, Hal Needham (Stunts); Francisco Ardura (Production Manager); Theodore Soderberg, Jim Willis (Sound); Kenneth

---

*Reddy was nominated for a 1975 Golden Globe for Most Promising Newcomer (must have been a lean year for that kinda stuff).

Hall (Music Editor); Dennis Moscher (Assistant Editor); Stanford C. Allen (Editor). Running time: 103 minutes

Honest black wrangler Pike promises his dying boss Morgan (Dana Andrews) that he will deliver the $86,000 from Morgan's last cattle drive to his widow and the families to whom it belongs. En route to Mexico, Pike is joined by mute kung fu-fighting Indian scout Kashtok and laconic black gambler Tyree, who has other plans for the money. As they trek across hundreds of miles of western wilderness, they are pursued by an army of thieves, including callous bounty hunter Kiefer and corrupt Sheriff Kane. In an uneasy alliance the trio fend off numerous attempts on their lives before they reach the end of the trail, where there is a face-to-face confrontation between Pike and Tyree.

Taglines: "It Rides with the Great Westerns"; "The West has never seen a team like this or the hunt that aims to destroy them!"

Take a Hard Ride was one of the last spaghetti westerns, arriving in the mid–'70s when big-screen westerns were generally on the decline. The film tried to squeeze one last drop out of the genre by also cashing in on the popularity of blaxploitation and kung fu films. Steely-eyed Lee Van Cleef provided the spaghetti angle, Jim Brown, Fred Williamson and Jim Kelly the black and kung fu elements, with Andrews (in a cameo role) and fellow Hollywood legends Barry Sullivan and Harry Carey, Jr., contributed the more traditional western qualities.

Three of the leads were accomplished sportsmen before Hollywood beckoned. Brown and Williamson were famous football stars, while Kelly was an international middleweight karate champion. Brown announced his retirement from football when he starred in *The Dirty Dozen* (1967); he went on to star in several films with Williamson including 1974's *Three the Hard Way* with Jim Kelly and *One Down, Two to Go* (1982).

Like Andrews, Lee Van Cleef enjoyed a brief career as an accountant before he caught the acting bug. He achieved iconic status for his spaghetti westerns in the '60s (*For a Few Dollars More* and *the Good, the Bad and the Ugly*).

When it came to pulling a middle-aged, stony face, Andrews met his match with Barry Sullivan, who tended to portray tough, aggressive characters with a ruthless streak. Like Andrews, he enjoyed a long career, but more often than not

in supporting roles, most notably in *The Bad and the Beautiful* (1952).

The real television buffs out there will spot British actor Ronald Howard (son of Leslie Howard) as the crooked preacher — a far cry from his respectable portrayal of Sherlock Holmes in the 1954 television series.

Although Andrews had favorably acquitted himself in several European spy and crime exploitation films, *Take a Hard Ride* was his first and only foray into the realms of the spaghetti western, which pretty much completed his comprehensive repertoire of film genres. (The only one missing was the sexploitation genre, but Andrews fans had no worries on that account, as the actor was a strong opponent of needless sex and nudity on film.) As in *Airport 1975*, Andrews's character, Morgan, suffers a fatal heart attack, bringing his guest appearance to an abrupt end within the first ten minutes.

The Harry Bernsen production was shot on location in the Canary Islands and full use was made of the sumptuous scenery including a memorable gunfight in a canyon. Much of the pace and action in the film was down to the second unit director and stunt boss, Hal Needham, who went on to direct action films such as *Smokey and the Bandit*. The film also benefits from a great Jerry Goldsmith score.

In his Western encyclopedia, Herb Fagen wrote, "A cut above the average, the movie's major asset is an effective cast, mostly Americans, many of whom had come to depend on the Italian film market for their income."[1]

Some critics felt that the film was simply a series of set action pieces, thin on plot and short on character development. I entirely agree — but are these not the classic ingredients of a spaghetti western, or am I missing the plot?

The Last Tycoon
Paramount, 1976

Cast: Robert De Niro (Monroe Stahr); Tony Curtis (Rodriguez); Robert Mitchum (Pat Brady); Jeanne Moreau (Didi); Jack Nicholson (Brimmer); Donald Pleasence (Boxley); Ray Milland (Fleishacker); Dana Andrews (Red Ridingwood); Ingrid Boulting (Kathleen Moore); Peter Strauss (Wylie); Theresa Russell (Cecilia Brady); Tige Andrews (Popolos); Morgan Farley (Marcus); John Carradine (Tour Guide); Jeff Corey (Doctor); Diane Shalet (Stahr's Secretary); Seymour Cassel (Seal Trainer); Anjelica

Huston (Edna); Bonnie Bartlett, Sharon Masters (Brady's Secretaries); Eric Christmas (Norman); Leslie Curtis (Mrs. Rodriguez); Lloyd Kino (Butler); Brendan Burns (Assistant Editor); Peggy Feury (Hairdresser); Betsy Jones-Moreland (Lady Writer); Patricia Singer (Girl on Beach).

Credits: Sam Spiegel (Producer); Elia Kazan (Director); F. Scott Fitzgerald (Unfinished Novel); Harold Pinter (Screenplay); Victor J. Kemper (Cinematography); Maurice Jarre (Music); Jack T. Collis (Art Direction); Jerry Wunderlich (Set Decorations); Anna Hill Johnstone, Anthea Sylbert (Costumes); Gary Liddiard (Makeup); Danny McCauley (Assistant Director); Barbara Fallick Marks, Ronald Poore, Robert M. Reitano, Winston Ryder, Dick Vorisek, Larry Jost (Sound); Henry Miller (Special Effects); Richard Marks (Editor). Running time: 122 minutes

Film director Red Ridingwood (Andrews) discusses his temperamental leading lady with studio boss Monroe Stahr (Robert De Niro) in Paramount's lavish 1976 film production of F. Scott Fitzgerald's unfinished novel *The Last Tycoon*.

A glimpse of 1930s Hollywood, loosely based on the career of MGM's "boy wonder," production chief Irving Thalberg. Tycoon Monroe Stahr is in a position of power at a major studio, juggling several productions and handling everyday crises with brilliant efficiency. Amidst the chaos that ensues after a small earthquake hits Los Angeles, Stahr catches sight of a girl, who reminds him of his dead wife. He is fixated on English beauty Kathleen Moore, and their romance becomes interwoven with the challenges and conflicts of running a studio and interacting with a number of characters: his friend and mentor, studio head Pat Brady; matinee idol Rodriguez, who is suffering a masculinity crisis; Fleishacker, a smart New York lawyer; Boxley, a highbrow screenwriter; Brimmer, a tough union organizer and communist agitator who comes west to plead the writers' cause; Brady's daughter Celia, who has her sights set on Stahr; and Red Ridingwood (Dana Andrews), an over-the-hill director replaced on a whim while filming his latest project, to satisfy the selfish temperament of pampered leading lady Didi.

As Stahr continues his affair with Moore, Brady becomes concerned that his protégé's obsession with the girl is at odds with his loyalties to the studio and he sides with the studio financiers and other board members in their quest to bring him down.

Tagline: "He has the power to make anyone's dream come true ... except his own."

The Last Tycoon provided Andrews with another opportunity to be part of the type of lavish, high-quality production he had enjoyed during his leading man days at Fox and Goldwyn in the 1940s. Based on F. Scott Fitzgerald's last, uncompleted novel, the story was a pet project of producer Sam Spiegel, who had been attempting to bring it to the screen for several years. Fitzgerald died in 1940 before finishing his portrait of 1930s Hollywood, which was based on his observations of the MGM studios and in particular film mogul Irving Thalberg, whose genius for filmmaking in the 1920s and '30s earned him the nickname "The Boy Wonder." The story was adapted by Nobel Prize–winning playwright Harold Pinter and direction was provided by Elia Kazan, who had earlier collaborated with Spiegel on the highly successful *On the Waterfront* (1954). Andrews worked with Kazan on the 1947 hit *Boomerang!*

The film provided a rare opportunity to contrast two of the greatest modern method actors of the day, De Niro and Jack Nicholson, with Hollywood legends Robert Mitchum, Tony Curtis, Andrews, Ray Milland and John Carradine.

"On paper," the film had everything going for it (a Fitzgerald story, Spiegel production, Pinter script, Kazan direction, De Niro as lead character and an awesome supporting cast), but the result from a box office perspective was a disappointment. In truth, both Pinter and Kazan were poor choices as neither was able to connect with the romantic spirit of Fitzgerald. It is also possible that Kazan was unable to give the film his best because his mother was terminally ill at the time of filming and he would rush to her side at every opportunity between scenes.[1] The lukewarm response was unfortunate for both Kazan and Spiegel, and neither made another film.

No one could fault De Niro's perfect performance in the film, which saw him at the peak of his career following his Oscar-winning work in *The Godfather II* (1974) and a nomination for *Taxi* (1976). Theresa Russell, in her debut role as Brady's daughter Celia, also made a strong impact. In contrast, model Ingrid Boulting (stepdaughter of English producer Roy Boulting) looks suitably ethereal as Stahr's mysterious English girlfriend, but had little to work with and made no lasting impression.

Mitchum's early career had certain parallels with Andrews's in that they had both fully established their acting credentials in 1945 as infantrymen in two of the great films about World War II, *A Walk in the Sun* (Andrews) and *The Story of G.I. Joe* (Mitchum). In the same period the two stars also reigned supreme in the realm of film noir with Mitchum's *Out of the Past* (1947) and Andrews's *Laura* ranking as two of the best of the '40s crop.

Even though Andrews's role as journeyman film director was minor, it helped to define the hard-nosed personality of the leading character, Monroe Stahr: The studio boss ruthlessly pulls Ridingwood off his current production in mid-take purely to keep the leading lady happy. There was little need for Andrews to use his photographic memory to learn his lines in this part, with the script simply requiring him to refer to his temperamental leading lady as a terrible bitch and Stahr as a bastard for replacing him with no notice. But if earning your spurs as an actor included a stint in an effeminate role, Andrews received his as the foppish director.

The limited success of the film continued the Hollywood trend of failing to do justice to Fitzgerald's novels. Both versions of *The Great Gatsby* (1949 and 1974), *The Last Time I Saw Paris* (1954, based on *Babylon Revisited*) and *Tender Is the Night* were all dull productions according to the critics.

A television version of *The Last Tycoon* was made in America in 1957 starring Jack Palance, Lee Remick and Peter Lorre.

Good Guys Wear Black
Mar Vista, 1978

Cast: Chuck Norris (John T. Booker); Anne Archer (Margaret); James Franciscus (Conrad Morgan); Lloyd Haynes (Murray Saunders); Dana Andrews (Edgar Harolds); Jim Backus (Doorman); Lawrence P. Casey (Mike Potter); Anthony Mannino (Gordie Jones); Soon-Tek Oh (Maj. Mhin Van Thieu); Joe Bennett (Lou Goldberg); Jerry Douglas (Joe Walker); Stack Pierce (Holly Washington); Michael Payne (Mitch); David Starwalt (Steagle); Aaron Norris (Al); Don Pike (Hank); Benjamin J. Perry (Finney); Kathy McCullen (Kelly); Michael Stark (Pitman); James Bacon (Senator); Hatsuo Uda (Shoeshine Man); Virginia Wing (Mrs. Mhin Van Thieu); Viola Harris (Airline Ticket Agent); Jacki Robins (Fat Lady); Pat. E. Johnson (CIA Agent); Warren Smith (Morgan's Chauffeur); Dick Shoemaker (Newscaster).

Credits: Michael Leone (Executive Producer); Allan F. Bodoh (Producer); Ted Post (Director); Joseph Fraley (Story); Bruce Cohn, Mark Medoff (Screenplay); Robert Steadman (Cinematography); Craig Safan (Music); Beala Neel (Art Direction); Robinson Royce (Set Decorations); Jean-Pierre Dorleac (Costumes); Robert Dawn (Makeup); Bob Dawson (Special Effects); Gene Marum, John Patterson, Bob Shue (Assistant Directors); Hubie Kerns, Jr. (Stunt Coordinator); Dean Gilmore (Sound): Millie Moore, William M. Moore (Editors). Running time: 96 minutes

Five years after the end of the Vietnam War, teacher John T. Booker, a former head of an elite army unit, discovers that during the conflict several of his army friends lost their lives unnecessarily due to a political conspiracy: It seems that on their last mission (a C.I.A. operation), most of the men were left behind in the jungle waiting for a rescue helicopter which never came. Booker suspects that they were set up by corrupt politicians as part of an expedient deal with the enemy to bring about an end to the war. In an obsessive quest for the truth, Booker sets off to track down the surviving members of his unit only to discover that they are being systematically killed off by unknown forces. With his martial arts skills, Booker blazes forward in his pursuit of the bad guys, ably assisted by a small group of investigators — Margaret, a journalist; Murray, an old army buddy; and alcoholic politician Edgar J. Harolds (Dana Andrews). After a series of martial arts confrontations, explosions and shootouts, the trail eventually leads to corrupt politician Conrad Morgan, who in an effort to conceal the truth arranges a plane explosion which kills Booker's girlfriend, Margaret. The only person who can expose Morgan is his former political aide Harolds, but Morgan has committed him to a psychiatric hospital to undermine his evidence. Undeterred and hell-bent on revenge, Booker chauffeurs Morgan to a watery grave at the bottom of the bay, and then swims away to join Murray.

Tagline: "The C.I.A. can't afford John T. Booker ... alive."

Having sampled the martial arts phenomenon in the spaghetti western *Take a Hard,* courtesy of Kim Kelly's mute, high-kicking half-breed, Andrews found himself fully immersed in the kung fu genre with the Ted Post actioner *Good Guys Wear Black*. From F. Scott Fitzgerald's literary classic *The Last Tycoon* to kung fu highjinks in one flying kick — if there was ever an award for sheer diversity of film work, Andrews would have won hands down. With such an active career in the 1970s, it was inevitable that Andrews's CV would eventually include a kung fu entry and one with a Vietnam flavor. *Good Guys Wear* combined the two.

Ted Post was no stranger to action-adventure, having directed *Beneath the Planet of the Apes* (1970), *Go Tell the Spartans* (1978) and two Clint Eastwood films, *Hang 'Em High* (1968) and *Magnum Force* (1973).

Born to half–Irish, half–Cherokee parents, Chuck Norris was the world middleweight karate champion between 1968 and 1974, and was perhaps America's home-grown answer to Bruce Lee. When his younger brother was killed in Vietnam, Norris dedicated his *Missing in Action* films (a series of POW rescue stories) to his memory. He sustained his popularity with further kung fu antics in *The Octagon* (1980) and *The Delta Force* (1986).

James Franciscus, playing against type as a villain, and the beautiful Anne Archer, in an early role, provide adequate support, but the most notable acting comes from Andrews as Edgar Harolds, a retired U.S. diplomat at the 1973 Paris Peace talks, who is locked away in a psychiatric hospital in an effort to discredit his evidence, which would confirm Morgan's betrayal. Even though Andrews's appearance is short, he makes it count, prompting a *Los Angeles Times* critic to comment: "Dana Andrews gives a poignant performance as an alcoholic career diplomat who can no longer control his better impulses."

Rather gaunt and with little makeup, Andrews very much looks his age in this film, but even at 69 his screen presence has lost none of its luster with a performance that memorably captures his natural ability to exude world-weary cynicism.

> EDGAR J. NAROLDS ON MEETING BOOKER: Oh, Major Booker — the shepherd of the betrayed flock.
>
> BOOKER: That's what we're here to talk about.
>
> Narolds: Well, normally I'd do what I've done in all the years I've served my country and feed you a line of shit. But I don't think I'll bother.
>
> ...
>
> Narolds: Most of us think that we know what we want out of life. Conrad is one of those few who knows how to get it.

Andrews was not alone on the veteran bench and was accompanied by the voice of Mr. Magoo, Jim Backus, in a cameo role as an over-aged bellboy. Backus was highly acknowledged for his role as James Dean's father in *Rebel Without a Cause* (1955); he worked with Andrews again in the political drama *Prince Jack* (1985). Like Andrews, Backus died from complications of pneumonia following a debilitating disease.

One of the most memorable action scenes has Norris delivering the assassin a martial arts kick by leaping through the windshield of a moving car. The spectacular stunt was actually performed by Norris's brother Aaron. *Good Guys Wear Black* did so well at the box office it prompted a sequel, *A Force of One* (1979).

The critical reviews were, in some instances, particularly scathing, with the *New York Times* setting the tone: "Martial-arts films can usually be counted on to be long on action and short on plot, characterization and so on. *Good Guys*

Wear Black ... manages to be short on both. ... Under the circumstances, there's little that Ted Post ... can do to bring the movie alive. Mr. Norris, a slim, blond fellow, does reasonably well, as do Anne Archer, James Franciscus, Dana Andrews and Lloyd Haynes."

Born Again
Avco Embassy, 1978

Cast: Dean Jones (Charles Colson); Anne Francis (Patty Colson); Jay Robinson (David Shapiro); Dana Andrews (Thomas I. Phillips); Raymond St. Jacques (Jimmy Newsom); George Brent (Judge Gerhard Gesell); Harold Hughes (Himself); Harry Spillman (President Richard Nixon); Scott Walker (Scanlon); Robert Gray (Kramer); Arthur Roberts (Al Quie); Ned Wilson (Douglas Coe); Dean Brooks (Dick Howard); Peter Jurasik (Henry Kissinger); Christopher Conrad (Chris Colson); Stuart Lee (Wendell Colson); Alicia Fleer (Emily Colson); Richard Caine (H.R. Haldeman); Brigid O'Brien (Holly Holm); Robert Broyles (John Erlichman); Byron Morrow (Archibald Cox); Bill Zuckert (E. Howard Hunt); William Benedict (Leon Jaworski); John Philip Dayton (Judge's Assistant); Bobb Hopkins (Prison Guard); Ray Nikolaison (Reporter).

Credits: Robert L. Munger (Executive Producer); Frank Capra, Jr. (Producer); Irving Rapper (Director); Paul Temple (Associate Producer); Charles Colson (Based on his Autobiography); Walter Bloch (Screenplay); Harry Stradling, Jr. (Cinematography); Les Baxter (Music); Bill Kenney (Production Designer); Bob Bender (Assistant Director); Richard Anderson (Sound); Axel Hubert Sr. (Editor). Running time: 110 minutes

A true story based on the autobiography of President Richard Nixon's legal counselor Charles Colson, who was sent to prison for his alleged involvement in the Watergate scandal. While serving his sentence, Colson finds his faith and is reborn with the help of his legal client, successful businessman Thomas I. Phillips (Dana Andrews). Realizing the error of his former ways, Colson is transformed from a cynical politician to a devout Christian whose faith helps him to survive prison and accept the injustice of his plight because, as the story suggests, he may have been an innocent pawn in the devious machinations of Washington.

Tagline: "For everyone who ever wanted a chance to start over."

Charles Colson acted as chief counsel to President Richard Nixon from 1969 to 1973, and was one of the Watergate Seven jailed for his

Having found God, Thomas L. Phillips (Andrews) imparts his newfound faith on cynical politician Charles Colson (Dean Jones) in the fact-based drama *Born Again* (Avco Embassy, 1978).

involvement in the scandal. Although Colson regarded himself as a sinner, he has always shown a reluctance to discuss his Watergate involvement, which is not surprising because, according to Watergate historian Stanley Kutler, as Nixon's "hard man," Colson considered hiring Teamster thugs to beat up anti-war demonstrators and also plotted to raid or firebomb the Brookings Institution (an independent Washington D.C. think tank). After serving seven months of a one- to three-year prison sentence, Colson was released due to family reasons and took up a new calling as a prison missionary.

Andrews plays Tom Phillips, a close friend of Colson who gave him a copy of *Mere Christianity* by C.S. Lewis when he was facing arrest; this apparently prompted his evangelical conversion. Many newspapers ridiculed this conversion, claiming it was simply a ploy to reduce his sentence. Andrews replaced Arthur Kennedy, who was originally earmarked for the role of Tom. Although Andrews only appears in two scenes, his character is central to the story, setting Colson on the road to Christianity after his own

conversion, which was heavily influenced by the preachings of evangelist Billy Graham. In contrast to many of Andrews's late-career characters, who were usually irascible in nature, Tom Phillips is a picture of serenity, with Andrews delivering his lines with great tenderness. When Colson makes the observation that he seems a different man from the one he knew, Tom explains, "Some exciting things have happened since I last saw you, Chuck. I have accepted Jesus Christ. I've committed my life to him." And later, reading at length from C.S. Lewis, Tom tells Charles that a proud man, who is always looking down at people, can never find God.

Although the film was made for television, there were some top oldtime talents involved: In addition to Andrews, the credits also included veteran director Irving Rapper. Rapper, who died in 1999 at the age of 101, was one of the last survivors of the Golden Age of Hollywood and the genius behind some of the Bette Davis classics such as *Now, Voyager* (1942) and *The Corn Is Green* (1945). *Born Again* was his last film. Another luminary from the Warner Brothers stable was Bette Davis's most frequent male co-star, George Brent, who retired from acting in 1956, but returned in 1978 to play the part of Judge Gerhard Gesell in *Born Again*. (Brent's glory days long behind him, you would be hard-pushed to recognize him, were it not for that distinctive voice.) Gesell ruled in 1974 that national security was not a valid reason for the 1971 Watergate break-in. This was to be Brent's last film as the actor died in 1979. Producer Frank Capra, Jr., is the son of legendary Hollywood director Frank Capra, best remembered for *It's a Wonderful Life* (1946).

Disney regular Dean Jones, who made his mark with the highly successful *Love Bug* series, took the part of Colson, which coincidently drew certain parallels with his own life (he too became a devout born-again Christian in the mid–'70s). Although he puts in a commendable performance playing against type, there are times that you feel he is simply too much of a nice guy to be portraying Nixon's hatchet man. It could be argued that with Andrews's natural ability to play flawed, ambiguous characters, the role of Colson could have been tailor-made for him if he had been 20 years younger.

The film also featured Harry Spillman doing his lookalike impression of President Nixon (when he appears, you half-expect the film to drift into lampoon mode) and interestingly, former Senator Harold Hughes playing himself.

The role of Colson's wife was played by Anne Francis; Andrews had almost become a regular feature in her films. In total they appeared together in four films which was only topped by the five with his perfect leading lady Gene Tierney. (Jeanne Crain was tied with Anne at four.)

Although the performances were admirable, the film's one-dimensional account of Colson's life left it open to much criticism. Director Rapper was apparently prevented from dramatizing the crimes of Colson, having to concentrate instead on his redemption as chronicled in his memoir.

The Pilot
(U.S. video title: Danger in the Skies)
New Line, 1979

Cast: Cliff Robertson (Mike Hagen); Diane Baker (Pat Simpson); Frank Converse (Jim Cochran); Milo O'Shea (Dr. O'Brian); Dana Andrews (Randolph Evers); Gordon MacRae (Joe Barnes); Ed Binns (Larry Zanoff); Jennifer Holton (Cricket); Kitty Sullivan (Nancy); Leigh Court (Jean Hagen); Bob Willis (Ken Howland); Hope Pomerance (Sandy Campbell); Ted Janus, Paul Stewart, Bill Bretz, Julian Byrd (Mechanics); Bob Kozlowski (First Engineer); Charles Pitts (Ralph); Bill Hindman (Roger); Bobby Sherman (Bob); Dick Liberty, Raymond Forchion (Advertising Personnel); Fred Buch (Gary); Laura Steckel (Stewardess); Dick Sterling, John Archie (Agents); Bruce McLaughlin (FAA Man); Will Knickerbocker (Man in Bar); Danny "Big Black" Rey (Bartender); Toomy Lane (Man Outside Bar); Judy Wilson (Mary); Jack McDermott (AA Leader); Herb Goldstein (Drunk at AA Meeting); Gerald Busby (Oliver); Russ Kartrude (Russ); Ronald Shelley (Controller); Al Torman (Taxi Driver); Al Kolker (Painter).

Credits: Gregory Earls (Producer); Cliff Robertson (Director); Robert P. Davis (Story & Screenplay); Walter Lassally (Cinematography); John Addison (Music); Dick Earls (Associate Producer); Sonny Persons, Norman Gewirtz (First Assistant Directors) James Bigham (Second Assistant Director); William De Seta (Art Director); Evan Lottman (Editor); Al Nahmias, Thomas Halpin, Harriot Fidlow (Sound Editors); Clay Lacey (Director of Aerial Photography); Rita Ogden (Makeup); Bonnie Derham (Set Dresser); Jody Mercurio (Wardrobe Mistress). Running time: 92 minutes

Veteran commercial pilot Mike Hagen is a candidate for "Best Pilot of the Year," but nobody is aware that his world is collapsing due to a severe alcohol problem. In his constant battle with the bottle he is destroying his life and putting passengers' lives at risk, but he won't accept that for professional reasons he should take time out to overcome his addiction. Flying is his life and at first he manages to juggle his drinking and flying timetables, but when a stewardess becomes suspicious of his regular visits to the toilet, she reports her concerns and a co-pilot is assigned to keep an eye on him. While trying to rehabilitate himself, his DC-8 crashes on take-off; the irony is that the crash is caused by the watchdog pilot.

Taglines: "He's the best damn pilot in the sky. Drunk or Sober"; "Alcohol and Aviation.... A deadly cocktail."

Don't worry, Andrews keeps his feet firmly on the ground in this aerial feature, but with Cliff Robertson taking over on the cold sweat front, you'd still be advised to check out the emergency landing instructions before you settle back with the in-flight magazine.

Having proved his flying colors in *633 Squadron* (1964), Cliff Robertson took to the air again in 1980, this time as a commercial airline pilot with a drink problem. Robertson's film career in many ways echoed that of Andrews's, in that both enjoyed successful leading man status for most of their professional life without ever becoming a major star.

Robertson only really came to the public's attention when he played a young John F. Kennedy in *PT 109* (1963). In 1968 he received a Best Actor Academy Award for his performance as a mentally retarded man in *Charly*. The actor was unfairly blacklisted for several years in Hollywood when he reported an incident of forgery by the head of Columbia. As well as taking the lead role in *The Pilot*, Robertson also directed the film, which has been described as one of the most realistic and technically accurate aviation movies ever produced. This is not surprising, as Robertson is himself an accomplished sailplane pilot.

Apart from the great aerial shots, the fun part of the film for me was watching the airborne Hagen sneak off to the john every now and then, to take a few swigs from his hidden stash of booze. When down to his last drop, he even diverts to a distant airport where he knows he can get a drink without discovery. Hagen's supportive sweetheart is played by demure beauty Diane Baker, who carved a respectable career in both film and television, but will best be remembered for her near-perfect performances in *Marnie* (1964) and *Mirage* (1965).

In addition to Andrews, the supporting cast also takes in Frank Converse, Irish character actor Milo O'Shea (Dr. Durand Durand in *Barbarella*) and actor-singer Gordon MacRae, who shot to fame with two big Rodgers and Hammerstein musicals, *Oklahoma!* (1955) and *Carousel* (1956). MacRae's film and night club work suffered in the late 1950s and 1960s when he became an alcoholic. *The Pilot* marked his return to films after an absence of 23 years, but it was his last film performance due to a 1982 stroke. It is a rather sad coincidence that a film about an alcoholic should feature two acknowledged real-life alcoholics amongst its cast list — but it is also true to say that for decades, heavy drinking was very much part of the Hollywood scene.

While MacRae enjoyed a few interesting scenes to mark his return to the big screen, Andrews by contrast had very little do in his one scene, which was nothing more than a "blink and you'll miss me" cameo. This is disappointing as one would have hoped for some interaction between his character and those played by MacRae and Robinson. Even though his appearance as airline head honcho Randolph Evers is brief, Andrews does deliver one memorable sales line that puts you in mind of his ad man Clint Lorimer, from *Madison Avenue* (1962): "Picture to oneself. What we are selling are well-packaged fantasies — hell, everybody flies jets."

In addition to the strong performances, the film also features some beautiful photography, particularly the low-level flying scenes over the desert. The artful aerial cinematography, courtesy of Walter Lassally, is perfectly accompanied by a stirring John Addison score.

The role of Colson in *Born Again* would have had Andrews's name written all over it had he been 20 years younger; the same could be said of the leading role in *The Pilot*, because when it comes to landing an aircraft against all odds, while fighting inner demons, Andrews is your man — even though you might have some serious doubts during the bumpy ride.

Prince Jack
Castle Hill Productions, Inc., 1985

Cast (in alphabetical order): Dana Andrews (The Cardinal); Jim Backus (Dealy); Theodore Bikel (Georgi); Aaron Greenberg (John F. Kennedy, Jr.); Robert Guillaume (Martin Luther King); Robert Hogan (Jack); James F. Kelly (Bobby); Kenneth Mars (Lyndon Johnson); Cameron Mitchell (Gen. Edwin Walker); Lloyd Nolan (Joe Kennedy); William Windom (Ferguson).
Credits: Jim Milo (Producer); Patrick Regan, Alain Silver (Associate Producers); Bert Lovitt (Director & Story); Hiro Narita (Cinematography); Elmer Berstein (Music); Michael Corenblith (Art Direction); Bobbie Mannix (Costume Design); Eric Fidler, Mark Landon (Makeup); Gary Wright, Trevor Black (Sound); Janice Hampton (Editor). Running time 100 minutes

A docudrama chronicling the main chapters in the political life of President John Fitzgerald Kennedy, focusing on his election, the Bay of Pigs debacle, the Cuban Missile Crisis and the civil rights movement. Combining fictionalized accounts with actual footage, this intimate insight is seen through the eyes of some of his closest advisers including his brother Bobby, who became his attorney general; his father Joe Kennedy; Martin Luther King, vice-president Lyndon Johnson, chief military advisor General Edwin Walker and his father's old friend and confidant, the cardinal (Dana Andrews).

In the opening scene, showing actual footage from the 1960 Democratic nomination campaign, we are treated to a politically charged version of "High Hopes," with Frank Sinatra singing.

As the PR put it, this is an intimate behind-the-scenes look at an American presidency through the eyes of ten powerful men. And one of those men, the cardinal, provided Andrews with his last major film role after a five-year absence from the big screen. In the intervening years since his 1979 cameo in *The Pilot*, Andrews's screen appearances were few, including a stint on *The Love Boat* and two episodes of *Falcon Crest* as vineyard owner Elliot McKay. The role of the elderly cardinal, a diplomatic character who was nobody's fool, gave Andrews another opportunity to show a softer, tender side to his screen persona, which we had previously observed in his worldly Father Roth from *Edge of Doom* (1950) and his born-again Christian Tom Phillips from *Born Again* (1978). And at 76 years of age, he still lit up the screen with his engaging and reassuring presence.

The film reunited Andrews with two stars from his earlier days, Jim Backus, who had worked with Andrews in *I Want You* (1951) and more recently *Good Guys Wear Black* (1978), and Cameron Mitchell, who played Greer Garson's wayward brother in *Strange Lady in Town* (1955). *Prince Jack* also featured a wonderfully ripe performance from Lloyd Nolan, who chewed up his every line in the role of Joe Kennedy, as if he knew it might be his last. The actor went on to make one more film, *Hannah and Her Sisters* (1986), before he passed away in 1985. When John Ford rather coyly asked young John Wayne who he thought might be good as the Ringo Kid in *Stagecoach*, Wayne suggested Nolan.

And let's not forget the youngsters in the film: regular soap star Robert Hogan in the role of Jack and James F. Kelly as his brother Bobby, who played the part so well, he reprised the same character in six different filmed projects, even taking on the role of JFK himself (no fear of typecasting there). In the role of Martin Luther King, *Benson* star Robert Guillaume acquitted himself with honors, as did Kenneth Mars in the role of "kick-ass" Vice-President Lyndon Johnson.

To reinforce the fact that in the 1960s the Oval Office was strictly a "man's world," there are no female characters in the film. Only a passing reference is made to JFK's wife Jacqueline, and as for Marilyn Monroe, by the tone of their locker talk, the boys simply saw her as a spaced-out plaything.

In an attempt to secure the release of those taken prisoner by Castro in the Bay of Pigs fiasco, Joe Kennedy seeks the cardinal's advice on paying off the dictator, claiming that their blood will be on the holy fathers' hands if they don't get them out. With the financial wheels clearly turning in his head, the wily cardinal replies, "Well, how can he ask people to donate money to Castro? It's not even tax deductible."

With the Bay of Pigs incident finally put to bed, the cardinal's attention is directed to the president's squeaky-clean image. Fearing that it might be tarnished if he hung out at Sinatra's pad in Palm Springs one weekend, he suggests to JFK that Bing Crosby's place might be a more appropriate choice. When Kennedy declares that he likes Frank, the cardinal replies, "So do I, but not publicly. Sometimes I think we would be better off with a protestant president. Someone who would court our support and not count on it as a birth right."

With its emphasis on the Bay of Pigs and the Cuban Missile Crisis, this version of the major events of the day stacks up as a blatant case of big boys playing hardball with the fate of mankind, or as Sinatra might have merrily crooned it, "Oops, there goes another planet, ker-plop." But that aside, the performances from all concerned are top drawer, and the riveting subject matter will definitely keep you in your seat until the usherette starts sweeping up the popcorn from around your feet.

Appendix:
Major Television, Theatre and Radio Credits

Television

Playhouse 90

Weekly 90-minute drama anthology series produced by CBS from 1956 to 1961. Andrews starred in two of the 133 episodes, taking the roles of Leo Bass and Mark Bragg respectively.

"The Right Hand Man" first aired March 20, 1958. A tale of ambition and friendships in the life of a Hollywood talent agent in which Andrews played Leo Bass.

"Alas, Babylon" first aired April 3, 1960. A grim vision of the world in the aftermath of a nuclear war. Andrews played Mark Bragg.

General Electric Theatre

Weekly one-hour drama anthology series broadcast by CBS from 1953 to 1962 (200 episodes). Andrews starred in the radio audition show, "The Token," which aired on January 18, 1953, before it debuted with CBS on July 9, 1953. Ronald Reagan hosted the show at the beginning of the 1954-55 season.

"The Playoff" (November 20, 1960)—Carl Anderson.

The Barbara Stanwyck Show

Weekly half-hour drama anthology series hosted by Hollywood actress Barbara Stanwyck, who also starred in some of the episodes, which were aired by NBC between 1960 and 1961. Jacques Tourneur directed the majority of the stories. The show was also used to try out pilots for new series, none of which saw the light.

"Yanqui Go Home" (1960)—Clint Evans

Checkmate

Weekly one-hour drama, telecast by CBS from September 1960 to September 1962, about an upscale San Francisco detective agency run by Don Corey (Anthony George) and Jed Stills (Doug McClure), who called themselves Checkmate, Inc.

"Trial by Midnight" (1962)—Judge Leland McIntyre

The DuPont Show of the Week

A late Sunday evening one-hour NBC show, showcasing a panorama of entertainment and informational programs. The show ran from September 1961 to September 1964, and attempted to show the latitude and potential of television as a means of communication.

"Emergency Ward" (November 18, 1962)—Narrator

"Mutiny" (December 2, 1962)—Commander Jason Vanning

The Twilight Zone

Long running series of offbeat and out of the ordinary tales, with an ironic twist in the tail, which ran from 1959 to 1965. Telecast by CBS, the show was hosted by playwright Rod Sterling, and filled a half-hour slot before expanding to an hour in January 1963. The success of the show led to two revival shows and a feature film.

"No Time Like the Past" aired on March 7, 1963, with Andrews playing scientist Paul Driscoll, who uses a time machine in an attempt to alter the past for the benefit of mankind.

The Dick Powell Show

Weekly one-hour anthology presented by 1930s star Dick Powell. The show was telecast by NBC and ran from September 1961 to September 1963.

"Crazy Sunday" (December 18, 1962). Budding Hollywood writer Joel Coles ignores the advice of old pro Nat Keough (Andrews).

"The Last of the Big Spenders" (April 16, 1963). Seriously ill novelist Paul Oakland (Andrews) gets reacquainted with his son, played by Robert Redford, whom he hasn't seen for 20 years.

Alcoa Premiere

Weekly hour-long drama series hosted by and occasionally starring Fred Astaire. Aired by ABC from 1961 to 1963, each episode presented a new story, which tended to focus on painful and sometimes controversial subjects.

"The Boy Who Wasn't Wanted" (June 5, 1962) — Pat Barrat

"The Town That Died" (April 25, 1963) — Adam Stark

Calhoun: County Agent

Unaired pilot show, produced in 1964, about a county agent.

Ben Casey

A medical drama series, starring handsome Vince Edwards. The one-hour weekly show ran from 1961 to 1966, and soon became the most successful program on the ABC network.

"The Light That Loses, the Night That Wins" (1964) — Dr. Ernest Farrow

Bob Hope Presents the Chrysler Theatre

Anthology series, presented in a mixture of formats, including musical, drama, and comedy. Hosted by Bob Hope and telecast by NBC, the one hour show ran from 1963 to 1967.

"A Wind of Hurricane Force" (1964) — Douglas Vinton

The Presidency: A Splendid Misery

A tale of presidential power politics produced in 1964.

Family Affair

Situation comedy series about "man about town" bachelor and highly paid civil engineer Bill Davis (Brian Keith), who, with the assistance of his English gentleman's gentleman, attempts to bring up his brother's orphaned children in his swank New York apartment. Produced by CBS, the half-hour series ran from 1966 to 1971 (138 episodes).

"The Wings of an Angel" (1969). Andrews guest stars as recently released ex con Harv Mullen, who drops in on Bill in the hope of securing a job.

Bright Promise

NBC daytime soap opera dealing with the turbulent lives of the students and staff at Bancroft College headed by college president Thomas Boswell, whom Andrews played in 1969–70. The series ran from 1969 to 1972.

The Name of the Game

Late evening, weekly NBC series that ran to 90 minutes, rotating between three characters (played by Robert Stack, Tony Franciosa and Gene Barry) who worked at a large Los Angeles publishing empire. Telecast by NBC, the show ran from 1968 to 1971 (76 episodes).

"The Time Is Now" (1970) — Marvin Taylor

The Failing of Raymond (TV Movie)

A spinster school teacher (Jane Wyman), on the eve of her retirement, discovers that she is marked for death by a deranged former student (Dean Stockwell) she had flunked ten years earlier. Andrews plays Allan McDonald.

Released November 27, 1971; Universal; 90 minutes

Night Gallery

A weekly collection of supernatural stories introduced by Rod Sterling, which was very much a follow-up to *The Twilight Zone*. Telecast by NBC, the show ran from 1970 to 1973.

"The Different Ones" (1971). Lost and asking directions, a woman gets a warning and possible glimpse into her future. Andrews plays Paul Koch.

Ironside

Police drama about the investigations of former chief of detectives, Robert Ironside (Raymond Burr), who is consigned to a wheelchair after a would-be assassin's bullet grazed his spine and left him paralyzed from the waist down. An hour long, the NBC weekly show ran from 1967 to 1975.

"The Lost Cotillion" (1974) — Courtenay Eliot

A Shadow in the Streets (TV movie)

In this pilot film for a potential series, a tough ex-convict attempts to make a life on the outside in the role of a parole officer as part of an experimental program. Andrews plays Len Raeburn.

Released January 28, 1975; Playboy Productions; 90 minutes

The First 36 Hours of Dr. Durant (TV movie)

An idealistic young surgical doctor confronts his medical ethics in his first demanding hours on call at a big-city hospital. (Dr. Hutchins.)

Released May 13, 1975; Columbia Pictures; 90 minutes

Ellery Queen

Detective drama series with mystery writer turned super sleuth Ellery Queen (Jim Hutton) wading through a mass of evidence and a generous helping of likely suspects in an attempt to nail the guilty party. The show ran intermittently for DUM, ABC and NBC from 1950 to 1976.

"The Adventures of the Judas Tree" (February 1, 1976). The super-sleuth investigates whether the murder of a wealthy man (found hanging from a Judas tree) was really a ritualistic killing. (Lewis Marshall).

The Last Hurrah (TV movie)

Despite challenges to his position from younger ambitious contenders, the ailing head of an age-old political regime pushes for victory in his last election campaign. A 1977 remake of the 1958 movie starring Spencer Tracy. (Roger Shanley).

Released November 6, 1977; O'Connor/Becker/ Productions/Columbia; two hours.

Ike

Emmy Award–winning miniseries about the life of General Eisenhower (Robert Duvall), focusing on his relationship with other wartime leaders and his personal moments with his driver, Kay Summersby (Lee Remick). Andrews played General George C. Marshall. The three episodes were later cut to fill a single four-hour slot and retitled *Ike: The War Years*. 1979; ABC Circle Films; 3 episodes of 96 minutes each

A Tree, a Rock, a Cloud

A short tale of youth, age, innocence and experience (1978).

The American Girls

The weekly adventures of two attractive female TV journalists. An hour-long show that aired in 1978 on CBS.

"The Cancelled Czech" (1978) — Phillips

The Hardy Boys/ Nancy Drew Mysteries

The cases of a pair of teen detective brothers and a teen girl amateur sleuth, which ran for the ABC channel between 1977 and 1979.

"Assault on a Tower" (1978) — Townley

The Love Boat

Situation romantic comedy series dealing with the loves of young and old aboard the luxurious cruise liner Pacific Princess. Each week, viewers were treated to guest appearances from famous movie and TV stars from past and present. The weekly one-hour show was broadcast on the ABC channel from 1977 to 1986.

"Command Performance/Hyde and Seek/ Sketchy Love" (1982)

Falcon Crest

Nighttime soap opera featuring the rich, feuding factions of the Gioberti/Channing family fighting for power in the California wine industry, starring Hollywood legend Jane Wyman as the matriarch of the Falcon Crest Winery. Telecast by CBS, the hour-long show ran from 1981 to 1990.

"The Candidate" (1982) — Elliot McKay
"Deliberate Disclosure" (1983) — Elliot McKay

Theatre

The Glass Menagerie

New England tour in 1952 with wife Mary Todd Andrews, Aline MacMahon and Walter Matthau. Tennessee Williams play about family hardship and delusion during the Depression. Andrews took the part of Tom Wingfield, an aspiring writer, who works in a dead-end job to look after his crippled sister, Laura, and his mother Amanda, a former southern belle who yearns for the Old South.

Two for the Seesaw

Andrews replaced Henry Fonda in the lead male role, making his Broadway debut on July 9, 1958 (until June 29, 1959). Anne Bancroft co-starred.

Written by William Gibson, the play revolves around recently separated lawyer, Jerry Ryan (Andrews), who meets up with an eccentric dancer while living in a shabby New York apartment awaiting his divorce.

The Captains and the Kings

The show was not a great success and only ran to seven performances at the Playhouse Theatre, New York, in January 1962. The supporting cast included Charlie Ruggles, Peter Graves, Conrad Nagel and Lee Grant. A tale of Naval politics written by Leon Lieberman, with Andrews in the role of Richard Kohner, a naval captain tasked with the launching of the first nuclear-powered submarine.

A Remedy for Winter

Leonard Spigelgass comedy about a noted historian (Andrews) and his involvement with an actress (Susan Oliver). Throughout 1965, the fifteen-week tour took in Holyoke, Mass; Westport, Conn; Falmouth, Mass; Philadelphia and Chicago.

A Man for All Seasons

The Royal Poinciana Playhouse, Palm Beach, Florida, February 1965. Andrews and Albert Dekker.

Plaza Suite

Neil Simon comedy, composed of three separate stories about people who book into suite 719 of New York's Plaza Hotel (1967).

The Odd Couple

Two divorced men, slobbish Oscar and over fussy Felix, share an apartment and gradually get on each other's nerves in this classic Neil Simon comedy (1967). Andrews took the part of Oscar.

Paint Your Wagon

Stage musical written by Lerner and Loewe, set in a mining camp in gold-rush era California where two gold prospectors share a wife (1969, Meadowbrook Dinner Theatre).

Is Anyone Listening?

Andrews played a lawyer who is subjected to blackmail following an affair with a teenage girl. The show, written by Joseph Hayes, premiered January 4, 1971, at Florida State University Theatre.

The Marriage-Go-Round

A saucy comedy about marriage written by Leslie Stevens. Andrews played Paul Delville. Once during the play's run (1972 and 1973 with wife Mary Todd), Andrews received a surprise during a curtain speech when television host Ralph Edwards unexpectedly appeared on the stage and informed him that he was to be the subject of "This Is Your Life" (January 1973 episode).

Our Town

A three act play written by American playwright Thornton Wilder about the highs and lows of community life in the early part of the twentieth century (England tour, 1973, with wife Mary Todd).

Together Tonight! Jefferson, Hamilton and Burr

Monte Markham's play concerning the political machinations of Thomas Jefferson, Alexander Hamilton and Aaron Burr at the end of the eighteenth century (U.S. tour 1976).

Come Back, Little Sheba

A domestic drama by William Inge exploring a barren marriage, with slovenly wife at odds with her alcoholic husband Doc (Andrews), a chiropractor who had once harbored aspirations of becoming a doctor. It played at the Berkshire Theatre in Stockbridge, Massachusetts. Rosemary Murphy co-starred (Aug. 1977).

Any Wednesday

Broadway sex comedy penned by Muriel Resnik (U.S. Dinner Theatres tour 1978).

Radio

Cavalcade of America

Factual anthology show, which dramatized the history of America.
"Weather is a Weapon" (May 14, 1945)

Family Theatre

Thirty minute anthology program which placed its emphasis on family prayer. Bing Crosby and Irene Dunne also featured in this episode.
"J. Smith and Wife" (February 27, 1947)

Hollywood Fights Back

A two part show (Part One: October 26, 1947, and Part Two: November 2, 1947), where Hollywood stars, as themselves, hit back at the House Un-American Activities Committee which investigated Communist party activities within the movie industry. Part one was hosted by Charles Boyer, with Frederic March taking the reins for the second installment.

Lux Radio Theatre

Hour-long drama show performed before a live audience, featuring many actors in radio adaptations of Broadway and Hollywood films (using as many of the original stars from theses productions as possible). Aired from 1935 to 1955, the shows were hosted by Cecil B. DeMille and Lionel Barrymore. Lux (soap products) commercials were delivered throughout the show.

Laura (February 5, 1945). A romantic murder mystery, with Andrews, Gene Tierney and Vincent Price reprising their roles from the noir movie classic. Otto Kruger took over from Clifton Webb in the role of Waldo Lydecker for this presentation.

Daisy Kenyon (April 5, 1948). Post World War II love triangle with Ida Lupino in the title role. Joan Crawford took the part in the film version and Andrews played Dan O'Mara.

Luck of the Irish (December 27, 1948). Romantic complications ensue when soon to be married New York reporter Stephen Fitzgerald (Andrews) meets a beautiful young girl (Anne Baxter) and a leprechaun while travelling in Ireland. Tyrone Power played the male lead in the film version.

Deep Waters. December 9, 1949. A lobster fisherman adopts a problem boy and finds love with his welfare worker. Donna Reed took the part of the love interest portrayed by Jean Peters in the film. (Hod Stillwell).

Night Song. May 29, 1950. A beautiful socialite (Joan Fontaine) falls in love with a blind pianist. Merle Oberon played the rich gal in the film version. (Dan Evans).

My Foolish Heart. August 28, 1950. Wartime tearjerker. With the film's female lead, Susan Hayward. (Walt Dreiser).

Where the Sidewalk Ends. April 2, 1951. A tough cop accidentally kills a suspect and tries to cover it up. Anne Baxter stepped into the shoes of Gene Tierney for this radio version.

Mister 880. October 15, 1951. An FBI agent tracks down an amiable old counterfeiter (Edmund Gwenn). Andrews took the part of the federal agent played by Burt Lancaster in the film (Steve Buchanan).

My Six Convicts (October 20, 1952). A prison psychologist's attempts to better understand his patients. (Doc)

One Foot in Heaven (July 27, 1953). The life of an itinerant minister and his family in 20th Century America. With Steve Forrest (Andrews's younger brother).

September Affair. February 22, 1954. Listed as dead in a plane crash, two lovers, one married, get an opportunity to continue their affair. Andrews played the part of the married man played by Joseph Cotton in the film. Eleanor Parker took the Joan Fontaine role. (David Lawrence).

Strangers on a Train (April 12, 1954). A thriller, with two men, one a psychotic, agreeing to swap murders following a chance meeting on a train journey. With Robert Cummings (Farley Granger and Robert Walker starred in the classic Hitchcock film version).

The Blue Gardenia (November 30, 1954). Murder mystery; Andrews played newspaperman Casey Mayo. (Richard Conte starred in the film version.)

War of the Worlds (February 8, 1955). H.G. Wells story about a Martian invasion adapted to 1950s America. With Les Tremayne. Andrews featured in the role of the scientist, played by Gene Barry in the film.

Screen Director's Playhouse

Dramatic anthology, aired from 1949 to 1951, featuring stars and directors from Hollywood films. Andrews' appearances were adapted from two of his films.

The Best Years of Our Lives (April 17, 1949). Three American servicemen return home after the war and try to readjust to civilian life. (Fred Derry)

No Minor Vices (February 22, 1951). An artist disrupts the household of a doctor and his beautiful wife in this romantic comedy.

Screen Guild Players

The Screen Guild Players radio program originated as means of raising money for the Motion Picture Relief Fund. Many big stars featured in this dramatic anthology show, waiving their fees to support, amongst other things, a retirement home for movie industry employees.

Laura (August 20, 1945). Romantic murder mystery. (Detective Mark McPherson)

Suspense

A CBS show that aired regularly from 1942 to 1962 focusing on chiller/thriller type themes.

"Two Birds with One Stone" (May 17, 1945). Andrews plays the part of a playwright who dupes his wife in to recording an audio suicide note so that he can kill her without anyone suspecting.

"If the Dead Could Talk" (January 20, 1949). A tale of bitter jealousy.

"The Crowd" (September 21, 1950). Andrews takes the part of a police lieutenant on the trail of a killer in New York.

"One Man Crime Wave" (January 11, 1954). A fact-based story concerning a big city in the grip of fear from a killer. Andrews is the cop on the case.

General Electric Theatre

Anthology series, which started on radio before moving to television on July 9, 1953, for CBS.

"The Token." Audition show which aired on January 18, 1953.

I Was a Communist for the FBI

Produced at the height of anti-communist hysteria in the early 1950s, the show was based on the book by Matt Cvetic covering his nine years as an undercover agent for the FBI — a secret even his family was not party to. Andrews played the part of Cvetic, and always ended each story with the closing words, "I was a Communist for the FBI. I walk alone." The show aired from 1952 to 1953. The FBI refused to provide any assistance with the series, which ran to 78 episodes, with each story running to approximately 28 minutes. "Little Red School House" was the pilot show aired in 1952, which was redone in episode three. Frank Lovejoy played Cvetic in the 1951 movie adaptation by the same name.

1952 Episodes

"I Walk Alone" (April 23)
"I Can't Sleep" (April 30)
"Little Red Schoolhouse" (May 5)
"Red Red Herring" (May 14)
"Pit Viper" (May 21)
"Traitors For Hire" (May 28)

"Card Game in the Clouds" (June 4)
"American Kremlin" (June 11)
"Tight Wire" (June 18)
"A Riot Made to Order" (June 25)
"Where the Red Men Roam" (July 2)
"The Dangerous Dollars" (July 9)
"Rich Man, Poor Man" (July 16)
"Canadian Crossfire" (July 23)
"Draw the Red Curtain" (July 30)
"Red Clouds on Good Earth" (August 6)
"Exit on the Left" (August 13)
"The Red Record" (August 20)
"Burnt Offering" (August 27)
"Squeeze Play" (September 3)
"Violence Preferred" (September 10)
"The Rat Race" (September 17)
"Jump to the Whip" (September 24)
"Pennies from the Dead" (October 1)
"A Suit for the Party" (October 8)
"The Party Got Rough" (October 15)
"The Little Boy Red" (October 22)
"The Unwelcome Hosts" (October 29)
"No Second Chance" (November 5)
"The Red Gate" (November 12)
"Red Rover, Red Rover" (November 19)
"Home Improvement" (November 26)
"Red Clay" (December 3)
"The Kiss of Death" (December 10)
"Treason comes in Cans" (December 17)
"The Flames Burned Red" (December 24)
"Hate Song" (December 31)

1953 Episodes

"Little Boy Blue Turned Red" (January 7)
"Red Gold" (January 14)
"Charter City Square Dance" (January 21)
"A Study in Oils" (January 28)
"The Sleeper" (February 4)
"Against the Middle" (February 11)
"Black Gospel" (February 18)
"The Red Ladies" (February 25)
"One Way Ticket" (March 4)
"Word Game" (March 11)
"The Red Waves" (March 18)
"Trial by Fear" (March 23)
"The Wrong Green" (April 1)
Unknown title (April 22)
Unknown title (April 29)
"The Brass Monkey" (April 8)
"Forged Faces" (April 15)
"An Unashamed Activity" (May 6)
"My Friend the Enemy" (May 13)

"The Canadian Backbone" (May 20)
"The Elspeth Club" (May 27)
"The Crossed Heart" (June 3)
"The Red Octopus" (June 10)
"Abby, as in Abbigale" (June 17)
"Tour of Duty" (June 24)
"Fifteen Minutes to Murder" (July 1)
"Use Only as Directed" (July 8)
"Double Exposure" (July 15)
"Courier of Disaster" (July 22)
"The Lion is Busy" (July 29)
"The Red Snow" (August 5)
"Very Private Funeral" (August 12)
"Rhapsody in Red" (August 19)
"Kangaroo Court" (August 26)
"The Inhuman Element" (September 2)
Unknown title (September 9)
Unknown title (September 16)
Unknown title (September 23)
Unknown title (September 30)
"Panic Plan" (October 7)
"Exit on the Left" (October 14)

The Screen Guild Theatre — Radio Anthology Series

Laura

August 20, 1945. With Andrews, Gene Tierney and Clifton Webb.

The Best Years of Our Lives

May 19, 1947. With Andrews, Virginia Mayo, Donna Reed, Cathy O'Donnell, and Warren William.

Boomerang!

November 10, 1947. With Andrews, Jane Wyatt, Richard Widmark and Reed Hadley.

Deep Waters

February 17, 1949. With Andrews, Jean Peters and Dean Stockwell.

Laura

February 23, 1950. With Andrews, Gene Tierney and Clifton Webb.

The Dark Mirror

November 9, 1950. With Andrews, Bette Davis and Gene Tierney.

Call Northside 777

December 27, 1951. With Andrews and Thomas Gomez.

Notes

Biography

1. *Modern Screen*, November 1945.
2. Ibid.
3. *Hollywood Album*, 1948.
4. *Modern Screen*, November 1945.
5. Imogen Sara Smith, "The Forties Hero and His Shadow."
6. Karen Burroughs Hannsberry, *Bad Boys: The Actors of Film Noir* (Jefferson, NC: McFarland, 2003), 16–17.
7. *Hollywood Album*, 1948.
8. James Robert Parish with Gregory W. Mank, *The Hollywood Reliables* (Westport, CT: Arlington House, 1980), 2.
9. The Reminiscences of Dana Andrews (1958), 6, in the Oral History Collection of Columbia University.
10. The Reminiscences of Dana Andrews (1958), 8.
11. *Modern Screen*, November 1945.
12. The Reminiscences of Dana Andrews (1958), 14.
13. *Hollywood Album*, 1948.
14. *Picturegoer*, October 9, 1948.
15. *Films Illustrated*, 1972.
16. *Modern Screen*, January 1945.
17. *Modern Screen*, September 1944.
18. *Modern Screen*, January 1946.
19. *Hollywood Album*, 1948.
20. *Evening Standard*, December 18, 1992, 14.
21. *Evening Standard*, March 11, 1956.
22. *Films Illustrated*, 1972.
23. The Reminiscences of Dana Andrews (1958), 41.
24. *Screen Parade* (issue unknown).
25. *Classic Images* #107 and #174.
26. *The Guardian* (obituary), December 19, 1992, 26.

Sailor's Lady (1940)

1. *Sailor's Lady* pressbook.

Kit Carson (1940)

1. *Modern Screen*, January 1945.

The Westerner (1940)

1. Interview with Allen Eyles, *Focus on Film* 26 (1977).
2. Hannsberry, *Bad Boys: The Actors of Film Noir* (Jefferson, NC: McFarland, 2003), 17.
3. The Reminiscences of Dana Andrews (1958), 15.

Tobacco Road (1941)

1. J.A. Place, *The Non-Western Films of John Ford* (New York: Citadel Press, 1979), 74.

2. Interview with Allen Eyles, *Focus on Film*.
3. *Modern Screen*, November 1945.
4. Michelle Vogel, *Gene Tierney: A Biography* (Jefferson, NC: McFarland, 2005), 30–31.

Belle Starr (1941)

1. *Modern Screen*, November 1945.
2. Vogel, *Gene Tierney*, 41–42.

Swamp Water (1941)

1. Ronald Bergan, *Jean Renoir: Projections of Paradise* (London: Bloomsbury, 1992), 225.
2. Ibid.
3. *Modern Screen*, September 1944.
4. Bergan, *Jean Renoir*, 226.

Ball of Fire (1941)

1. Axel Madsen, *Stanwyck* (New York: Harper Collins, 1994), 202.
2. Todd McCarthy, *Howard Hawks: The Grey Fox of Hollywood* (New York: Grove Press, 1997), 325–27.
3. A. Scott Berg, *Goldwyn* (London: Sphere Books, 1990), 363.

Crash Dive (1943)

1. *Modern Screen*, May 1946.
2. Lawrence Suid, *Sailing on the Silver Screen: Hollywood and the U.S. Navy* (Annapolis, MD: Naval Institute Press, 1996), 59–60.
3. *Modern Screen*, "The Guy Next Door," September 1944.

The Ox-Bow Incident (1943)

1. William Meyer, *The Making of the Great Westerns* (New Rochelle, NY: Arlington House, 1979), 132–33.
2. Ibid.
3. The Reminiscences of Dana Andrews (1958), 32–33.

The North Star (1943)

1. Farley Granger and Robert Calhoun, *Include Me Out: My Life from Goldwyn to Broadway* (New York: St. Martin's Press, 2007), 22.

Up in Arms (1944)

1. James Robert Parish with Gregory W. Mank, *The Hollywood Reliables* (Arlington House, 1980), 8.

2. A. Scott Berg, *Goldwyn* (London: Sphere Books, 1990), 385–86.

3. Martin Cottfried, *Nobody's Fool: The Lives of Danny Kaye* (New York: Simon & Schuster, 1994), 94.

The Purple Heart (1944)

1. The Reminiscences of Dana Andrews (1958), 18.

Wing and a Prayer (1944)

1. Ben Ohmart, *Don Ameche: The Kenosha Comeback Kid* (Albany, GA: BearManor Media, 2007), 109.

2. The Reminiscences of Dana Andrews (1958), 38.

3. Rudy Behlmer (edited and annotator), *Henry Hathaway — A Director's Guild of America Oral History* (Lanham, MD: Scarecrow Press, 2001), 207.

4. Suid, *Sailing on the Silver Screen*, 76.

Laura (1944)

1. George F. Custen, *Twentieth Century's Fox: Darryl Zanuck and the Culture of Hollywood* (New York: Basic Books, 1997), 289.

2. Chris Fujiwara, *The World and Its Double: The Life and Work of Otto Preminger* (New York: Faber and Faber, 2008), 39.

3. The Reminiscences of Dana Andrews (1958), 19–20.

4. Ibid.

5. *Music from the Movies of Dana Andrews 1944–1949* CD booklet (released in November 2008).

6. Victoria Price, *Vincent Price: A Daughter's Biography* (London: Sidgwick & Jackson, 1999), 155.

7. Vogel, *Gene Tierney*, 193.

State Fair (1945)

1. Esther Williams with Digby Diehl, *Esther Williams — The Million Dollar Mermaid: An Autobiography* (New York: Simon & Schuster, 1999), 275.

A Walk in the Sun (1945)

1. Lawrence J. Quirk, *The Great War Films* (New York: Citadel Press, 1994), 102–04.

2. The Reminiscences of Dana Andrews (1958), 34.

3. Interview with Allen Eyles.

Fallen Angel (1945)

1. Interview with Allen Eyles.

2. Chris Fujiwara, *The World and Its Double: The Life and Work of Otto Preminger* (New York: Faber and Faber, 2008), 63.

3. Jane Lenz Elder, *Alice Faye: A Life Beyond the Silver Screen* (Jackson: University Press of Mississippi, 2002), 179, 181.

4. Fujiwara, *The World and Its Double*, 63.

5. Ronald L. Davis, *Hollywood Beauty: Linda Darnell and the American Dream* (Norman: University of Oklahoma Press, 1991), 89.

6. Ibid.

7. Foster Hirsch, *Otto Preminger: The Man Who Would Be King* (New York: Alfred A. Knopf, 2007), 127.

Canyon Passage (1946)

1. Robert Laguardia and Gene Arceri, *Red: The Tempestuous Life of Susan Hayward* (London: Robson Books, 1985), 55.

2. Chris Fujiwara, *Jacques Tourneur: The Cinema of Nightfall* (Baltimore: Johns Hopkins University Press, 2000), 126 and 137.

3. Brian Garfield, *Western Films: A Complete Guide* (London: Da Capo Press, 1982), 132.

4. Fujiwara, *Jacques Tourneur*, 126 and 137.

The Best Years of Our Lives (1946)

1. A. Scott Berg, *Goldwyn* (London: Sphere Books, 1990), 410.

2. Interview with Allen Eyles.

3. Axel Madsen, *William Wyler: The Authorized Biography* (London: W.H. Allen, 1974), 266.

4. Jan Herman, *A Talent for Trouble: The Life of Hollywood's Most Acclaimed Director, William Wyler* (New York: G.P. Putnam's Sons, 1995), 283 and 288.

5. The Reminiscences of Dana Andrews (1958), 32.

6. Herman, *A Talent for Trouble*, 283 and 288.

7. Carol Easton, *The Search for Sam Goldwyn: A Biography* (New York: Quill William Morrow, 1975), 238.

8. *Music from the Movies of Dana Andrews 1944–1949* CD booklet (released in November 2008).

9. Michael Freedland, *The Goldwyn Touch: A Biography of Sam Goldwyn* (London: Harrap, 1986), 195.

Boomerang! (1947)

1. Karl Malden with Carla Malden, *When Do I Start? A Memoir* (New York: Simon & Schuster, 1997), 163–64.

2. The Reminiscences of Dana Andrews (1958), 40.

Daisy Kenyon (1947)

1. Jane Ellen Wayne, *Crawford's Men* (London: Robson Books, 1988), 188.

2. Interview with Allen Eyles.

3. Ibid., 189.

4. Foster Hirsch, *Otto Preminger: The Man Who Would Be King* (New York: Alfred A. Knopf, 2007), 149.

5. Ibid.

Night Song (1948)

1. The Reminiscences of Dana Andrews (1958), 33–34.

2. *Modern Screen*, September 1947.

3. Ibid.

4. Charles Higham and Roy Moseley, *Merle: A Biography of Merle Oberon* (Sevenoaks, Kent: New English Library, 1983), 129.

The Iron Curtain (1948)

1. George F. Custen, *Twentieth Century's Fox — Darryl Zanuck and the Culture of Hollywood* (Basic Books, 1997), 307.

2. James Robert Parish with Gregory W. Mank, *The Hollywood Reliables* (Arlington House, 1980), 16.

3. Custen, *Twentieth Century's Fox*, 307.

4. Frank T. Thompson, *William A. Wellman* (Metuchen, NJ: Scarecrow Press, 1983), 221.

5. *Johnny Reno* pressbook.

Deep Waters (1948)

1. Richard Hack, *Hughes: The Private Diaries, Memos and Letters* (Beverly Hills, CA: New Millennium Press, 2001), 188.
2. Deep Waters Pressbook.

No Minor Vices (1948)

1. Interview with Allen Eyles.
2. Allen Eyles, "Films of Enterprise. A Studio History," *Focus on Film*, April 1980.

The Forbidden Street (1949)

1. Maureen O'Hara with John Nicoletti, *'Tis Herself— A Memoir* (New York: Simon & Schuster, 2004), 129.
2. Penelope Smith, "Dana on the Up and Up," *Picturegoer*, October 1948.
3. Karen Burroughs Hannsberry, *Bad Boys: The Actors of Film Noir* (Jefferson, NC: McFarland, 2003), 19–20.
4. Penelope Smith, "Dana on the Up and Up," *Picturegoer*, October 1948.
5. *Hollywood Album,* circa 1954.
6. Jean Negulesco, *Things I Did and Things I Think I Did: A Hollywood Memoir* (New York: Linden Press/Simon & Schuster, 1984), 147.

Sword in the Desert (1949)

1. Jack G. Shaheen, *Reel Bad Arabs — How Hollywood Vilifies a People* (Moreton-in-Marsh: Arris Books, 2003), 463.
2. Jeff Wells, *Jeff Chandler* (Jefferson, NC: McFarland, 2005), 46–47.
3. Ibid., 47.

My Foolish Heart (1949)

1. Christopher P. Andersen, *A Star, Is a Star, Is a Star: The Lives and Loves of Susan Hayward* (London: Robson Books, 1981), 110.

Where the Sidewalk Ends (1950)

1. Interview with Allen Eyles.
2. Karl Malden with Carla Malden, *When Do I Start? A Memoir* (New York: Simon & Schuster, 1997), 221.
3. Gary Merrill, *Bette, Rita and the Rest of My Life* (New York: Berkley Books, 1990), 74.
4. Gene Tierney with Mickey Herskowitz, *Self-Portrait* (New York: Berkley Books, 1980), 150.
5. Alain Silver and Elizabeth Ward (editors), *Film Noir: An Encyclopedic Reference to the American Style* (Woodstock, NY: The Overlook Press, 1992), 310.

Edge of Doom (1950)

1. Carol Easton, *The Search for Sam Goldwyn: A Biography* (New York: Quill William Morrow, 1975), 270–71.
2. A. Scott Berg, *Goldwyn* (London: Sphere Books, 1990), 453.
3. Farley Granger and Robert Calhoun, *Include Me Out: My Life from Goldwyn to Broadway* (New York: St. Martin's Press, 2007), 92.

The Frogmen (1951)

1. Gary Merrill, *Bette, Rita and the Rest of My Life* (New York: Berkley Books, 1990), 86.

2. Lawrence Suid, *Sailing on the Silver Screen: Hollywood and the U.S. Navy* (Annapolis, MD: Naval Institute Press, 1996), 115.
3. Ibid., 117.

I Want You (1951)

1. A. Scott Berg, *Goldwyn* (London: Sphere Books, 1990), 457.
2. Robert J. Lentz, *Korean War Filmography* (Jefferson, NC: McFarland, 2003), 168.
3. Berg, *Goldwyn*, 458.

Assignment Paris (1952)

1. *Assignment Paris* pressbook.
2. Eddie Muller, *Dark City Dames: The Wicked Women of Film Noir* (New York: Regan Books, 2001), 197.
3. *Assignment Paris* pressbook.
4. James Robert Parish and Michael R. Pitts, *The Great Spy Pictures II* (Metuchen, NJ: Scarecrow Press, 1986), 25.

Elephant Walk (1954)

1. Jerry Vermilye and Mark Ricci, *The Films of Elizabeth Taylor* (New York: Citadel Press, 1989), 106.
2. Elaine Dundy, *Finch, Bloody Finch: A Biography of Peter Finch* (London: Michael Joseph Ltd., 1980), 178.
3. Ibid., 180.
4. James Robert Parish with Gregory W. Mank, *The Hollywood Reliables* (Westport, CT: Arlington House, 1980), 22.
5. Ibid., 21–22.
6. Vermilye and Ricci, *The Films of Elizabeth Taylor*, 107.
7. Alexander Walker, *Elizabeth* (London: Weidenfeld & Nicolson, 1990), 151.
8. Ibid.
9. Dundy, *Finch, Bloody Finch*, 181.
10. *Hollywood Album,* circa 1954
11. Ibid.

Duel in the Jungle (1954)

1. Jay Fultz, *In Search of Donna Reed* (Iowa City: University of Iowa Press, 1998), 96.
2. *Hollywood Album,* circa 1954.
3. *Picture Show & Film Pictorial*, September 11, 1954.
4. *Picturegoer*, October 24, 1953.
5. Ibid.
6. Ibid.
7. Phil Booker, *Jeanne Crain, the Beautiful Dreamer* (New York: Carlton Press, 1977), 29.
8. *Hollywood Album,* circa 1954

Three Hours to Kill (1954)

1. Phil Hardy, *The Aurum Film Encyclopedia — The Western* (London: Aurum Press, 1995), 235.
2. Ibid.
3. Jay Fultz, *In Search of Donna Reed* (Iowa City: University of Iowa Press, 1998), 99.

Smoke Signal (1955)

1. Brian Garfield, *Western Films: A Complete Guide* (London: Da Capo Press, 1982), 297.
2. Herb Fagen, *The Encyclopedia of Westerns* (New York: Facts on File, 2003), 398.

Strange Lady in Town (1955)

1. Michael Troyan, *A Rose for Mrs. Miniver: The Life of Greer Garson* (Lexington: University Press of Kentucky, 1999), 261.
2. Ibid., 263.
3. Ibid., 264.
4. Phil Hardy, *The Aurum Film Encyclopedia — The Western* (London: Aurum Press, 1995), 252.

Comanche (1956)

1. *Leonard Maltin's Movie and Video Guide 1996* (New York: Signet, 1996), 249.
2. *Halliwell's Film Guide,* 10th Edition.

While the City Sleeps (1956)

1. William Donati, *Ida Lupino: A Biography* (Lexington: University Press of Kentucky, 1996), 212.

Beyond a Reasonable Doubt (1956)

1. *TV Times Film & Video Guide 1995* (London: Mandarin, 1995), 61.
2. Patrick McGilligan, *Fritz Lang: The Nature of the Beast* (New York: Faber & Faber, 1997), 418.
3. Ibid., 420.
4. Ibid., 418.
5. Interview with Allen Eyles.

Spring Reunion (1957)

1. Kirk Douglas, *The Ragman's Son: An Autobiography* (New York: Simon & Schuster, 1988), 293.

Zero Hour! (1957)

1. *Zero Hour!* pressbook.
2. Ibid.

Night of the Demon (1957)

1. Chris Fujiwara, *Jacques Tourneur: The Cinema of Nightfall* (Baltimore: Johns Hopkins University Press, 2000), 242.
2. Tony Earnshaw, *Beating the Devil: The Making of Night of the Demon* (Sheffield: Tomahawk, 2005), 28.
3. Fujiwara, *Jacques Tourneur*, 243.
4. Ibid., 245.
5. Earnshaw, *Beating the Devil*, 28.
6. Ibid., 63.
7. Ibid., 32.

The Fearmakers (1958)

1. Robert J. Lentz, *Korean War Filmography* (Jefferson, NC: McFarland, 2003), 100.
2. Chris Fujiwara, *Jacques Tourneur: The Cinema of Nightfall* (Baltimore: Johns Hopkins University Press, 2000), 256.
3. Ibid., xi.
4. Mel Torme, *It Wasn't All Velvet: An Autobiography* (New York: Viking Penguin, 1988), 184.
5. Lentz, *Korean War Filmography*, 104–05.
6. Fujiwara, *Jacques Tourneur*, 256.
7. Ibid., 260.

Enchanted Island (1958)

1. Peter Bogdanovich, *Allan Dwan; The Last Pioneer* (New York: Praeger Publishers, 1971), 166.
2. Ibid.
3. Ibid.
4. Karen Burroughs Hannsberry, *Bad Boys: The Actors of Film Noir* (Jefferson, NC: McFarland, 2003), 22.
5. Jane Powell, *The Girl Next Door ... and How She Grew* (New York: William Morrow, 1988), 178.
6. *Enchanted Island* pressbook.
7. Powell, *The Girl Next Door*, 178.
8. *Enchanted Island* pressbook.

The Crowded Sky (1960)

1. *The Crowded Sky* pressbook.

Madison Avenue (1962)

1. Doug McClelland, *Eleanor Parker: Woman of a Thousand Faces* (Metuchen, NJ: Scarecrow Press, 1989), 103.
2. James Robert Parish with Gregory W. Mank, *The Hollywood Reliables* (Westport, CT: Arlington House, 1980), 26.

Crack in the World (1965)

1. James Robert Parish with Gregory W. Mank, *The Hollywood Reliables* (Westport, CT: Arlington House, 1980), 27.

The Satan Bug (1965)

1. The Reminiscences of Dana Andrews (1958), 17.

In Harm's Way (1965)

1. Foster Hirsch, *Otto Preminger: The Man Who Would Be King* (New York: Alfred A. Knopf, 2007), 394.
2. Kirk Douglas, *The Ragman's Son: An Autobiography* (New York: Simon & Schuster, 1988), 380.
3. Interview with Allen Eyles.

Brainstorm (1965)

1. Alain Silver and Elizabeth Ward (editors), *Film Noir: An Encyclopedic Reference to the American Style* (Woodstock, NY: The Overlook Press, 1992), 41.

Town Tamer (1965)

1. *Leonard Maltin's Movie and Video Guide 1996*, 249.

The Loved One (1965)

1. Interview with Allen Eyles.

Battle of the Bulge (1965)

1. Ken Annakin, *So You Wanna Be a Director?* (Sheffield: Tomahawk Press, 2001), 169, 173, 175 and 176.
2. Lawrence H. Suid, *Guts & Glory: Great American War Movies* (Reading, MA: Addison-Wesley, 1978), 243.
3. Lawrence J. Quirk, *The Great War Films* (New York: Citadel Press, 1994), 192.

Johnny Reno (1966)

1. *Johnny Reno* pressbook.
2. Ibid.
3. Don G. Smith, *Lon Chaney, Jr.* (Jefferson, NC: McFarland, 1996), 170.

Spy in Your Eye (1966)

2. Phil Hardy (editor), *The Aurum Film Encyclopedia: Science Fiction* (London: Aurum Press, 1984), 236.

Hot Rods to Hell (1967)

1. Phil Booker, *Jeanne Crain, the Beautiful Dreamer* (New York: Carlton Press, 1977), 44.
2. *Hot Rods to Hell* pressbook.
3. Ibid.

Il Cobra (1968)

1. Matt Blake and David Deal, *The Eurospy Guide* (Baltimore: Luminary Press, 2004), 51.

The Devil's Brigade (1968)

1. The Reminiscences of Dana Andrews (1958), 41–42, 45.

2. Lawrence H. Suid, *Guts & Glory: Great American War Movies* (Reading, MA: Addison-Wesley, 1978), 238.

Innocent Bystanders (1972)

1. *Innocent Bystanders* pressbook.
2. Ibid.
3. Ibid.
4. Ibid.

Airport 1975 (1974)

1. Jeff Rovin, *The Films of Charlton Heston* (Secaucus, NJ: Citadel Press, 1977), 216.
2. Ibid.

Take a Hard Ride (1975)

1. Herb Fagen, *The Encyclopedia of Westerns* (New York: Facts on File, 2003), 419.

The Last Tycoon (1976)

1. Richard Schickel, *Elia Kazan: A Biography* (New York: Harper Collins, 2005), 437.

Bibliography

Andersen, Christopher P. *A Star, Is a Star, Is a Star: The Lives and Loves of Susan Hayward*. London: Robson Books, 1981.

Annakin, Ken. *So You Wanna Be a Director?* Sheffield: Tomahawk Press, 2001.

Annan, David. *Catastrophe: The End of the Cinema?* London: Lorrimer, 1975.

Barson, Michael. *The Illustrated Who's Who of Hollywood Directors. Volume 1: The Sound Era*. New York: Noonday Press, 1995.

Behlmer, Rudy, ed. *Henry Hathaway: A Director's Guild of America Oral History*. Lanham, MD: Scarecrow Press, 2001.

Belafonte, Dennis. *The Films of Tyrone Power*. Secaucus, NJ: Citadel Press, 1979.

Berg, A. Scott. *Goldwyn*. London: Sphere Books, 1989.

Bergan, Ronald. *Jean Renoir: Projections of Paradise*. London: Bloomsbury, 1992.

_____. *The United Artists Story*. New York: Crown, 1986.

Blake, Matt, and David Deal. *The Eurospy Guide*. Baltimore: Luminary Press, 2004.

Bogdanovich, Peter. *Allan Dwan; The Last Pioneer*. New York: Praeger, 1971.

_____. *John Ford*. Berkeley: University of California Press, 1978.

Booker, Phil. *Jeanne Crain, the Beautiful Dreamer*. New York: Carlton Press, 1977.

Brown, Peter Harry, and Pat H. Broeske. *Howard Hughes: The Untold Story*. New York: Dutton, 1996.

Cocchi, John. *Second Feature: The Best of the "B" Features*. Secaucus, NJ: Carol, 1991.

Coppedge, Walter. *Henry King's America*. Metuchen, NJ: Scarecrow Press, 1986.

Cottfried, Martin. *Nobody's Fool: The Lives of Danny Kaye*. New York: Simon & Schuster, 1994.

Crow, Jefferson Brim, III. *Randolph Scott: The Gentleman from Virginia*. Carrollton, TX: WindRiver Books, 1987.

Crowther, Bruce. *Film Noir — Reflections in a Dark Mirror*. London: Virgin, 1990.

Custen, George F. *Twentieth Century's Fox: Darryl F. Zanuck and the Culture of Hollywood*. New York: Basic Books, 1997.

Davenport, Robert. *The Encyclopedia of War Movies: The Authoritative Guide to Movies About Wars of the Twentieth Century*. New York: Facts on File, 2004.

Davis, Ronald L. *Hollywood Beauty: Linda Darnell and the American Dream*. Norman: University of Oklahoma, 1991.

Denton, Clive, Kingsley Canham, and Tony Thomas. *The Hollywood Professionals: Henry King, Lewis Milestone, Sam Wood*. New York: A.S. Barnes, 1974.

Dickens, Homer. *The Films of Gary Cooper*. New York: Citadel Press, 1971.

Doherty, Thomas. *Projections of War: Hollywood, American Culture, and World War II*. New York: Columbia University Press, 1993.

Donati, William. *Ida Lupino: A Biography*. Lexington: University Press of Kentucky, 1996.

Douglas, Kirk. *The Ragman's Son: An Autobiography*. New York: Simon & Schuster, 1988.

Dundy, Elaine. *Finch, Bloody Finch: A Biography of Peter Finch*. London: Michael Joseph, 1980.

Durgnat, Raymond. *Jean Renoir*. London: Cassell and Collier Macmillan, 1975.

Eames, John Douglas. *The MGM Story*. London: Octopus Books, 1975.

_____. *The Paramount Story*. London: Octopus Books, 1985.

Earnshaw, Tony. *Beating The Devil: The Making of Night of the Demon*. Sheffield: Tomahawk, 2005.

Easton, Carol. *The Search for Sam Goldwyn: A Biography*. New York: Quill William Morrow, 1975.

Edwards, Anne. *Vivien Leigh: A Biography*. London: W.H. Allen, 1977.

Elder, Jane Lenz. *Alice Faye: A Life Beyond the Silver Screen*. Jackson: University Press of Mississippi, 2002.

Evans, Alun. *Brassey's Guide to War Films*. Washington, D.C.: Brassey's, 2000.

Everson, William K. *Classics of the Horror Film*. New York: Citadel Press, 1974.

Fagen, Herb. *The Encyclopedia of Westerns*. New York: Facts on File, 2003.

Fonda, Henry, as told to Howard Teichmann. *Fonda, My Life*. New York: New American Library, 1981.

Fowler, Karen J. *Anne Baxter: A Bio-Bibliography*. New York: Greenwood Press, 1991.

Frank, Alan. *Frank's 500: The Thriller Film Guide*. London: B.T. Batsford, 1997.

_____. *The Science Fiction and Fantasy Film Handbook*. London: B.T. Batsford, 1982.

Freedland, Michael. *The Goldwyn Touch: A Biography of Sam Goldwyn*. London: Harrap, 1986.

Frischauer, Willi. *Behind the Scenes of Otto Preminger*. London: Michael Joesph, 1973.

Fujiwara, Chris. *Jacques Tourneur: The Cinema of Nightfall*. Baltimore: Johns Hopkins University Press, 1998.

_____. *The World and Its Double: The Life and Work of Otto Preminger*. New York: Faber and Faber, 2008.

Fultz, Jay. *In Search of Donna Reed*. Iowa City: University of Iowa Press, 1998.

Garfield, Brian. *Western Films: A Complete Guide*. London: Da Capo Press, 1982.

Garland, Brock. *War Movies*. New York: Facts on File, 1987.

Gifford, Barry. *Out of the Past: Adventures in Film Noir*. Jackson: University Press of Mississippi, 2001.

Granger, Farley, with Robert Calhoun. *Include Me Out: My Life from Goldwyn to Broadway*. New York: St. Martin's Press, 2007.

Green, Stanley. *Encyclopedia of the Musical Film*. New York: Oxford University Press, 1981.

Guiles, Fred Lawrence. *Joan Crawford: The Last Word*. London: Pavilion Books, 1995.

Gunning, Tom. *The Films of Fritz Lang — Allegories of Vision and Modernity*. London: British Film Institute, 2000.

Hack, Richard. *Hughes: The Private Diaries, Memos and Letters*. Beverly Hills: New Millennium Press, 2001.

Halliwell, Leslie. *Halliwell's Film Guide,* Tenth Edition. London: Harper Collins, 1994.

_____. *Halliwell's Harvest: A Further Choice of Entertainment Movies from the Golden Age*. London: Grafton Books, 1986.

Hannsberry, Karen Burroughs. *Bad Boys: The Actors of Film Noir*. Jefferson, NC: McFarland, 2003.

Hardy, Phil. *The Aurum Film Encyclopedia: Gangsters*. London: Aurum Press, 1998.

_____. *The Aurum Film Encyclopedia: Horror*. London: Aurum Press, 1985.

_____. *The Aurum Film Encyclopedia: Science Fiction*. London: Aurum Press, 1984.

_____. *The Aurum Film Encyclopedia: Westerns*. London: Aurum Press, 1983, 1984, 1991, 1995.

_____, ed. *The BFI Companion to Crime*. London: Cassel, 1997.

Hathaway, Henry, edited and annotated by Rudy Behlmer. *Henry Hathaway. A Directors Guild of America Oral History*. Lanham, MD: Scarecrow Press, 2001.

Herman, Jan. *A Talent for Trouble: The Life of Hollywood's Most Acclaimed Director, William Wyler*. New York: G.P Putman's, 1995

Higham, Charles, and Roy Moseley. *Merle: A Biography of Merle Oberon*. Sevenoaks, Kent: New English Library, 1983.

Hirsch, Foster. *Otto Preminger: The Man Who Would Be King*. New York: Alfred A. Knopf, 2007.

Hirschhorn, Clive. *The Columbia Story*. London: Octopus Books, 1989.

_____. *The Hollywood Musical*. London: Octopus Books, 1981.

_____. *The Universal Story*. London: Octopus Books, 1983

_____. *The Warner Bros Story*. London: Octopus Books, 1979.

Holston, Kim. *Richard Widmark: A Bio-Bibliography*. New York: Greenwood Press, 1990.

Jeavons, Clyde. *A Pictorial History of War Films*. New York: Hamlyn, 1974.

Jensen, Paul M. *The Cinema of Fritz Lang*. New York: A.S. Barnes, 1969.

Jewel, Richard B., with Vernon Harbin. *The RKO Story*. London: Octopus Books, 1982.

Katz, Ephraim. *The Macmillan Film Guide, Encyclopedia*. New York: Macmillan, 1998.

Kay, Glen, and Michael Rose. *Disaster Movies*. Chicago: Chicago Review Press, 2006.

Kirk, Marilyn. *Jeff Chandler. A Biography*. Bloomington, IN: 1st Books Library, 1999.

Kotsilibas-Davis, James, and Myrna Loy. *Myrna Loy: Being and Becoming*. London: Bloomsbury, 1987.

Krutnik, Frank. *A Lonely Street: Film Noir, Genre, Masculinity*. New York: Routledge, 1991.

Laguardia, Robert, and Gene Arceri. *Red: The Tempestuous Life of Susan Hayward*. London: Robson Books, 1985.

Langman, Larry, and David Ebner. *Encyclopedia of American Spy Films*. New York: Garland, 1990.

Lentz, Robert J. *Korean War Filmography*. Jefferson, NC: McFarland, 2003.

LeRoy, Mervyn. *Take One. An Autobiography by Mervyn LeRoy*. London: W.H. Allen, 1974.

Macksoud, Meredith C., with Craig R. Smith and Jackie Lohrke. *Arthur Kennedy, Man of Characters*. Jefferson, NC: McFarland, 2003.

Madsen, Axel. *Stanwyck*. New York: Harper Collins, 1994.

_____. *William Wyler: The Authorised Biography*. London: W.H. Allen, 1974.

Malden, Karl, with Carla Malden, *When Do I Start? A Memoir*. New York: Simon & Schuster, 1997.

Margulies, Edward, and Stephen Rebello. *Bad Movies We Love*. London: Marion Boyars, 1993, 1995.

Marx, Arthur. *Goldwyn: The Man Behind the Myth*. Badley Head, 1976.

Mayo, Virginia, LC Van Savage. *Virginia Mayo: The Best Years of My Life*. Chesterfield, MS: Beachhouse Books, 2002.

McArthur, Colin. *Underworld USA*. New York: Viking Press, 1974.

McBride, Joseph. *Searching for John Ford: A Life*. New York: St. Martin's Press, 1999.

McCarthy, Todd. *Howard Hawks: The Grey Fox of Hollywood*. New York: Grove Press, 1997.

McCarty, John. *The Modern Horror Film*. New York: Citadel Press, 1990.

McClelland, Doug. *Eleanor Parker: Woman of a Thousand Faces*. Metuchen, NJ: Scarecrow Press, 1989.

McFarlane, Brian. *An Autobiography of British Cinema: By the Actors and Filmmakers Who Made It.* London: Methuen, 1997.

McGilligan, Patrick. *Fritz Lang: The Nature of the Beast.* New York: Faber and Faber, 1997.

Merrill, Gary. *Bette, Rita, and the Rest of My Life.* New York: Berkley Books, 1990.

Meyer, William R. *The Making of the Great Westerns.* New Rochelle, NY: Arlington House, 1979.

Milne, Tom. *Rouben Mamoulian.* London: Thames & Hudson, 1969.

Montgomery, Bill. *A Seat in the Second Circle.* Liverpool: Bluecoat Press, 2002.

Morella, Joe, Edward Z. Epstein, and John Griggs. *The Films of World War II.* New York: Citadel Press, 1975.

Moreno, Eduardo. *The Films of Susan Hayward.* New York: Citadel Press, 1979.

Moshier, W. Franklyn. *The Alice Faye Movie Book.* Harrisburg, PA: Stackpole Books, 1974.

Mosley, Leonard. *Zanuck: The Rise and Fall of Hollywood's Last Tycoon.* London: Granada, 1984.

Muller, Eddie. *Dark City Dames: The Wicked Women of Film Noir.* New York: Regan Books, 2001.

Negulesco, Jean. *Things I Did ... and Things I Think I Did: A Hollywood Memoir.* New York: Linden Press/Simon & Schuster, 1984.

Newman, Kim. *Apocalypse Movies: End of the World Cinema.* New York: St. Martin's, 2000.

_____. *Wild West Movies or How The West Was Found, Won, Lost, Lied About, Filmed and Forgotten.* New York: Bloomsbury, 1990.

Nolan, Frederick. *The Sound of Their Music — The Story of Rodgers & Hammerstein.* London: J. M. Dent, 1978.

Nott, Robert. *Last of the Cowboy Heroes: The Westerns of Randolph Scott, Joel McCrea, and Audie Murphy.* Jefferson, NC: McFarland, 2000.

O'Brien, Geoffrey. "Dana Andrews, or the Frozen Mask." In *O.K. You Mugs: Writers on Movie Actors.* Edited by Luc Sante and Melissa Holbrook Pierson. London: Granta Books, 1999

O'Hara, Maureen, with John Nicoletti. *'Tis Herself: A Memoir.* New York: Simon & Schuster, 2004.

Ohmart, Ben. *Don Ameche: The Kenosha Comeback Kid.* Albany, GA: BearManor Media, 2007.

Ott, Frederick W. *The Films of Fritz Lang.* New York: Citadel Press, 1979.

Ottoson, Robert. *A Reference Guide to the American Film Noir: 1940–1958.* Metuchen, NJ: Scarecrow Press, 1981.

Paris, Michael. *From the Wright Brothers to* Top Gun*: Aviation, Nationalism and Popular Cinema.* Manchester: Manchester University Press, 1995.

Parish, James Robert. *The Fox Girls.* Secaucus, NJ: Castle Books, 1972.

_____. *The Great Combat Pictures.* Metuchen, NJ: Scarecrow Press, 1990.

_____. *The Great Cop Pictures.* Metuchen, NJ: Scarecrow Press, 1990.

_____. *The Paramount Pretties.* Secaucus, NJ: Castle Books, 1972.

_____, and Michael R. Pitts. *The Great Spy Pictures.* Metuchen, NJ: Scarecrow Press, 1974.

_____, and Michael R. Pitts. *The Great Spy Pictures II.* Metuchen, NJ: Scarecrow Press, 1986.

_____, and Michael R. Pitts. *The Great Westerns.* Metuchen, NJ: Scarecrow Press, 1988.

_____, with Gregory Mank. *The Hollywood Reliables.* Westport, CT: Arlington House, 1980.

Place, J. A. *The Non-Western Films of John Ford.* New York: Citadel Press, 1979.

Powell, Jane. *The Girl Next Door ... and How She Grew.* New York: William Morrow, 1988.

Pratley, Gerald. *The Cinema of Otto Preminger.* New York: A.S. Barnes, 1971.

Price, Victoria. *Vincent Price: A Daughter's Biography.* London: Sidgwick & Jackson, 1999.

Quinlan, David. *British Sound Films: The Studio Years 1928–1959.* London: B.T. Batsford, 1984.

_____. *Quinlan's Illustrated Directory of Film Stars.* London: B.T. Batsford, 1981.

Quirk, Lawrence J. *The Films of Fredric March.* New York: Citadel Press, 1974.

_____. *The Films of Joan Crawford.* New York: Citadel Press, 1970.

_____. *The Films of Myrna Loy.* New York: Citadel Press, 1987.

_____. *The Great Romantic Films.* New York: Citadel Press, 1974.

_____. *The Great War Films: From* The Birth of a Nation *to* Today. New York: Citadel Press, 1994.

Radio Times Guide to Films. London: BBC Worldwide, 2000.

Roberts, Randy, and James S. Olson. *John Wayne America.* New York: Free Press, 1995.

Rovin, Jeff. *The Films of Charlton Heston.* Secaucus, NJ: Citadel Press, 1977.

_____. *A Pictorial History of Science Fiction Films.* New York: Citadel Press, 1975.

Royce, Brenda Scott. *Donna Reed: A Bio-Bibliography.* New York: Greenwood Press, 1990.

Rubenstein, Leonard. *The Great Spy Films: A Pictorial History.* New York: Citadel Press, 1979.

Schickel, Richard. *Elia Kazan: A Biography.* New York: Harper Collins, 2005.

Selby, Spencer. *Dark City: The Film Noir.* Jefferson, NC: McFarland, 1984.

Shaheen, Jack G. *Reel Bad Arabs: How Hollywood Vilifies a People.* Moreton-in-Marsh: Arris Books, 2003.

Shipman, David. *The Great Movie Stars: The International Years,* New York: St. Martin's Press, 1972.

_____. *The Great Movie Stars: The International Years,* New York: Hill and Wang, 1980.

_____. *The Great Movie Stars: The International Years, 2,* London: Warner Books, 1989.

Silver, Alain, and Elizabeth Ward, editors. *Film Noir: An Encyclopedic Reference to the American Style (Third Edition).* Woodstock, NY: Overlook Press, 1979, 1992.

Skogsberg, Bertil. *Wings on the Screen: A Pictorial History of Air Movies.* San Diego: A.S. Barnes, 1981.

Smith, Don G. *Lon Chaney, Jr.: Horror Film Star, 1906–1973*. Jefferson, NC: McFarland, 1996.

Smith, Ella. *Starring Miss Barbara Stanwyck*. New York: Crown, 1974.

Soister, John T., with JoAnna Wioskowski. *Claude Rains: A Comprehensive Illustrated Reference*. Jefferson, NC: McFarland, 1999.

Springer, John. *The Fondas: The Films and Careers of Henry, Jane & Peter Fonda*. New York: Citadel Press, 1974.

Stanley, John. *Creature Features: The Science Fiction, Fantasy and Horror Movie Guide*. New York: Berkley Boulevard, 2000.

Sudhalter, Richard M. *Stardust Melody: The Life and Music of Hoagy Carmichael*. New York: Oxford University Press, 2002.

Suid, Lawrence H. *Guts & Glory: Great American War Movies*. Reading, MA: Addison-Wesley, 1978.

_____. *Sailing on the Silver Screen: Hollywood and the U.S. Navy*. Annapolis, MD: Naval Institute Press, 1996.

Swindell, Larry. *The Last Hero. A Biography of Gary Cooper*. New York: Doubleday, 1980.

Taraborrelli, J. Randy. *Elizabeth*. London: Sidgwick & Jackson, 2006.

Telotte. J. P. *Voices in the Dark: The Narrative of Patterns of Film Noir*. Urbana: University of Illinois Press, 1989.

Thomas, Tony. *The Films of Henry Fonda*. New York: Citadel Press, 1983.

_____. *The Films of Kirk Douglas*. New York: Citadel Press, 1972.

_____. *The Films of the Forties*. New York: Citadel Press, 1975.

_____, and Aubrey Solomon. *The Films of 20th Century–Fox: A Pictorial History*. New York: Citadel Press, 1979.

Thomson, David. *The New Biographical Dictionary of Film*. New York: Alfred A. Knopf, 2002.

Thompson, Frank T. *William A. Wellman. Filmakers No. 4*. Metuchen, NJ: Scarecrow Press, 1983.

Tierney, Gene, with Mickey Herskowitz. *Self-Portrait: Gene Tierney*. New York: Berkley Books, 1980.

Torme, Mel. *It Wasn't All Velvet: An Autobiography*. New York: Viking Penguin, 1988.

Troyan, Michael. *A Rose for Mrs. Miniver: The Life of Greer Garson*. Lexington: University Press of Kentucky, 1999.

Tyler, Parker. *The Magic and Myths of the Movies*. New York: Henry Holt, 1947.

Vermilye, Jerry, and Mark Ricci. *The Films of Elizabeth Taylor*. New York: Citadel Press, 1989.

Vinson, James (editor). *The International Dictionary of Films and Filmmakers— Actors and Actresses*. London: Papermac, 1986.

Vogel, Michelle. *Gene Tierney: A Biography*. Jefferson, NC: McFarland, 2005.

Walker, Alexander. *Elizabeth*. London: Weidenfeld and Nicolson, 1990.

Warren, Patricia. *Elstree: The British Hollywood*. London: Columbus Books, 1988.

Wayne, Jane Ellen. *Crawford's Men*. London: Robson Books, 1988.

Wells, Jeff. *Jeff Chandler*. Jefferson, NC: McFarland, 2005.

Williams, Esther, with Digby Diehl. *Esther Williams, the Million Dollar Mermaid: An Autobiography*. New York: Simon & Schuster, 1999.

Williams, Lucy Chase. *The Complete Films of Vincent Price*. New York: Citadel Press 1995.

Wilson, Ivy Crane (editor). *Hollywood Album; The Wonderful City and Its Famous Inhabitants*. London: Sampson Low Marston.

Wood, Michael. *America in the Movies*. New York: Columbia University Press, 1975, 1989.

Miscellaneous

Doyle, Neil. "Flawed Hero." *Films of the Golden Age* #25 (2001).

Eyles, Allen, interview, *Focus on Film* #26. Tantivy Press, 1977.

Film Dope.

Film Illustrated Monthly.

Films Illustrated.

Internet databases— e.g., IMDb and Wikipedia.

Modern Screen.

Picture Show & Film Pictorial, 1954.

Picturegoer.

Reminiscences of Dana Andrews (1958), in the Oral History Collection of Columbia University.

Screen Parade.

Screenland.

Pressbooks

Assignment Paris

Deep Waters

The Crowded Sky

Enchanted Island

Hot Rods to Hell

Innocent Bystanders

Johnny Reno

Laura

Sailor's Lady

Zero Hour!

Index

Aames, Marlene 79
Abbot, Anthony (Foulton Oursler) 84, 85
"Abby, as in Abbigale" 221
ABC Circle Films 217
ABC-TV (American Broadcasting Company) 65, 216, 217
Abril, Anton Garcia 197
Academy Award 11, 25, 26, 30, 32, 34, 37, 40, 44, 45, 48, 51, 60, 66, 68, 73, 77, 78, 80, 81, 83, 85, 101, 103, 108, 117, 118, 121, 124, 130, 135, 147, 150, 167, 175, 180, 182, 185, 197, 201, 208, 213
Acapulco, Mexico 162
Acuff, Eddie 25
Adam, Ken 155
Adams, Dorothy 61, 79
Adams, Nick 139
Addison, John 181, 212, 213
Adleman, Robert H. 199
Adrejew, Andrew 102
"Adventures of the Judas Tree" 217
"Against the Middle" 220
Agar, John 22, 186, 188
Agee, James 96
Ahern, Lloyd 192
Aiken, Joseph E. 41
Airplane 17, 153, 182
Airport 204
Airport 1975 19, 153, 166, 204–205
Airport 77 204
"Alas, Babylon" 215
Albert, Eddie 166, 167, 168
Albertini, Bitto 190
Alberty, Karl Otto 183
Alcoa, Premiere 216
Aldem, Norman 199
Aldridge, Kay 24, 26, 27
All Quiet on the Western Front 50, 59, 71, 100
Allen, Fred 23, 25, 41
Allen, June 101
Allen, Robert 161
Allen, Stanford C. 205
Allied Artists 161
Alper, Murray 25, 59
Ambler, Buster 102,
Ameche, Don 59, 60
The American Girls 217
American International 188, 189, 197, 198

"American Kremlin" 220
"Anchors Aweigh" (song) 61
Anderson, Eugene, Jr. 158
Anderson, Glenn E. 104
Anderson, Herbert 148
Anderson, Howard A. 27
Anderson, John 171
Anderson, Judith 61, 63
Anderson, Richard 210
Anderson, William H. 23, 25
Andrade, Fran 158
Andrei, Franco 190
Andrews, Anice (mother) 3
Andrews, Betti 166
Andrews, Charles (brother) 3
Andrews, Charles Forrest (father) 3
Andrews, Dana: addiction to drink 12; becomes president of the Screen Actor's Guild 18; birth 3; birth of first son 5; death of first child 18; delves into property development 18; first film role 6; first marriage 5; goes independent 12; move to Hollywood 4; returns to the theatre 12; runs away from home 4; second marriage and birth of children Katherine, Stephen and Susan 6; signs with Samuel Goldwyn 6
Andrews, David (son) 5, 8, 13, 18, 27, 37, 144, 145
Andrews, Harlan (brother) 3
Andrews, Jack 41
Andrews, Katherine (daughter) 6, 8, 13, 15, 47
Andrews, Mary Todd (second wife) 6, 7, 8, 12, 13, 22, 31, 217, 218
Andrews, Stanley 27
Andrews, Stephen (son) 6, 8, 13, 15
Andrews, Susan (daughter) 6, 13, 14
Andrews, Tige 206
Andrews, Tod 174
Andrews, Witon (brother) 3
Andriot, Lucien N. 23
The Andromeda Strain 171
Angeli, Pier 183, 188, 190
Angels with Dirty Faces 115

Angiolillo, Luciana 188
Anhalt, Edward 171, 172
Annakin, Ken 183, 184
Annie Get Your Gun 150
The Anniversary 196
Anthony and Cleopatra 5
Any Wednesday 13, 218
Appley, Chris 158
Arch of Triumph 100, 101
Archer, Anne 209, 210
Archie, John 212
Ardura, Francisco 205
Arleen, Richard 118
Arlen, Harold 52
Arlen, Richard 178, 179, 186, 187
Arlen, Roxanne 181
Armand, Eddie 151
Armoured Attack 52
Arno, Sig 52
Arnold, Malcolm 102
Arnold, Newton 199
Arnt, Charles 39, 52
Arodin, Sidney 79
Arthur, Jean 40
Ashby, Hal 181
Asher, Ed 171, 173
Asher, Irving 127, 128
Ashley, Edward 127
Ashley, Herbert 72
Ashley, John 151
Askew, Luke 199
Askin, Leon 124
"Assault on a Tower" 217
Assignment in Brittany 49
Assignment Paris 12, 67, 124–127, 145, 150, 159
Assola, Charles-Henri 169
Astaire, Fred 216
Astar, Ben 124
At Gun Point 134, 135
Atkins, Claude 199, 201
Aurthur, Robert Alan 149
Austin, Frank 37
Avco Embassy 210, 211
Aymo 191
Ayres, Lew 67

Bacher, William A. 60
Backus, Jim 122, 209, 210, 213, 214
Bacon, Irving 31
Bacon, James 209
Bacon, Lloyd 116, 117, 118

Bailey, Robert 59
Bainter, Fay 65
Bakaleinikoff, C. 90
Baker, Art 87
Baker, Benny 52
Baker, Diane 212, 213
Baker, Fay 99
Baker, Stanley 184, 201, 202, 203
Baldini, Renato 188
Baldwin, Walter 79, 122
Balenda, Carla 119, 120, 121, 180
Ball of Fire 7, 39–41
Ballard, Lucien 90, 91, 93
Bambi 43
Bancroft, Anne 217
The Bandit Queen 36
Banks, Don 195
Banton, Travis 76
Baracco, Adriano 188
The Barbara Stanwyck Show 215
Bardette, Trevor 29
Bari, Lynn 27, 29, 150
Barker, Jess 76
Barnes, George 99
The Baron 203
Baron, Kathy 191
Barr, Patrick 131
Barrett, Hoyle 176
Barrie, Lesley 93
Barrow, Janet 155
Barry, Don "Red" 25, 27, 55, 56, 58, 178
Barry, Gene 216, 219
Barrymore, Drew 145
Barrymore, Ethel 90, 93
Barrymore, John Drew 144, 145
Barrymore, Lionel 219
Barsha, Leon 149
Bartlett, Bonnie 206
Bartlett, Hall 151, 152, 153, 154
Baseheart, Richard 171, 172
Basevi, James 30, 31, 46, 55
Basinger, Jeanine 64
Bassett, James 174, 175
Bates, Charles 49
Bates, Florence 6
Battle, John Tucker 116
Battle of the Bulge 18, 175, 183–186, 190, 200
Battleground 150
Bau, Gordon 90, 164, 176
Baxter, Anne 36, 37, 38, 43, 44, 49, 51, 52, 150, 219
Baxter, Les 210
Baxter, Warner 23
Bazin, Abdul-Rahim 188
Beakeley, Ballard 155
Bean, Judge Roy 29, 30, 31 35
Beard, Matthew 72
Beavers, Louise 34
Beckwith, Reginald 155
Beddoe, Don 79
The Bedford Incident 117
Bedoya, Alfonso 23
Begley, Ed 84, 85, 87, 96, 98
Behlmer, Rudy 64
Behm, Joseph 97
Bell, Vereen 37
Belle Starr 7, 24, 34–36, 44, 112, 150, 184

Beltramme, Franco 188
Benda, George K. 102
Bender, Bob 210
Benedict, Richard 67, 148
Benedict, William 210
Bennett, Charles 155, 156
Bennett, Joan 76
Bennett, Joe 209
Benson, Sam 37, 46, 50, 55, 60, 61, 65, 68, 116
Benton, Robert 186
Benvenuti, Jolanda 190
Bercovici, Eric 205
Berenguer, Manuel 169
Berghof, Herbert 124
Bergman, Ingrid 100, 126
Berkshire Theatre (Stockbridge, Mass) 218
Berle, Milton 181
Berlin Correspondent 7, 41–43, 54, 67, 108, 126, 184
Berlin Express 91
Berlino — Appuntamento per le spie (*Spy in Your Eye*) 18, 188–190
Bernard, Barry 127
Berne, Jack R. 166
Berner, Sara 148
Bernsen, Harry 205, 206
Bernstein, Elmer 213
Bertisch, Max 68
Bertoya, Paul 192, 194
Beryl, Tunia 188
Best, Edna 93
Best, Richard 102
The Best Years of Our Lives 1, 2, 11, 12, 17, 30, 51, 79–84, 87, 90, 93, 96, 112, 113, 123, 124, 153, 165, 194, 197
"The Best Years of Our Lives" (radio) 219, 221
Bettger, Lyle 18, 178, 179, 186, 187
Beumont, Roger 191
Beyond a Reasonable Doubt 15, 41, 67, 87, 90, 122, 145, 146–148, 157, 177, 178
Beyond Mombasa 132
Bianchi, Tino 188
Biberman, Abner 127
Bickford, Charles 59, 60, 71, 74, 180
The Big Heat 112
Biggs, Douglas 55
Bigham, James 212
Bikel, Theodore 213
Binger, R.O. 49, 52
Binns, Ed 146, 212
The Birds 128
Bissell, Whit 123
Black, Karen 204
Black, Trevor 213
"Black Gospel" 220
Blackmer, Sidney 146
Blackwell, George 155
Blaine, Martin 171
Blaine, Vivian 65, 66, 67
Blair, Linda 204
Blake, Larry J. 144
Blake, Oliver 158
Blanchard, Susan 117
Blangstead, Folmar 139

Blech, Hans Christian 183
Bloch, Walter 210
Blood Alley 96, 106
The Bloody Spur 144, 145
"The Blue Gardenia" 17, 219
Blumenthal, Herman A. 171
Blyth, Ann 106
Bob Hope Presents the Chrysler Theatre 216
Bodeen, Dewitt 6, 90
Bodoh, Allan F. 209
Boetticher, Budd 36
Bogart, Humphrey 40, 115, 126
Bogeaus, Benedict 161, 163
Bohnen, Roman 79
Bolzoni, Adrianno 188, 197
Bond, James 172, 189, 190, 203
Bond, Lilian 29
Bond, Ward 25, 27, 29, 31, 34, 37, 75, 78
Boomerang! 12, 58, 84–87, 98, 101, 111, 114, 115, 148, 208
Boomerang! (radio) 221
Boone, Pat 67, 73
Booth, Karen 107
Boretz, Allen 52
Borg, Veda Ann 158
Borionko, Yuri 201
Born Again 20, 210–212, 213
Bouchet, Barbara 174
Bouchey, Willis 124, 151
Boulting, Ingrid 206, 208
Boulton, Davis 195
Bourneuf, Philip 146
Bowers, William 125
Bowker, Aldrich 39
Bowman, Tom 201
"The Boy Who Wasn't Wanted" 216
Boyer, Charles 219
Boyle, Edward G. 27, 99
Boyle, Joseph 79
Boys Town 115
Brackett, Charles 39, 115
Bradburn, Arthur 155
Brady, Leo 113
Brahm, John 192, 194
The Brain That Wouldn't Die 196
Brainstorm 18, 41, 176–178, 184
Brandi, Rose 176
Brando, Marlon 18, 86, 137, 163
Brandon, Henry 22, 141, 142, 143
Brandt, Janet 158, 183
"The Brass Monkey" 220
Breck, Kathleen 195, 197
Brega, Mario 191
Brennan, Frederick Hazlitt 25
Brennan, Walter 6, 29, 31, 36, 37, 39, 49, 50, 51, 52, 143
Brent, George 210, 211
Bresler, Jerry 125, 149, 150
Bretz, Bill 212
Bridge on the River Kwai 201
Bridgeport, Connecticut 84, 85
Bridges, Beau 99, 101
Bridges, Lloyd 67, 68, 75, 153, 182
Brigandi, Phil 119
Briggs, Matt 46
Bright Promise 19, 21, 216
Brissac, Virginia 113
Bristol, Howard 39, 49, 52, 122

Britannia Mews (novel) 102
British Museum Library 155
Britt, Leo 127
Broadway 217, 218, 219
Brodie, Steve 67, 68
Brodine, Norbert 84, 16, 118
Bronson, Charles 183, 185
Brookes, George 134
Brooks, Dene 210
Broussard, Eddie 136
Brown, Bernard 76
Brown, Charles D. 25, 52
Brown, George H. 201
Brown, Harry 68
Brown, Harry Joe 36, 134
Brown, James 178
Brown, Jim 205, 206
Brown, Kathie 176
Brown, Malcolm 186
Brown, Phil 65
Broyles, Robert 210
Bruce, George 27
Brunn, Frederic 43
Bruzlin, Alfred 37, 46, 55, 60, 110
Bryant, Gene 31
Bryce, Hope 174, 175
Bryna Company 151
Brynner, Yul 43
Buch, Fred 212
Buckner, Robert 104, 105
Budapest 126
"Buffalo Gals Won't You Come Out Tonight" 29
The Build Up Boys 166, 167
Bull, Richard 171, 173
Burch, John 149
Burnett, W.R. 43
Burns, Brendon 207
Burns, Mel 119
Burns, Paul E. 34, 37, 72
"Burnt Offering" 220
Burton, R. 204
Burton, Richard 12, 128
Busby, Gerald 212
Busch, Niven 30, 34, 51
Busch, Paul 199
Bush, Kate 158
Butchart, Anne 101
Butler, Frank 139, 141
Butler, Lawrence W. 174
Buttolph, David 31, 37, 41, 43, 84
Byrd, Julian 212
Byron, Jeffrey 192, 193

The Caballero's Way 23
Cabot, Bruce 71, 72, 174, 178, 179, 180
Cacavas, John 204
Cady, Jerome 55, 60, 61
Caesar, Sid 204
Cagney, James 1, 27, 40, 83, 85, 163
Cagney, Jeanne 178
Caine, Richard 210
Caldwell, Erskine 7
Calhern, Louis 52
"Call Northside 777" 221
Calley, John 81
Camden, Joan 139
Campbell, Clay 125
"The Canadian Backbone" 221

"Canadian Crossfire" 220
Canary Islands 206
"The Candidate" 217
Cantor, Eddie 8, 52
Canty, Marietta 107
Canutt, Joe 204
Canyon Passage 11, 29, 75–79, 93, 156, 159, 180
Capps, McClure 49, 52
Capra, Frank 99
Capra, Frank, Jr. 210, 211
Captain from Castile 97, 98
Captains and the Kings 13, 20, 218
Captains Courageous 99
Carbajal, Tony 141
"Card Game in the Clouds" 220
Cardi, Pat 176
Cardwell, James 67, 75
Carey, Harry, Jr. 199, 205, 206
Carey, Leslie I. 136
Carey, Philip 178, 180
Carmichael, Hoagy 75, 77, 79, 80, 81, 90, 93
Carmona, Nick 104
Caroll, Madeleine 153
Carpenter, Claude E. 178
Carpenter, Paul 131
Carradine, John 36, 37, 39, 71, 74, 206, 208
Carruth, Milton 76, 136
Carruth, Richard 174
Carson, Robert 158
Carter, Ann 49
Carter, Ben 43, 44
Carter, Eric 195
Carter, Maurice 201
Cartwright, William 199
Casablanca 48, 64
Casey, Lawrence P. 207
Cash, Don L. 27
Cashin, Bonnie 61, 72, 93
Caspary, Vera 61, 63
Cass, Maurice 52
The Cassandra Crossing 172
Cassel, Seymour 206
Cassini, Oleg 109, 112
Cast a Giant Shadow 106
Casting the Runes 155
Castle Hill Productions Inc. 213
Catlett, Walter 52
Cavalcade of America 218
CBS Television 65
Ceylon 14, 127, 128, 130
Chamberlain, Howland 113
Champion, John C. 151
Chandler, George 31, 148
Chandler, Jeff 104, 105
Chandler, Lane 61
Chaney, Lon, Jr. 18, 178, 179, 180, 186, 187, 188
Chaney, Stewart 32
Chang, E. 197
Chano, Peter 55
Chaplin, Charlie 117
Chaplin, Geraldine 201, 202, 203
"Charter City Square Dance" 220
Charters, Spencer 31
Chester, Hal E. 155, 157, 158
Chicago (city) 218
Chicago Deadline 65

Chooluck, Leon 158
"Chopsticks" 82
Christie, Agatha 148
Christie, Howard 136
Christmas, Eric 207
Churchill, Winston 94, 201
The Cinema of Nightfall 156
Cinquini, Renato 188
Cinquini, Robert 188
Citizen Kane 88
Clark, Carroll 144, 146
Clark, Cliff 96
Clark, Dort 174
Clark, Marie 107
Clark, Susan 204
Clark, Walter Van Tilbury 46, 47
Clarke, Charles G. 93, 166
Clarke, John 171
Clavell, James 171, 172
Claxton, William F. 27
Cleef, Lee Van 205, 206
Clothier, Willian H. 199
Cobb, Edmund 186
Cobb, Lee J. 84, 85, 87
Il cobra 18, 197–199
Coburn, James 181, 182
Cochran, Steve 79, 165
Cody, Iron Eyes 27, 141
Coe, Peter 104, 136
Coe, Weldon 161
Cohen, Cal 31
Cohn, Bruce 209
Collins, Chick 72
Collins, Covington County 3, 4
Collins, Joan 167
Collins, John 201
Collins, Ray 79, 122
Collis, Jack T. 207
Collison, Peter 201, 202, 203
Colorado River 136, 137, 138
Colson, Charles 210
Columbia Studio 19, 124, 125, 134, 135, 155, 213, 217
Comanche 25, 134, 141–144
Come Back, Little Sheba 218
Comer, Anjanette 181, 182
Comer, Sam 127
"Command Performance" 217
Commonweal 124
Compton, Fay 101
Concorde: Airport 79 204
Confessions of a Nazi Spy 94
Conlin, Jimmy 71
Connecticut (state) 84, 85
Conrad, Christopher 210
Conrad, William 176, 177
Conroy, Frank 46, 47
Conte, Richard 55, 58, 67, 68, 70, 117, 219
Converse, Frank 212, 213
Coogan, Richard 134
Cook, Elisha, Jr. 39, 52
Cook, Rowena 27
Cooke, Malcolm 96
Coolidge, Philip 84
Cooper, Gary 6, 7, 29, 30, 39, 41
Cooper, Maxine 151
Cope, John 127
Copelin, Campbell 104
Copland, Aaron 49

Corby, Ellen 113
Corenblith, Michael 213
Corey, Jeff 206
Corwin, Norman 166
Cory, Ray 125
Cosgrove, Jack 27
Costello, Dolores 145
Cotten, Joseph 128, 146, 219
Coulouris, George 131
Country Girl 103
"Courier of Disaster" 221
Court, Leigh 212
Covington County 3
Cox, Hal Wilson 161
Crabbe, Larry, "Buster" 24, 26
Crack in the World 18, 153, 169–171, 172, 184, 197
Crafford, Charles 155
Craig, James 144, 145, 199
Crain, Jeanne 65, 66, 67, 131, 192, 193, 194, 195, 212
Craine, Richard 59
Cramer, Duncan 166
Crash Dive 7, 43–46, 52, 60 86, 150, 151
Cravat, Noel 93
Craven, John 55
Crawford, Joan 2, 12, 32, 87, 88, 90, 113, 121, 150, 196, 219
Creber, Lewis H. 25, 41, 55, 60, 65
Cregar, Laird 5, 63
Crisanti, Gabriele 191
Cristal, Linda 141, 143
Cromwell, John 90, 92
Cronjager, Edward 76, 77
Crosby, Bing 103, 151, 218
Crosland, Alan, Jr. 204
Cross, Melville 55, 57 see Zanuck, Daryl
"The Crossed Heart" 221
"The Crowd" 220
The Crowded Sky 18, 97, 153, 164–66, 178, 204, 205
Crowley, Aleister 156
Crowther, Bosley 49, 52, 108, 130
Cugat, Xavier 52
Cummings, Homer 85
Cummings, Robert 219
Cummins, Irving 34, 36
Cummins, Peggy 155, 156, 157
Curran, Pamela 181
Curse of the Demon see Night of the Demon
Curtis, Donald 90
Curtis, Ken 148
Curtis, Leslie 207
Curtis, Ray 43
Curtis, Tony 138, 206, 208
Cuthbertson, Ian 158
Cutler, Victor 67, 75, 79
Cvetic, Matt 220

D'Achile, Luciano 205
D'Agostino, Albert S. 90, 119
Daily Telegraph 64
Daisy Kenyon 8, 12, 87–90, 101, 157
"Daisy Kenyon" (radio) 219
Dale, Esther 49
Dale, Ted 151
Damon, Peter 169

Dane, Peter 197
"The Dangerous Dollars" 220
Daniel, Paul 186
Daniell, Henry 166
Daniels, Bill 201
Darin, Bobby 67
"The Dark Mirror" 221
Darnell, Linda 17, 37, 71, 73, 74, 75, 151, 152, 153, 165
Darwell, Jane 46, 47, 73
Davenport, Doris 29, 31
Davenport, Harry 46, 47
Daves, Michael 174
Davidson, William B. 25
Davies, Marion 6
Davis, Bette 117, 221
Davis, George 87, 97, 192
Davis, Joan 24, 26, 27
Davis, Robert P. 212
Davis, William 52
Dawn, Robert 209
Dawson, Bob 209
Dawson, Gordon T. 174
Dawson, Ralph 119
Dawson, Richard 199
Day, Doris 153
Day, Francisco 127
Day, Richard 23, 25, 31, 34, 41, 43, 46, 84, 107, 113, 122, 124
The Day the Earth Caught Fire 169
Dayton, John Philip 210
The Dead End Kids 156
Dearing, Edgar 25
December 7th 8
de'Corsia, Ted 161, 163
Deep Water 118
Deep Waters 12, 24, 96–99, 117, 121, 180
"Deep Waters" (radio) 219, 221
Dehaven, Carter 125
de Havilland, Olivia 73, 80, 108
Dekker, Albert 218
DeKova, Frank 139
Delaplain, Warren B. 166
Del Greco, Luciano 188
"Deliberate Disclosure" 217
del Ray, Pedro 197
DeMille, Cecil B. 29, 188, 219
Denham, Maurice 155, 158
De Niro, Robert 206, 207, 208
Derham, Bonnie 212
De Rochemont, Louis 84
D'Esco, Phil 84
De Seta, William 212
Destination Gobi 117
Destination Tokyo 60
Detective Story 112
Deterle, William 127, 128
The Devil's Brigade 199–201
Devil's Canyon 134
Devine, Andy 75, 77
Devine, Denny 76, 77
Devine, Tad 76, 77
Devlin, J.G. 201
De Weese, Richard 79
De Wilde, Brandon 174
De Witt, Elina 190
I diamanti che nessuno voleva rubare 191–192
The Dick Powell Show 215

Dickson, Donald 52
Dietrich, Marlene 63
"Different Ones" 216
Diggings, Cliff 201
The Dirty Dozen 201
Dirty Harry 112
Diskant, George E. 119
Dive Bomber 25
Dr. Strangelove 182, 183
Donahue, Troy 164, 165
Donlevy, Brian 75, 77, 78
Donnelly, Dennis 199
Donnelly, Ruth 109
Donner, Robert 205
Donoghue, Quinn 183
Donovan's Brain 196
Don't, Covington County 3
Doohan, James 171, 173
Doolittle, Jimmy 56
Doolittle Raid 5, 56
Dorleac, Jean-Pierre 209
Dorn, Philip 119
Dorr, Lester 25
"Double Exposure" 221
Double Indemnity 64, 177
Douglas, Jerry 209
Douglas, John 169
Douglas, Kirk 22, 112, 137, 151, 174, 175
Dow, Peggy 122
Dowd, Ross 151
Dowling, Constance 52, 53
Down to the Sea in Ships 99
Downing, Joe 34
Doyle, Mimi 148
Drake, Chris 67
Drake, Col. Thomas D. 68
Drake, Tom 186
Dratler, Jay 61
"Draw the Red Curtain" 220
Drayton, Noel 127, 151
Drew, Barbara 148
Dru, Joanne 68
Dubbins, Don 161, 163
Dudley, Tom 61, 72, 77, 78
Duel in the Jungle 14, 66, 131–134, 167, 194
Duff, Howard 144, 145
Duff, William 119
Dugan, Tom 52
Dumont, Margaret 52
Dunham, William A. 178, 186
Dunn, Ralph 61
Dunne, Irene 218
Dunning, George 125, 176
Dunnock, Mildred 122
DuPont Show of the Week 215, 218
Durango, New Mexico 142
Duryea, Dan 39, 40, 41
Duvall, Robert 217
Dwan, Allan 161
Dynarski, Gene 204

Eagle-Lion Films 119
Earle, Marilee 158, 159, 160
Earls, Dick 212
Earls, Gregory 212
Eastman, George 197
Easton, Robert 181
Eastwood, Clint 18, 112, 190

Eckhardt, William 94
The Eddy Duchin Story 92
Edge of Darkness 49
Edge of Doom 108, 113–115, 124, 214
Edmunds, William 41
Edouart, Farciot 174
Edwards, Ralph 21
Edwards, Vince 199, 201, 216
Einstein, Charles 144, 145
Ekberg, Anita 197
Elephant Walk 13, 93, 127–131, 133, 150
Ellery Queen 217
Ellington, Duke 64
Elliot, John 191
Elliot, Peter 155
Elliot, Stephen 134
Ellis, Robert 23
"The Elspeth Club" 221
Elstree Studios (UK) 133
"Emergency Ward" 215
Emmy Award 217
Enchanted Island 17, 25, 97, 118, 120, 161–164
Engel, Samuel C. 97, 116, 117, 118
England 12, 15, 18, 104, 156, 196, 218
Enterprise-MGM 99
Epstein, Julius J. 107
Epstein, Philip G. 107
Essler, Fred 52
Estrada, Erik 204
Europe 12, 18, 190
Evans, Charles 146
Evans, Joan 113
The Evening Telegraph 105
Every, Dale Van 119
Executive Suite 167
"Exit on the Left" 220, 221
Exodus 106
Eythe, William 46, 59, 60

Fagen, Herb 138, 206
The Failing of Raymond 19, 216
Fair Wind to Java 163
Fairbanks, Douglas, Sr. 25
Falcon Crest 214, 217
Fallen Angel 8, 11, 25, 39, 60, 89, 98, 106, 110, 112, 145, 148, 150, 153, 157, 169, 177, 180
Falmouth (Mass.) 218
Family Affair 216
Family Theatre 218
Farley, Morgan 119, 206
Farmer, Mimsy 192, 194
Farnum, William 27
Farrar, David 131, 132, 133
Farrara, Romano 188
Farrell, Amy 204
Faye, Alice 67, 71, 72, 74, 165
The Fear Machine 158, 159
Feldary, Eric 119
Fell, Norman 204
Fenton, Frank 90
Ferguson, Perry 39, 49, 52, 79
Fernandez, Augustine 161
Ferrell, Raymond 151
Feury, Peggy 207
Fidenco, Vico 190, 191
Fidler, Eric 213
Fidlow, Harriot 212

Field, Mary 39, 113
Fields, A. Rolands 104
Fields, Verna 144
Fields, W.C. 128
Fiferman, Stan 181
"Fifteen Minutes to Murder" 221
The Fighting Lady 61
Figland, Lyle 151
Filippini, Angelo 191
Fillmore, Clyde 61
Film Review 104
Finch, Peter 127, 128, 130
Fine, Sylvia 52
Finley, Evelyn 22
First Lady 6
First Special Service Force (FSSF) 201
The First 36 Hours of Dr. Durant 19, 217
Fisher, Steve 41, 186
Fitzgerald, F. Scott 207, 208, 209
"The Flames Burned Red" 220
Flannery, Jerrilyn 122
Flavin, James 34, 61
Fleer, Alicia 210
Fleming, Rhonda 144, 145, 146, 153, 164
Fletcher, Bill 199
Fletcher, Charlotte 134
Flick, W.D. 84
Flight into Danger 151, 153
Florida State University Theatre 218
Flynn, Erroll 1, 36, 44, 68, 73, 153
Fonda, Henry 7, 18, 35, 44, 46, 47, 48, 50, 60, 87, 88, 89, 90, 117, 174, 175, 183, 184, 190, 217
Fontaine, Joan 40, 146, 147, 219
Foo, Lee Tung 61
For a Few Dollars More 194
For Me and My Gal 65
Foran, Dick 158, 160
Forbes, Louis 52
The Forbidden Street 12, 101–104, 133, 160, 190
Force of Evil 99
Forchion, Raymond 212
Ford, Francis 23, 31, 47
Ford, Glenn 122
Ford, John 7, 8, 25, 29, 31, 32, 34, 37, 47, 102, 143, 177, 214
Forde, Eugene 41, 43
"Forged Faces" 220
"The Forgotten War" 124
Forrest, Sally 144, 145
Forrest, Steve 3, 44, 70, 95, 160, 203, 219
Forte, Joseph 124
Fortier, Robert 158
Foster, Art 104
Foster, Dianne 134, 136
Foster, Eddie 39, 40
The Four Lads 161
Fowler, Gene, Jr. 144, 148
Fowler, Hugh S. 174
Fowley, Douglas 113
Fox, Arthur 134
Fox, Edward 195, 197
Fox, Paul 43
Fox, Richard K. 36
Foy, Bryan 41, 42

Fraley, Joseph 209
Francesco, Aldo De 188
Franciosa, Tony 216
Francis, Jan 158
Franciscus, James 209, 210
Frank, Fred 76
Frankel, Benjamin 183, 185
Frankenheimer, John 160
Franz, Arthur 146
Franz, Eduard 93, 95
Frazee, Logan 199
Frederick, Maj. Gen. Robert 201
Freed, Bert 109
Freeman, Kathlene 166
Freemont, John C. 27, 28
Freericks, Bernard 23, 65, 72, 94, 97
French, Hugh 104
Friedhofer, Hugo 60, 79, 83
Friedlob, Bert E. 144, 145, 146, 147, 148
Friend, Philip 104
The Frogmen 12, 61, 115–119, 138, 163, 177
Frogmen in Korea 118
"From A to Z" 39
From Here to Eternity 135
The Frozen Dead 18, 41, 194, 195–197
Frye, William 204
Fudge, Alan 204
Fujiwara, Chris 78, 157, 160
Fuller, John C. 151
Fuller, Leland 61, 72, 166
Fullmer, Gene 199
Fulton, John P. 107, 127, 151
Fultz, Jay 136
Furburg, Curt 41
Fury 144

Gable, Clark 1, 29, 137
Gabor, Magda 126
Gabor, Zsa Zsa 126
Gage, Ben 66
Gallico, Paul 125
Gallico, Pauline 125
Gallitti, Alberto 191
Garcia, Luis 183
Garden of Eden 138
Gardiner, Reginald 63
Garfield Brian 78, 138
Garland, Beverly 204
Garland, Judy 27, 150
Garmes, Lee 107
Garner, Peggy Ann 87, 88
Garrett, Oliver H.P. 119
Garrison, Michael 164
Garson, Greer 2, 138, 139, 141, 214
Garvin, Eddie 113
The Gaunt Woman 119
Gausman, Russell A. 76, 104, 136
Gaynor, Janet 66
Geer, Will 96
General Electric Theatre 215, 220
Genge, Paul 164, 192
Gentleman's Agreement 96
George, Christopher 174
George, George W. 136, 137
George, Gladys 79
Georgette 161
Germonprez, Louis 52

Gershenson, Joseph 136
Gerswin, Ira 49, 64
Gertz, Irving 136, 158
Gerwirtz, Norman 212
Ghost Stories of an Antiquary 156
Giandalia, Roberto 191
Giant 130
Gibbons, Ayllene 181
Gibbs, Susanne 101
Gibson, Mary 195
Gibson, William 218
Gielgud, John 181, 182
Giglio, Sandro 124
Gilbert, Herschel Burke 141, 144, 145, 146
Gilbert, Philip 195, 197
Gillen, Jim 169
Gilligan, Edmund 119
Gilmore, Dean 209
Gilmore, Lowell 104, 141
Gilmore, Virginia 36, 41, 43
Gilson, Tom 164
Gittens, George A. 178
Glass, Gaston 65
The Glass Menagerie 217
Glassberg, Irving 104
Glasser, Bernard 169
Glazier, Peter 155
Gleason, F. Keogh 192
Gleason, James 43, 44, 148, 151
Gless, Sharon 204
Glory for Me 79
Goddard, Paulette 106
Goell, Kermit 72
Goetz, William 41
Goldner, Charles 131
Goldsmith, Jerry 171, 172, 174, 175, 205
Goldstar Production 196
Goldstein, Herb 212
Goldstein, Robert 195
Goldwyn, Francis 113
Goldwyn, Sammy 123
Goldwyn, Samuel 6, 7, 8, 12, 19, 25, 31, 31, 39, 40, 41, 49, 50, 51, 52, 53, 79, 81, 83, 84, 103, 107, 108, 113, 122, 123, 124, 208
Goldwyn Studio 6, 24
Golitzen, Alexander 76, 104, 136
Gombell, Minna 79
Gomez, Thomas 221
Gone with the Wind 31, 36, 83
Gonzalez-Gonzalez, Pedro 138
Good Guys Wear Black 20, 209–210, 214
Goodman, John B. 76
Goodrich, Jack A. 125
Goorney, Howard 201
Gordon, C. Henry 27
Gordon, Michael 155
Gordon, Roy 151, 158
Gore, Chester 84
Gortz, Walter 125
Gosery, Bernard 99
Gottlieb, Alex 134
Gouzenko, Igor 93, 94, 95, 96
Grable, Betty 73
Grace, Henry 192
Grace, Howard 176
Grand Canyon 137, 138

Granger, Farley 8, 49, 51, 55, 58, 65, 80, 113, 114, 115, 122, 123, 219
Granger, Stewart 18, 138, 145, 191
Grant, Lee 218
The Grapes of Wrath 34, 37, 47, 96
Grapewin, Charley 31, 32
Graves, Peter 218
Gray, Coleen 178
Gray, Robert 210
Grayson, Dave 158
The Great Sioux Uprising 142
Green, Paul 65
Greenberg, Aaron 213
Greenleaf, Raymond 96
Greenwood, Rosamund 155
Gregory, Grace 127
Grenzbach, Charles 151, 174
Griggs, Loyal 127, 130, 174, 175
Groesse, Paul 149
Gross, Jack J. 90
Grossman, Eugene 25, 87
Gruba, Anna 190
Gruber, Frank 178
The Guardian Obituary 22
Guest, Val 169
Guffey, Burnett 125
Gugliemi, Marco 188
Guiffre, Aldo 191
Guilfoyle, Paul 49
Gwenn, Edmund 219

Haade, William 72
Hackforth-Jones, Gilbert 97
Hadley, Reed 59, 85, 93, 221
Hadyn, Richard 39
Hagen, Earl 149
Hagen, Jean 148, 151
Haggerty, Don 148, 174, 181
Hagman, Larry 174
Hailey, Arthur 17, 151, 153, 204
Hall, Huntz 67, 68
Hall, John 24, 26, 27, 28, 29, 150
Hall, Kenneth 205
Halliwell, Leslie 144
Halls of Montezuma 70, 117
Halpin, Thomas 212
Halsey, Brett 189, 190, 192
Halton, Charles 29, 31, 52, 79
Hamilton, Guy 102
Hamilton, Lloyd 117
Hammer, Alvin 67
Hammerstein, Oscar, II 10, 65, 66, 67
Hammond, Len 37
Hampton, Bruce 25, 26
Hampton, Janice 213
Hampton, Walter 138
Hansard, Helen 72
Hansen, Chuck 164
Hanson, Arthur 151
Harding, Ann 49, 51
Hardwicke, Cedric 59
Hardy, Phil 134
The Hardy Boys/Nancy Drew Mysteries 217
Hare, Ernest 102
Harlan, Russell 67
Harline, Leigh 122
Harris, Brad 190, 192
Harris, Harry 166

Harris, Stacy 141, 143, 176
Harris, Viola 209
Harrison, Linda 204
Harrison, Rex 101
Harrold, Scott 102
Hart, Diane 101
Hartley, Neil 181
Hartman, Don 52
Harvey, Paul 25
Haskell, Jimmie 178, 186
Haszillo, Louis 186
"Hate Song" 220
Hathaway, Henry 60, 61
Hatton, Raymond 27
Haulani, My Lee 127
Havens, James Curtis 192
Havoc, June 43, 93, 95
Hawaii 175
Hawks, Howard 39, 40
Haworth, Jill 174
Haycox, Ernest 76
Hayden, Harry 52
Hayden, Sterling 17, 151, 153, 182
Haydin, Ty 183, 190
Hayes, Helen 137
Hayes, Joseph 218
Haymes, Dick 65, 66, 72
Haynes, Lloyd 209, 210
Haywood, Susan 2, 12, 75, 78, 103, 107, 108, 109, 121, 219
Hayworth, Rita 117
Head, Edith 39, 107, 127, 186, 204
Hearn, Chick 181
Hecht, Ben 109, 111, 112, 115
Heermane, Richard V. 27
Heflin, Van 18, 106
Heindorf, Ray 52
The Heiress 108
Hellman, Les 161
Hellman, Lillian 49, 51, 52
Hellman, Martin 131
Helm, Matt 168, 189
Heman, Roger 84
Heman, Roger, Sr. 37, 43, 44, 46, 65, 84, 97, 116
Henagan, Jim 192
Henderson, Charles 65
Henry, Maxwell 90, 146
Henry, O. 23
Henson, Basil 195
Herbert, Percy 155
Herbert, Pitt 144
Herman, Hal 41
Hermes, Douglas 195
Hernfield, Kurt 183
Heron, Julia 30, 39, 79, 107, 113
Hertz, David 87
Hertzburn, Bernard 104
Heston, Charlton 137, 204, 205
Heyward, Louis M. 188
Hickman, Howard C. 34
Hickox, Harry 192
Hicks, Chuck 186
The High and the Mighty 153
High Noon 135
Highman, Charles 92
Hiller, Erwin 131
Hilyard, David 183
Hilyard, Jack 183
Hindman, Bill 212

Hinsdale, Oliver 5
Hinton, Ed 144
Hipkins, Ben 102
Hirsch, Elroy "Crazy Legs" 151, 154
His Majesty O'Keefe 163
Hitchcock, Alfred 146, 147, 219
Hobart, Rose 75
Hobbes, Halliwell 75
Hobbes, Peter 102, 155
Hodiak, John 63
Hoffenstein, Samuel 61
Hoffman, Morris 174, 199
Hoffman, Otto 23
Hogan, Louanne 66
Hogan, Pat 136
Hogan, Robert 213, 214
Hogsett, Albert 116
Holden, Fay 75
Holden, William 5, 12, 115, 137, 199, 200, 201
Holland, Edna 107
Holland, Marty 72
Holloway, Stanley 174
Holloway, Sterling 67, 68
Hollywood 1, 4, 7, 10, 18, 22, 23, 24, 25, 32, 35, 37, 41, 43, 46, 51, 52, 53, 60, 63, 65, 66, 76, 77, 91, 93, 94, 95, 97, 101, 103, 104, 105, 113, 115, 118, 121, 126, 128, 131, 138, 140, 142, 143, 153, 169, 178, 182, 187, 190, 191, 205, 206, 208, 209, 212, 213, 215, 219
The Hollywood Citizen News 115
The Hollywood Fights Back 218
The Hollywood Reporter 34, 146, 154
Holmes, Taylor 84
Holton, Jennifer 212
Holyoke (Mass.) 218
"Home Improvement" 220
Homeier, Skip 119
Homolka, Oscar 39
Hondo 142
Hong, James 171
Hooker, Buddy Joe 205
Hope, Bob 83, 84, 216
Hopkins, Bobb 210
Hopper, Hedda 4, 63
Hopper, Jerry 136, 137
The Hornet 57, 61
Hornung, Paul 199
Horvath, Charles 186
Hot Rods to Hell 18, 66, 93, 167, 192–195
Hounds of Love 158
Howard, Kathleen 39, 61
Howard, Mary 36
Howard, Ronald 205, 206
Howe, James Wong 49
Howell, Kenneth 39
Howland, Olin 34, 71, 74
Hoyt, Robert 204
Huber, Harold 27, 29
Hubert, Axel, Sr. 210
Hubert, Rene 65
Huggins, Roy 119, 154
Hughes, Sen. Harold 211, 212
Hughes, Howard 98, 121, 180, 199
Hughes, Mary Beth 23, 24, 46, 47
Hughes, Thomas 46
Hugo, Laurence 134

Hugo, Mauritz 93
Humberstone, Bruce 23, 166, 167
Hunter, Jeffrey 39, 115, 116, 117, 176, 177, 190
Hunter, Tab 178
Huntsville, Texas 4
Hurst, Paul 29, 46, 47
Huston, Anjelica 206
Huston, Walter 36, 49, 51, 52
Hutton, Betty 15, 148, 149, 150, 151
Hutton, Jim 217
Hyatt, Robert 99
"Hyde and Seek" 217
Hyde-White, Wilfred 101, 131, 133
Hyland, Dick Irving 90

"I Can't Begin to Tell You" 99
"I Can't Sleep" 220
I Saw What You Did 196
I Wake Up Screaming 24
"I Walk Alone" 220
I Want You 12, 108, 122–124, 214,
I Was a Communist Spy for the F.B.I. 13, 220–221
"If the Dead Could Talk" 220
Ihnene, Wiard B. 43
Ike 217
Ike: The War Years 217
I'll Cry Tomorrow 77
"I'm Getting Married in the Morning" 77
Imazu, Eddie 164
In Harm's Way 174–176, 184, 200
Independent Film Journal 154
The Indian Fighter 151
Indian Uprising 142
Inescort, Frieda 164
Ingalls, Don 204, 205
Inge, William 218
"Inhuman Element" 221
Innes, Jean 113
Innocent Bystanders 41, 201–204
"Into the Wild Blue Yonder" 58, 61
Ipale, Aharon 201
Ireland, John 67, 68
The Iron Curtain 12, 43, 93–96, 112, 159
Irving, Hollis 164
Irving Thalberg trophy 83
Is Anyone Listening? 218
Isherwood, Christopher 181
"Isn't It Kinda Fun" 66
It! 196
"It Might as Well Be Spring" 66
"It's a Grand Night for Singing" 66
It's a Wonderful Life 99, 136, 212
Ivan, Rosalind 127
Ivers, Robert 178
Ives, George 192

Jackson, Selmer 25
Jacobson, Artie 55
Jaekel, Richard 59, 178, 179, 180, 199
Jafor, Pal 124
Jagger, Dean 49, 51
James, Montague R. 155, 156
Janeway, Elizabeth 87
Janis, Conrad 204
Janis, Vivi 148
Janus, Ted 212

Jarre, Maurice 207
Jarvis, Edward B. 131
"Jeanie with the Light Brown Hair" 29
Jeffries, Wesley 171
Jenkins, Allen 39, 40, 41
Jenkins, George 79
Jergens, Adele 113, 115, 139
Johannesburg 133
John Douglas French Centre for Alzheimers 22
Johnny Reno 18, 96, 186–188
Johnson, Anna Hill 207
Johnson, J. McMillan 127
Johnson, Julian 23
Johnson, Nunnally 31
Johnson, Russell 139
Jones, Bob 186
Jones, Carolyn 134
Jones, Clifton 201
Jones, Dean 210, 211
Jones, Gordon 136, 148
Jones, Harman 84
Jones, Jane 90
Jones, Jennifer 63, 128
Jones, John Paul 174
Jones-Moreland, Betsy 207
Jory, Victor 92
Joslin, Howard 174
Jost, Larry 207
Jourdan, Louis 99, 100, 150
Journey into Fear 133
Joy, Nicholas 87, 93
Julie 153
"Jump to the Whip" 220
Juran, Nathan 34
Jurasik, Peter 210

Kager, Fred 192
Kalser, Erwin 41
"Kangaroo Court" 221
Kantor, MacKinlay 79, 80
Karlsen, John 169
Karns, Todd 107
Karter, Ehsane Sadek 197
Kartrude, Russ 212
Katch, Kurt 41
Katzman, Sam 192, 193
Kaye, Danny 8, 26, 41, 52, 53, 54, 55, 83, 150
Kaylin, Samuel 25
Kazan, Elia 12, 53, 84, 85, 86, 207, 208
Kean, John 158
Keating, John 21
Keaton, Buster 42
Keith, Brian 85, 216
Keith, Richard 151
Keith, Robert 84, 107, 108, 113, 114, 122
Kelley, Barry 84
Kellogg, John 68
Kellum, Terry 146
Kelly, Claire 181
Kelly, DeForest 178, 180
Kelly, James F. 213, 214
Kelly, Jim 205, 206, 209
Kelly, Nancy 24, 26
Kelly, Patsy 164
Kelly, Tony 131, 133

Kemmer, Ed 164
Kemper, Victor J. 207
Kennedy, Arthur 84, 85, 86, 211
Kennedy, Douglas 139
Kennedy, George 174, 204, 205
Kennedy, Jacqueline 65
Kenney, Bill 210
Kenny, Joseph E. 136
Kent, Robert E. 109
Kentucky 4
Kerns, Hubie, Jr. 209
Kerr, John 164, 165
Kerrigan, J.M. 119
Kerrigan, S.K. 131
Keyes, Marion Herwood 99
Keys, Basil 155
Khachaturian, Aram 93, 96
Kiel, Richard 178
Kilbride, Percy 65, 71, 73, 74
Kilian, Victor 46
Kimball, Charles L. 141
Kine Weekly 174
King, Aldine 204
King, Harold V. 131
King, Henry 97
King, Peggy 151, 154
Kino, Lloyd 207
King Solomon's Mines 131
Kinskey, Leonid 39
Kirk, Jeremy 166, 167
Kirk, Joe 146
Kirk, Mark-Lee 93
Kirkland, Jack 31, 32
Kirkpatrick, M.K. (Commander U.S.N.) 43
Kirkwood, Gene 192, 194
Kish, Joseph 90
Kiss of Death 117
"Kiss of Death" (radio) 220
Kissel, William 139
Korda, Alexander 91
The Korean War 12, 122, 123, 159, 160
Korvin, Charles 90
Kosleck, Martin 41, 43
Kozlowski, Bob 212
Kreig, Frank 99
Krims, Milton 93, 94
Krizman, Serge 158
Kroeger, Barry 93, 95
Krueger, Carl 141
Krueger, Otto 219
Kruger Park Game Reserve 133
Krupa, Gene 39
Kuehl, William L. 164
Kutler, Stanley 211

Lacava, Lou 146
Lacey, Clay 212
Ladd, Alan 14, 65, 134

Lady in the Dark 100
Lake, Stuart N. 30
Lamarr, Hedy 63
Lambert, Edward P. 27
Lambert, Father George A. 85
Lamble, Lloyd 155
Lamont, Marten 104
Lampell, Milliard 68
Lancaster, Burt 137, 219
Lancer, Martin 158
The Lancers 143
Landis, Jessie Royce 107
Landon, Mark 213
Lane, Charles 39
Lane, Rusty 146
Lane, Tommy 212
Lang, Fritz 2, 15, 37, 122, 144, 145, 146, 147, 148, 159
Lang, Jennings 204, 205
Lang, Walter 65, 66
Langan, Glenn 59
Langley, Bryon 155
Langtry, Lily 29, 30
La Plant, Laura 148, 151
Lardner, Ring, Jr. 102
Larkin, John 171, 173
La Rue, Frank 61
Lasdun, Gary 169
LaShelle, Joseph 61, 63, 72, 75, 97, 109, 111
Lassaly, Walter 212, 213
The Last Hurrah 217
"The Last of the Big Spenders" 216
The Last Possee 134
The Last Tycoon 19, 207–209
Laszlo, Ernest 144, 145
Latell, Lyle 158
Latham, Heather 102
Lathrop, Philip H. 204
Lau, Fred 30, 49, 52, 107, 113, 122
Laune, Paul 158
Laura 2, 8, 9, 10, 22, 26, 36, 61–65, 72, 74, 101, 110, 112, 115, 121, 145, 172, 180, 208
"Laura" (radio) 13, 219, 220, 221
Laurence, Ken 176
Laurie, Piper 136, 137, 138
Lauter, Harry 171
Lava, William 136
LaVigne, Emile 104, 171, 181
Lavista, Paul 161, 163
Lawrence, Marc 22, 46
Lawrence Productions 12
Lawton, Charles, Jr. 134
Leavitt, Sam 158, 176
Ledebur, Friedrich 161, 163
Leder, Herbert J. 195, 196
Lee, Betty 155
Lee, Earl 124
Lee, Gipsy Rose 95
Lee, Stuart 210
Lee, William A. 39
Leech, Richard 155
The Left Hand of God 115
Leicester, James 161
Leicester, William F. 146
Leigh, Vivien 128, 129
Leighton, Margaret 181
Le Maire, Charles 87, 93, 97, 109, 112, 116

Lembeck, Harvey 115
Lentz, Robert J. 160
Leonard, Harry M. 41, 61, 72, 94, 110
Leone, Michael 209
LePore, Richard 174
Lerner, Alan J. 218
LeRoy, Mervyn 139, 141
Lerpae, Paul K. 127, 178, 186
Leslie, Nan 164
Levein, Sonya 65
Levene, Sam 55, 56, 57, 58, 84
Leverett, Lewis 84
Leverett, Winston H. 116
Levitt, Robert 205
Lewis, Ben 192
Lewis, Harold 171, 174, 186
Lewis, Sylvia 149
Lewton, Val 156
Liberace 181
Liberty, Dick 212
Liberty Films 99
Liberty Journal 146
Lichine, David 49
Liddiard, Gary 207
Lieberman, Leon 218
Liebman, Max 52
The Life and Times of Roy Bean 31
"The Light That Loses, the Night That Wins" 216
Linder, Cec 201
Lindfors, Viveca 176, 178
"The Lion Is Busy" 221
Lipstein, Harold 149
Litel, John 141
Little, Thomas 233, 25, 31, 34, 41, 43, 44, 55, 60, 61, 65, 72, 84, 87, 93, 97, 109, 116
"Little Boy Blue Turned Red" 220
"The Little Boy Red" 220
"Little Red Schoolhouse" 220
Littlefield, Lucien 29
Livadary, John P. 134
Lloyd, Norman 67, 99
Lloyd, Sue 201, 202
Loeffler, Louis R. 61, 87, 94, 110
Loew, Arthur M. 99
Loew, David 99
Loew, Marcus 99
Loewe, Frederick 218
Loew's 52
Logan, Helen 23
Logan, Stanley 104
Lollobrigida, Guido 197
Lombard, Carole 40
London (UK) 104, 133
London, Steve 151
Loo, Richard 55, 57, 58
Loper, Don 149
Lord Jim 164
Lorre, Peter 209
Los Alamitos Medical Centre 22
Los Angeles 4, 45
Los Angeles Herald Examiner 141
Los Angeles Times 124, 210
Lossman, Ed 199
"The Lost Cotillion" 216
The Lost Weekend 103
Lottman, Evan 212
Louis, Jean 125

Louisville, Kentucky 4
Lourie, Eugene 169, 170, 183
Lourie, Laure 169, 183
The Love Boat 214, 217
The Loved One 181–183, 184
Lovejoy, Frank 220
Lovitt, Bert 213
Lovsky, Celia 144
Lowery, Robert 49, 186
Loy, Myrna 22, 79, 80, 81, 204, 205
"The Luck of the Irish" 219
Lucky Cisco Kid 6, 7, 23–24, 25, 98
Ludwig, Jerry L. 205
Ludwig, Julian 199
Ludwig, Otto 104
Lupino, Ida 144, 145, 219
Lupton, John 204
Lure of the Wilderness 39
Lux Radio Theatre 13, 17, 65, 219
Lynn, George 27

M 145
MacArthur, James 183, 185
MacDonald, Edmund 25
MacGinnis, Niall 155, 156
Macgowan, Kenneth 34
MacGreevy, Oliver 195
MacGregor, Scott 195
MacKenzie, Mary 131
MacLean, Alistair (as Ian Stuart) 171, 172
MacLean, Barton 178
MacMahon, Aline 217
MacMurray, Fred 14, 80, 134
MacRae, Gordon 212, 213
Maculani, Guilio 188
MacWilliams, Glen 60
Madison Avenue 18, 24, 25, 66, 75, 89, 166–169, 194, 213
Maharis, George 171, 172, 173
Maher, Frank 201
Mahin, John Lee 127
Maine 97, 98, 99
Maitland, Scott 205
Majan, Juan 205
Malden, Karl 84, 85, 86, 109, 111
Maley, Peggy 122
The Maltese Falcon 64
Maltin, Leonard 143, 180
Mamoulian, Rouben 63
A Man for All Seasons 187, 218
Man from U.N.C.L.E. 173, 189
The Manchurian Candidate 160
Mancini, Henry 136
Mandell, Daniel 30, 39, 49, 52, 79, 83, 107, 113, 122
Mangini, Gino 191
Mann, Anthony 178
Manning, Knox 52
Mannino, Anthony 209
Mannix, Bobbie 213
Manoff, Arnold 99
Mansfield, Duncan 68
Mansfield, Richard 174
Mantell, Joe 164, 165
Mantovani, Lilly 191
"Many Dreams Ago" 130
Mar Vista 209
March, Fredric 79, 80, 81, 83, 219
March of Times series 84

Marcus, Larry 176
Marcuzzo, Luciano 188, 191
Maret, Harry 97
Margaret, Ann 67
Margheriti, Antonio 205
Marion, Paul 104
Maris, Mona 41, 43
Marker, Harry 90
Marks, Barbara Fallick 207
Marks, Richard 207
Marley, Peverell 37
Marlowe, Hugh 65
Marquesas Islands 161
The Marriage-Go-Round 218
Mars, Kenneth 213, 214
Marsh, Mae 96, 144
Marshall, Connie 87
Marshall, George 76, 131, 132
Marshall, Trudy 55
Marshall, Tully 39
Marshall, William 65
Marston, Joel 158
Martel, Peter 192, 197, 198
Martien, Robert 144
Martin, Carmen 205
Martin, Chris-Pin 23, 24, 46
Martin, Gene 199
Martin, Strother 176, 178
Martin, Todd 169
Marton, Andrew 169, 171
Marty Kaye Trio 149
Marum, Gene 209
Marx, Sam 131
Marx, Samuel 125
Masters, Monty 176
Masters, Sharon 207
Mataka, Michael 131
Mather, Aubrey 39
Mathews, George 52, 59
Mathieson, Muir 102, 155
Matis, Bernard 186
Matlew, Mary 101
Matthau, Walter 217
Matthews, A.E. 101
Mattingly, Phil 174
Mature, Victor 5, 65, 66
Maxwell, Edwin 27
May, Donald 164
Maybery, Richard 116
Mayes, Wendell 174
Mayne, Ferdy 201
Maynor, Asa 181
Mayo, Archie 43
Mayo, Virginia 22, 52, 53, 79, 81, 83, 115, 118, 165, 221
Mayo, Walter 30
Mazurki, Mike 141, 143
McAdoo, Tom 164
McCallum, Gordon C. 183, 201
McCarthy Era 96
McCauley, Daniel 174
McCauley, Danny 207
McClure, Doug 154
McCoy, Herschel 25, 41
McCullen, Kathy 209
McDermott, Jack 212
McDonald, Francis 134
McDowell, Roddy 181
McEvoy, Renny 59
McGregor, Charles 205

McGuire, Dorothy 122, 123, 124
McHugh, Frank 65
McIntyre, Lelia 71
McKay, Don 166
McKinney, Mira 71
McLaglen, Andrew V. 199, 200
McLaughlin, Bruce 212
McLean, Barbara 31, 97
McMahon, Ben 204
McManus, Sharon 99
McNally, Pat 122
McNally, Stephen 104, 105, 106
McNeal, Allen 46
McQueeney, Robert 176
McWhorter, Frank 99
Meadowbrook Dinner Theatre (New Jersey) 218
Mears, Martha 107
Medoff, Mark 209
Meehan, John 125
Meek, Donald 65, 66
Meeker, David 93
Meeker, George 52
Meeker, Ralph 118
Meet Me in St. Louis 65
Megowan, Don 199
Melson, John 183
Melville, Herman 17, 161, 162, 163
Menzies, William Cameron 49
Mercer, Johnny 61, 64, 149
Mercurio, Jody 212
Meredith, Burgess 106, 174
Merrall, Mary 131, 133
Merrick, M.A. 164, 176
Merrill, Gary 109, 110, 111, 115, 117
Merrill, Lew 27
Merritt, Gene 127
Mescall, John J. 27
Metcalfe, Melvin M., Sr. 204
Metropolis 145
Meyer, Torben 41
Meyerink, Paige 176
Meyler, Fintan 151
MGM (Metro-Goldwyn-Mayer) 6, 20, 65, 99, 100, 128, 165, 181, 192
Michaels, Mickey S. 204
Middleton, Charles 34
Milestone, Lewis 2, 8, 10, 12, 49, 51, 52, 55, 57, 63, 68, 69, 70, 71, 99, 100, 101, 159
Millan, Victor 127
Milland, Ray 14, 103, 134, 196, 206, 208
Miller, Arthur C. 31, 46, 55
Miller, Doris 44
Miller, Henry 207
Miller, Virgil 41, 43
Mills, Jack 144
Milner, Martin 122
Milo, Jim 213
Mims, William 192
Mission to Moscow 51
Mississippi 3, 21, 22
Mississippi State University 21
"Mister 880" 219
Mitchel, Shirley 148
Mitchell, Cameron 138
Mitchell, Grant 31, 61
Mitchell, James 201, 202

Mitchell, Thomas 144, 145
Mitchell, Warren 201, 202
Mitchum, Cameron 49, 213, 214
Mitchum, James 174
Mitchum, John 178
Mitchum, Robert 24, 115, 122, 138, 159, 178, 188 206, 208
Moby Dick 163
Mock, Laurie 192, 193, 194
Mockridge, Cyril J. 23, 46, 97, 99, 109, 116
Molina, Antonio 205
Molina, Julio 205
Moll, Elick 149
Mollo, Cumersindo 197
Monroe, Marilyn 138, 214
Monroe, Thomas 39
Montes, Elisa 197
Montez, Maria 26
Montgomery, Elizabeth 36
Montgomery, George 22, 52, 183, 185
Montgomery, Robert 106
Moore, Clayton 22, 27, 29
Moore, Dennis 158
Moore, Eleanor 96
Moore, John 195
Moore, Kieron 169, 170
Moore, Millie 209
Moore, Pat 201
Moore, Ruth 97
Moore, Terry 178, 180
Moore, William M. 209
Moreau, Jeanne 206
Morgan, Henry "Harry" 43, 44, 46, 59, 65, 92
Morley, Robert 181, 182
The Morning Telegraph 46
Morosco, Walter 60
Morris, Dave 37, 72
Morris, Frances 113
Morrison, Brian 204
Morrow, Byron 210
Morrow, Douglas 146, 147
Morse, Robert 181
Morse, Terry, Jr. 199
Moscher, Dennis 295
Moschin, Gastone 188
Moss, Stuart 174
Motion Picture Daily 154
Motion Picture Herald 106
Moulton, Thomas T. 39
Mrs. Miniver 51
Mudie, Leonard 41
Munger, Robert L. 210
Munroe, James 201, 202
Muntz, Paul 164
Murphy, Sen. George 96
Murphy, Horace 72
Murphy, Richard 84, 97
Murphy, Rosemary 218
Murray, Angie 5, 6
Murray, Janet 5, 13, 27
Murray, Dr. Margaret 158
"Mutiny" 215
My Foolish Heart 12, 25, 77, 107–109, 113, 124, 142, 150
"My Foolish Heart" (radio) 219
"My Foolish Heart" (song) 108
"My Friend the Enemy" 220

"My Six Convicts" 219
Myers, Buddy 144
Myron, Helen A. 23

Nader, George 191
Nagel, Conrad 20, 218
Nahmias, Al 212
The Naked Jungle 128
The Name of the Game 216
Napier, Alan 181
Narita, Hiro 213
Nash, Mary 24
NBC-TV (National Broadcasting Company) 19, 21, 215, 216, 217
Neal, Patricia 174, 175
Needham, Hal 205, 206
Neel, Beala 209
Negulesco, Jean 39, 102, 104
Nelson, Charles 125
Nelson, Ed 204
Nelson, Kay 84
Nelson, Ruth 49
Nelson, Sam 49, 134
The Nervous Wreck 52
Nesbitt, Derren 201, 202
Neumann, Dorothy 148
Neumann, Kurt 181
New Line 212
New York (city) 30, 32, 43, 65, 76, 81, 111, 115, 138, 218
The New York Daily Mirror 54
The New York Daily News 204
The New York Herald Tribune 36, 43, 71, 90, 96, 125
The New York Morning Telegraph 31
New York Philharmonic Orchestra 93
The New York Post 66, 83
The New York Times 7, 29, 41, 43, 44, 49, 52, 59, 61, 64, 71, 75, 78, 87, 90, 101, 104, 107, 108, 115, 118, 122, 127, 130, 134, 136, 138, 141, 146, 147, 150, 154, 162, 168, 171, 174, 195, 197, 201, 204, 210
The New York World-Telegraph 64
The New Yorker 183
Newell, Norman 131
Newhouse, Edward 122
Newman, Alfred 34, 39, 40, 55, 65, 84, 87, 90, 93, 110
Newman, Emil 41, 43, 60, 61, 72, 79, 107, 113
Newman, Lionel 97, 109, 116
Newman, Paul 18, 31, 137, 178
Newsweek magazine 57, 124
Newton, Mary 151
Nichols, Barbara 146, 181
Nichols, Dudley 37
Nicholson, Jack 206, 208
Nicoli, Attilio 190
Nielsen, Erik 122
Nigh, Jane 65
Night Cry 109, 111
Night Gallery 216
Night of the Demon 1, 2, 15, 19, 76, 101, 106, 13, 155–158, 159, 185
Night Song 12, 90–93, 150
"Night Song" (radio) 219
Nightingale, Laura 201
Nikolaison, Ray 210

Niles, Wendy 146
Niven, Kip 204
No Minor Vices 12, 49, 99–101, 150
"No Minor Vices" (radio) 219
"No Second Chance" 220
"No Time Like the Past" 215
Nolan, Lloyd 213
Norin, Gustav 99, 144
Norris, Aaron 209
Norris, Christopher 204
Norris, Chuck 209
Norris, Jay 67
North, Alex 199
North, Ted 46
The North Star 7, 49–52, 94, 113
Nugent, Elliot 52
Numkena, Anthony 139
Nye, Ben 60, 72, 84, 93, 97, 109, 116, 166

Oakland, Simon 171
Oberon, Merle 2, 12, 90, 91, 121, 219
O'Brian, Hugh 174
O'Brien, Brigid 210
O'Brien, Pat 64, 115, 178, 179, 180
Ochoa, José Maria 169
O'Connor, Carroll 174, 199
O'Connor, Donald 27
O'Connor/Becker/Productions/Columbia 217
The Odd Couple 218
O'Donnell, Cathy 79, 221
O'Donnell, Gene 49
O'Farrell, Broderick 71
O'Fearna, Edward 31
Offerman, George 67
Ogden, Rita 212
Oh, Soon-Tek 209
Oh Evening Star 6
O'Hanlon, George 25
O'Hara, Maureen 12, 101, 103, 104
O'Hara, Scarlett 31, 32, 76
Okey, Jack 90
"Ole Buttermilk Sky" 77
Oliphant, Peter 192
Oliver, Susan 218
Olivier, Laurence 128
Olsen, Christopher Robin 93
Olsen, Tracy 186
Olson, Nancy 204
On Dangerous Ground 112
"On the Atchison, Topeka, and Santa Fe" 78
"One Foot in Heaven" 219
"One Man Crime Wave" 220
"One Way Ticket" 220
O'Neal, Patrick 174
Onions, S.D. 155
Operation Manhunt 96
Orenbach, Al 65
Ormandy, Eugene 90, 93
Ortolani, Pietro 191
Ortolani, Riz 188
Oscars *see* Academy Awards
O'Shea, Kevin 55, 59
O'Shea, Milo 212, 213
Oshrin, Harry 31
O'Skeete, Norman 151
"Our State Fair" 66
Our Town 218

Oursler, Fulton 84, 85
Out of the Past 208
Outbreak 172
Overton, Al 199
Owen, Garry 72
Owen, Tony 131, 132
The Ox-Bow Incident 2, 7, 8, 11, 24, 44, 46–49, 52, 58, 60, 92, 96, 109, 114, 136, 145, 162, 178, 186

Pack, Charles Lloyd 155
Paige, Mabel 113
Paint Your Wagon 218
Palacios, Ricardo 205
Palance, Jack 177, 209
Palk, Anna 195, 197
Pallette, Eugene 36
Palm Springs Desert 172
Palmdale, California 194
Palmer, Ernest 25, 34
Palmer, Lilli 99, 100, 101, 150
Palmer, Paul 72
"Panic Plan" 220
Paramount Pictures 54, 127, 129, 130, 131, 151, 152, 169, 170, 174, 178, 179, 186, 187, 201, 202, 207
Paris 125, 126
Paris, Jerry 107, 151, 154
Parish, James Robert 127
Parker, Clifton 155, 157
Parker, Eleanor 166, 167, 168, 169, 219
Parker, Suzy 167
Parrish, Robert 99, 101, 125
Parsons, Derek 169, 183
Parsons, Harriett 90, 92
Parsons, Lindsley, Jr. 141
Parsons, Louella 92, 103
Parton, Regis 186
"The Party Got Rough" 220
Pasadena Community Playhouse 5, 6, 10, 31, 92
Pascal, Ernest 76
Pate, Michael 176
Paths of Glory 5
Patterns 167
Patterson, Elizabeth 31, 34
Patterson, John 209
Pattillo, Alan 201
Pavese, Cesare 53
Pavia, Nestor 141, 143
Payne, James W. 181
Payne, John 161, 162
Payne, Michael 209
Peake, Michael 155
Pearce, Guy 37, 46, 61
Pearl Harbor 8, 41, 44, 60, 61, 174, 175
Pelling, George 176
Pendleton, Steve 25
"Pennies from the Dead" 220
Pepper, Barbara 25
Pereira, Hal 127, 178, 186
The Perfect Case 85
Peri, Arrigo 190
Perinal, George 102
Perlberg, William 65, 102
Perreau, Gigi 107
Perry, Alfred 146
Perry, Benjamin J. 209

Persons, Sonny 212
Peters, Jean 39, 96, 97, 98, 121, 180, 219, 221
Peters, Ralph 39, 144
Peters, Werner 183, 185
Petra, Hortense 192
Petrucci, Giovanni 197
Pevney, Joseph 164
Peyton Place 151
Philidelphia 218
Phipps, William 136
Pichel, Irving 37
Pickens, Slim 174
Pickford, Mary 25, 54
Picturegoer magazine 104
Pidgeon, Walter 77
Pierce, Jack P. 76
Pierce, Stack 209
Piergentili, Bruno 191
Pigozzi, Luciano 188
Pigozzi, Ugo 188
Pike, Don 209
The Pilot 153, 212–213, 214
Pin Up Girl 24
Pine, Phillip 107, 176
Pinter, Harold 207, 208
Pirosh, Robert 149, 150
Pisani, Sergio 191
"Pit Viper" 220
Pittack, Robert 27
Pitts, Charles 212
Pitts, Michael R. 127
Plague 172
Playboy Production 217
Playhouse 90 215
Playhouse Theatre (New York) 218
"The Playoff" 215
Plaza Suite 218
Poggioni, Vera 191
Pohlenz, Peter 49
Pollard, Paul 171
Pomerance, Hope 212
Poole, Michael 201
Poore, Ronald 207
Pork Chop Hill 70
Portman, Clem 90, 119, 199
Portrait of Jenny 93, 99
Possessed 89
Post, Ted 209, 210
Powell, Dick 156
Powell, Dinny 178
Powell, Edward 65
Powell, Jane 161, 163, 164
Powell, Michael 132
Power, Tyrone 1, 7, 43, 44, 45, 50, 60, 86, 92, 98, 137, 150, 219
Powers, Leona 96
Powers, Mala 113
Powers, Richard 52
"Prairie Schooner" 29
Preminger, Otto 2, 8, 9, 10, 11, 12, 61, 63, 64, 72, 73, 74, 87, 88, 89, 90, 109, 110, 111, 112, 138, 148, 159, 174, 175, 176
Prentiss, Paula 174
The Presidency: A Splendid Misery 216
Pressburger, Emeric 132
Preston, Robert 5, 92
Pretoria 133

Price, Vincent 9, 61, 63, 65, 144, 145, 219
Prince Jack 20, 213–214
Prine, Andrew 199
Prisoner of War 160
Pritchard, David 199
Pritchard, Robert 136
Probyn, Brian 201
Prokofiev, Serge 93, 96
Puente, Jesus 197
The Purple Heart 7, 8, 27, 49, 55–59, 63, 113, 153
Pye, Merrill 192

Queen Elizabeth II 157
Quinlivan, Charles 151
Quinn, Anthony 46, 47
Quinn, Fred 54
Quinn, Louis 164
Quirk, Lawrence J. 68, 186

Racca, Claudio 197
The Rack 158
Radio City Music Hall 40, 41
Radio Times Guide to Films 134
Radziwell, Lee 65
Rage 172
Rain, Jack 127
Rains, Claude 12, 85, 119, 121
Rambeau, Marjorie 31, 32
Rameau, Ramil 104
Rando, Salvo 191
Rank, J. Arthur 77
Rapper, Irving 210, 211
Raskin, David 61, 64, 72, 74, 87, 88, 172
"The Rat Race" 220
Ray, Danny "Big Black" 212
Raymond, Robin 146
Reader's Digest 85
Reagan, Ronald 77, 96, 160, 215
Real, Nacio 161
Reason, Rex 136, 138
Rebecca 130, 147
"Red Clay" 220
"Red Clouds on Good Earth" 220
"The Red Gate" 220
"Red Gold" 220
"The Red Ladies" 220
"The Red Octopus" 221
"The Red Record" 220
"Red Red Herring" 220
"Red Rover, Red Rover" 220
"The Red Snow" 221
"The Red Waves" 220
Reddish, Jack N. 171
Reddy, Helen 204, 205
Redford, Robert 18
Redmond, Liam 104, 106, 155
Redwing, Rod 186
Reed, Clive 201
Reed, Donna 65, 132, 134, 135, 136, 219, 221
Reed, Walter 90
Regan, Patrick 213
Regis, Billy 154
Reid, Carl Benton 49
Reiguera, Francisco 161
Reimers, Edwin 181
Reinhardt, Betty 61

Reitano, Robert M. 207
Reliance Pictures 28
Remedy for Winter 187, 218
Remick, Lee 209, 217
Remisoff, Nicholai 99
Renaldo, Duncan 23
Renay, Liz 192
Rennahan, Ray 34, 52
Rennie, Michael 199
Renoir, Jean 7, 31, 34, 37, 38, 39
Republic Pictures 27, 58
Resnik, Muriel 218
Return to Paradise 163
The Revenge of Frankenstein 157
Revenge of the Zombies 196
Revere, Anne 71, 74, 96, 98
Reynolds, Burt 53
Reynolds, Harry 72
Reynolds, William 116
"Rhapsody in Red" 221
Rhein, Alan 39
Rhodes, Hari 171
Rhodesia 131, 133
Riano, Renie 27
Ricciardello, Fiorella 191
Rich, Dick 23
Rich, Frederic Efrem 68
"Rich Man, Poor Man" 220
Richards, Addison 39
Richards, Lloyd 119
Richardson, Tony 181, 182
Ridges, Stanley 75
Ridgley, John 113
Riedel, Richard H. 76, 136
Rififi 190
Righi, Massimo 188
"Right Hand Man" 215
Riordan, Christopher 192
"A Riot Made to Order" 220
River of No Return 138
RKO (Radio-Keith-Orpheum) 12,
   39, 40, 49, 50, 52, 54, 79, 80, 82,
   90, 91, 92, 107, 109, 113, 114, 119,
   120, 122, 123, 144, 145, 146, 147,
   148, 158, 162, 172, 199
Roach, James 158
Roberts, Arthur 210
Roberts, Eric 49
Roberts, Ewan 155
Roberts, Roy 99
Roberts, Stephen 176
Roberts, William 199
Robertson, Cliff 153, 212, 213
Robertson, Donald W. 199
Robertson, Willard 23, 46
Robinson, Casey 144, 146, 199, 201
Robinson, Earl 68
Robinson, Edward G. 18
Robinson, Jay 210
Robson, Mark 107, 108, 113, 115, 122
Roc, Patricia 75, 77
Rockwell, Robert 115
Roddan, Jim 195
Rode, Fred J. 60, 116
Rodero, Jose Lopez 183, 205
Roelofs, Al 174, 178
Roessel, Howard 178
Rogers, Cameron 34
Rogers, Ginger 32, 39
Rogers, Richard 10, 65, 66, 67

Rogers, Rita 199
Rogers, Will 66
"Rogue River Valley" 77
Roland, Gilbert 23
Rolla, Stefano 188, 197
Roman, Ruth 17, 36
Romero, Cesar 23, 24, 96, 98
Rondell, Ronnie 144
Rooney, Mickey 27
Rooney, Mickey, Jr. 192, 194
Roosevelt, Franklin 85
Ropp, Carl 183
Rorke, Hayden 104
Rosenberg, Frank P. 109
Rosenberger, Jim 186
Rosenman, Leonard 164
Rossen, Robert 68
Rossi, Gino 191
Rosson, Harold 139, 141
Rowland, Sig 41
Rowland, Steve 183
Royal Command Film Perfor-
   mance 157
The Royal Poinciana Playhouse
   (Palm Beach, Florida) 218
Royce, Robinson 209
Royle, William 23
Rub, Christian 41
Rubin, Mann 176
Rubinstein, Artur 90, 93
Rudley, Herbert 67, 70
Ruggles, Charlie 218
Ruman, Sig 41
Runway Zero-Eight 153
Russell, Charles 55
Russell, Harold 79, 80, 83
Russell, Jane 36, 186, 187, 188
Russell, Theresa 206, 208
Rustichelli, Carlo 191
Ryan, Irene 148, 151
Ryan, Peggy 25, 26
Ryan, Robert 112, 183, 184, 185, 202
Ryan, Tim 39
Ryder, Winston 207

Sacristan, Martin 183
Sacs, Tom 195
Sad, Ben 176
Saenz, Eddie 161
Safan, Craig 209
Sage, Will 151
Sailor's Lady 6, 7, 29, 24–27
St. James, Raymond 210
St. John, Howard 166
Sakall, S.Z. 39
Sala, Vittoria 188
Salerno Beachhead (*A Walk in the
   Sun* retitled) 71,
Salew, John 155
Salinger, J.D. 107, 108
Saltern, Irene 30
Sam Houston Teacher College 4
San Antonio 4
Sand, Walter 122
Sanders, George 65, 124, 125, 126,
   144, 145,
Sansom, Ken 204
Sansom, Lester A. 169
Santa Fe 139, 140
The Satan Bug 171–174, 178, 184

Satan Never Sleeps 115
Saturday Evening Post 106, 126, 193
Saturday Review of Literature 118
Saunders, Robert 61
Saunders, Russ 139
Savalas, Telly 183, 185, 190
Sawtell, Paul 134
Sawyer, Joe 23, 34, 37
Scaife, Ted 155
Schallert, William 136
Schioppa, Franco 190
Schlickenmayer, Harold 61
Schmidhauser, Hannes 191
Schnabel, Stefan 93
Schnee, Charles 164
Schneiderman, Wally 210
Schultz, John DuCasse 27
Schumn, Hans 41
Scognamillo, Gabriel 139
Scott, George C. 182
Scott, Gordon 191
Scott, Janette 169, 170
Scott, Martha 204
Scott, Randolph 7, 34, 35, 36, 60,
   150, 192
Scott, Sydna 169
Scott, Walter M. 55, 87, 109, 166
Screen Actors Guild 18
Screen Director's Playhouse 219
Screen Guide 108
Screen Guild Players 219
The Screen Guild Theatre 221
Sealed Cargo 12, 97, 119–122, 180
The Searchers 143
Searls, Hank 164
Seitz, George B 27, 29
Selander, Lesley 178, 179
Selwart, Tonio 49
Selznick, David O. 99, 123
Sempere, Julio 183
Sennett, Max 117
"September Affair" 219
Sequi, Mario 197, 199
Sersen, Fred 43, 44, 55, 60, 61, 65,
   72, 87, 94, 97, 110, 116
Seven Little Foys 42
Seyler, Athene 155
Seymour, Dan 146
Shadow in the Streets 19, 217
Shadow of a Doubt 146
Shaffeen, Jack G 105
Shalet, Diane 206
Shamroy, Leon 43, 65, 87
Shane 177
Shannon, Harry 24
Shannon, Richard 148
Sharaff, Irene 79
Sharp, Margery 102
Shaw, Frank 104
Shaw, Irvin 122, 123
Shaw, Rita 181
Shaw, Robert 183, 184
Shay, John 93
The Shearwater (yacht) 159
Sheerwood, Robert E. 79, 80, 83
Sheffield, Johnny 23
Shelley, Ronald 212
Sheman, Reed 141
Shepperton Studio 104
Sherman, Bobby 212

Sherman, George 104, 105, 141, 142
Sheybal, Vladek 201, 202
Shields, Arthur 119, 120, 161, 163
Shore, Dinah 52, 53, 55
Shoshtakovich, Dimitri 93, 96
Shoup, Howard 164
Shue, Bob 209
Siegel, Benjamin "Bugsy" 41
Siegel, Sol C. 93, 96
Silver, Alain 112, 213
Silver and Ward 178
Silvera, Darrell 90, 119, 146
Simminger, Charles 183
Simmons, Richard Alan 134
Simon, Neil 218
Simon, Robert F. 148, 151
Simpson, Albert 61
Simpson, Robert L. 34
Simpson, Russell 31, 37
Simpson, Tom 195
Sinatra, Frank 64
"Sinews of Peace" address 94
Singer, Patricia 207
Sitting Bull 142
"Sketchy Love" 217
Skinner, Frank 76, 78, 104
Skouras, Spyros 57, 58
Slate, Henry 115
Slate, Jeremy 199
Slavin, George F. 136, 137
"The Sleeper" 220
Slifer, Clarence 49, 52
"Slowly" 74
Small, Edward 27, 28, 29
Smash Up: The Story of a Woman 77, 103
Smedley-Aston, Brian 181
Smight, Jack 204
Smith, Dick 94
Smith, Harold Jacob 161
Smith, Kent 107, 141, 142, 143
Smith, Leigh 76
Smith, Leonard 205
Smith, Louis 138
Smith, Robert 176
Smoke Signal 15, 26, 134, 136–138, 143
Snel, Otto 183
"Snow White and the Seven Dwarfs" 41
Snyder, William 146
Society of Independent Motion Picture Producers 54
Soderberg, Theodore 205
Sofaer, Abraham 127
Sokoloff, Vladimir 144
A Song Is Born 41
Song of Russia 51
A Song to Remember 92
"Sophisticated Lady" 64
South Africa 133
Southern, Terry 181, 182
Southern Californian Motion Picture Council 141
Spaak, Catherine 205
Spadaro, Adriana 190
Spaghetti Western 206
Spain 18, 185, 190
Spang, Laurette 204
Spellbound 100

Spencer, Douglas 136, 138
Spencer, Herbert 149
Spencer, Russell 109
Sperli, Alessandro 188
Sperling, Milton 43, 183
Spiegel, Sam 207, 208
Spielman, Fred 90
Spigelgass, Leonard 218
Spillman, Harry 210, 211
Spitz, Henry 141
Spitzer, Jackie 144
Spoliansky, Mischa 131
Spoonhandle 97
Spring Reunion 15, 44, 148–151
"Spring Reunion" (radio) 149
Springsteen, R.G. 186
"Squeeze Play" 220
Stack, Robert 65, 216
Stader, Paul 161
Stagecoach 66, 76, 214
Stahl, George, Jr. 161
Stahl, Jorge, Jr. 141
Stalmaker, Charles 183
Stamford, Connecticut 84
Stander, Lionel 181
Standish, Robert 127
Stanwyck, Barbara 7, 36, 39, 40
Stany, Jacques 197
Stark, Michael 209
Starwalt, David 209
State Fair 10, 25, 34, 65–67, 131, 167, 194
State of the Union 99
Steadman, Robert 209
Steckel, Laura 212
Steele, Bob 178
Steen, Mike 169
Stehanoff, Robert 79
Steiger, Rod 181, 182
Steinberg, Betty 166
Stepanek, Karel 195, 196
Stephanoff, Robert 113
Sterling, Dick 212
Sterling, Rod 215, 216
Stern, Tom 199
Stevens, Charles 27
Stevens, Craig 109, 111
Stevens, George 99
Stevens, Leith 90, 93
Stevens, Leslie 218
Stevens, Onslow 75, 119
Stevens, Warren 115
Stevens, William 119
Stevenson, Houseley 113
Stevenson, Robert 151
Stewart, Martha 87
Stewart, Paul 113, 115, 212
Stiller, Jerry 204
Stine, Clifford 136, 137
Stine, Hal 186
Stockwell, Dean 96, 99, 216, 221
Stockwell, Guy 204
Stoker, Austin 204
Stoker, H.G. 97
Stoloff, Morris 125
Stone, Fred 29
Stone, John 23
Stone, Milburn 136
Stonehenge 155, 156
Stong, Philip 65, 66

Storch, Larry 204
The Story of G.I. Joe 208
Stradling, Harry, Jr. 113, 115, 210
Stradling, Harry, Sr. 122, 164
Strang, Harry 27, 61
Strange Lady in Town 15, 134, 138–141, 214
"Strangers on a Train" 219
Stratton, Chet 174
Strauss, Peter 206
Strauss, Theodore 199
Street Scene Theme 110
Streeter, Alban 183
Strudwick, Shepperd 34, 37, 146
Stuart, Gilchrist 104
Stuart, William L. 109, 111
Studio City 22
"A Study in Oils" 220
Sturges, John 171, 172
Sturtevant, John 166
Suess, Maurice M. 68
"A Suit for the Party" 220
Sukman, Harry 166, 167
Sullivan, Barry 205, 206
Sullivan, Kitty 212
Summers, Hope 151
"Summertime" 64
Summerville, Slim 31
Sundstrom, Florence 148
Supercolpo da 7 miliardi (*The Ten Million Dollar Grab*) 190–191
Surtees, Robert 171
"Suspense" 220
Suspicion 147
Sutton, Frank 171
Swamp Water 7, 29, 31, 34, 36–39, 43, 92, 97, 114, 162
Swanson, Gloria 204, 205
Sweeney, Al, Jr. 199
Sweetheart of Turrret One 26
Swerling, Jo 30, 43
Swift, Joan 176
Sword, Roger 204
Sword in the Desert 12, 26, 97, 101, 104–107, 114, 126, 142
Sylbert, Anthea 207

Take a Hard Ride 205–206, 209
Talbot, Lyle 52
Talman, William 136, 138
Talton, Alix 199
Tancred, Anthony 101
"Taps" 29
Tatar, Ben 169
Taylor, Elizabeth 13, 93, 127, 128, 129, 130, 150
Taylor, Joyce 146
Taylor, Nell 131
Taylor, Robert 5, 156
Teal, Ray 79, 113
Teilhet, Darwin L. 158, 159
Temple, Paul 210
Ter-Arutunian, Rouben 181
Terror in the Sky 154
"Tess's Torch Song" 55
Test Pilot 25
Tetrick, Ted 199
Texas 4
Texas Oil Corporation 4
Thalberg, Irving 20, 208

"That Old Feeling" 151
Thatcher, Heather 131
"That's for Me" 66
They Saved Hitler's Brain 196
They Were Expendable 25
The Thing with Two Heads 196
Thinnes, Roy 204
This Is Your Life 21, 218
This Love of Ours 92
Thomas, Bill 136
Thomas, Tony 67
Thompson, Charles P. 192
Thompson, Walter 37, 43
Thompson, William 176
Thor, Larry 151
Thordsen, Kelly 158
Thorndike, Sybil 101, 102
Thorson, Arthur 151
Three Hours to Kill 14, 132, 134–136, 138, 178, 186
Thrett, Maggie 199
Thursday, David 151
Tibbett, Lawrence 5
Tiernan, Patricia 151
Tierney, Gene 2, 7, 9, 10, 12, 16, 22, 24, 31, 34, 35, 36, 61, 62, 65, 93, 94, 95, 109, 110, 112, 121, 150, 165, 212, 219, 221
Tiffin, Pamela 67
"Tight Wire" 220
Tilbury, Zeffie 31
Tillar, Jack K. 199
Tilvern, Alan 195, 196, 197
Time (magazine) 45, 52, 59, 66, 75, 78, 79, 176, 201
"The Time Is Now" 216
Time Limit 158
The Times 101
Tiomkin, Dimitri 30, 139, 141
Tirard, Anne 195
Tobacco Road 7, 31–34, 112, 114
Together Tonight! Jefferson, Hamilton and Burr 218
"The Token" 215, 220
Toland, Gregg 30, 39, 79, 82
Tomak, Sid 148
Tomasini, George 127, 174
Tone, Franchot 174
Tonge, Philip 127
Toomey, Stanley 5
Toone, Geoffrey 151, 154
Topete, Manuel 141
Toran, Enrique 197
Toren, Marta 104, 105, 106, 121, 124, 125, 131
Torman, Al 212
Torme, Mel 158, 159, 160, 170
Torre, Jania 90
Torrey, Roger 178
Torvay, Jose 139
Totter, Audrey 124, 125, 126
Tou, Yui Chang Pio 188
"Tour of Duty" 221
Tourneur, Jacques 2, 11, 15, 17, 76, 78, 155, 156, 157, 158, 159
Tovey, Arthur 192
Town Tamer 18, 178–181, 182, 184
"The Town That Died" 216
Tozere, Frederic 93
Tracy, Lynn 155

Tracy, Spencer 64, 115, 217
Tracy, William 31
Trader Horn 131
"Traitors for Hire" 220
Travers, Henry 39
"Treason Comes in Cans" 220
Treasure of the Sierra Madre 23
A Tree, a Rock, a Cloud 217
Tremayne, Les 219
"Trial by Fear" 220
"Trial by Midnight" 215
Trial of Terror 125, 126
Tribby, John 90
Trivas, Victor 109
Trotti, Lamar 34, 46, 47
Troupe, Tom 199
Troutman, James 204
Trowbridge, Charles 34
The True Story of Lynn Stuart 158
Tsu, Irene 204
Tucker, Forrest 29, 31
Tucson, Arizona 140
Tufts, Sonny 178, 180
Tully, Tom 109
Turich, Felipe 134
Tuttle, Frank 125, 134, 192
12 Angry Men 87
20th Century-Fox 6, 7, 8, 9, 10, 12, 16, 23, 24, 25, 28, 29, 30, 31, 32, 33, 34, 35, 36, 38, 39, 41, 42, 43, 44, 46, 48, 55, 56, 57, 58, 59, 60, 61, 62, 63, 65, 66, 67, 69, 71, 73, 74, 75, 84, 86, 87, 88, 93, 95, 96, 98, 101, 102, 103, 109, 112, 115, 116, 157, 166, 167, 168, 169, 175, 205, 208,
20th Century Pictures 117
20 Million Miles to Earth 158
The Twilight Zone 215
Two Arabian Knights 101
"Two Birds with One Stone" 220
Two for the Seesaw 13, 18, 217
Two Rode Together 143
Tyler, Harry 31, 96
Tyler, Leon 148
Tyler, Tom 29
Tyne, George 67, 68, 104
Typee 17, 161, 162
Tyron, Tom 174, 175

Uda, Hatsuo 209
Uncle Wiggily in Connecticut 107, 108
United Artists 6, 27, 28, 29, 30, 100, 141, 142, 145, 149, 158, 159
United Kingdom *see* England
Universal Studio 27, 30, 75, 78, 104, 105, 106, 126, 136, 137, 138, 204
"The Unwelcome Hosts" 220
Up in Arms 8, 26, 52–55, 66, 150, 216
"Use Only as Directed" 221
Utah 201

Valdermarin, Mario 188
Valerie, Jeanne 191
Van Nuys Amateur Theatre 5
Van Nuys filling station 5
Variety 8, 39, 54, 59, 71, 83, 87, 112, 146, 158, 166, 174, 176, 201

Variety Movie Guide 104
Varriano, Emilio 109
Vassar, Chuck 171
Veevers, Wally 155
Venable, Evelyn 23
Verity, Terence 131
Vermilyea, Harold 113
Vernon, Wally 24, 25, 26, 27
"Very Private Funeral" 221
Victoria Falls 133, 134
Vignon, Jean-Paul 199
Vinalhaven 97
Vincenzi, Luciana 197
"Violence Preferred" 220
Vogan, Emmett 25
Vogeler, Robert A. 126
Volkman, Ivan 107, 122
Von Homburg, Wilhelm 199
Vorisek, Dick 207
Votrian, Peter J. 124
Voyage to the Bottom of the Sea 172

Wade, Charles 195
Wade, Jo Ann 151
Wagner, Robert 115, 117
Walcott, Gregory 139
Wale, Wally 71
A Walk in the Sun 2, 11, 49, 58, 67–71, 100, 150, 185
Walker, Robert 219
Walker, Scott 210
Wallace, Jerry 186
Wallace, Regina 107
Walters, James M. 136
Walton, Col. George 199
Walton, Herbert C. 101
Wang, George 188
Wanger, Walter 76, 77, 78
"War of the Worlds" 219
Ward, Clayton 61
Ward, Edmund 27
Ward, Elizabeth 112
Wardlow, Mr. 5
Warner Brothers 51, 54, 65, 73, 117, 131, 132, 138, 161, 162, 164, 165, 176, 183, 184, 195, 196, 212
Warner Brothers–Seven Arts 195
Warning Sign 172
Warren, Harry 149
Warren, John F. 151
Warwick, Robert 144
Warwick, Ruth 87, 88
Washington, Ned 107, 108, 139, 141
Watergate 210, 211
Watkin, Pierre 25
Watson, Jack 199, 201
Watt, Nate 99
Waugh, Evelyn 181, 182
Waverley Productions 163
Waxman, Franz 99, 127, 130
Wayne, John 1, 24, 25, 102, 106, 142, 153, 161, 174, 175, 177, 180, 188, 190, 198, 214
Wead, Lt. Cmdr. Frank "Spig" 25
"Weather Is a Weapon" 218
Webb, Clifton 61, 63, 64, 219, 221
Webb, George C. 204
Webb, J. Watson, Jr. 60, 65
Webb, Richard 22, 134, 178
Webb, Roy 119

Webster, Ferris 171
Weinberger, Henry 60, 110
Welch, Jerry 186
Welcome to Arrow Beach 196
Weldon, Alex 169, 170, 183
Wellman, William 46, 47, 93, 94, 153
Wells, Evelyn 27
Wells, H.G. 219
Wentworth, Martha 72
Werker, Alfred 119, 122, 134
Werle, Barbara 183
West, Elliot 158
West, Pat 39
Westerfield, James 134
The Westerner 6, 24, 25, 29–31, 35, 81
Westmore, Bud 104, 136
Westmore, Wally 127, 178, 186
Westport (Conn.) 218
Wexler, Haskell 181
Wheeler, Lois 107
Wheeler, Lyle R. 60, 61, 65, 72, 87, 93, 97, 109, 116, 174
"Where the Red Men Roam" 220
Where the Sidewalk Ends 8, 12, 13, 16, 41, 109–112, 117, 145, 148, 157, 166, 177, 178
"Where the Sidewalk Ends" (radio) 219
While the City Sleeps 15, 67, 122, 126, 144–146, 157, 169
The Whip Hand 172
Whipper, Leigh 46, 47
Whitby, Gwynne 102
White, Charles 204
White, David 166, 167
White, Jack Palmer 125
White, Jacqueline 90
White, John Manchip 169
White, Sandy 144
White, Will J. 151
White Plains, New York 84
Whitmore, James 118
Whitney, Peter 93
Whittage, J.R. 158
Whitty, Dame May 43
"Who Killed 'Er" 93
Whoopee! 52

Wick, Bruno 96
Widmark, Richard 12, 115, 117, 221
Wiehle, Kurt 183
Wilcox, Frank 49
Wilde, Brian 155, 157
Wilde, Cornel 92
Wilder, Billy 39, 40, 41, 177
Wilder, Thornton 218
Wilke, Robert J. 136, 139
Wilkinson, John 178, 186
Willes, Jean 164
William, Warren 221
Williams, Cara 84
Williams, Clyde 22
Williams, Esther 66
Williams, Guin "Big Boy" 37
Williams, Kay 99
Williams, Paul 181
Williams, Terry 204
Williamson, Fred 205, 206
Willis, Bob 212
Willis, Jim 205
Willis, Matt 37, 67
Willock, Dave 59
Wills, Chill 29, 34
Wills, Mary 107, 113, 122
Wilson 57
Wilson, Judy 212
Wilson, Ned 210
Winchell, Walter 113
"A Wind of Hurricane Force" 216
Windom, William 213
Wing, Virginia 209
Wing and a Prayer 7, 59–61, 63, 117, 138, 153, 180
Winged Victory 111
Wings 47
"Wings of an Angel" 216
Wings of Eagles 25
Winninger, Charles 65
Winters, Jonathan 181, 182
Winthrop, Lynn 49
Withers, Jane 49
Wolfe, David 104
Woman's World 167
Wood, Natalie 12
Wood, Victor 93
Woodell, Barbara 107
Woods, Robert 183

Woolley, Monty 63
"Word Game" 220
Woulfe, Michael 119
The Wrath of God 115
Wright, Gary 213
Wright, Joseph C. 37
Wright, Teresa 51, 79, 80, 81, 82, 83, 165
Wroe, Trudy 146
"The Wrong Green" 220
Wulff, Georgina 124
Wunderlich, Jerry 207
Wurtzel, Sol M. 23, 25
Wurtzel film unit 32
Wuthering Heights 115
Wyatt, Jane 84, 85, 86, 99, 101, 221
Wyler, Gretchen 199
Wyler, William 6, 30, 51, 79, 80, 81, 83, 99
Wyman, Jane 19, 216, 217
Wynn, Keenan 164
Wynter, Dana 65

Yankee Doodle Dandy 65
"Yanqui Go Home" 215
Yates, Herbert 58
Yong, Soo 174
Yordan, Philip 113, 169, 183
Yorkshire Television 158
Young, Carlton 146
Young, Victor 107, 108
The Young Lions 123

Zago, Emilio 191
Zambezi River 133
Zanuck, Darryl 7, 31, 34, 37, 47, 53, 55, 57, 58, 60, 63, 64, 66, 73, 74, 84, 94, 96, 104, 117
Zavitz, Lee 161
Zero Hour 17, 151–154, 194, 204
Ziegler, William 176
Zimbalist, Efrem, Jr. 164, 165, 166, 190, 204, 205
Zimet, Julian 169
Zolficar, Omar 197
Zorro 23
Zuccoli, Fausto 188
Zuckert, Bill 210

Ingram Content Group UK Ltd.
Milton Keynes UK
UKHW031814130423
419801UK00018B/315

9 780786 446148